Adolf Hitler

The Final Analysis

In July 1922 Hitler declared: 'It was he [the Aryan] alone, in the final analysis, who knew how to establish states.' *(Der Volkischer Beobachter*, Munich, 28 July 1922) Here however, it is the MIND of the 'Führer' which is under the microscope, metaphorically speaking, of course, and the analysis of HIM, which is the subject of *Adolf Hitler: the Final Analysis*.

ADOLF HITLER

THE FINAL ANALYSIS

by

Dr Andrew Norman

SPELLMOUNT
Staplehurst

British Library Cataloguing in Publication Data:
A catalogue record for this book is available
from the British Library

Copyright © Dr Andrew Norman 2005

ISBN 1-86227-314-6

First published in the UK in 2005 by
Spellmount Limited
The Village Centre
Staplehurst
Kent TN12 0BJ

Tel: 01580 893730
Fax: 01580 893731
E-mail: enquiries@spellmount.com
Website: www.spellmount.com

1 3 5 7 9 8 6 4 2

Printed in Great Britain by
Oaklands Book Services
Stonehouse, Gloucestershire GL10 3RQ

Contents

Also By Andrew Norman

HMS Hood: Pride of the Royal Navy.
(2001) Stackpole Books, Mechanicsburg, PA, USA.
ISBN 0-8117-0789-X. (Avaliable from Spellmount Ltd., UK.)

By Swords Divided: Corfe Castle in the Civil War.
(2003) Halsgrove, UK. ISBN 1-84114-228-X.

Thomas Hardy: Behind the Inscrutable Smile
(2003) Halsgrove, Tiverton, UK. ISBN 1-84114-324-3.
(Order from Halsgrove Direct, Lower Moor Way, Tiverton, Devon, EX16 6SS. Tel. 01884-243242).

Tyneham: The Lost Village of Dorset.
(2003) Halsgrove, UK. ISBN 1-84114-322-7.

TE Lawrence: Unravelling the Enigma.
(2003) Halsgrove, UK. ISBN 1-84114-321-9.

Sir Francis Drake: Behind the Pirate's Mask.
(2004) Halsgrove, UK. ISBN 1-84114-371-5

Dunshay: Reflections on a Dorset Manor House.
(2004) Halsgrove, UK. ISBN 1-84114-403-7.

Robert Mugabe and the Betrayal of Zimbabwe.
(2004) McFarland & Company Inc., Jefferson, North Carolina, USA. ISBN 0-7864-1686-6. (Available from Eurospan, Covent Garden, London, UK.)

Enid Blyton and her Enchantment with Dorset.
(2005) Halsgrove, UK. ISBN 1-8411-4480-0.

Thomas Hardy: Christmas Carollings.
(2005) Halsgrove, UK. ISBN 1-8411-4479-7.

Acknowledgements

The British Library, London; The National Archives, Kew, Richmond, Surrey, UK; King's College (Liddell Hart Centre for Military Archives,) University of London; the manager and staff of Poole Library; Isle of Wight Record Office, Newport, Isle of Wight; Ventnor and District Local History Society, Ventnor, Isle of Wight.

The Daily Telegraph; The Times.

The Rt Hon. The Earl Jellicoe; Lord Angus Douglas-Hamilton; Martin A Clay; Peter Devlin; Nicholas Dragffy; Tom Gillibrand; Howard Waldin; Peter Tewkesbury.

Oberösterreichisches Landesarchiv, Linz; The Kunsthistorisches Museum, Vienna.

I am especially grateful to my dear wife, Rachel, for all her help, expertise and encouragement.

Introduction

In this book, Andrew Norman examines the origins and validity of Hitler's beliefs: that Germany was not defeated in the First World War, but 'stabbed in the back' by its politicians: that the German nation and its culture were being corrupted and weakened by Jewish influence, and particularly by Jewish international finance: that Bolshevism in the 1930s was threatening to overwhelm Germany, just as it had taken over Russia in the Revolution of October 1917.

We follow Hitler as he bludgeons his way to power, using violence whenever it suits him, and breaking treaties with other nations without compunction. We watch as the 'Führer' assumes command of Germany's armed forces, and through a mixture of ignorance and incompetence, leads that nation to a catastrophic defeat at the hands of the Allies.

We examine the validity of Hitler's claim that he obtained his ideas from the great philosophers and politicians, whose works he claims to have read. Instead, we find that his ideas on anti-Semitism, Aryan superiority, and the necessity to exterminate the Jews, were derived from a quite different source, which he failed to acknowledge in his book *Mein Kampf*, even though much of that volume was plagiarised, almost verbatim, from this other source.

Finally, we look at Hitler himself, and attempt to categorise, in psychiatric terms, a man who was clearly suffering from paranoia, and whose bizarre sexual practices can only be explained in pathological terms. And yet this appears not always to have been the case. Hitler's family physician, Dr Eduard Bloch, paints a picture of the young Adolf as a charming and caring youth, if a little 'strange'. *So what occurred to change him into a hate-driven, homicidal maniac?*

Having established that Hitler was definitely suffering from a 'Personality Disorder', we ask the reason why: could it be that this was brought about by his upbringing, or life experiences; or was there a deeper reason, connected with the fact that his parents were closely related, and may have unwittingly passed on to their son, Adolf, the defective gene which would have the effect of totally changing the history of the world in the 20th Century? Is it possible that herein lies the answer to the riddle of Hitler's personality – one that has lain undiscovered for over sixty years?

***

In studying Adolf Hitler, the modern biographer has a number of advantages not available to those of previous generations. In recent years a great number of television documentaries have been made about Hitler and his times: these convey a freshness and a reality in a way which books are unable to achieve. They also give an opportunity for people to express their views, and perhaps give their own unique insight into past events, which they would not otherwise have been able to do. Another advantage is the recent release of a large amount of material from the National Archives at Kew (particularly in respect of the Duke and Duchess of Windsor, and Sir Oswald and Lady Diana Mosley, and the personalities associated with those organisations which existed in Britain in the 1930s, which were sympathetic to the Nazi cause).

CHAPTER I

Germany In Crisis

On 11 November 1918 Germany and the Allies signed the Armistice, thus bringing the First World War to an end. This was despite the fact, that just prior to the cessation of hostilities, Holland, a large area of Belgium, and parts of France and Luxemburg were still in German hands. Nonetheless, the armies of Germany were being progressively driven back at this time. According to German soldier Herbert Richter:

> Of course we were angry. The Front Line troops did not feel defeated, and we wondered why the Armistice occurred so quickly, and why we had to vacate all our positions in such a hurry, because everywhere we were still on enemy territory.[1]

German soldier and statesman Paul von Hindenburg later declared: 'As an English general has very truly said, the German Army was "stabbed in the back".'[2]

The blame was attributed to the Social Democratic and Republican Parties who were accused of betraying Germany, and thereafter branded as the 'November Criminals'; also to Marxists and Jews who had fomented dissent back at home.

The truth of the matter, however, was that the offensive at Amiens, launched by the British and the French on 8 August 1918 had been catastrophic for Germany, having resulted in the capture of 30,000 German prisoners. In the words of General Erich von Ludendorff:

> The 8th August demonstrated the collapse of our fighting strength, and in the light of our recruiting situation it took from me any hope of discovering some strategic measure which would re-establish the position in our favour … An end must be put to the war.[3]

The German Kaiser Wilhelm II reached the same conclusion, stating when the battle was still in progress: 'I see that we must strike the balance. We are at the limits of our endurance. The war must be brought to an end.'[4] Senior Staff Officer General Hermann von Kuhl, in evidence to the Reichstag Committee of Inquiry said: 'The heavy losses could no longer be replaced. Our reinforcements were exhausted.'[5]

However, Adolf Hitler (a serving a corporal in the German Army, who would one day become leader of the nation) refused to accept the fact of Germany's defeat. In his opinion there was no doubt as to where the true blame lay:

> I intensely loathe the whole gang of miserable party politicians who had betrayed the people. I had long ago realised that the interests of the nation played only a very small part with this disreputable crew, and that what counted with them was the possibility of filling their own empty pockets. My opinion was that those people thoroughly deserve to be hanged, because they were ready to sacrifice the peace and if necessary, allow Germany to be defeated, just to serve their own ends. To consider their wishes would mean to sacrifice the interests of the working classes for the benefit of a gang of thieves. To meet their wishes meant that one should agree to sacrifice Germany.[6]

Hitler never forgot what he perceived as this humiliation, which would rankle with him for the rest of his life. It was 'The fighting Siegfried' (i.e. the German nation) who had, 'succumbed to the dagger plunged in his back'[7] (i.e. by those Germans who, in Hitler's eyes, had betrayed their country by seeking an armistice at the end of the First World War). 'Germany once laid down its arms at a quarter to twelve,' he later said, and therefore, 'On principle, I've never stopped [work] until five past twelve.'[8] Not only that, but Germany's situation was now made worse by the Allies who continued to blockade that country, causing hunger and debilitation amongst the population with resulting outbreaks of tuberculosis and influenza.

***

Prior to the Armistice being signed, the political unrest in Germany had been considerable, opinions tending to become polarised, with people lending their support either to the fascists, or to the socialists, or to the communists, gangs of whom marched through the streets fighting for control of Germany's cities and towns.

On 3 November 1918 the seriousness of the situation manifested itself, when at Germany's Baltic port of Kiel, some 20,000 or so sailors from her Baltic fleet mutinied, demanding the abdication of the Kaiser and the setting up of 'Workers and Soldiers Councils'. On 7 November 1918 in Munich, capital of Germany's south-eastern region of Bavaria, a 'Workers and Soldiers Council', led by journalist and politician Kurt Eisner (who the previous year had founded the Bavarian branch of the Independent Socialist Party), proclaimed in a bloodless revolt, a Bavarian Socialist Republic. There would now be a proliferation of such Workers and Soldiers Councils throughout Germany.

On 9 November 1918 a general strike commenced in many German cities including the capital Berlin, where hostile crowds converged on the chancellery building, forcing Prince Max of Baden (Germany's last Imperial Chancellor, who had been appointed on 3 October by Wilhelm II) to announce the abdication of the Kaiser, before he himself resigned. That same day the so-called Majority Socialists, under the leadership of Friedrich Ebert and Philipp Scheidemann, proclaimed the new German Republic, and a deal was struck between Ebert and General Paul von Hindenburg (commander of the entire army on the Western Front) when it was agreed that if Ebert acted against the communists, then the Army would, in return, support his new government and him personally, as the legitimate Chancellor of Germany. On 10 November 1918 a Council of People's Representatives was elected to govern the country with Ebert at its head. Meanwhile, Prince Max was seeking an armistice with the Allies and had despatched a commission to meet with Allied representatives in France's Compiègne Forest accordingly.

For Ebert, there now arose a major problem in that armed Spartacists, under the command of communist revolutionary Karl Liebknecht (a German barrister and politician), had established themselves in the former Kaiser's Imperial Palace, from the roof of which now flew a red flag. Liebknecht had founded the Spartacus League in Berlin at the outbreak of World War I, with Rosa Luxemburg, a left-wing revolutionary, who had been born in Russian Poland in 1871. Luxemburg and fellow revolutionary Liebknecht had created the International Group which in 1915 became the Spartacus League; this in turn became firstly, part of the Social Democratic Party (SDP – later the Independent SDP) and finally, the Communist Party of Germany. Luxemburg now joined Liebknecht in Berlin.

***

Hitler returned to Munich in November 1918 shortly after the signing of the Armistice, to find the streets littered with cripples and amputees; these were ex-servicemen with no pensions and no possessions. There were demonstrations in which the cry was 'Give us bread!' 'Give us work!' By this time, Hitler had already developed a deep-seated, not to say pathological hatred of Bolshevism as epitomised by the Bolshevik Revolutionaries who, in November 1917 had overthrown Russia's tsarist regime. 'The menace to which Russia once succumbed,' he said in his book *Mein Kampf* (*My Struggle*), 'is hanging steadily over Germany.'[9] As events unfolded in Germany, so this hatred would grow.

***

On 5 January 1919 the Spartacists and Independent Socialists staged a huge demonstration in Berlin, and the following morning called a general strike with in excess of 200,000 workers, many of them armed, parading through the city.

The Free Corps, on the other hand, was a body of right-wing mercenaries, largely composed of veteran soldiers from Germany's defeated army, whose officers were trained professional soldiers, and whose weapons and ammunition were supplied covertly by the army. The Free Corps troops now moved against the Spartacists. They marched into Berlin, and between 10 and 17 January – so-called

Bloody Week – put down the Communist uprising with much brutality. 500 or so lives were lost, including those of Luxemburg and Liebknecht who were both hunted down and executed.

On 19 January 1919 when elections were held for the new National Assembly, the Social Democrats (Majority and Independent Socialists) won 185 of the 421 seats; insufficient to form a majority. On 6 February 1919 the National Assembly met at Weimar, 130 miles south of Berlin on the Elbe river (instead of Berlin, because of continuing violence in that city). A coalition was formed between the Social Democratic Party (SDP), the Democratic Party, and the centre parties, with Philipp Scheidemann of the SDP as Chancellor. Five days later, Friedrich Ebert was elected First President of the so-called Weimar Republic. Germany now had a national assembly with a democratic constitution (as opposed to the previous semi-autocratic monarchy of Kaiser Wilhelm II).

The fact that so many communist revolutionaries, not only in Germany but elsewhere, were Jews, gave rise to the impression in that country that Bolshevism and Judaism were virtually one and the same thing. On 21 February Munich socialist revolutionary Kurt Eisner, a Jew, was murdered by a disgruntled Austrian army officer. In late March 1919 Béla Kun, a 33-year-old Hungarian Jew and founder of the Hungarian Communist Party, staged a coup in that country and proclaimed the Hungarian Soviet Republic.

Many Germans now came to despise the Weimar Republic for being a talking shop, and for kow-towing to Germany's enemies. They believed that parliamentary democracy had failed them. Many soldiers refused to shed their uniforms, and instead formed right-wing militias (Free Corps) which indulged in physical battles with communists. This then, was the atmosphere in Germany long before Hitler came to power.

On 4 April 1919 there was a second revolt in Bavaria, when, encouraged by the success of the communists in Hungary, a coalition of German radical left-wing parties, led by Eugen Levine, proclaimed the Bavarian Soviet Republic. With its own Red Army and control of the press, the Republic's aim was to form an alliance with Soviet Russia, and with the Hungarian Soviet Republic. Its reign, however, was to be short lived: on 1 May regular army troops and Free Corps entered Munich, and in a bloody massacre overturned the communist regime. Now, a moderate socialist government was established under Johannes Hoffmann. In June that year, Levine was executed; according to his son Eugene, he (Levine) met his death bravely, crying out: 'Long live the World Revolution!'

***

Under the terms of the Treaty of Versailles signed on 28 June 1919 Germany was forced to surrender territory to France (Alsace-Lorraine); to Poland (the Polish corridor – between Germany and East Prussia – and Silesia); to Czechoslovakia; to Denmark, and to Belgium. This amounted to one eighth of Germany's territory. Moreover, Germany had already lost her African colonies of South West Africa (Namibia), which was invaded and seized by South Africa in 1915, and

German East Africa (Tanzania), which was conquered by British and South African forces in 1916.

Germany was also forbidden to keep troops in her western provinces, namely the Rhineland – a thirty mile wide strip of land to the west side of the Rhine river. (This region would now be demilitarised and occupied by the Allies for a minimum period of fifteen years.) She was also required to limit her army to 100,000 men, and to pay heavy reparations for damage caused during the war. In this year 1919 the League of Nations was created, although it was not until 1926 that Germany became a member.

***

The questions now for Germany were: would she drift to the left, or to the right? How could she pay the punitive war reparations demanded of her by the Allies, and at the same time revitalise her shattered economy? The answer would come in the personage of the hitherto unknown future 'Führer' (leader) Adolf Hitler, but the situation would get considerably worse before it got better.

Notes

1. *The Nazis: A Warning from History, Part 1.*
2. Shirer, William L, *The Rise and Fall of the Third Reich,* p.31.
3. Lloyd George, David, *War Memoirs of David Lloyd George,* Vol.2, p.1870.
4. Ibid, p.1871.
5. Ibid, p.1872.
6. Hitler, Adolf, *Mein Kampf,* p.118.
7. Ibid, p.344.
8. *Hitler: a Profile, The Seducer.*
9. Hitler, op. cit., p.364.

* Film Documentary.

CHAPTER II

The 'Saviour' Cometh

A constant theme of Hitler's was that he had been chosen to lead the German people.

> I can give expression to my deepest feeling only in the form of humble thanks to Providence who called upon me and vouchsafed to me, once an unknown soldier of the Great War, to rise to be the leader of my people so dear to me.[1]

So how did this come about? As will be seen, one of Hitler's methods was the use of strong-arm tactics.

Hitler, who had served in World War I as a corporal and was still a serving soldier, was now employed by the army to infiltrate left-wing organisations which were seen by it as a threat. To this end he was,

> ordered to appear before the Inquiry Commission which had been set up in the 2nd Infantry Regiment for the purpose of watching revolutionary activities.

This, he said, was his, 'first incursion into the more or less political field.'[2]

A few weeks later, Hitler was ordered to, 'attend a course of lectures which were being given for members of the army', their purpose being, 'to inculcate certain fundamental principles on which the soldier could base his political ideas.'[3] He and others were convinced at that time that Germany,

> could not be saved from imminent disaster by those who had participated in the November treachery [i.e. the signing by Germany of the Armistice with the Allies on 11 November 1918] – that is to say, the Centre … , the Social-Democrats … , and the so-called Bourgeois-National group ….[4]

Hitler and his 'small circle' now 'discussed the project of forming a new party': it would be called the Social Revolutionary Party.[5] In this desire however, he would be overtaken by events. One day, as a result of attending his lectures, Hitler volunteered to take part in a discussion group. Having found that, 'an

6

overwhelming number of those who attended the lecture course supported my views', he was a few days later, 'assigned to a regiment then stationed in Munich and given a position there as "instruction officer".'[6] This gave him, 'an opportunity of speaking before quite a large audience', and he was now, 'able to confirm what I had hitherto merely felt, namely that I had a talent for public speaking.'[7] Not only that, but becoming a 'platform orator at mass meetings' gave Hitler, by his own admission, 'practice in the pathos and gesture required in large halls that held thousands of people.' In other words, he appreciated the importance of 'body language' as a way of captivating his audience.[8]

In September 1919 Hitler received an order from the army's Political Department to investigate a small political group in Munich known as the German Labour Party (GLP).[9] This he duly did on the 12th of that month. At the meeting, the National President of the Party, Anton Drexler, a locksmith by trade, gave him a small booklet entitled *My Political Awakening,* the theme of which was 'A Greater Germany and German Unity'. Hitler read it and to his surprise, found himself much in sympathy with Drexler's aim of creating a political party which would appeal to the working classes, but which unlike the Social Democrats, would be strongly nationalistic.[10] He was even more surprised the following morning, to receive a postcard telling him that he had been accepted as a member of the party.

'When I entered the German Labour Party,' said Hitler, 'I at once took charge of the propaganda, believing this branch to be far the most important for the time being.'[11] 'The receptive powers of the masses are very restricted,' he affirmed,

and their understanding is feeble. On the other hand, they quickly forget. Such being the case, all effective propaganda must be confined to a few bare essentials and those must be expressed, as far as possible, in stereotyped formulae. These slogans should be persistently repeated until the very last individual has come to grasp the idea that has been put forward.[12]

Captain Ernst Röhm of District Command was already a member of the GLP, who had brought with him covertly and illegally, volunteers and funding from the army which was sympathetic to the GLP. An influential member of the GLP was Dietrich Eckart, poet, playwright, drunkard and one-time drug addict, who regarded Hitler as his protégé.

In October 1919 Hitler addressed the German Workers Party on the subject of the Treaty of Versailles (the terms of which he considered to be grossly unfair to Germany), and the Treaty of Brest-Litovsk which he described as, 'one of the most scandalous acts of violence in the history of the world.'[13]

***

On 24 February 1920 'the first great mass meeting under the auspices of the new movement took place' in the Banquet Hall of the Munich Hofbräuhaus (beer hall for drinking and singing) owned by the brewery Hofbrau.[14] The committees were meeting to elect members and, 'to revise the old programme and draw up a new one,' said Hitler, who was not impressed by what he saw. Here, he said,

> the swindle begins anew. Once we understand the impenetrable stupidity of our public we cannot be surprised that such tactics turn out [to be] successful. Led by the press and blinded once again by the alluring appearance of the new programme, the bourgeois as well as the proletarian herds of voters, faithfully return to the common stall and re-elect their old deceivers. Scarcely anything else can be so depressing as to watch this process in sober reality, and to be the eyewitness of this repeatedly recurring fraud.[15]

At this meeting, the Party was renamed the Nationalsozialistische Deutsche Arbeiterpartei (National Socialist German Workers Party [NSDAP] or Nazi Party). This convinced Hitler that,

> ... during the first stages of founding our movement, we had to take special care that our militant group which fought for the establishment of a new and exalted political faith should not degenerate into a society for the promotion of parliamentarian interests.[16]

On 13 March 1920 sections of the 'Reichswehr' rose up in revolt against the (Weimar) republican government of President Friedrich Ebert, marching into Berlin and installing the sixty-two year old civilian Wolfgang Kapp as Chancellor of the Reich. However, Reichswehr units in other parts of the country failed to lend their support and the Reich government was able to suppress the so-called 'Kapp Putsch'.

On 14 March 1920 the Munich government of Johannes Hoffman was overthrown by the Reichswehr, and replaced by a right-wing one under Gustav von Kahr. Munich now became the focus for extremist groups anxious to overthrow the German Republic and repudiate the Treaty of Versailles, the terms of which they considered to be excessively harsh. Included amongst them was German General Erich von Ludendorff, and many former army officers. Meanwhile, the Reichswehr had overthrown the Social Democratic government of Munich and from then on Bavaria was ruled by a state government which had right-wing leanings – in contrast to the central government in Berlin.

The communists remained a potent threat. By 20 March 1920 a Red Army of 50,000 workers had occupied most of the Ruhr, and on this day their newspaper, *Das Ruhr Echo* (*The Ruhr Echo*), declared that,

> Germany must become a republic of Soviets and, in union with Russia, the springboard for the coming victory of the World Revolution and World Socialism.[17]

On 31 March 1920 Hitler left the army and became a private citizen. As for the Party, 'It was imperative from the start to introduce rigid discipline into our meetings,' said Hitler, 'and establish the authority of the chairman absolutely.' To this end, 'as early as the summer of 1920, the organisation of squads of men as hall guards for maintaining order at our meetings was gradually assuming definite shape.'[18]

***

On 22 June 1921 an attempt was made by right-wing extremists to assassinate Philipp Scheidemann, the socialist who had proclaimed the Republic. On 21 July 1921 Hitler was confirmed as chairman of the NSDAP, having won the election for the post by the margin of 543 votes to one.

On 26 August 1921 Matthias Erzberger, a Catholic politician who had signed the Armistice Agreement (when the generals had demurred) and who was therefore seen as a traitor, was murdered by right-wing extremists. On the evening of 14 September 1921 at the Munich Löwenbraukeller (beer hall owned by the brewery Löwenbrau), Hitler and his SA disrupted a left-wing meeting of the Bavarian League, dragging its leader away and assaulting him. This resulted in Hitler's appearance in court and his being given the minimum sentence possible – three months imprisonment. However, for the time being he would remain a free man.

The NSDAP's paramilitary unit led by Rohm, which had now effectively become a uniformed, private army, was largely composed of First World War veteran volunteers, or Free Corps (Freikorps). From November 1921 it was known as the 'Sturmabteilung' (Storm Detachment, abbreviated to SA). Within the SA was a small, elite unit, established in 1928 as Hitler's personal bodyguard, known as the SS ('Schutzstaffel' – Defence Squadron).

The SA was put to the test on 4 November 1921 on the occasion of Hitler's addressing an evening meeting of the Party at the Munich Hofbrauhaus when, 'like wolves', they, 'threw themselves on the enemy [the communists – or Reds] again and again in parties of eight or ten, and began steadily to thrash them out of the hall.'[19]

***

On 16 April 1922 Germany's Foreign Minister, Walther Rathenau (a Jew), signed the Treaty of Rapallo with the Soviet Union: in essence a trade agreement, this treaty also included secret agreements for military co-operation between the two countries, both of which regarded themselves as outcasts from the international community. The result was that the anti-Bolsheviks were incensed and on 4 June Rathenau was assassinated by two former members of the Free Corps.

The Bavarian Government now insisted that Hitler serve the prison sentence which he had been given the previous year. However, following representations in support of Hitler by the presiding judge at the trial to the Appeal Court, the sentence was reduced from three months to just over one month (i.e. 24 June to 27 July).

***

On 11 January 1923 French and Belgian troops occupied the Ruhr – the heartland of Germany's heavy industry – in an attempt to enforce reparation payments owed to them. Passive resistance by the local population involved the government in extra expense, which contributed to the already high level of inflation in the country.

Hitler took the opportunity to vent his anger at this, 'most humiliating kind of capitulation ...', and described the French 'invasion' as 'insolent'.

> ... indignation against such a betrayal of our unhappy country broke out into a blaze. Millions of [Deutschmarks] German money had been spent in vain and thousands of young Germans had been sacrificed, who were foolish enough to trust in the promises made by the rulers of the Reich. [By this, Hitler was presumably referring to German losses in World War I.] Millions of people now became clearly convinced that Germany could be saved only if the whole prevailing system were destroyed root and branch.
>
> There never had been a more propitious moment for such a solution. On the one side, an act of high treason had been committed against the country, openly and shamelessly; on the other side, a nation found itself delivered over to die slowly of hunger. Since the State itself had trodden down all the prospects of faith and loyalty, made a mockery of the rights of its citizens, rendered the sacrifices of millions of its most loyal sons fruitless, and robbed other millions of their last penny, such a state could no longer expect anything but hatred from its subjects. This hatred against those who had ruined the people and the country, was bound to find an outlet in one form or another.20

By September 1923 the communists remained highly influential in Saxony and in industrial centres like Hamburg and the Ruhr where they threatened to revolt. By the end of October, however, a communist rising in Hamburg had been suppressed by the police; a socialist-communist government in Saxony was arrested by the local Reichswehr and a Reich Commissioner appointed to rule in its place; a communist government in Thuringia had similarly been removed.

In Munich, on the evening of 8 November 1923 Hitler and 600 'Storm Troopers' (the brown shirted paramilitary wing of the National Socialist or Nazi Party, whose job it was to protect Nazi political meetings) launched a surprise attack on the Munich Bürgerbraukeller (beer hall owned by Bürgerbrau), where high ranking members of the Bavarian administration (including State Commissioner Gustav Ritter von Kahr, local army commander General Otto von Lossow, and police chief Colonel Hans Ritter von Seisser) were holding a political meeting. Hitler himself mounted the stage and shouted: 'The National Revolution has begun!'21 and demanded the overthrow of the left-wing government in Berlin.

This 'Putsch' (during the course of which the Nazis seized a local bank, hoping to use it for their central offices) was swiftly put down by the Munich police who, in the ensuing fracas, shot dead sixteen of Hitler's men. One of those who lost his life was Theodor von der Pfordten, councillor to the Superior Provincial Court, who was part Jewish – though this latter fact was never acknowledged by Hitler. Hitler fled the scene but was soon captured and imprisoned in Bavaria's Landsberg Fortress. Revolutionaries Rudolf Hess (who had been seriously wounded in the action), Hermann Göring, Julius Streicher, Ernst ('Putzi') Hanfstaengl and others fled to Austria. The Nazi Party was now proscribed and its newspaper *Der Volkischer Beobachter* (The People's Observer) suppressed.

***

In February 1924 Hitler and nine of his collaborators, including the distinguished military leader of the First World War, General Erich von Ludendorff, together with Captain Ernst Röhm, found themselves appearing before the same judge who had presided over Hitler's previous trial (the Bavarian authorities having deliberately chosen this particular person whom they knew would be lenient towards Hitler). At the conclusion of the trial Hitler states in *Mein Kampf* that he made the following speech:

> The judges of this State may tranquilly condemn us [i.e. himself and his fellow conspirators] for our conduct at that time, but history, the goddess of a higher truth and a better legal code, will smile as she tears up this verdict and will acquit us all of the crime for which this verdict demands punishment.[22]

Nevertheless, Hitler was sentenced to a period of five years imprisonment. (General Ludendorff himself escaped prison.) In the event, he would only serve thirteen months.

NOTES

1. Prange, Gordon W (ed.), *Hitler's Words*, p.94.
2. Hitler, Adolf, *Mein Kampf*, p.121.
3. Ibid.
4. Ibid.
5. Ibid, p.122.
6. Ibid, p.125.
7. Ibid.
8. Ibid, p.262.
9. Ibid, p.126.
10. Shirer, William L, *The Rise and Fall of the Third Reich*, p.37.
11. Hitler, op. cit.,p.318.
12. Ibid, p.108.
13. Ibid, p.261.
14. Ibid, p.210.

15. Ibid, p.211.
16. Ibid, p.213.
17. Toland, John, *Adolf Hitler*, pp.100–1.
18. Hitler, op. cit., p.274.
19. Ibid, p.281.
20. Ibid, p.377.
21. Bullock, Alan, *Hitler: A Study in Tyranny*, p.106.
22. Hitler, op. cit., p.377.

CHAPTER III

'Mein Kampf' – Hitler's 'Manifesto'

Mein Kampf (*My Struggle*) was written by Hitler between November 1923 and December 1924 during his imprisonment in the Landsberg Fortress, situated on the Lech river, he having been tried for participating in a failed right-wing 'Putsch' (or revolution) in Munich the previous year. In his book, he recounts the details of his upbringing in Austria, and the time he spent as a young man in its capital Vienna; he also explains his philosophy. More importantly, however, he leaves the reader in no doubt as to his intentions, were he ever to come to power.

He wrote that his time in Vienna (where he mainly lived between the autumn of 1907 when he was aged 18, and June of 1913 when he was 24) provided him with a unique insight into the problems of the poor; knowledge which would be of immense benefit in his subsequent efforts to persuade the German people to accept him as their leader. During that period of his life he lived first in lodgings, then in hostels for the homeless, and finally, on the streets. His ambition had been to enter the city's art college, but he failed to gain admission due to the mediocrity of the grades he had obtained whilst at school, and also because of a lack of aptitude.

The Poor

'Abject poverty confronted the wealth of the aristocracy and the merchant class face to face,' wrote Hitler. 'Thousands of unemployed loitered in front of the palaces on the Ring Strasse; and below that Via Triumphalis of the old Austria, the homeless huddled together in the murk and filth of the canals.'[1]

In a typical household [said Hitler] ... the week's earnings are spent in common at home within two or three days. The family eat and drink together as long as the money lasts, and at the end of the week they hunger together. Then the wife wanders about furtively in the neighbourhood, borrows a little, and runs up small debts with the shopkeepers in an effort to pull through the lean days towards the end of the week. They sit down

13

together to the midday meal with only meagre fare on the table, and often even nothing to eat. They wait for the coming pay-day, talking of it and making plans; and while they are thus hungry they dream of the plenty that is to come. And so the little children become acquainted with misery in their early years.[2]

The manual labourers of Vienna, wrote Hitler,

lived in surroundings of appalling misery. I shudder even today when I think of the woeful dens in which people dwelt, the night shelters and the slums, and all tenebrous spectacles of ordure, loathsome filth and wickedness. [Then, ominously] What will happen one day when hordes of emancipated slaves [i.e. the poor and the oppressed] come forth from these dens of misery to swoop down on their unsuspecting fellow men...? Sooner or later destiny will take its vengeance unless it will have been appeased in time.

As far as Hitler was concerned,

there was a two-fold method by which alone it would be possible to bring about an amelioration of these conditions .... First, to create better funda-mental conditions of social development by establishing a profound feeling for social responsibility among the public; second to combine this feeling for social responsibilities with a ruthless determination to prune away all excrescences which are incapable of being improved.[3]

Prostitution and Syphilis

Hitler, who regarded the Weimar Republic as decadent, even though it was generally considered that Berlin had outstripped even Paris as a city of culture, took a lively interest in what he perceived as other social problems. For example, he had much to say about prostitution and the venereal disease syphilis, which may result from it.

... those who want seriously to combat prostitution must first of all assist in removing the spiritual conditions on which it thrives. They will have to clean up the moral pollution of our city 'culture' fearlessly and without regard for the outcry that will follow. If we do not drag our youth out of the morass of their present environment, they will be engulfed by it. The fight against syphilis and its pace-maker, prostitution, is one of the gigantic tasks of mankind ....[4]

... the primary cause [of syphilis] is to be found in the manner in which love has been prostituted. Even though this did not directly bring about the fearful disease itself, the nation must still suffer serious damage thereby, for the moral havoc resulting from this prostitution would be sufficient to bring about the destruction of the nation, slowly but surely. This Judaising of our spiritual life and mammonising of our natural instinct for procreation will sooner or later work havoc with our whole posterity. For instead of strong, healthy children, blessed with natural feelings, we shall see miserable specimens of humanity resulting from economic calculation. For economic considerations are becoming more and more the foundations of marriage ....[5]

The Institution of Marriage

Hitler regarded marriage not as,

an end in itself, but [something which] must serve the greater end, which is that of increasing and maintaining the human species and the race [by which Hitler meant his own so-called 'Aryan' race]. This is its only meaning and purpose.[6]

Bourgeois (Middle Class) Parties and Trade Unions

Hitler directed his wrath towards the bourgeois parties,

who had opposed every social demand put forward by the working class. The short-sighted refusal to make an effort towards improving labour conditions; the refusal to adopt measures to insure the workman in case of accidents in the factories; the refusal to forbid child labour; the refusal to consider protective measures for female workers, especially expectant mothers.

As a result of this failure of the bourgeois parties the masses had no alternative but to join the Social Democratic Party who could claim, 'that they alone stand up for the interests of the working class.'

This became the principal ground for the moral justification of the actual existence of the trades unions, so that the labour organisations became from that time onwards the chief political recruiting ground to swell the ranks of the Social Democratic Party.[7]

However, by the time he had reached the age of 20, Hitler had,

learned to distinguish between the trade union as a means of defending the social rights of the employees and fighting for better living conditions for them and, on the other hand, the trade union as a political instrument used by the Party in the class struggle.

On balance, therefore, Hitler decided that as far as the trade unions were concerned, he would recommend members of his Party either to leave those unions, 'in which they were enrolled, or to remain in them with the idea of causing as much destruction in them as possible.'[8] Employers and employees would, 'no longer find themselves drawn into mutual conflict over wages and hours of work …' but,

> questions that are now fought over through a quarrel which involves millions of people will then be settled in the representative chambers of trades and professions, and in the Central Economic Parliament.[9]

Here, Hitler was already indicating to the German people what they might expect were he to come to power. In other words, a centralised, authoritarian state.

The Press

Hitler, in *Mein Kampf*, made his intentions perfectly clear. With regard to the so-called 'freedom of the Press', he stated that,

> with ruthless determination, the State must keep control of this instrument of popular education and place it at the service of the State and the Nation.[10]

The Arts

Hitler was also concerned about what he described as 'the Bolshevisation of art ….' A person,

> need only take a glance at those lucky [sarcasm on Hitler's part] states which had become Bolshevised and, to his horror, he will there recognise those morbid monstrosities which have been produced by insane and degenerate people. All those artistic aberrations which are classified under the names of cubism and dadaism … [which] showed signs not only of political, but also of cultural decadence.[11]

Race

Mein Kampf is riddled with racist overtones: 'The worth of the State can be determined only by asking how far it actually succeeds in promoting the well-being of a definite race, and not by the role which it plays in the world at large.'[12]

'Those states which do not serve this purpose have no justification for their existence. They are monstrosities.'[13] Referring to his home country of Austria, Hitler describes, 'forces ... that had their origin in the nationalist yearnings of the various ethnic groups.'[14] In Hitler's opinion, Archduke Franz Ferdinand, 'was the chief patron of the movement to make Austria a Slav state,'[15] to which Hitler was bitterly opposed.

In respect of matters racial, France was not to escape the wrath of Hitler who was already angered by that country's occupation of Germany's Ruhr in 1923. The fact that the French had included native colonial soldiers in their army of occupation angered him still further. 'France is and will remain by far the most dangerous enemy,' he said.

The French people, who are becoming more and more obsessed by negroid ideas, represent a threatening menace to the existence of the white race in Europe. For the contamination caused by the influx of negroid blood on the Rhine, in the very heart of Europe, is in accord with the sadist[ic] and perverse lust for vengeance on the part of the hereditary enemy of our people, just as it suits the purpose of the cool, calculating Jew, who would use this means of introducing a process of bastardisation in the very centre of the European continent and, by infecting the white race with the blood of an inferior stock, would destroy the foundations of its independent existence.[16]

Eugenics

Not only would Hitler's State be organised on racial lines, but he would ensure that within its boundaries only the fittest would survive. He bewailed the fact that:

In this present State of ours ... our national bourgeoisie look upon it as a crime to make procreation impossible for syphilitics and those who suffer from tuberculosis or other hereditary diseases, also cripples and imbeciles.[17]

It was his professed view that in the 'struggle between the various species',

nature looks on calmly, and is even pleased with what happens .... The struggle for the daily livelihood leaves behind in the ruck everything that is weak or diseased or wavering ... and this struggle is a means of further-ing the health and powers of resistance in the species. Thus, it is one of the causes underlying the process of development towards a higher quality of being.[18]

If for a period of only 600 years those individuals would be sterilised, who are physically degenerate or mentally diseased, humanity would not only be delivered from an immense misfortune, but also restored to a state of general health such as we at present can hardly imagine.

Religion

It perhaps comes as a surprise to know that at the time of writing *Mein Kampf,* Hitler regarded himself as a Christian and a 'champion of truth and right'.[19] He was equally in no doubt that '[Jesus] Christ was an Aryan ...'[20] and that, 'Jesus was certainly not a Jew.'[21]

Hitler admired the Catholic church which he said had 'a lesson to teach us'. Even though,

> its dogmatic system is in conflict with the exact sciences and with scientific discoveries, it [the Church] is not disposed to sacrifice a syllable of its teachings. It has rightly recognised that its powers of resistance would be weakened by introducing greater or less trial adaptations to meet the temporary conclusions of science, which in reality are always vacillating.[22]

However, he was soon to make it clear that his objective was change. 'Without a religion of its own the German people has no permanence,' said Hitler. 'What this religion will be, we do not yet know. We feel it, but that is not enough.'[23] This new religion would be based on, 'the old beliefs,' which, 'will be brought back to honour again .... We shall wash off the Christian veneer and bring out a religion peculiar to our race.'[24]

The State

Democracy, 'as practised in Western Europe today,' said Hitler, was, 'the forerunner of Marxism ... Democracy is the breeding ground in which the bacilli of the Marxist world pest can grow and spread.'[25] Therefore, in the 'People's State' which he envisaged, 'no vote would be taken in the chambers or senate' which were to be,

> organisations for work, and not voting machines ... The right of decision belongs exclusively to the president, who must be entirely responsible for the matter under discussion ... this principle of combining absolute authority with absolute responsibility will gradually cause a select group of leaders to emerge; which is not even thinkable in our present epoch of irresponsible parliamentarianism.[26]

'The act of inauguration in citizenship [of this new State], shall be a solemn ceremony,' Hitler declared. 'It entitles him [the new citizen] to exercise all the rights of a citizen and to enjoy all the privileges attached thereto.'[27] Quite what these 'privileges' were was not spelt out.

Education

Hitler was in favour of education, but for him this appears to be with the purpose of fostering nationalistic feelings in the German people, rather than encouraging them to acquire a broader knowledge and wisdom.

> ... only when family upbringing and school education have inculcated in the individual a knowledge of the cultural and economic and, above all, the political greatness of his own country – then, and then only, will it be possible for him to feel proud of being a citizen of such a country. I can fight only for something that I love. I can love only what I respect. And in order to respect a thing, I must at least have some knowledge of it.[28]

***

Volume 1 of *Mein Kampf* ends with the stirring words:

> A fire was enkindled from whose glowing heat the sword would be fashioned which would restore freedom to the German Siegfried [a Wagnerian reference] and bring back life to the German nation. Beside the revival which I then foresaw, I also felt that the Goddess of Vengeance was now getting ready to redress the treason of the 9th November, 1918 .... The movement was on the march.[29]

Notes

1. Hitler, Adolf, *Mein Kampf*, p.24.
2. Ibid, p.26.
3. Ibid, p.27.
4. Ibid, p.146.
5. Ibid, pp.141–2.
6. Ibid, p.144.
7. Ibid, p.36.
8. Ibid, p.333.
9. Ibid, p.331.
10. Ibid, p.139.
11. Ibid, p.147.
12. Ibid, p.222.
13. Ibid, p.221.
14. Ibid, p.51.
15. Ibid, p.19.
16. Ibid, p.343.

17. Ibid, p.226.
18. Ibid, p.161.
19. Prange, Gordon W (ed.), *Hitler's Words*, p.71.
20. *Hitler's Secret Conversations*, 1941–1944, The New American Library of World Literature Inc., p. 75.
21. Ibid, p.328.
22. Hitler, op. cit., p.257.
23. Rauschning, Hermann, *Hitler Speaks*, p.59.
24. Ibid, p.63.
25. Hitler, op. cit., p.53.
26. Ibid, p.252.
27. Ibid, p.247.
28. Ibid, p.29.
29. Ibid, p.209.

CHAPTER IV

The Jews and Bolshevism

Hitler applied some of his most caustic comments to his two pet hates, namely the Jews and the Bolsheviks, against whom his accusations were many and various. (Though as in Germany, the Jews numbered only around 600,000, or slightly less than 1% of the population, it is difficult to see how he could have come to regard them as any kind of threat. However, he had long perceived them as his mortal enemy.)

World War I

On 7 October 1916 Hitler, having been wounded in the leg by shrapnel during the Battle of the Somme, was sent back to hospital in Germany, and once he was able to walk again he obtained leave to visit Berlin. Here, it was his opinion that,

> The art of shirking was looked upon almost as proof of higher intelligence, and devotion to duty was considered a sign of weakness or bigotry. Government offices were staffed by Jews. Almost every clerk was a Jew and every Jew was a clerk. I was amazed at this multitude of combatants who belonged to the chosen people and could not help comparing it with their slender numbers in the fighting lines. In the business world the situation was even worse. Here the Jews had actually become 'indispensable'. Like leeches, they were slowly sucking the blood from the pores of the national body. By means of newly floated War Companies, an instrument had been discovered whereby all national trade was throttled so that no business could be carried on freely. Special emphasis was laid on the necessity for unhampered centralisation. Hence as early as 1916/17 practically all production was under the control of Jewish finance.[1]

The Bolshevik Revolution

When on 7 November 1917 the Russian provisional government of Alexander Kerensky was ousted in a Bolshevik coup, Hitler believed that it was Jews who had helped the Bolsheviks come to power through the doctrine of Marxism which they had invented.

> By categorically repudiating the personal worth of the individual and also the nation and its racial constituent, this doctrine destroys the fundamental basis of all civilisation; for civilization essentially depends on these very factors ... The destruction of the concept of personality and of race removes the chief obstacle which barred the way to domination of the social body by its inferior elements, which are Jews ... To all external appearances, this movement strives to ameliorate the conditions under which the workers live; but in reality its aim is to enslave and thereby annihilate the non-Jewish races.[2]

Germany's Wartime Defeat

When Germany was defeated in World War I, Hitler once again blamed the Jews.

The Revolt in Bavaria

The Soviet uprising in Munich in April/May 1919 which Hitler had witnessed at first hand, was organised by Eugen Levine, Max Levien, Kurt Eisner, Ernst Toller, and Gustav Landauer, all of whom were Jews. Therefore, in the mind of Hitler, as with many millions of Germans, all Marxists were Jews, and all Jews were Marxists. And, of course, Karl Marx – who, paradoxically, had been brought up and educated in Germany – was himself a Jew.

Jewish Finance and Prosperity

In *Mein Kampf*, Hitler wrote, '... as early as 1916–17, practically all [German economic] production was under the control of Jewish finance ... Jewry was busy despoiling the nation and tightening the screws of its despoliation.'[3] However, as usual, Hitler was selective in his analysis and omitted to mention for example, Krupps, (the largest producer of armaments in Germany at that time), which was a German but not a Jewish firm.

In January 1922 Hitler, speaking to Josef Hell, a resident of Munich who was an editor on the staff of the weekly magazine *Der Gerade Weg* (*The Straight Way*) said,

> There are few Germans who are not angered here and there about the behaviour of the Jews, or who have not been injured by Jews. In their relatively small number they control an enormous part of the German National

Wealth. That is money you can confiscate and use for the state and the general public, just as was done with the property of the monasteries, the bishops, and the nobility .... Once the hate and the battle against the Jews is really fanned and stirred up, their resistance will collapse in the shortest possible time. They cannot even protect themselves, and no-one else will provide protection for them.[4]

The fact that Hitler may have envied the Jews for their prosperity is indicated by his description of a visit he made to Berlin where: 'the luxury, the perversion, the iniquity, the wanton display, and the Jewish materialism disgusted me so thoroughly, that I was almost beside myself.'[5]

Civilisation, Art, Literature, the Press

In Vienna there came what appeared to be the turning point in Hitler's life:

In my eyes the charge against Judaism became a grave one the moment I discovered the Jewish activities in the press, in art, in literature and the theatre .... One needed only to look at the posters announcing the hideous productions of the cinema and theatre, and study the names of the authors who were highly lauded there, in order to become permanently adamant on Jewish questions. Here was a pestilence, a moral pestilence, with which the public was being infected. It was worse than the Black Plague of long ago .... The fact that nine-tenths of all the smutty literature, artistic tripe and theatrical banalities, had to be charged to the account of people who formed scarcely one percent of the nation – that fact could not be gain said [i.e. contradicted].[6]

Perhaps Hitler summed up his attitude to the Jews most succinctly thus:

The Jew has never yet founded a civilisation, but he has destroyed hundreds. He can show nothing of his own creation. Everything that he has is stolen. He has foreign people, foreign workers to build his temples; foreigners create and work for him; foreigners shed their blood for him. He has no art of his own; everything has either been stolen from other peoples, or imitated. He does not even know how to preserve these costly possessions. In his hands they turn immediately to filth and dung.

In contrast: 'It was through the Aryan that art and science flourished.'[7]

The State

'It was he [the Aryan] alone, in the final analysis, who knew how to establish states,' said Hitler.

The Jew is incapable of all this. His revolutions, therefore, must be 'international'. They must spread like a disease .... And how long? Until the whole world falls in ruins and brings him down with it in the midst of the ruins.[8]

In the course of a few years he [the Jew] endeavours to exterminate all those who represent the national intelligence. And by this depriving the peoples of their natural intellectual leaders he fits them for their fate as slaves under a lasting despotism. Russia furnishes the most terrible example of such a slavery. In that country the Jew killed or starved 30 million of the people, in a bout of savage fanaticism and partly by the employment of inhuman torture.[9]

Marxism

From the experiences he had of meeting with Jews while he was a resident in the hostel for the homeless in Vienna, Hitler declared that in his opinion, 'a Jew can never be rescued from his fixed notions,' even though he, 'talked to them until my throat ached and my voice grew hoarse. I believed that I could finally convince them of the danger inherent in their Marxist follies. But I achieved only the contrary result.'[10]

Prostitution

The part which the Jews played in the social phenomenon of prostitution, and more especially in the white slave traffic, could be studied here [in Vienna] better than in any other western European city, with the possible exception of certain ports in southern France .... A cold shiver ran down my spine when I first ascertained that it was the same kind of cold blooded, thick skinned and shameless Jew who showed his consummate skill in conducting that revolting exploitation of the dregs of the big city. Then I became fired with wrath.

Having '... learned to track down the Jew in all the different spheres of cultural, artistic life ...,' said Hitler,

I suddenly came upon him in a position where I had least expected to find him. I now realised that the Jews were the leaders of social democracy. In the face of that revelation the scales fell from my eyes. My long inner struggle was at an end.[11]

Vienna as a 'Mongrelised' City

In Vienna, said Hitler,

My inner aversion to the Habsburg State was increasing daily .... The conglomerate spectacle of heterogeneous races which the capital of the dual monarchy [i.e. Austro–Hungarian] presented, this motley of Czechs, Poles, Hungarians, Ruthenians, Serbs and Croats etc. – and always that bacillus which is the solvent of human society, the Jew, here and there and everywhere – the whole spectacle was repugnant to me. The gigantic city seemed to be the incarnation of mongrel depravity.[12]

The Jews as Aliens

In Vienna, it was the Jews who were to attract his attention most. '... the more I saw of them, the more strikingly they stood out as a different people from other citizens ... in outer appearance [they] bore no similarity to the Germans.'[13] It was obvious that for Adolf Hitler the early stages of anti-Semitism were beginning to take root.

It appears that simply being in the presence of a Jew induced in him a feeling of physical revulsion. 'That they were water-shy was obvious ... The odour of those people in caftans often used to make me feel ill. Beyond that there were the unkempt clothes and the ignoble exterior.' Hitler then extrapolated these thoughts to give them a wider meaning.

Was there any shady undertaking, any form of foulness, especially in cultural life, in which at least one Jew did not participate? On putting the probing knife carefully to that kind of abscess one immediately discovered, like a maggot in a putrescent body, a little Jew who was often blinded by the sudden light.[14]

In the Jew I still saw only a man who was of a different religion, and therefore, on grounds of human tolerance, I was against the idea that he should be attacked because he had a different faith. And so I considered that the tone adopted by the anti-Semitic press was unworthy of the cultural traditions of a great people.[15]

Gradually however, Hitler's attitude towards the Jews was to harden:

Once, when passing through the inner city [of Vienna] I suddenly encountered a phenomenon in a long caftan and growing black side-locks. My first thought was: is this a Jew? They certainly did not have this appearance in Linz. I watched the man stealthily and cautiously, but the longer I gazed at the strange countenance and examined it feature by feature, the more the question shaped itself in my brain: Is this a German? Wherever I now went

I saw Jews, and the more I saw of them the more strikingly and clearly they stood out as a different people from the other citizens. Especially the inner city and the district northwards from the Danube Canal swarmed with people who, even in outward appearance, bore no similarity to the Germans.[16]

Hitler went on to describe 'mischievous' articles which he had read in the Marxist press, and discovered that, 'From the publisher downwards, all of them were Jews.' Then he, 'recalled to mind the names of the public leaders of Marxism,' and,

> realised that most of them belonged to the Chosen Race – the social democratic representatives of the Imperial Cabinet as well as the secretaries of the trades unions and the street agitators. Everywhere, the same sinister picture presented itself. I shall never forget the row of names – [Friedrich] Austerlitz, [Anton] David, [Victor] Adler, and [Wilhelm] Ellenbogen and others. One fact became quite evident to me. It was this alien race [that] held in its hands the leadership of that Social Democratic Party with whose minor representatives I had been disputing for months past. I was happy at last to know for certain that the Jew is not of German stock.[17]

Religion

So how did Hitler reconcile his own faith – he was a Catholic and received Communion during the First World War – with his attitude towards the Jews? He reveals this in a speech delivered on 12 April 1922:

> My feeling as a Christian points me to my Lord and Saviour as a fighter. It points to the man who once lonely and with only a few followers, recognized these Jews for what they were, and called men to fight them, and who, so help me, was greatest not as a sufferer but as a fighter. With boundless love, as a Christian and as a man, I read the passage which relates how the Lord finally gathered His strength, and made use of the whip, in order to drive the usurpers, the vipers, and cheats, from the temple. Today, 2,000 years later, I recognise with deep emotion Christ's tremendous fight for the world against the Jewish poison.[18]

But then, paradoxically: 'The heaviest blow that ever struck humanity was the coming of Christianity,' said Hitler, and 'Bolshevism is Christianity's illegitimate child. Both are inventions of the Jew.'[19]

***

In Hitler's opinion the Jew was to blame for virtually everything. 'Not satisfied with the economic conquest of the world,' he states, 'the Jew was now also demanding that it must come under his political control ....'[20] 'In the field of politics,' says Hitler, 'he [the Jew] now begins to replace the idea of democracy by introducing the dictatorship of the proletariat ... so as to subjugate and rule in a dictatorial fashion by the aid of brute force.[21] Was not the Jew, in political life, always on the side of analysis and criticism?' asked Hitler, as if to imply that these two were some kind of crime.[22] It was

> no longer princes or their courtesans who contend and bargain about state frontiers, but the inexorable cosmopolitan Jew, who is fighting for his own dominion over the nation. The sword is the only means whereby a nation can thrust that clutch from his throat. Only when national sentiment is organised and concentrated into an effective force can it defy that international menace which tends towards an enslavement of the nation. But this road is, and will always be marked with bloodshed. [A blunt forewarning of the Holocaust.][23]

As for the Bolsheviks:

> ... the present rulers of Russia are blood-stained criminals, but here we have the dregs of humanity which, favoured by the circumstances of the tragic moment, overran a great State, degraded and extirpated [rooted out] millions of educated people out of sheer blood-lust ... One does not form an alliance with a partner whose only aim is the destruction of his fellow partner. Above all, one does not enter into alliances with people for whom no treaty is sacred: because they do not move about this earth as men of honour and sincerity but as the representatives of lies and deception, thievery and plunder and robbery ....

[Fine words from Hitler, which in the light of his future conduct, can be seen in retrospect to be entirely vapid!]

In Hitler's mind Bolsheviks and Jews were inexorably linked. 'The Bolshevisation of Germany' with, 'the extermination of the patriotic and national German intellectuals' had forced German Labour, 'to bear the yoke of international Jewish finance,' he states.[24] 'In Russian Bolshevism, we ought to recognise the kind of attempt which is being made by the Jew in the Twentieth Century to secure dominion over the world.'[25]

Hitler described Germany's, 'position in relation to Russia' as, 'the most important problem in our foreign policy.'[26]

To restore Germany's frontiers, 'as they existed in 1914' would be, 'thoroughly illogical,' in the sense that this would not include, 'all the members of the German nation' nor was such a course of action to be considered, 'reasonable, in view of the geographical exigencies of military defence.'[27] 'We, as National Socialists, must stick firmly to the aim that we have set for our foreign policy,' said Hitler, 'namely that the German people must be assured [of] the territorial area which is necessary for it to exist on this earth.'[28] In future, this territory would not be obtained, 'as a favour from other people, but we will have to win it by the power of a triumphant sword.'[29]

In a final, ominous warning, Hitler declared: 'Today, Germany is the next battlefield for Russian Bolshevism!'[30]

***

Why did Hitler not take the opposite view and look on the Bolsheviks and Jews in a friendly and constructive light? The reason is that this would have gone against the man whose teachings were the principal source of Hitler's philosophy, namely the former monk, Jörg Adolf Lanz, alias Baron Adolf Jörg Lanz von Liebenfels, Ph.D., who wrote the following passages:

> The socialistic-bolshevistic primitive race has given us notice. Fine, we will give them notice that we've given up charity and humanity. They want class warfare, they shall have race warfare, race warfare from our side until the castration knife.[31]
>
> The Jews – as hybrid beasts of historical and prehistorical races, and from the dross of all fallen cultures – are the living witnesses and testimony of Frauja's (the Lord Jesus Christ's) suffering, the death (Christ's crucifixion) caused by blending of the ancient heroic peoples of venerable manhood.[32]

Here Liebenfels appears to apportion the blame for Christ's crucifixion on racial intermingling, rather than on the Jews specifically.

> A culture without slaves is not possible. Therefore, the enslavement of the inferior race is a real and economic demand.[33]

Liebenfels and his influence on Hitler will be discussed shortly.

Notes

1. Hitler, Adolf, *Mein Kampf*, p.114.
2. Ibid, p.181–2.
3. Ibid, p.114.
4. Josef Hell manuscript in Charles Bracelen Flood, 1922, p.245 and p.649.
5. Langer, Walter, Information obtained from Ernst Hanfstaengl(901), p.35.
6. Hitler, op. cit., p.42.
7. Ibid, p.171.
8. *Der Volkischer Beobachter*, Munich, 28 July 1922; 16 Aug. 1922, in Prange, Gordon W (ed.), *Hitler's Words*, p.75.
9. Hitler, op. cit., p.185.

10. Ibid, p.44.

11. Ibid, p.43.

12. Ibid, p.79.

13. Ibid, p.41

14. Ibid, p.42.

15. Ibid, p.39.

16. Ibid, p.41.

17. Ibid, p.44.

18. *Der Volkischer Beobachter*, Munich, 12 April 1922; 22 April 1922, in Prange, op. cit., p.71.

19 Trevor-Roper, H R (ed.), *Hitler's Table Talk, 1941–1944*, p.7.

20. Hitler, op. cit., p.182.

21. Ibid, p.185.

22. Rauschning, Hermann, *Hitler Speaks,* p.232.

23. Hitler, op. cit., p.364.

24. Ibid, p.342–3.

25. Ibid, p.364.

26 Ibid, p.353.

27. Ibid, p.357.

28. Ibid, p.359.

29. Ibid, p.360.

30. Ibid, p.364.

31. *Ostara*, III/4 [see below], in Daim, p.30.

32. *Die Priesterschaft St Bernhards von Clairvaux*, II. Teil. Szt Balazs 1930, in Daim, p.196.

33. *Ostara*, III/19, in Daim, p.272.

N.B. *Ostara* references (Series I, Nos 1–100); Series II, No. 1; Series III, Nos 1–101) are
to text in Daim (principally pp. 195–207, translated by Martin Clay and Nicholas
Dragffy); and from 'Grey Lodge Occult Review' by Manfred Nagl (in www.
antiqillum.com/glor/glor_005/nazimyth.htm., translated by Sabine Kurth).

CHAPTER V

The Origins of Hitler's Ideas

In view of the fact that Hitler was soon to become the most powerful man in the world, and to impose his will on large portions of it, it is pertinent to enquire as to the source of his ideas.

School

Hitler's performance at school, and in particular at 'Realschule' (secondary school) was undistinguished, and he left having failed to obtain his vital 'Abitur' (school leaving examination diploma at 16). Highly critical of his school teachers, he complained that, 'they had no sympathy with youth ....' 'If any pupil showed the slightest trace of originality they persecuted him relentlessly, and the only model pupils whom I have ever known have all been failures in later life.'[1] There was one teacher, however, whom Adolf did admire, namely Dr Leopold Poetsch, a fervent German Nationalist. Adolf describes the two of them sitting together, 'often aflame with enthusiasm, sometimes even moved to tears .... The national fervour which we felt in our own small way, was used by him [Potsch] as an instrument of our education ...' It was for this reason that history became Hitler's favourite subject.[2]

Georg Ritter von Schönerer

It was while he was living as a 19-year-old in the Austrian town of Linz (in early 1908) that Hitler became acquainted with the teachings of Georg Ritter von Schönerer, a Viennese born in 1842.

Schönerer, founder of Austria's Pan-German Nationalist Party, had been elected to the Austrian Reichsrat (Upper House of Parliament) in 1873 where he made anti-Semitic speeches. He was vigorously opposed to liberals, socialists, Catholics, Jews, and the Habsburgs, and demanded the separation of the German-speaking provinces of Austria from the multi-national Hapsburg Empire, in favour of their economical and political union with the German Reich.

The Schönerer 'code' advocated celibacy until the age of 25; the avoidance of eating meat and drinking alcohol (which were seen as aphrodisiacs); the avoidance of consorting with prostitutes due to the danger of infection. (Hitler himself is believed to have been a teetotaller and to have preferred a vegetarian diet.) It was Schönerer who bestowed the title of 'Führer' on himself, and instituted the 'Heil' greeting.

As Hitler said in *Mein Kampf*, 'When I came to Vienna, all my sympathies were exclusively with the Pan-German movement.'[3] However, in his view, the way Schönerer's party supported the parliamentary system of democracy, and its failure to win over the support of the 'establishment' and in particular the army, was a weakness.

Hitler, instead, found himself to be more in sympathy with Doctor Karl Lueger, head of Austria's Christian Socialists, whom he admired for his ability to

adopt all available means for winning the support of long established institutions, so as to be able to derive the greatest possible advantage for his movement from those old sources of power.[4]

However, in Hitler's opinion, both these parties had weaknesses: the Pan-German Party in its failure to arouse the broad masses of the people; the Christian Socialists for their failure to embrace Pan-Germanism.

Authors whom Hitler professed to have read

Referring to his time spent in Vienna from 1908 Hitler said: 'I now often turn to the *Volksblat*' – a reference to the anti-Semitic Viennese newspaper. Subsequently, during his period of incarceration in the Landsberg Fortress (1923–4), which he described as his, 'university paid for by the state,' Hitler declared that he, 'devoured book after book, pamphlet after pamphlet.'[5] In *Mein Kampf* he mentions by name the works of von Ranke (Professor of History in Berlin); Treitschke; H S Chamberlain (writer and propagandist); Nietzsche (German philosopher, scholar and writer); Marx (German social, political and economic theorist); Prince Otto von Bismark (Prusso–German statesman and the first Chancellor of the German Empire); together with the war memoirs of German and Allied soldiers and statesmen.[6]

In this, Hitler may well have been telling the truth – after all at school, history had been a favourite subject, and in prison he would have had ample time to read. He also mentions H S Chamberlain, the German philosopher Schopenhauer, and his former schoolteacher Leopold Poetsch. It is interesting, therefore, to discover what these authors actually had to say, and to what extent their ideas coincided with those of Hitler.

Arthur Schopenhauer

Arthur Schopenhauer (1788–1860), German philosopher of metaphysics, postulated a world of suffering and disappointment, and took an atheistic and pessimistic view of the world; pessimistic because of what he perceived as an irrational force in human beings which produces an ever frustrating cycle of desire, from which the only escape is aesthetic contemplation or absorption into nothingness. Perhaps one reason why Hitler admired him was because of his reference to the Jew as, 'The great master of lies.'[7]

Heinrich von Treitschke

Heinrich von Treitschke (1834–1896), German historian, regarded war not only as an inevitability, but something to be glorified.

> ... martial glory is the basis of all the political virtues; in the rich treasure of Germany's glories the Prussian military glory is a jewel as precious as the masterpieces of our poets and thinkers. War is not only a practical necessity, it is also a theoretical necessity, an exigency of logic. The concept of the state implies the concept of war, for the essence of the state is power .... That war should ever be banished from the world is a hope, not only absurd, but profoundly immoral. It would involve the atrophy of many of the essential and sublime forces of the human soul .... The people which become attached to the chimerical hope of perpetual peace finishes irremediably by decaying in its proud isolation ....

Treitschke also affirmed that, 'It does not matter what you think, so long as you obey.'[8]

Houston Stewart Chamberlain

Houston Stewart Chamberlain (1855–1927), writer and propagandist, was born in Southsea, Hampshire on 9 September 1855. Aged 14, because of poor health, he left England to visit health resorts on the Continent, accompanied by Prussian tutor Otto Kuntze, who extolled to him the virtues of Prussian militarism, and introduced him to German history, literature and philosophy, including the works of composers and poets such as Beethoven, Schiller, Goethe and Wagner. Kuntze remained his tutor for four years. At the University of Geneva Chamberlain embarked upon a three-year study of various subjects, including philosophy, physics, chemistry and medicine.

Having married Anna Horst, a Prussian, Chamberlain and his wife set up home in Dresden where they spent four years, before moving to Vienna in 1889. Here, he researched into plant physiology.

Chamberlain began his writing career in January 1892. His *Foundations of the Nineteenth Century* was published in 1899, with an introduction written by the Englishman Algernon Bertram Mitford (grandfather of the famous Mitford sisters), known as Bertie, who in 1906 became Lord Redesdale. The book attributes the moral, cultural, scientific and technological superiority of western civilisation to the positive influence of the 'Germanic race' (which for him included Slavs and Celts).

As far as Christianity was concerned, Chamberlain believed that it had developed into a murderous, totalitarian system because of two factors, namely the Catholic church whose influence relied on terror, and the laws of the Old Testament which he attributed to a Jewish influence. In fact, he opposed any cultural, religious or political system which had global aspirations, such as the Catholic church, capitalism and socialism.

Foundations of the Nineteenth Century was greeted with rapture by German Kaiser Wilhelm II, who invited the author to his Court; thus began a lifelong friendship and correspondence between the two of them. 'It was God who sent your book to the German people, and you personally to me,' wrote Wilhelm to Chamberlain.

Chamberlain was in turn influenced by the writings of Joseph Arthur, Compte de Gobineau (1816–82) whose *Essai sur l'Inégalité des Races Humaines* made the case for the superiority of Nordics and Aryans, peoples who he, Gobineau, forecast would decline owing to their intermingling with other races.

In 1905 Chamberlain divorced his wife Anna, and three years later married Eva, the daughter of the late composer Richard Wagner (who had died in 1883). Chamberlain had first met Wagner and his wife Cosima, in Bayreuth in 1882 and it was in that city that the couple would settle.

In 1915 Chamberlain, who regarded it as an act of treason that Britain had opposed Germany during World War I, was awarded the Iron Cross for services to the German Empire; in 1916 he adopted German nationality.

On 30 September 1923 Hitler, who was visiting Wagner's widow, the 86-year-old Cosima, at Bayreuth, crossed the road to call on the aged Chamberlain, who was by this time blind, paralysed and confined to a wheel chair. As Hitler took his leave the old man wept with grief.

A few days later, Chamberlain wrote to Hitler:

My belief in the Germans has already been strong although – I confess – it had ebbed. With one stroke, you have changed the state of my soul. That Germany gives birth to a Hitler in the time of direst need is proof of her vitality ... may God protect you.[9]

In no way do you resemble the descriptions depicting you as a fanatic. I even believe that you are the absolute opposite of a fanatic ... The fanatic wants to persuade people, you want to convince them and to convince only.[10]

On the question of Christianity, Hitler and Chamberlain parted company. 'In my view, H S Chamberlain was mistaken in regarding Christianity as a reality upon the spiritual level,' said Hitler. Whereas, 'We have no reason to wish that the Italians and Spaniards should free themselves from the drug of Christianity. Let us be the only people who are immunised against the disease.'[11]

Had Chamberlain been able to read Hitler's mind, perhaps he would not have been so distraught at their parting. Hitler, for his part, knew that one day, if he had his way, he would betray Chamberlain's ideals, for it was the latter's wish that no harm should come to the Jews.

Chamberlain died on 9 January 1927 aged 71; by which time he had written books on German philosopher Immanuel Kant, and German poet Johann Wolfgang von Goethe, as well as a biography of Wagner.

Friedrich Wilhelm Nietzsche

Friedrich Wilhelm Nietzsche (1844–1900), German philosopher, scholar and writer, was an admirer of Richard Wagner, regarding that composer's operas as the true successors to Greek tragedy. However, he broke with Wagner in 1876, ostensibly because he believed that the Christian convictions expressed in Wagner's opera 'Parsival' were 'mere play-acting'.

In essays published between 1873 and 1876, Nietzsche repudiated Christian and liberal ethics and democratic ideals, seeing the deeds of the great as being more historically significant than the movements of the masses. Christianity was a 'slave morality', and democracy was a means by which quantity was made to prevail over quality. As far as nationalism and racialism were concerned, Nietzsche despised them both.

> God is dead, but considering the state the species Man is in, there will perhaps be caves, for ages yet, in which his shadow will be shown. Morality is the herd-instinct of the individual. The Christian resolution to find the world ugly and bad has made the world ugly and bad. Believe me! The secret of reaping the greatest fruit from us and the greatest enjoyment from life is to live dangerously![12]

For Nietzsche the decadent western Christian civilisation had to be swept away, and the heroic superman who took its place would be above conventional morality. 'A daring and ruler race is building itself up...,' said Nietzsche.

> The aim should be to prepare a trans-valuation of values for a particularly strong kind of man, most highly gifted in intellect and will. This man and the elite around him will become the 'Lords of the Earth'.[13]

'I teach you Superman,' said Nietzsche. 'Man is something to be surpassed.'[14]

Nietzsche described this heroic leader thus:

Such beings are incalculable, they come like fate without cause or reason, inconsiderably and without pretext. Suddenly they are here like lightning: too terrible, too sudden, too compelling and too 'different' even to be hated ... What moves them is the terrible egotism of the artist of the brazen glance, who knows himself to be justified for all eternity in his 'work' as the mother is justified in her child.[15]

When Nietzsche died in 1900, Hitler was only 20 years old. However, two other statements made by Nietzsche may be considered to be prophetic as far as the rise of Hitler is concerned:

1. *In all great deceivers a remarkable process is at work to which they owe their power. In the very act of deception with all its preparations, the dreadful voice, expression and gestures, they are overcome by their belief in themselves; it is this belief which then speaks, so persuasively, so miracle-like, to the audience.*[16]

2. *He who fights with monsters might take care lest he thereby become a monster. And if you gaze for long into an abyss, the abyss gazes also into you.*[17]

Leopold Poetsch

According to Hitler in *Mein Kampf*, it appears that the concept of racism was first put into his mind by his teacher Doctor Leopold Poetsch of the Realschule in Linz. In Hitler's words, 'The national fervour which we felt in our own small way was utilised by him [Poetsch] as an instrument of our education ....'[18]

***

Is Hitler to be believed when he says that he read – and therefore by implication had a detailed knowledge of – the works of these philosophers and teachers? Professor Robert G L Waite believes this to be unlikely. In his opinion, 'Hitler lacked the intellectual patience and discipline to read long books.'[19]

Instead, the truth appears to be that although Hitler would undoubtedly have been acquainted and identified with some aspects of the above, there were other more contemporary, more graphic, and more immediately intelligible, sources upon which his philosophy rested.

Before examining these sources, however, it is first necessary to enquire as to the meaning of the word 'Aryan', for it was on the concept of 'Aryan supremacy' that the Third Reich was founded.

Notes

1. Bullock, Alan, *Hitler: A Study in Tyranny*, p. 27.
2. Ibid.
3. Hitler, Adolf, *Mein Kampf*, p. 64.
4. Ibid, p. 65.
5. Ibid, p. 40.
6. Frank, Hans, 1953, *Im Angesicht des Galgen*, Munich-Grafelfing. pp. 46–7.
7. Hitler, op. cit., p. 173.
8. Shirer, William L, *The Rise and Fall of the Third Reich*, p. 99.
9. Chamberlain to Hitler, October 7, 1923. American Historical Association, German Records Collection, Roll 4. Microcopy number T84. Folder 8. Frames 3715 to 3721.
10. Briefe (letters) 1882–1924, Und Briefwechsel mit Kaiser Wilhelm II, vol. 2, page 124.
11. Hitler's Secret Conversations, 1941–1944, The New American Library of World Literature Inc. Speech. December 13, 1941.
12. Nietzsche, Friedrich, 1910, *Die Fröhliche Wissenschaft* (*The Joyful Wisdom*), pp. 3, 18, 116, 130, 283.
13. Nietzsche, Friedrich, *The Will to Power*.
14. Nietzsche, Friedrich, *Die Begrüssung*.
15. Nietzsche, Friedrich, 1887, *Zur Genealogie der Moral* (*A Genealogy of Morals*), section 2, para. 17.
16. Nietzsche, Friedrich, 1878, *Human, All Too Human*, para. 52, quoted by J P Stern, p. 35.
17. Nietzsche, Friedrich. *Jenseits von Gut und Bose* (*Beyond Good and Evil*), 1b, 146.
18. Hitler, op. cit., p. 19.
19. Wolman, Benjamin (ed.), *The Psychoanalytic Interpretation of History*, p. 197.

CHAPTER VI

The Concept of the 'Aryan'

'If we divide mankind into three categories: founders of culture, bearers of culture, destroyers of culture,' said Hitler in *Mein Kampf*, '[then] the Aryan alone can be considered as representing the first category.'

Every manifestation of human culture, every product of art, science and technical skill, which we see before our eye today, is almost exclusively the product of the Aryan creative power. This very fact fully justifies the conclusion that it was the Aryan alone who founded a superior type of humanity. Therefore, he represents the archetype of what we understand by the term MAN. He is the Prometheus of mankind from whose shining brow the divine spark of genius has at all times flashed forth ....

'Should he [the Aryan] be forced to disappear, a profound darkness will descend on the Earth; within a few thousand years human culture will vanish and the world will become a desert.'[1] If the Aryan should be 'exterminated or subjugated,' said Hitler, 'Then the dark shroud of a new barbarian era would enfold the Earth.' (In the light of what he himself was shortly to inflict upon the world, one might consider the reverse to be the case!)

Curiously enough, Hitler regarded the inhabitants of the USA as 'Aryans', even though the time would come when he would plot the destruction of that country.[2]

So who, in Hitler's opinion, were the Aryans, and how had they come into such prominence?

Aryan tribes, often almost ridiculously small in number, subjugated foreign peoples and, stimulated by the conditions of life which their new country afforded them, and profiting also by the abundance of manual labour furnished them by the inferior race, they developed intellectual and organising faculties which had hitherto been dormant in these conquering tribes. Within the course of a few thousand years, or even centuries [Hitler was apparently not quite sure which] they gave life to cultures whose primitive traits completely corresponded to the character of the founders, then modified by adaptation to the peculiarities of the soil and the character-

37

istics of the subjugated people. But finally the conquering race offended against the principles which they first had observed namely the maintenance of their racial stock unmixed, and they began to intermingle with the subjugated people. Thus they put an end to their own separate [self-contained] existence; for the original sin committed in paradise has always been followed by the expulsion of the guilty parties.[3]

***

In the light of the evidence, it is astonishing that the leader of a hitherto literate and cultured country, i.e. Germany, should have had the arrogance to believe that his particular peoples were superior, and that 'non-Aryans' were inferior. It would have been interesting, therefore, to enquire of Hitler, how he accounted for the emergence in Russia, for example, of composers such as Tchaikovsky, Borodin (who was also a scientist), Glinka and Mussorgsky; poets such as Pushkin and Blok; writers such as Tolstoy, Dostoevsky and Chekhov, to name but a few. (By a quirk of fate, it was Tolstoy who wrote *War and Peace* – arguably the finest novel in world literature – about the French Emperor Napoleon Bonaparte's disastrous military campaign in Russia.)

***

So how do Hitler's notions about the 'Aryan race' measure up to reality? According to the *Oxford English Dictionary*, the term 'Aryan' referred to, 'the worshippers of the gods of the Brahmans (of the highest Hindu caste.)'[4] 'It also applies to a family of languages (which includes Sanskrit, Zend, Greek, Persian, Latin, Celtic, Teutonic and Slavonic, with their modern representatives)', although historically, 'only the ancient Indian and Iranian members of the family are known... to have called themselves, "Aria, Arya or Ariya".'

> The idea current in the 19th century of an Aryan race corresponding to a definite Aryan language was taken up by nationalistic and historical and romantic writers. It was given a special currency by de Gobineau, who linked it with the theory of the essential inferiority of certain races. The term 'Aryan race' was later revived and used for purposes of political propaganda in Nazi Germany.[5]

However, J S Huxley (English biologist and humanist) stated that, 'Biologically, it is almost as illegitimate to speak of a "Jewish race" as of an "Aryan race".'[6] Madison Grant declared that, 'the name "Aryan race" must (also) be frankly discarded as a term of racial significance.'[7] Even H S Chamberlain admitted that, 'It were [i.e. has been] proved that there never was an Aryan race in the past ....'[8]

***

Did it ever cross the minds of Hitler's acolytes that their very own 'Führer' had none of the attributes of the Aryan, that 'Superman' whom he affected so greatly to espouse – with the exception of blue eyes, that is? (Perhaps this is why he included the Nordic peoples as being equally worthy members of the 'superior race', since his own features were definitely more Nordic than they were Aryan!)

As for the acolytes themselves, there was hardly one amongst them, from the diminutive Goebbels, to the corpulent Himmler – whom one might be likely to mistake for a member of the Master Race!

NOTES

1. Hitler, Adolf, *Mein Kampf*, p.164.
2. Ibid.
3. Ibid, p.165.
4, 5.*The Oxford English Dictionary*, 2nd edn. 1989, Vol. 1. Oxford: Clarendon Press.
6. Huxley, J S, *Race in Europe*, p.24.
7. Grant, Madison, *Passing of Great Race*, 1917, V.62.
8. Chamberlain, H S, *Foundations of the 19th Century*, iv.266.

CHAPTER VII

Guido Von List

As will be demonstrated, Guido von List (1848–1919) was important to Hitler, not only as a primary source of inspiration, but also because he was a formative influence on a person who was to be pre-eminent in providing Hitler with his ideas (namely Lanz von Liebenfels).

List was born in Vienna on 5 October 1848 into a Catholic family. After the death of his father, a prosperous leather merchant, List left the family business. As a newspaper journalist he also became a contributor of articles for periodical magazines or journals, and a prolific writer of books.

List was a staunch supporter of the Hapsburg monarchy and imperial dynasty … (a sentiment with which Hitler would most certainly not have approved.)[1] In the early 1900s he claimed that he was descended from the aristocracy and added the title 'von' to his name.

Elsa Schmidt-Falk, wife of an SA (Stormtrooper) leader, was honorary director of the Department of Family Research in the NSDAP's Nazi Party's Munich-North Executive District Committee, and also Honorary Assistant Advisor for Genealogy in the National Socialist women's organisation.

She affirmed that Hitler rated List's work very highly and above all, his two-volume work *Deutsch-Mythologische Landschaftsbilder* (*Images of German Mythological Landscapes*). Hitler also expressed the opinion that, with these two volumes of List, the Austrians possessed such a treasure that other German countries should acquire something similar. Hitler commissioned Frau Falk to make drawings of these Bavarian mythological landscapes (which she did), and, according to the author Wilfried Daim, 'she showed me copies which she had prepared, on the occasion of our conversation.'[2]

Frau Falk also affirmed that Hitler believed that the reference by List to the advent of the 'invincible', 'strong man from above' referred specifically to himself.[3] In fact this was a reference to the discovery in 1891 by List of a prophetic verse in the *Voluspa* (which is contained in a collection of mythological and heroic old Norse poetry, dating from the 12th century and known as the *Edda* – meaning literally, 'The wisdom of the prophetess'), which predicted that a messianic figure, the 'Starke von Oben' ('Strong one from the Skies') would come and set up an eternal order.

As a pan-Germanist (democratic, social-reformist, but anti-liberal and anti-Semitic), List was in favour of promoting German culture and language, and attempted to establish links between modern German place names and the ancient pagan religions. In a speech delivered in 1878, he demanded the, 'economic and political union of German-speaking Austria with the German Reich.'[4] In 1911 List predicted war prophesying that,

> The Aryo–German–Austrian battleships shall once more … shoot sizzling from the giant guns of our dreadnoughts; our national armies shall once more storm southwards and westwards to smash the enemy and create order.[5]

List called for, 'the ruthless subjection of non-Aryans to Aryan masters in a highly structured, hierarchical state.'[6] The church, he said, had, 'encouraged a deviation from strict eugenics of "the old Aryan sexual morality" ....'[7]

> The qualification for candidates for education or positions in public service, the professions and commerce rested solely on their racial purity. The heroic Aryo-German race was to be relieved of all wage labour and demeaning tasks, in order to rule as an exalted elite over the slave castes of non-Aryan peoples. Strict racial and marital laws were to be observed; a patriarchal society was to be fostered in which only the male head of the house had full majority, and only Aryo-Germans enjoyed the privileges of freedom and citizenship; each family was to keep a genealogical record attesting [to] its racial purity ....

These ideas were published in 1911.[8]

***

It was List's belief, articulated in 1893, that the ancient native Germans (whom he called 'Aryo-Germans') once possessed their own language and their own religion, Wotanism (after Wotan, the Germanic god of war). 'The central tenet of Wotanism was the cyclical nature of the universe which proceeded through a series of transformations: "birth", "being", "death", and "rebirth".'[9]

According to the *Edda*, it was Wotan who first gained an understanding of the runes, which, according to Norse legend, were not only a system of writing, but also possessed an inherent, magical power.[10]

The Secret of the Runes was published by List in 1908. He convinced himself that the runes were 'the script of our Germanic ancestors' (i.e. the 'Aryans')[11] being divided into 'letter-runes' and 'hieroglyph-runes' (holy-signs).

The sixth rune embraces the concept of the Aryan tribe or race which, 'is to be purely preserved; it may not be defiled by the roots of the foreign tree.' 'Therefore: "Your blood, [is] your highest possession".'[12]

The eleventh or 'sig' rune ('victory-rune') was, according to List, associated with the 'millenia-old Aryan greeting and battle-cry …' (namely, 'sal and sig!' – meaning salvation and victory). The message of the sig rune is therefore: 'The creative spirit must conquer!'[13]

List states that, 'the seventeenth or "eh-rune" plays off against the sixteenth'. Just as the former warns against frivolous transitory love affairs, so the 'marriage ('ehe-rune') confirms the concept of lasting love on the basis of marriage as the legal bond between a man and a woman. Marriage is the basis of the folk [people], and according to an ancient legal formula the, 'raw-root of the continuance of Teutondom.' Therefore: 'Marriage is the raw-root of the Aryans!'[14]

List classified the 'social levels' of the Aryans into 'provider class', 'teacher class', and 'soldier class'. However, because, 'All Aryans or Teutons felt themselves to be one folk,' then, 'every individual, be he free man or king, had to belong to the "provider class" in order to prevent this class from being devalued'. In effect, this meant that, 'Everyone had, therefore, to be a farmer ....'[15]

'In the Aryan world,' said List,

There was no personal ownership of land and soil, only familial estates: the elder governed it for his clan, the members of which only had rights of usage over it. If their number became too great for the ownership of land, then the serfs would have to migrate, never to return. Such migratory expeditions were known as 'colonisation efforts' and the resulting, Aryan foundations were to be found throughout the whole world ... reaching all the way back into prehistoric times.[16]

It was possible, 'to recognise in the old Aryan sexual morality the truly traditional and true wisdom – which must and will lead our folk to salvation.'[17] The, 'old Aryo–Germanic world view,' said List, 'was that "Wuotanism" [Wotanism] assures those who fall in battle of a heroic heaven with eternal joy in Walhalla [Valhalla – celestial resting place of the souls of fallen heroes.]'[18]

***

Hitler would certainly have found himself in tune with List's antagonistic feelings towards, 'democracy, parliamentarianism, feminism and "Jewish" influences in the arts, press and business.' Also with List's prescription for, 'a rigid hierarchy of offices, levels of authority and traditional administrative districts ['Gaue' – to be administered by 'Gauleiters' – regional party leaders.][19] Finally, for Hitler, the concept of himself as a new messianic, 'strong one from the skies' would clearly have been a difficult one to resist.

NOTES

1. Goodrick-Clarke, Nicholas, *The Occult Roots of Nazism*, p. 65.
2. Daim, Dr Wilfried, *Der Mann, der Hitler die Ideen gab*, p. 96.
3. Hamann, Brigitte, *Hitler's Vienna: a Dictator's Apprenticeship*, p. 212–13.
4. Goodrick-Clarke, op. cit., p. 37.
5. List, Guido von, *Das Geheimnis der Runen*. 2a., p.81f. (in Goodrick-Clarke, p. 85).

6. Goodrick-Clarke, op. cit., p. 63.
7. Ibid, p. 68.
8. List, Guido von, op. cit., 2a. p. 70 ff. (in Goodrick-Clarke, p. 64).
9. Barker, Alan, *Invisible Eagle: The History of Nazi Occultism*, p. 41.
10. Ibid.
11. List, Guido von, *The Secret of the Runes* (translated 1988 by Stephen Flowers), Destiny Books, Vermont, USA, p. 42.
12. Ibid, p. 53.
13. Ibid, p. 57.
14. Ibid, p. 63.
15. Ibid, p. 75.
16. Ibid, p. 76.
17. Ibid, p. 98.
18. Ibid, p. 107.
19. Goodrick-Clarke, op. cit., p. 200.

CHAPTER VIII

Lanz Von Liebenfels

In *Mein Kampf*, Hitler, referring to his sojourn in Vienna (which commenced in 1908) stated that here, 'For the first time in my life, I bought myself some anti-Semitic pamphlets for a few pence.'[1]

In his book, *Der Mann, der Hitler die Ideen gab* (*The Man who gave Hitler his Ideas* – published in 1958), Wilfried Daim (Viennese psychologist, psychotherapist and writer) sheds light on what these pamphlets were, and on who wrote them. Daim describes how in 1951 he was told by a friend, Dr Erwin von Watersrat,

> about the sect of a certain Lanz von Liebenfels. In his [Watersrat's] opinion I ought to meet the people who would interest me, from the psychological standpoint, about the sect.[2]

By coincidence,

> shortly after that, on 27 March 1951 Professor A M Knoll [August Maria Knoll, Professor of Sociology at the University of Vienna] mentioned, in the company of some friends [one of whom presumably was Daim], a certain Lanz von Liebenfels, who in his opinion had given Hitler some decisive ideas. He [Knoll] mentioned the *Ostara*, a journal which Lanz [Daim's preferred name for Liebenfels] had founded in 1905; adding that the ideas propagated in this organ were completely mad.[3]
>
> Professor Knoll possessed six copies of *Ostara* from the years before the First World War, and he had concluded that there was a significant influence [of Lanz von Liebenfels on Hitler] from the ideological congruence between the theories contained in *Ostara* and those of Hitler.

So obvious was the 'identity [i.e. identicalness] of the theories of the *Ostara* journals with those of National Socialism,' that Knoll was able to conclude, 'that Lanz was Hitler's ideological father.' 'But what interested us above everything was whether Lanz had known Hitler personally,' said Daim.[4]

On being informed by Daim that Liebenfels was still alive, Knoll expressed the opinion that,

one ought to get to know Lanz because he had made world history, and in his effect he was distantly comparable with that of Karl Marx. He [Knoll] said that he had, in his lectures [at the university] between 1934 and 1938 often surprised the students [the largest number of whom were Nazis] by referring to the *Ostara* as the source of Hitler; for the primitiveness and the madness of these ideas was pretty obvious.

Knoll then asked Daim, 'immediately to organise a meeting with Lanz von Liebenfels.' The result was that, 'on a rainy morning on May 11, 1951,' Daim, Knoll and Watersrat, 'looked up Lanz von Liebenfels in his Vienna flat at 32 Grinzingerstrasse.' So who was Liebenfels?

***

Josef Adolf Lanz (1874–1954) was born in Vienna to a middle class family, his father being a teacher. In July 1893, when he was aged 19, he entered the Cistercian Chapter of the Holy Cross ('Heiligenkreuz' – situated in the Vienna Woods), as 'Brother George'. However, on 27 April 1900 six years after he had been ordained into the priesthood, he left the Order, the Abbey's register recording that this was because of his, 'surrender to the lies of the world and to carnal love.'[5]

In 1902 Lanz (in order to disguise the fact that his mother Katharina, née Hoffenreich, was of Jewish descent) assumed a new identity. He claimed (falsely) that his father was Baron Johannes Lanz de Liebenfels, and that he himself had been born in Messina, Sicily, in 1872. He also awarded himself a fake doctorate in philosophy. He now became, 'Baron Adolf Georg (Jörg) Lanz von Liebenfels, Ph.D.'

In 1905 Liebenfels (to use his newly adopted name) became editor, publisher and contributor to the anti-Semitic monthly journal *Ostara* (named after the ancient Germanic goddess of Spring), whose logo was the swastika.[6] His writings are appropriately described as, 'a potpourri of contemporary theories, most importantly of [Guido von] List's race theories.'[7]

Ostara was dedicated to the, 'practical application of anthropological research for the purpose of preserving the European master race from destruction by the maintenance of racial purity.' It was lavishly illustrated with erotic pictures of blond beauties being seduced by undesirable creatures, referred to by Liebenfels as 'beast-men' or 'ape-people'.

On 25 December 1907 Liebenfels, inspired by the deeds of the Templar Knights (a Christian Order of Chivalry that was in existence at the time of the Crusades), founded his 'Order of the New Templars' ('Ordo Novi Templi'). This was a secret society devoted to his teachings, by which means he hoped that the Aryan 'race' could be salvaged. For its headquarters, Liebenfels chose the ruined castle of Burg Werfenstein, situated on the Danube river between

Linz and Vienna. Membership was of course restricted to 'Aryans', one of whom Liebenfels (Lanz) could now pretend to be, having expunged the details of his Jewish ancestry from the record books.

***

Liebenfels was undoubtedly influenced by the works of Guido von List (who was twenty-six years his senior), and belonged to the Guido von List Society, not merely as an honorary member, but also as an actual member. List, for his part, was a member of Liebenfels' Order of the New Templars.[8]

***

'When I remember this meeting [of May 1951],' said Daim,

> I have to say that the old man [i.e. Liebenfels/Lanz], who was at that time not quite 77, made a very sympathetic impression. You could speak quite pleasantly with him; he was kind and conciliatory, even if as Professor Knoll thought he noticed, he was a little nervous, because he was very conscious of his significance with regard to Hitler's ideology.

Liebenfels' story was as follows:

> One day in 1909, Hitler visited Lanz in his office. Hitler said that he lived in the Felberstrasse and had regularly bought copies of the *Ostara* in a tobacco/newsagent's kiosk [Tabac-Trafik] there. (*Ostara* being the organ of Lanz.) He bought it almost [fairly] regularly.[9]
> But now he [Hitler] said that a few numbers [copies] were missing and that he wanted to get them all and he asked Lanz for these numbers. Lanz noticed that Hitler seemed to be particularly poverty stricken, and therefore let him have the required copies without charge, and apart from that, gave him a couple of Crowns so that he could travel back home. Hitler was very grateful for this.
> In 1908 Hitler abruptly broke off his friendship with Kubizek [August Kubizek, son of a Linz upholsterer and student of music]. Round about that time however, he got to know [engineer Josef] Greiner; in fact, if we can believe him, Greiner already knew Hitler at a time when he was still friendly with Kubizek. [Reinhold Hanisch, an acquaintance of Hitler, confirms that Greiner was present in a men's hostel in Vienna at the time in question.][10]
> Kubizek and Greiner had a different attitude towards Hitler. Whereas Kubizek understands [i.e. believes in] loyalty to one's friend ... even if he [the friend, in this case Kubizek] had an awful lot on his conscience, Greiner is more concerned with showing that he didn't identify himself with all of the ghastly side of Hitler; so that his temporary participation in the National Socialist trend shouldn't be taken the wrong way.[11]

'With Kubizek,' said Liebenfels, 'we can find no reference to *Ostara* or to Lanz.'[12] (The most likely reason for this is that Hitler's interest in them may only have begun after he and Kubizek went their separate ways in 1908.)

In the light of what Liebenfels had told him, Daim, 'sought contact with diploma engineer Greiner …', and at the ensuing meeting, Daim asked Greiner about *Ostara* and Lanz von Liebenfels.

Greiner immediately knew what I was talking about, and … told me several things that he had not, because of the editor's wish, put in his book entitled *Das Ende des Hitler-Mythos*. The memories came to him [i.e. Greiner] so spontaneously, and the details were so vivid to him, that I have no doubt about the genuineness, at least of the first reminiscences.

He [Greiner] said that in the 'Mannerheim' [men's hostel] in the Meldemannstrasse [in the north-east district of Vienna], there was, besides Hitler, a certain person called Grill who lived there. (His [Grill's] real name was, for Austrian tongues, difficult to pronounce.) This Grill was a fallen Roman Catholic priest who was concerned with founding a religion of pure love for one's neighbour without any church apparatus. He was, as he told Greiner in confidence, but not Hitler, the son of a Polish-Russian rabbi who had been brought up in a Catholic monastery.

This Grill talked about several theories, three of which Greiner had written about. Grill, above all, was Hitler's main partner in discussion. From him [Grill] we have many of his [Hitler's] anti-Catholic, in particular anti-Christian arguments.

Greiner also told Daim that,

Hitler possessed a great number of magazines, above all *Ostara* numbers. Greiner thought that there was a pile of them about 25 or 30 centimetres thick. He [Hitler] was very interested in the content and also took the side of Lanz von Liebenfels very enthusiastically in discussions, above all with Grill.

With Grill he [Hitler] unambiguously agreed in the rejection of Christianity, but he did not subscribe to Grill's thesis, [which was] the necessity of a general, 'love one's neighbour'. Instead, he [Hitler] wanted to exclude the Jews, whereas Grill naturally, did not wish to permit that.

Hitler represented intensively the racial standpoint of Lanz. Grill, on the other hand, thought that there were rabbits with blue and red eyes, but they were all rabbits without any particular distinction. Hitler, very emphatically, disagreed with this; he wanted to divide them into better and worse.[13]

Greiner remembered Numbers 2, 3 and 4 [of *Ostara*] which portrayed on its cover an ascending [astronomical] comet. [The comet was in fact depicted on the front cover of *Ostara*, Issue Number 3, dated 1906.] He remembered exactly that he had seen at least one of these with [in the possession of] Hitler. Also, he well remembered the cover of another copy. Of all the *Ostara* numbers, especially these had a particularly striking cover [said Greiner], so that you do not forget them easily.[14]

As for the name *Ostara*, Lanz adopted it from the English writer, 'Beda Venerabilis' (the 'Venerable Bede', c.673–735), who stated that the ancient English tribes named the month of Easter after the goddess 'Eostra', signifying 'a new beginning'.[15]

***

These statements are proof that Hitler not only possessed significant numbers of Liebenfels' *Ostara* journals, but also that he was anxious to obtain more of them. Amongst the surviving remnants of Hitler's personal library is to be found Liebenfels' *Das Buch der Psalmen teutsch* (published 1926).[16]

However, in order to ascertain what influence, if any, *Ostara* had on Hitler, it is necessary to compare his sentiments with those expressed therein.

Notes

1. Hitler, Adolf, *Mein Kampf*, p. 41.
2. Daim, Dr Wilfried, *Der Mann, der Hitler die Ideen gab*, p. 18.
3. Ibid.
4. Ibid, p. 20.
5. Ibid, p. 252.
6. *The Swastika and the Nazis: 14. The Ostara Connection*.www.intelinet.org/swastika14. htm.
7. Hamann, Brigitte, *Hitler's Vienna: a Dictator's Apprenticeship*, p. 217.
8. Daim, op. cit., p. 96.
9. Ibid, p. 25.
10. Hanisch, Reinhold, *I was Hitler's Buddy*, 5 April 1939, pp. 239–42 (I); 12 April pp. 270–2 (II); 19 April 1939, pp. 297–300 (III).
11. Daim, op. cit., p. 33.
12. Ibid, p. 34.
13. Ibid, p. 37.
14. Ibid, p. 38.
15. Ibid, p. 116.
16. Goodrick-Clarke, Nicholas, *The Occult Roots of Nazism*, p. 199, ref 13.

CHAPTER IX

Ostara

Between 1905 and 1931 a total of 137 *Ostara* pamphlets were published (Series I, II and III – of which fifty-four were re-issued in Series III); of these all but a handful were composed by Liebenfels himself.

Viennese historian and magazine editor Friedrich Heer describes how, 'The *Ostara* publications were widely distributed throughout Germany to persons liable to lend a sympathetic ear to its writings. Lanz [i.e. Liebenfels] himself referred to a total circulation of around 500,000 copies. These found their way through to the fanatical agitators in the German theo-political underground ...'[1] Daim states that *Ostara* was distributed free of charge. 'It became more of a secret publication,' no copies of it being kept in the Austrian National Library.[2]

To begin with, Liebenfels in his publication appeared reasonably well disposed towards the Jews. For example, when a subscriber to a first copy of *Ostara* wrote an anonymous letter complaining to him that, 'only a Jew could write your book,' Liebenfels declared, 'I couldn't explain to him that I was not a Jew, though it would not worry me if I were.'[3] However, as time went by, 'Lanz became progressively more aggressive [to the Jews], the more he published.'[4]

For one particular Jew, Austrian writer, editor and satirist Karl Krause, Liebenfels was full of admiration, describing him as, 'a genius, a genuine genius, for his work is that of a pioneer and creator.' This, despite the fact that Liebenfels had, 'never personally associated with Karl Krause,' and did not, 'know the exact measurement of his skull.'[5]

This hardening of Liebenfels' attitude towards Jews was probably the result of a positive decision by him to jump, as it were, onto the Nazi bandwagon of increasing anti-Semitism, and it is reflected in the pictures on the covers of the *Ostara* journals. For example, those of *Ostara* Nos 10 and 13 of 1906 depict an ape-like creature appearing to hurl a boulder. Issue No. 1 of Series II, dated 1922, depicts a knight in armour, and in the lower right-hand corner, a Jewish face in caricature with the caption, 'Who shall lead, who shall be Duke? An Enlightenment through "*Ostara*".' The implication is clear: it is the knightly duke who will lead, not the Jew.[6]

As Heer points out, although, 'Hitler himself never referred to Jörg Lanz-Liebenfels,' nevertheless, Hitler's, 'talks on "diabolical" Jewish plutocracies, Russian "bog/marsh people", the "satanic" Bolsheviks and his theo-political messages of salvation, illustrate how close his beliefs were to enthusiasts such as Lanz ...'[7]

Liebenfels based much of his life's work on the notion, that in ancient times, human beings had practised bestiality – and produced, what he described as, 'ape-people' or 'Sodom-apelings.' In this way, the pure, Aryan race had been corrupted. Liebenfels, who was a well-read person, was undoubtedly acquainted with English naturalist Charles Darwin's 'Theory of Evolution and Natural Selection', to which his own theory was in direct opposition. Therefore, the basis of the realms of racially motivated vitriolic verbiage which emanated from Liebenfels' pen was, to say the least, unscientific.

***

In order to ascertain what influence, if any, *Ostara* had on Hitler, it is necessary to compare his sentiments with those expressed in that journal. The first page of the first edition of *Ostara* in 1905 set the tone for future publications:

> *Ostara* is the first and only illustrated Aryo–aristocratic collection of publications, which, in both words and pictures, depicts the heroic blond peoples, the beautiful, moral, noble, idealistic, gifted and religious people; the creator and keeper of all knowledge, art and culture; and the main-bearer of divinity. All iniquity and ugliness originates from the cross-breeding of races, in respect of which, for physiological reasons, the woman has always been and remains more submissive than the man. Thus, the arrival of *Ostara* comes at a time when women and the inferior races are taking it upon themselves to procreate and thereby ruthlessly to eradicate the heroic blond race of men, who epitomise all outstanding beauty, truth, ambition and seekers of God.[8]

1. Cultivation of the Land

According to *Ostara* (Series I, Nos 22–23), 'Only a person who is intimately involved with the soil – the country farmer – is a human being in the real sense. Therefore, the Aryan race prospers only in the cultivation of the land.'[9] Reflecting this view, an earlier issue of *Ostara* was entitled, *The Austro–German Regions of the Alps as Meat and Milk Producers: a Study of the Local Economy*.[10] How does this compare with Hitler's ideas? This can be established from Hitler's known utterances, for example:

> No concept, no political theory is sound which is not based on the principle that the existence of the people depends upon its soil and territory. A people which does not find its support in its soil and does not establish an affinity with its soil will perish miserably and wretchedly ....[11]

2. Eugenics (improving the race by judicious mating)

This philosophy lies at the heart of Liebenfels' teachings, and more articles appear in *Ostara* on this than on any other subject. 'All calamities in the history of the world … have been caused by the liberated woman.'[12] Racial mixing [i.e. miscegenation] is the crime of all crimes, that is the mortal sin.'[13]

Ostara I/47, entitled *The Art of Good Living and in Being Happily Married: a Racial Purity Breviary (instruction manual) for People in Love,* discusses a method of preventing conception during intercourse, 'by the use of chemical or mechanical means … for the purpose of breeding a pure race.'[14]

'The perfect man [i.e. the 'Aryan'] has, in accordance with the policy of pure breeding of all Aryan people, the right to put himself forward to several women [i.e. to impregnate them] in order to go on creating numerous people: he is permitted to have more children than those of an inferior race.'[15]

Ostara I/21 introduces the idea of the 'marriage helper,' whose, 'role is to create sperm for the wife in the place of a person [husband] who is impotent, but Lykurg [Lycurgus – law giver of Sparta, 9th century BC] emphasises that these marriage helpers must specifically be young, strong and efficient.'[16]

'We must now set up reservations [i.e. breeding colonies] for the blond heroic races in remote, secret places.[17] The breeding mothers are required to live in strict isolation, so there is no temptation for adultery.'[18]

In such, 'ecclesia – or communities of the elite for the chosen people, the improvement of mankind will take place. For the time being [however] it is sufficient if we succeed in founding even a small but closed community of highly bred heroic people, who also can dispose of sufficient wealth, and a milieu (environment) which is appropriate to them.'[19]

Liebenfels even produced a 'Rassenwertigkeitsindex' (racial composition index) to enable an individual to assess his degree of 'Aryanness', awarding 12 points for blue or blue-grey eyes, and minus 12 points for black (dark) eyes. Similar points were awarded or deducted for hair and skin colour, facial features and so forth.[20] In respect of the shape of the skull for example, Liebenfels declared, 'The percentage of mad Jews is quite enormous.'[21]

Hitler: '*What makes a people, or to be more correct a race, is not language but blood.*'[22] '*Whenever Aryans have mingled their blood with that of an inferior race, the result has been the downfall of the people who were the standard-bearers of a higher culture.*'[23] '*A person of mixed blood is not only relatively inferior to a person of pure blood, but is almost doomed to become extinct more rapidly. In innumerable cases wherein the pure race holds its ground, the mongrel breaks down* [presumably disintegrates].'[24] *Vienna was described by Hitler as,* '*the incarnation of mongrel depravity*'.[25]

The purpose of the State, said Hitler was, '*to preserve and promote a community of human beings who are physically as well as spiritually kindred.*'[26] '*A folk state* [from the German 'volk' – meaning people] *should in the first place raise matrimony from the level of being a constant scandal for the race. The state should consecrate it as an institution which is called upon to produce creatures made in the likeness of the Lord, and not create monsters that are a mixture of man and ape.'[27] 'This triumph* [i.e. of the idea of a People's State] *can be assured only through a militant movement ....*[28]

'The great leaders of Jewry are confident that the day is near at hand when the command given in the Old Testament will be carried out and the Jews will devour the other nations of the Earth.'[29] 'This pestilential adulteration of the blood, of which hundreds of thousands of our people take no account, is being systematically practised by the Jew today. Systematically, these negroid parasites in our national body corrupt our innocent fair-haired girls and thus destroy something which can no longer be replaced in this world.'[30]

3. Euthanasia (putting painlessly to death)

'What I prophesied thirty years ago,' said Liebenfels, 'has become true. The hordes of untouchables have eaten up and destroyed all our economic reserves. The insoluble economic chaos is here: the chaos from which civilised and Aryan Christian humanity can save itself only by means of a bloodless and painless destruction and damming up of the dark, untouchable elements.'[31]

'The first source of sick bodies of inferior races and people incapable of proper work must be destroyed straight away. The modern economy cannot put up any more with these sinister hordes of people, millions of whom are incapable of work and are simply unsocial, racial curs.'[32]

4. Genocide (deliberate extermination of a race)

Liebenfels: 'The struggle for nationality made the German-Austrians and other Austrian peoples [both] conscious of their nationality and [also] anti-Semitic.'[33]

'We must therefore, throw away people of inferior race – the monkey people and the primeval people. We must throw away and get rid of it in us, around us and after us.[34] Everywhere, the earth will steam from the blood of the people of mixed race.[35] The basis of all wars is race war.'[36]

'We must join up with [rifle] shooting clubs and armed corps.'[37] 'We will not be able to shoot millions of inferior races with our rapid fire cannons, but a much better means would be to strangle them with rubber.'[38]

In *Ostara* III / 2, Liebenfels expresses the opinion that, '[Lord] Kitchener [British soldier and statesman, 1850–1916], in the time before the war [i.e. World War I], was busy with eugenics. He constructed a racially more pure group. By the time he had enough people as reserves capable of fighting, he sent the coloured ones, without any consideration at all, to face the fire of the enemy. If only the Germans had spared their blond racial reserves in this way, and sent the dark, unruly urban mob of untouchables into the Front Line as canon fodder! If only the Germans had done that!'[39] [In fact, what Liebenfels is accusing Kitchener of here is genocide.]

Hitler: *'For the good of the German people, we must wish for a war every fifteen or twenty years.'[40] 'The new German Empire should have set out on its march along the same road as was formerly trodden by the Teutonic Knights, this time to acquire soil for the German plough by means of the German sword, and thus provide the nation with its daily bread.'[41]*

5. Religion

It was Liebenfels' belief that both the Old and New Testaments (of the Bible) were in favour of racial 'Hygiene' and 'Renewal' viz. *Ostara* journals entitled: *Leviticus or Moses as a Racial Hygienist; Numeri* [i.e. the Book of Numbers] *or Moses as a Renewer of the Race*; and *Racial Mystique: An Introduction to the Aryo-Christian Esoteric Doctrine*.[42] Furthermore, *Ostara* Journal I/59 describes, 'Aryan Christendom as a Racial Cult Religion of The Blonds.'

'Racial purity (care of the race) cannot exist without a religion of the cult of the races, and vice versa – no religion can preserve its purity without the nurturing of the races.'[43] 'Racial breeding and purity of race will be and must be the only religion and church of the future.'[44]

'Therefore our religion must become an ariosophic religion of the cult of races.'[45] [Ariosophy means the combination of German 'volkisch' national-ism and racism with occult notions borrowed from the philosophy of Helena Petrovna Blavatsky, and 'volkisch' (after 'Volk') implying something which is anti-democratic, anti-liberal, anti-bourgeois, anti-capitalistic, and promotes a national community of the racially pure.] 'It must change from a religion which has become distorted by our being gagged. It has been distorted into an altruism, and it must become once more a religion of the superior people, an ariosophic cult religion of racism, which it was right from the beginning. Purity of the race, breeding of the race, cannot be carried out by the state, or by officials, or in a ministerial way, but only through religion and as a sacred idea.'[46]

'The higher races stem from God: the lower races from Lucifer, a fallen God. The evil must always be under the control of the good, as must the lesser always be under the control of the higher.'[47] 'Through the crushing and destruction of the primitive and inferior human beings, the superior heroic place will rise up out of the grave of racial mix and racial degeneration and will rise up to immor-tality and divinity and become divine men, both in the seed and the race.'[48]

'In this holy name and sign we will conquer like our ancestors or, if it has to be, die in the attempt'.[49] (These final four words WERE PERHAPS THE MOST PROPHETIC TO BE FOUND IN THE WHOLE OF *OSTARA*, in view of what would one day befall the Third Reich.)

Hitler: *(Referring to Jesus Christ, Hitler wrote:) 'Today, 2,000 years later, I recognise with deep emotion Christ's tremendous fight for this world against the Jewish poison. I recognise it most profoundly by the fact that He had to shed His blood on the cross for this fight. As a Christian it is not my duty to permit myself to be cheated, but it is my duty to be a champion of truth and of right.'[50]*

6. The 'Aristocratic Principle' (of Governance)

Ostara I/9 is entitled, *The People's Thoughts: The Aristocratic Principle of Our Time*. This principle was enunciated by Benedict de Spinoza (1632–77), a Jew of Portuguese origin who was born in Amsterdam. In his book, *A Preface To Morals*, he wrote: 'There is an aristocratic principle in all the religions which has attained wide acceptance. It is significant that Jesus was content to leave the governance of the mass of men to Caesar, and that he created no organisation during his lifetime beyond the appointment of the Apostles. It is significant because it shows how much more he was concerned with the few who could be saved than with arranging the affairs of the mass of mankind.'

Spinoza also believed that the love of God 'involves the love of our fellow creatures'; that 'the State exists to give liberty, not hold in slavery'; and that 'the sovereign in his own interest must rule with justice and wisdom, nor must the State interfere with the freedom of thought'.[51]

Hitler: Complained that, 'The Jewish doctrine of Marxism repudiates the aristocratic principle of Nature and substitutes for it the eternal privilege of force and energy, numerical mass and its dead weight.'[52]

7. Prostitution and Venereal Disease

Ostara I/58[53] is concerned with *The Immoral and Criminal Woman's Lifestyle of Our Times*, and *Ostara* I/76[54] with *Prostitution in Women and Men's Rights: A Judgement*.

Hitler: 'The population of our great towns and cities is tending more and more to avail of prostitution in the exercise of its amorous instincts, and is thus becoming more and more contaminated by the scourge of venereal disease.'[55]

The primary cause of syphilis, said Hitler, was 'to be found in the manner in which love was being prostituted'.[56] *'To wage war against syphilis means fighting against prostitution ...'*[57] *'The first remedy [for prostitution] must always be to establish such conditions as will make early marriages possible, especially for young men – for women are, after all, only passive subjects in this matter.'*[58]

8. Charity

In *Ostara* I/18, entitled, *Race and Welfare Work: A Call for a Boycott of Indiscriminate Charity*, Liebenfels adopts the philosophy: 'Everything for the pearls and nothing for the rotten fish. At least one third of diseases are the result of one's own fault or one's own race,' he declares. In particular, 'People with mixed parentage have a great tendency towards it [i.e. disease], and often sexual excesses are the underlying reason. All those disgusting skin diseases originate in the East and are really diseases of filth and race. Even those of a higher race will be infected, as modern life (which no longer knows any boundaries between races) forces them to associate with members of lower races.' Liebenfels now offers the solution: 'If the federal government pursued a racial economy and gently annihilated those families with hereditary impairments, it would be possible to save a considerable part of the nine million Kronen per annum!'

'How could it be', he asks, 'that there were "charitable institutions" for hospitals, foundling [deserted infant of no known parents] hospitals, illegitimate children and fallen girls,' when there were, 'no such institutions for the preservation of pure and noble blood and for legitimate children?' And yet he, Liebenfels, believed that, 'the old, and those of good Germanic descent, and ... those of true Israeli descent ... should be supported.' [This latter sentiment would certainly not have pleased Hitler!][59]

Therefore the only people worthy of receiving charitable donations, states *Ostara* I/18, were those with 'gold-blond hair, blue (or blue-grey) eyes, a rosy complexion, elongated skulls and elongated faces, high and small straight noses, well-proportioned mouths, healthy white teeth, round chins, a balanced, tall physique, narrow hands and narrow feet.'[60]

Hitler: *'During my struggle for existence in Vienna I perceived very clearly that the aim of all social activity must never be merely charitable relief, which is ridiculous and useless ....'*[61]

9. Marxism and Bolshevism

In *Ostara* I/61, Karl Marx is described as a 'dark, inferior mongrel'. 'In the course of its further development,' states *Ostara* III/13,[62] 'the Talmudic-Tachandalic Empire [Talmud – the sacred writings of Orthodox Judaism; Tachandalic – pertaining to the original race of inferior humans] succeeded in harnessing the intelligence of the Aryan Christians to its purposes by way of the ... secret society of Free-Masons. This society of obscurantists is responsible for the so-called "Enlightenment" – the various revolutions, liberalism, socialism and materialism in the 19th century – and for the Bolshevism in the 20th .... During the Middle Ages ... there was no proletariat and no proletarian problem. This class only came into being through the daemonic efforts of modern Free-Masons and their false doctrines of the so-called "Enlightenment".'[63]

'The conceptual manure-heaps, the mental excrement that is materialistic-rationalistic-social democratic-Bolshevist-Tachandalic philosophy and science of the modern period will not be of even historic interest in future generations.'[64]

'Bolshevism, Marxism, sovietism, communism, socialism, democratism ... are offshoots ... of these primaeval, base, and inferior racial origins.'[65]

Hitler: *'Bolshevism is Christianity's illegitimate child. Both are inventions of the Jew.'*[66]
'To be sure, our Christian Cross should be the most exalted symbol of the struggle against the Jewish-Marxist-Bolshevik spirit.'[67]

10. Other threats to the Aryan

Aside from Bolshevism and the Jews, *Ostara* I/72: *Race and External Politics*[68] is concerned with the, 'attrition [wearing down] of the heroic Aryans here in Europe, by numerous successive challenges to the Aryan people, through intellectualism, the Press, financial markets, industrialisation, overpopulation, through feminism and exploitation, through major capitalism.'

11. World Revolution

Ostara III/15: 'Greater than the howl of triumph of the untouchables is the terror when [they are] faced with the aryo-heroic world revolution.'[69]

12. Culture

Ostara titles include: *The Blonds as Creators of Language: A Summary of the Creation of Ancient Languages*[70]; *The Blonds as Creators of Music*[71]; *Race and Poetry*[72]; *Race and Philosophy*[73]; *Race and Painting*[74] and *Race and Architecture in the New Age*'[75] all of which extol the pre-eminent virtues of the 'Blonds'.

Hitler: *'Every manifestation of human culture, every product of art, science, and technical skill which we see before our eyes today, is almost exclusively the product of the Aryan creative power. This very fact fully justifies the conclusion that it was the Aryan alone who founded the superior type of humanity....'*[76]

'On this planet of ours, human culture and civilization are indissolubly bound up with the presence of the Aryan. If he should be exterminated or subjugated, then the dark shroud of a new barbaric era would enfold the earth.'[77]

13. Freedom of the Press

Ostara I/3: 'The monkey press has got to be stifled.'

Hitler: *'With ruthless determination the state must keep control of this instrument of popular education* [i.e. the Press] *and place it at the service of the state and nation.'*[78]

14. Animals

Ostara I/22–23: 'The superior man is one who is fond of animals.'

15. The Law and Legal Rights

Ostara I/58 asserts that, 'The origin of all questions of law has to do with race, and moreover superior races. For those who are plaintiffs, or witnesses, or defendants, the question of their race has to be considered. With a legal right based on race, all other questions are solved by themselves'. [In other words, the rights of the superior races are paramount.] *Ostara* III/4 declares, 'We will famously castrate habitual criminals, and sterilise habitual female criminals.'

16. Forced Labour

Ostara III/13–14: 'By means of ariosophic running of the economy' said Hitler, 'the whole problem of unemployment will be solved. All unemployed people who haven't accepted any work by a certain date will have to be organized to become miners.' 'It will be assumed that we view work in mines as the sort of work which is unworthy of the heroic type of person. This work should be done only by untouchables, or rather criminals.' *Ostara* III/15: 'One ought to introduce again slavery and castration.'

17. Deportation

Ostara I/13–14: 'If the untouchables don't want this [i.e. to accept working in mines], then away with the stones, and then throw them out into the deserts with the jackals and into the forest of the monkeys, where they will greet gorillas and baboons as comrades and people of a similar race. There, they can put into reality their socialist, Bolshevik, democratic, proletarian state utopia, where everybody has an equal right to vote in secret.'

Hitler: *The sentiments expressed in 14–17 above are entirely in accordance with those of Hitler. In respect of the law, Hitler would simply adapt it for his own ends. Forced labour and deportation would certainly become a feature of Nazism in practice. As for world revolution, he preferred the less subtle approach, i.e. military conquest, as will shortly be seen.*

***

It is clear from the above therefore, that Hitler's core beliefs were almost exclusively derived from *Ostara*. However, in other respects, he was not entirely in tune as it were, with Liebenfels' teachings. For example, when he stated that, 'Whoever leads Austria will also be the spiritual leader of the world',[79] Hitler demurred, it was because he (in contrast with Liebenfels) saw himself primarily as the leader of a German state which would swiftly move to incorporate Austria. Nor would the Führer have identified with such Ostarian concepts as embodied in the title, *World Peace as an Achievement and Victory for the Blonds*.[80]

***

A child reading a comic newspaper or magazine will usually, with education and maturity, learn to tell the difference between fact and fiction, and may even recognise propaganda for what it is. However, although in chronological terms, Hitler was a young man when he read *Ostara*, his mind did not reach a sufficient level of maturity for him to realise that the so-called facts and opinions being put before him (as articulated by Liebenfels and other contributors to *Ostara*) represented the bizarre wanderings of a deranged mind, and had no basis whatsoever in science, history or morality.

Notes

1. Heer, Friedrich, *Der Glaube des Adolf Hitler*, p. 710.
2. Daim, Dr Wilfried, *Der Mann, der Hitler die Ideen gab*, p. 169.
3. Ibid, p. 12.
4. Ibid, p. 169.
5. *Ostara*, I/52.
6. Daim, op. cit., p. 168.
7. Heer, op. cit., p. 710.
8. Ibid, p. 710.
9. *Ostara*, I/22–3.
10. Ibid, I/8.
11. Prange, Gordon W (ed.), *Hitler's Words*, p. 24.
12. *Ostara*, I/33.
13. Ibid, I/38.
14. Ibid, I/47.
15. Ibid, I/21.
16. Ibid.
17. Ibid, III/4.
18. Ibid, I/21.
19. Ibid, I/47.
20. Ibid, I/31.
21. Ibid, I/18.
22. Hitler, Adolf, *Mein Kampf*, p. 219.
23. Ibid, p. 162.
24. Ibid, p. 225.
25. Ibid, p. 79.
26. Ibid, p. 221.
27. Ibid, p. 226.

28. Ibid, p. 257.
29. Ibid, p. 351.
30. Ibid, p. 310.
31. *Ostara*, III/4.
32. Ibid, III/4.
33. Ibid, I/72.
34. Ibid, III/4.
35. Ibid, I/70.
36. Ibid, I/10 and I/13.
37. Ibid, I/3.
38. Ibid, I/34.
39. Ibid, III/2.
40. Trevor-Roper, H R (ed.), *Hitler's Table Talk, 1941–1944*, p. 55.
41. Hitler, op. cit., p. 87.
42. *Ostara*, I/95, 97, 98.
43. Ibid, III/13.
44. Ibid, III/19.
45. Goodrick-Clarke, Nicholas, *The Occult Roots of Nazism*, p. 2.
46. *Ostara*, III/4.
47. Ibid, I/74.
48. Ibid, III/18.
49. Ibid, I/1.
50. Prange, op. cit., 12 April 1922, Munich, p. 71.
51. *Oxford Companion to Literature*, Sir Paul Harvey (ed.), 1933, Oxford: Clarendon Press.
52. Hitler, op. cit., p. 46.
53. *Ostara*, I/58.
54. Ibid, I/76.
55. Hitler, op. cit., p. 142.
56. Ibid, p. 141.
57. Ibid, p. 143.
58. Ibid, p. 144.
59. Liebenfels, Dr Jorg Lanz von, *Theozoology*. Europa Germanic Translations Ltd, 2003, PO Box 175, Sandusky, Ohio, USA, p. 65.
60. Ibid, I/18 (in Hamann, pp.151–2).
61. Hitler, op. cit., p. 27.
62. *Ostara*, III/13–14.
63. Ibid, (in Grey Lodge Occult Review, SF, *Occult Sciences and Nazi Myths*, by Manfred Nagl, 1974, www.antiquillum.com/glor/glor_005/nazimyth.htm).
64. Ibid, III/15 (in antiquillum, op. cit.).
65. Ibid, I/13–14 (in antiquillum, op. cit.).
66. Trevor-Roper, op. cit., p. 37.
67. Prange, op. cit., 25 October 1930, Munich, p. 88.
68. *Ostara*, I/72.
69. Ibid, III/13–14.
70. Ibid, I/52.
71. Ibid, I/73.
72. Ibid, I/83.
73. Ibid, I/84.
74. Ibid, I/86.
75. Ibid, I/85.

76. Hitler, op. cit., p. 164.
77. Ibid, p. 216.
78. Ibid, p. 139.
79. *Ostara*, I/83
80. Ibid, III/4

CHAPTER X

Liebenfels' Wilder Notions

Liebenfels' writings ascended to new heights of preposterous farce, not only in *Ostara*, but in other works such as *Theozoology: or the Tale of the Apelings of Sodom and the Gods Electron* (published in Vienna in 1905).

The Gods

According to Liebenfels, the Bible and other ancient religious texts were written in a code which only he could understand.

> Every enquiry concerning the gods explores the old notions and fables, while the ancients concealed their natural ideas, which they preserved ... in parables, and always mixed their enquiries with the fables.[1] The original oriental text and various ancient translations and commentaries of the more ancient Fathers, give us the key to this secret language, and from this we may receive the unfathomable wisdom of the ancients.[2] In our search for god, we neophytes (novices) have lost our way because we have forgotten the basic principle of all wisdom of the ancients ..., and because we have forgotten the goal and the beginning of all investigation: the human body.[3]

Liebenfels therefore, drawing on his knowledge of the Bible, anthropology and ancient Greek and Hebrew texts, together with ancient bas-reliefs and sculptures which he had encountered on his travels, would now make it his business to unlock this 'unfathomable wisdom'. In doing so, he often interpreted the apocryphal stories contained therein literally, and so it is not surprising that in so doing, he arrived at the most bizarre conclusions!

61

Racial Development

Liebenfels described his work *Practical, Racial Metaphysics* [4] as being,

> concerned with research into the history of the races before their earthly development cycle (pre-terrestrial) … into the future of the races following their earthly period (post-terrestrial), and finally with research into the extrasensory, extra-terrestrial, cosmic forces that influence racial development in the present.
>
> The race of full-blooded and whole Aryan Man was not the result of natural selection alone. Instead, as the esoteric writings indicate, he was the result of a careful and conscious breeding process by higher and different kinds of being, such as the Theozoa, Elektrozoa, Angels, et sim., which once lived on this Earth. [5]

The Theozoa, Elektrozoa, etc. from whom Aryan Man developed were,

> perfect electro-biotic machines, characterised by their supernatural knowledge and power. Their knowledge encompassed everything to be found in the universe and beyond, in the metaphysical spaces of the fourth, fifth and ninth dimensions: they perceived such objects by way of their electro-magneto-radiophotic eye on their forehead, the rudiment of which is the human pineal gland. They had knowledge of all things, and could read past, present and future from the ether [upper air]. This is why they performed the office of oracles until well into historical times and live on, even today, in mediums. They possessed supernatural, 'divine' powers, whose centre is located in the lumbar brain. Their bodies exude rays of fire and light, which … materialise on the one hand and dematerialise on the other, breaking down atoms and reconstructing them, cancelling out gravity. [6]

Sodomy (the copulation of mankind with animals)

Liebenfels' volume, *Theozoology*, mentioned above (as well as no fewer than ten *Ostara* journals which appeared in the Third Series of that publication, 1927–31), revolves entirely around the subject of sodomy, and is concerned with the alleged historical mating of human beings with animals, to produce his so-called 'beast-men'.

The original sin of the blond, god-like 'homo sapiens or, more precisely, the homo arioheroicus women', [7] was in copulating with 'the male anthropo-saurians' [with their 'penis bone'!] and to their descendants, the man-animal races', to whom they were attracted on account of 'the magnitude of the member [i.e. penis].' [8]

As 'evidence' for this, he used as an example the so-called 'sea-men', as depicted on a relief 'found in Nimrud, in ancient Kalach' (in the north of present day Iraq), who were described as 'two-legged beasts about 1.2 metres tall with scaly skin.'[9] He also quotes Roman historian Tacitus' description of,

> a sodomistic orgy in which 'sea-beasts' took part, such that the lascivious Roman noble women would flock around them [the beasts] in large numbers.
>
> Almost the whole world has succumbed to ape-nature [i.e. the offspring of the union of man and beasts], right up to the Germanic countries which have not been fully spared either.[10] All of mankind, including [people in] the Germanic lands, is today dying the sodomistic death ...[11]

'Bolshy-Jewish bloodhounds (especially) remind us even today of the horrible faces of antediluvian dragon-monsters' who are the direct, 'descendants of ... the two-legged dinosaur hominids'. Rosa Luxemburg, the German Jewish left-wing revolutionary who was murdered by government troops in 1919 is described as a 'small, pure breed Bezah-dwarf ... [Wadi Bezah, in Egypt] just like those bred 2,000 years ago in the temple-zoos of Palestine.'[12]

'Our blood, our seed,' said Liebenfels, was 'something divine, the most precious heritage of our fathers.' Although,

> the blood of each and every one of us is more or less mixed with the water of Sodom ..., from this point forward a halt should be called to this mixing. It followed from many passages in the bible, that the European white man (in short, the Germanic man) is the Son of Heaven. He is the White Stone, the White Rider who conquers the coloured people ....[13]
>
> Adultery by wives and their quite strange preference for lusty, satyr-like so-called 'interesting men', must be obviated as much as possible ... A precipitin [i.e. precipitation] reaction will make it clear to each and every individual how closely or distantly his blood is related to the blood of apes ....[14]
>
> Unilateral woman's rights would make the world into a big brothel in which everything revolves around penises and pussies in a silly and absurd satyrs' 'orgy', and the proper wife, the loyal mother of the house and the healthy, strong troop of children will be mercilessly driven out of the chaste and legitimate home. The adulterous and sensual woman belongs to the whore house, the honour of motherhood is withdrawn from her and her name is blotted out of the book of life. Likewise criminals, the mentally ill, or those with hereditary diseases, should be prevented from reproducing. If we only allow fit persons to reproduce, the hospitals, prisons and the giant criminal justice system will become superfluous.[15]
>
> Dear ladies, tell me honestly, whose wives would you be today if noble men, if god-like Siegfrieds, had not torn you away from the sodomistic monsters, if they had not put you in a warm nest, if they had not defended you, sword in hand, throughout thousands of years, against Slavs, Mongols, Moors and Turks? Choose between us and those sons of Sodom ....[16]

Everybody must begin in himself therefore to carry out the struggle against the Sodom monkeys, and particularly [take care] with the choice of his wife. Only then can he defeat the Sodom ape around himself.[17]

'Woman, still today, loves pleasure-apes and makes the effort to bring humanity downward,' lamented Liebenfels.

Only when we become similar to the electrical god-men physically ... we will again become pure gods. We must take off the dark pelt of the ape and put on the shining breast-plate of the god-man. He who abides in love devoid of the ape-like nature, abides in God, and God in him.[18]

In the *Koran* [Muslim scriptures], said Liebenfels,

It is said that paradise is certain for the whites. The kingdom of heaven will be reached through intervention in the sexual life of man. Those of lesser value must be exterminated in a gentle way; by castration and sterilisation.[19]
For these elements [of the arioheroic people] who have no idea about [i.e care little about the significance of] race, they deserve to perish, because they are also the enemies of our race. They commit the sin against the Holy Ghost, and this sin will never be forgiven.[20]

Atlantis

In *Theozoology*, Liebenfels asserts his belief in the concept of 'Atlantis' (the alleged lost continent) and speaks of how Ludwig Wilser, 'in his scientific articles' had, 'convincingly proven that the tall, white man emerged from Europe [actually Atlantis]'.[21]

Sacrifice

'Bring sacrifices to Frauja [Liebenfels' word for Jesus Christ], you sons of God. Up, up and bring to Him the children of the forest demons and sacrifice them to Jesus. We are not thinking of preaching pogroms because they will occur without any preaching.'[22]

'Godman'

'If we are striving to bring the angelic men to rulership, we should improve the human body through selective breeding ....[23] Our bodies are the temples of God, they are the members of the future superman which will be formed in us'.
'Through conscious and goal-oriented influencing of the secreting glands, we shall be able in the coming two centuries to rebuild atoms and cells of all living

beings and ... finally to create a new human race, which will develop out of the arioheroical one.'[24]

'Everywhere and always, we must protect the institution of marriage, for it is the secure refuge of the race, the warm nest of the young phoenix, and the future God-Man .... Marital fidelity must be required of all women in all circumstances ... but marital fidelity on the husband's part is also necessary.'[25]

'The technology [of creating a new human race] ... [and] all higher scientific wisdom ... is to remain the secret knowledge of a numerically small, pure-bred, heroic-Aryan ruling elite.'[26]

Robotic Machines

'A newly bred slave being with crude nerves and strong hands whose mental potential has been carefully limited ... will perform for us all those jobs for which we have not invented machines ... The proletariat and the under-humanity cannot be improved or saved or made happy. They are the work of the Devil and must simply be, of course humanely and without pain, eliminated. In their place, we will have biological machines, whose advantage over mechanical machines will be that they repair and procreate themselves .... This "robot" will be the key to the future since his existence will solve not only the technological but also the social and racio-economic problems – and thereby all political problems that beset us. Total equality is nonsense! The social question is a racial question and not an economic one .... Who can say where the equality of rights should stop? Why should it stop with the Australian aborigine? Gorillas, chimpanzees and bats have exactly the same claim to socialist "human rights".'[27]

Liebenfels' Concept of Divinity

'If I were asked what I understood divinity to be,' said Liebenfels, 'I would say: by that I understand the living beings of the ultra-violet and ultra-red forces and world. In former times they were embodied and moved about in complete purity. Today they live on in human beings. The gods slumber in bestialised human bodies, but the day is coming when they will rise up again. We were electric, we will be electric, to be electric and to be divine is the same thing!'[28]

***

In 1932 the publisher of a new work by Liebenfels entitled *The Book of Psalms in German: The Aryosophes, Racial Mystics, and Anti-Semites Prayer Book*, sent a copy to Hitler, together with a dedication.[29]

In that year, on the occasion of his (alleged) 60th birthday, Liebenfels required that his guests toast him with the words, 'The pioneer of National Socialism is the modest, simple monk, Jörg Lanz Liebenfels.'[30]

However, at his meeting with psychologist Wilfried Daim in 1951 Liebenfels described how, from the year 1938 Hitler had banned him from writing, 'obviously to hide his sources from foreign countries – you know, other people.' More plausible reasons however, were firstly *that Hitler would have preferred that people did not discover that he himself had lifted, as it were, his philosophy straight from the pages of Liebenfels'* Ostara *(instead of thinking it out for himself)*, and secondly that Hitler may have feared being held up to ridicule, if it became known that he had associated with a man, whose more extravagant ideas might be described in modern terms as 'science fiction.'[31]

Liebenfels also confided to Daim, 'that he had rejected National Socialism as it eventually developed'. Can this be true, bearing in mind the intensity and fervour of his ideas as expressed in *Ostara* and other works? No. The truth is more likely to lie in the fact that National Socialism, which had brought ruin on the German people, had been utterly defeated, and Liebenfels felt it would be unfashionable to continue to support a lost cause.

***

Undoubtedly, Hitler 'cherry picked' those aspects of Liebenfels' philosophy which suited his purpose, while discarding or ignoring those which did not. As for Liebenfels' wilder assertions, the Führer would have greeted them with a mixture of amusement and derision. In Daim's words: 'Hitler tried to avoid some of the more comical and extreme of the Lanz [Liebenfels] writings.'[32]

***

Nevertheless, many of the outlandish theories of Liebenfels would (as will be demonstrated) find strong resonances in the policies adopted by Hitler and his Nazi Party, when time and again, *Ostara* ideas were embraced and put into practical effect.

In other words, many, if not the majority of the core tenets of the philosophy of Nazism were lifted (by Hitler) straight from the pages of the works of Lanz von Liebenfels, and from Ostara *in particular.*

***

Although Hitler's interest in Liebenfels' most fanciful notions would have been only marginal, the same was not true of his 'Reichsführer' SS Heinrich Himmler, who seized upon them avidly, and went to enormous trouble and expense to investigate them with the object of proving that they were true! Nevertheless, thanks to his factotum Hitler, Liebenfels and his catch phrases such as: 'Racial Purity', 'Inferior Races', 'Race War', 'Selective Breeding', 'Sterilisation', 'Deportation', 'Pogroms' and 'Extermination', would echo along the corridors of power of the Third Reich.

Notes

1. Liebenfels, Dr Jörg Lanz von, *Theozoology*, Europa Germanic Translations Ltd, 2003, PO Box 175, Sandusky, Ohio, USA, pp. 65, 9.
2. Ibid, p. 9.
3. Ibid, p. 10.
4. *Ostara*, I/80.
5. Liebenfels, Dr Jörg Lanz von, *Bibliomystikon*, Vol.II. p. 158 (in *Occult Sciences and Nazi Myths*, by Manfred Nagl. www.antiqillum.com/glor/glor_005/nazimyth.htm).
6. Ibid, Vol.III. p. 40.
7. Ibid, Vol.I. p. 90.
8. *Ostara*, I/21 (in antiqillum, op. cit.).
9. Liebenfels, *Theozoology*, op. cit., pp. 65, 23.
10. Ibid, p. 53.
11. Ibid, p. 61.
12. *Ostara*, I/13–14 (in antiqillum, op. cit.).
13. Liebenfels, *Theozoology*, op. cit., p. 66, A reference to the Bible: Book of Revelation.
14. Ibid, p. 67.
15. Ibid, p. 68.
16. Ibid.
17. *Ostara*, III/101.
18. Liebenfels, *Theozoology*, op. cit., pp. 69–70.
19. Ibid, p. 67.
20. *Ostara*, III/4.
21. Liebenfels, *Theozoology*, op. cit., p. 51.
22. *Ostara*, III/3.
23. Liebenfels, *Theozoology*, op. cit., p. 62.
24. *Ostara*, III/15, 19 (in antiqillum, op. cit.).
25. Liebenfels, *Theozoology*, op. cit., p. 67.
26. *Ostara*, I/75 (in antiqillum, op. cit.).
27. Ibid, I/19.
28. Liebenfels, *Theozoology*, op. cit., p. 44.
29. Krause, Karl, *Die Fackel*, 21 October 1913, pp. 6ff.
30. Becker, Peter Emil, 1988, *Zur Geschichte der Rassenhygiene: Weige ins Dritte Reich*. Stuttgart, p. 384.
31. Daim, Dr Wilfried, *Der Mann, der Hitler die Ideen gab*, p. 182.
32. Ibid.

CHAPTER XI

Heinrich Himmler

Heinrich Himmler, commander of the SS ('Reichsführer' SS – Hitler's personal bodyguard) and of the German police, was the son of devout Catholic parents. His father, a school teacher, had once been tutor to the Crown Prince of Bavaria.

Whilst studying agriculture in Munich, Himmler had joined the right-wing militia or Free Corps. It was he who had carried the flag through the streets of Munich for the Nazis in the failed coup of 1923.

A one-time chicken farmer, Himmler in 1935 declared,

> I, as leader of the SS and as a farmer born and bred, want to make it clear here today that the idea of 'blood', which has been upheld in the SS from the very beginning, would have been worthless if it were not inexorably linked to the belief in the sanctity of the soil.[1]

Just as Hitler enjoyed planning his expansionist wars, so Himmler, anxious to conjoin Nazi ideology with German history, preferred to look backwards into the past, and there were no lengths to which he would not go in order to prove his point.

The SS (Schutzstaffel)

Up until 1935, recruits to the SS were hand-picked by Himmler in person, great importance being attached to eye and hair colour (blue and blond respectively being the colours of choice), and to the shape of the skull, as defining a person's degree of 'Aryanism'.

The SS were regularly indoctrinated with theories of Aryan superiority. According to Father Gereon Goldmann (SS Police Division), SS men were told that, 'We are the race that must rule the world ... and all other races must be subordinated to the Aryan race. They are no more than slaves. We rule the whole world.' There was, 'not a word about religion. Their religion was simply the Aryan race, which was what they took as their creed.'[2] Himmler, for his part, believed that the breeding of the superior German race involved the adoption of a vegetarian diet and complete abstinence from alcohol and tobacco.

As for Hitler, his obsession with racial purity led him to require the SS to keep a genealogical register of its members. The discovery of a Jew in the ancestry, however long ago this might be, would result in the swift removal of the SS officer from his post.[3]

The SS and the Teutonic Knights

'When world history later proclaims Adolf Hitler not only the greatest German leader, but also the greatest Aryan,' said Himmler, 'then they will say that we, his closest followers, his chosen knights, were loyal, obedient believers, that we were steadfast and worthy of being his heroic champions.'[4]

And to SS officers stationed at the Dachau concentration camp:

> Never forget we are a knightly order from which one cannot withdraw; to which one is recruited by blood, and within which one remains, body and soul.[5]

Perhaps in this, Himmler had in mind the 'Order of Teutonic Knights', founded by Heinrich Walpot von Bassenheim in 1198 and originally established to care for crusader knights who had been wounded, or who had fallen ill during the Crusades. An exclusively Germanic Order, it was instrumental in the 13th century in expanding German domination over Prussia and the Baltic states. However, on 15 July 1410 the Teutonic Knights were defeated by a combined force of Poles, Lithuanians and Mongols at the Battle of Tannenberg, and their power was broken.

Himmler undoubtedly also drew inspiration from Liebenfels, who in 1907 had founded the ritualistic and virulently racist 'Order of the New Templars', which would serve as the prototype for Himmler's SS.[6]

The Nazis delighted in recreating this 'medieval era' by staging elaborate pageants with knights on horseback, wearing chained mail and flamboyant swastikas emblazoned on their breast, and comely maidens attired in long, flowing, white dresses.

Wewelsburg Castle

In 1934 Himmler discovered the ruined mountain fortress of Wewelsburg, near Paderborn in Westphalia. Adopting it for the peppercorn rent of one Mark a year, he spent 13 million Reichsmarks on its refurbishment as the headquarters of the SS, employing (between 1935 and 1945) 4,000 slave labourers on the project. Again, he appears to have taken his inspiration from Liebenfels, who had himself chosen an Austrian castle, Burg Werfenstein, as headquarters for his 'Order of New Templars'.

Soon, not only at Wewelsburg, but in each SS region (Oberabschnitte) educational and cultural centres would be created, devoted to enlightening members of the SS about their Germanic past.

In the manner of the legendary Arthur, 6th-century King of the Britons, Himmler installed in the banqueting hall a huge, round conference table, with thirteen seats to accommodate himself and his twelve most senior commanders – 'Obergruppenführeren'.

According to Florentine Rost von Tollingen (a friend of Himmler), '… if an SS man got married, he could go there [to Wewelsburg] and receive his SS (wedding) ring. If he later fell in battle, the SS ring was to be brought back to Wewelsburg and kept there.' When a senior SS man died, his body would be returned to Wewelsburg to be cremated, the ashes then to be interred in the castle's crypt.[7]

The Death's Head Ring

By 1939 all SS officers with more than three years of service were entitled to wear the SS 'Totenkopf' (skull and crossbones), or so-called 'Death's Head' Ring. This was first used as a motif on the caps of Prussian cavalry regiments in the 18th century. It was subsequently adopted as a distinctive emblem by all SS formations.

The Totenkopf ring was designed by 'Brigadeführer' Karl-Maria Wiligut-Weisthor, an expert on runes and encoded symbolism (under whose influence the Wewelsburg Castle had been transformed).[8] Each ring was inscribed on the outside with ancient Germanic and runic symbols (ancient Germanic or Scandinavian alphabetical letters) and embossed with the 'Death's Head' motif, and on the inside with the name of the recipient, the date and Himmler's signature.

Karl-Maria Wiligut-Weisthor (1866–1946)

Wiligut was a professional soldier who had seen service on the Russian and Italian Fronts during the First World War. He claimed to be a clairvoyant and a possessor of extra-sensory powers who could recall the time, 'around 228,000 BC, when there were three suns in the sky, and the earth was populated with giants, dwarfs and other supposedly mythical beings'.[9] In September 1933 he had been recruited by Himmler to the SS and appointed head of its Department of Pre- and Early History within the Race and Settlement headquarters, based in Munich.

Wiligut and the Runic Alphabet

Wiligut used a runic alphabet which, according to Nordic legend, was given to mankind by Odin, the supreme god of Norse mythology. Members of the SS were taught about the runes, each of which had a special meaning. The Vikings had used such emblems on their ships, shields and spears. In fact the 'double S' logo of the SS was a representation of the double 'sig' rune: the sig being the symbol of the sun or conquering energy. The single sig rune (single 'S') was the logo of the Hitler Youth. The runes could be cast (thrown like dice) and their meaning read. These mystic tools were used to tell fortunes, invoke magic powers and cast spells.

In November 1924 Wiligut was committed to the Salzburg mental asylum and declared to be insane.[10]

King Heinrich

Himmler was fascinated by the Saxon King Heinrich, regarded as the protector of Germany from the eastern hordes. On 2 July 1936 at Quedlinburg Cathedral, he delivered a eulogy on Heinrich, to mark the one thousandth anniversary of his death, and afterwards laid a wreath on the king's tomb.

According to Heinz Müller (eye witness at Quedlinburg), Himmler genuinely believed himself to be the reincarnation of Heinrich. 'He [Himmler] was the Aryan type [which] he presumed Heinrich to be, and in his mind [he] believed he was his descendant.'[11]

Himmler, obsessional as ever, was anxious that Heinrich's bones (which were missing) be found, and according to Müller he, 'gave the order to find the remains of Heinrich at all costs. They just had to be somewhere.' When the SS failed to find the king's remains however, they improvised and, 'out of the catacombs of the crypt they unearthed the bones of noble women who were buried there; a year later they claimed them to be Heinrich's remains.'[12]

The Ahnenerbe

In July 1935 in a villa in a suburb of Berlin, Himmler created the SS 'Ahnenerbe' ('Society for the Research and Teaching of Ancestral Heritage'). Its remit included the performing of medical experiments on human beings, the checking of blood lines for purity, and the resurrection of ancient occult and pagan practices. At the same time, any occult organisation not associated with Himmler was suppressed, including the freemasons whom the Nazis believed were created by the Jews to conspire against German people.

The official 'Ahnenerbe' teaching was based on the theories of Viennese engineer and technician Hans Horbiger (and expounded by him in his book *Glazialkosmogonie*, published in 1913). Horbiger believed that the Earth repeatedly traps planets from outer space into its orbit which finally crash into the Earth. In his view, it was the result of just such a collision that caused the Great Flood, and the destruction of the island of Atlantis (named after the Greek god 'Atlas') – original home of the master race.[13]

Atlantis

According to ancient myth, 'Atlantis' (mentioned by the Greek philosopher Plato in the 4th century BC) was an extensive island in the Atlantic Ocean and, '... said to have been a powerful kingdom before it was overwhelmed by the sea.'[14]

A forceful proponent of the notion of Atlantis was Ukranian born theosophist Helena Petrovna Blavatsky (1831–91). According to Blavatsky's 'Secret Doctrine', there lived in Atlantis a race of 'super beings' who had fallen from grace through evil and vice. When the floods came however, not all the Atlantians perished; for certain priests escaped by boat to India and in particular, to Tibet. This race of Tibetans eventually made its way to Northern Europe where its descendents became the Nordic or Aryan race. Lanz von Liebenfels was another firm believer in the concept of Atlantis.

In 1884 Blavatsky was accused by the Indian press of concocting fictitious, spiritualist phenomena. The following year, the Hodgson Report, commissioned by the London Society for Psychical Research, declared her to be a fraud.

***

The notion that there may once have been a 'lost continent' of Atlantis somewhere in the North Atlantic Ocean, can easily be dispelled by the most cursory glance at a topographical atlas of the area. Running down, roughly through the centre of the Atlantic Ocean, is a line where the Eurasian and African tectonic plates meet with the North American and South American tectonic plates. This is defined by the so-called Mid-Atlantic Ridge – a line of subterranean mountains which run roughly midway between the west coast of the British Isles, Spain and North Africa, and the east coast of North America.

In the North Atlantic Ocean, Iceland and the small archipelago of the Azores mark the only places where the North Atlantic Ridge is visible above the surface of the water. Furthermore, the subterranean topography indicates that these areas could not possibly have formed a continent, at any rate during the period that mankind has been present on the Earth.

Nowadays, the consensus is that if there ever was an island or continent of Atlantis, then the most likely candidate for this is the former Mediterranean island of Strongyle (now the Italian island of Stromboli) which, 'collapsed after catastrophic volcanic action, and was submerged' around 1500 BC.[15]

So where had the people of Germany actually originated from? There was an element of truth in Hitler's belief that the Germans were related to the Scandinavians (who, in his view, were fellow Aryans), for around 1000 BC Germanic tribes from Scandinavia began to settle between the Rhine, Elbe and Danube rivers. However, they came not via 'Atlantis' or India/Nepal, but directly, possibly crossing the Baltic Sea to do so.

***

Unhindered by factual historical and geographical impedimenta such as these, the 'Ahnenerbe', in its quest to discover the origins of the Aryan race, sent expeditions to Iceland, the Middle East, North Africa, the Caucasus and Venezuela. An expedition to Amazonia was led by SS 'researcher' Edmund Kiss (who was by profession a popular playwright).

Dr Ernst Schäfer, an SS scientist who led one such expedition in April 1938 later described (to his post war US army interrogator) a meeting that he had once had with Himmler.

Himmler mentioned his belief that the Nordic race did not evolve, but came directly down from Heaven to settle on the Atlantic continent [Atlantis] and that [after Atlantis became submerged under the sea] ancient immigrants from Atlantis had founded a great civilisation in Central Asia.[16]

Wherever the expeditions went, the accompanying Nazi scientists convinced themselves that the edifices and ruins which they found were vastly superior to anything which could have been built by the indigenous population. Instead, they must have been built by a former superior Aryan civilisation, and this included the Great Pyramids of Egypt.[17]

Several 'Ahnenerbe' expeditions were dispatched to Tibet at enormous expense, the most recent being in the winter of 1938–9. Here, Nazi researchers proceeded to inspect the bemused Tibetans for typical Aryan traits, such as narrow foreheads, long limbs and angular features. For this, detailed measurements were taken using metal callipers. Even the shades of eye and colour of skin were recorded, using colour code charts. Liebenfels, it will be remembered, was a strong advocate of using physical features to determine degree of 'Aryanness', one of his journals being entitled *Character Assessment relative to Skull Shape: an Elementary Racial Phrenology.*[18]

As if this were not enough, the researchers, in order to achieve an exact likeness of the subject, had plaster moulds made of the facial features which, on their return to Germany, were transformed into model heads – to be compared with the heads of non-Aryans (preferably captured Bolshevik commissars, and Jews, who were selected by the 'Ahnenerbe' scientists from the concentration camps, to be gassed and then decapitated). 'Ahnenerbe' researcher Dr August Hirt, Professor of Anatomy at the University of Strasburg, went so far as to make a collection of human skulls from the victims of the Auschwitz concentration camp, and used them to make, 'comparative anthropomorphic measurements'.[19]

By such methods, Himmler hoped to prove that the ancestors of these Tibetans (who he believed were also the ancestors of the Nazis) were gods, and having done so, it should then be possible to recreate a new race of Aryan 'godmen' through selective breeding. As for the breeding stock, this would consist of Himmler's highly selected SS men, all of whom must be at least five foot nine inches tall and be able to prove their German ancestry back to the year 1750.

This was entirely in keeping with Liebenfels' notion that,

Gods and goddesses with hair like the sun, and with eyes like the blue sky, with rosy cheeks, with eternal health and eternal youth, they will sing the praises of their suffering breed mothers, as the women who created them.[20]

***

As the role of the 'Ahnenerbe' expanded to take charge of all Germany's archaeological excavation programmes (again in the hope of linking Nazi Germany with her past), so did its staff, which included in excess of thirty university professors. Himmler, with great enthusiasm, ordered excavations to take place at Luneburg in north Germany, home of ancient Germanic tribes. Again this research, far from being objective, was designed to try to prove how artefacts from the past could be used to explain and justify current Nazi ideology.

Traditional scientific research requires not only the observation and recording of facts, but also the formulation of a theory based on these facts; finally the testing of that theory to see whether it is true or false. Himmler's method however, and that of his entourage, was to invent the theory first, and then attempt to find facts to fit in with it. This was not only unscientific; it may be described as anti-scientific.

The Holy Grail

An advisor of Himmler's, the author and historian Otto Rahn (1904–39), had a particular interest in the Holy Grail, which he believed was hidden somewhere in the caves of southern France, and it was his lifelong ambition to find it.

The principal early accounts concerning the Holy Grail – the vessel from which the Saviour Christ drank at the Last Supper – were those of German author Wolfram von Eschenbach, whose story *Parzival* was completed in 1207; the anonymously written *Perlesvaus* of around 1225 and English writer Sir Thomas Malory's *Morte d'Arthur* of 1485.

There are, however, other legends surrounding the Holy Grail dating back to the time of the ancient Greeks, and also to the Celts. One such legend concerns Joseph of Arimathaea, a Jew into whose care Christ's body was entrusted for burial. When he was washing the body prior to entombment, Joseph collected the blood which oozed from the dead Christ's wounds into a cup, which became known as the Holy Grail. Christ then appeared to Joseph in a blaze of light and entrusted the Grail, which is believed to have supernatural powers, to his care.

The notion that the Grail had once contained the pure blood of Christ was in keeping with the Nazi ideology that people of pure Aryan blood were necessary to breed their ideal race of supermen, and it therefore comes as no surprise to learn that a replica of the Grail was to be found in the banqueting hall at Wewelsburg Castle.

Joseph then sailed to England where he established the first Christian church at Glastonbury in Somerset, which is where the Grail (perhaps one of many?) was housed.

Another such legend surrounding the Grail concerns Arthur, the 6th-century King of the Britons, whose twelve knights congregated around the Round Table and pledged themselves to search for the Grail. It was believed that the whereabouts of the Grail could only be discovered by the purest of knights, one who had been thoroughly cleansed of his sins.

The Holy Grail is central to Richard Wagner's final work (and Hitler's favourite opera) *Parsival*. A measure of the composer's interest in the Grail is demonstrated by a visit he made in 1855 to Nanteos in North Wales, to view a wooden cup purported to be the original holy vessel.

Liebenfels was himself a devotee of grail mythology, the title of his *Ostara* I/69 being, *The Holy Grail as the Mystery of Aryan Christendom: a Racial Cult Religion*. In fact, to Liebenfels, the grail was indelibly linked to the concept of the maintenance of the pure and noble Aryan bloodline.

Hitler's Views on the Subject

When attempting to judge the extent to which Hitler concurred with Himmler in these matters, it is necessary to exercise a certain caution, for according to historian Dr Nicholas Goodrick-Clarke:

Books written about Nazi occultism between 1960 and 1975 were typically sensational and under-researched. A complete ignorance of the primary sources was common to most authors, and inaccuracies and wild claims were repeated by each newcomer to the genre until an abundant literature existed, based on wholly spurious 'facts' concerning the Thule Society, the Nazi links with the East, and Hitler's occult initiation.[21] [The Thule Society was founded by German nationalists in 1912; its name deriving from 'Ultima Thule' or 'Land at the End of The World' – supposedly the birthplace of the Germanic race. Anti-Bolshevik and anti-Semitic, its aim was a unified Europe under the leadership of a greater Germanic Reich.]

Albert Speer for one, was in no doubt as to what he thought of Hitler's 'Reichsführer' SS.

Himmler ... obviously was going his absurd way, which was compounded of beliefs about an original Germanic race, a brand of elitism, and an assortment of health food notions. The whole thing was beginning to assume far-fetched, pseudo-religious forms. Goebbels, with Hitler, took the lead in ridiculing these dreams of Himmler's, with Himmler himself adding to the comedy by his vanity and obsessiveness. When, for example, the Japanese presented him with a Samurai sword, he at once discovered kinships between Japanese and Teutonic cults and called upon scientists to help him trace these similarities to a racial common denominator.[22]

It is significant that the 'Führer' never visited Wewelsburg Castle, the epicentre of Himmler's activities, of which he was openly scornful:

What nonsense! Here we have at last reached an age that has left all mysticism behind it, and now he wants to start all over again. We might just as well have stayed with the Church. At least it had tradition. To think that I may some day be turned into an SS saint! Can you imagine it? I would turn over in my grave....[23]

As for Himmler's archaeological excavations, Hitler remarked:

Why do we call the whole world's attention to the fact that we have no past? Isn't it enough that the Romans were erecting great buildings when our forefathers were still living in mud huts? Now Himmler is starting to dig up these villages of mud huts and enthusing over every potsherd [fragment of pottery] and stone axe he finds. All we prove by that is that we were still throwing stone hatchets and crouching around open fires, when Greece and Rome had already reached the higher state of culture. We really should do our best to keep quiet about this past. Instead, Himmler makes a great fuss about it all. The present day Romans must be having a laugh at these relegations.[24]

As for the notion that Hitler was interested in astrology and took the advice of astrologers (as Himmler was reputed to have done), the American psychoanalyst and author Walter Langer (who made a study of Hitler for the US Office of Strategic Studies) had this to say:

All of our informants who have known Hitler rather intimately discard the idea [of Hitler's belief] as absurd. They all agree that nothing is more foreign to Hitler's personality than to seek help from outside sources of this type.[25]

**

Hitler was therefore prepared to tolerate the eccentric peregrinations of his 'Reichsführer' SS, just so long as they remained harmless. The fact is that the Führer had other and more important fish to fry, as it were.

Notes

1. *Secret History: The Nazi Expedition.*
2. *The SS: Himmler's Madness.*
3. Lumsden, Robin, *SS Regalia: A Collector's Guide to Third Reich Militaria*, p. 66.
4. *The SS: Himmler's Madness.*
5. *Nazis: The Occult Conspiracy.*
6. Barker, Alan, *Invisible Eagle: The History of Nazi Occultism*, p. 54.
7. www.richarddeacon,spyclopaedia
8. Lumsden, op. cit., p. 148.
9. Goodrick-Clarke, Nicholas, *The Occult Roots of Nazism*, p. 181.
10. Ibid, p. 182.
11. *The SS: Himmler's Madness.*
12. Ibid.
13. *Secret History: The Nazi Expedition.*
14, 15.   *Brewer's Dictionary of Phrase and Fable*, 2001. London: Cassell.
16. *Nazis: The Occult Conspiracy.*
17. *Secret History: The Nazi Expedition.*
18. *Ostara*, I/37.
19. Lumsden, op. cit., p. 128.
20. *Ostara*, I/21.
21. Goodrick-Clarke, op. cit., pp. 224–5.
22. Speer, Albert, *Inside the Third Reich*, p. 183.
23. Ibid, p. 147.
24. Ibid, p. 148.
25. Langer, Walter, *The Mind of Adolf Hitler*, p. 31.

CHAPTER XII

Hitler's Magnetism

The reason why the German people came to find Hitler and his message so appealing was simply one of supply and demand. World War I had left a legacy of bitterness and anger; Hitler offered a solution to what they saw as otherwise insuperable problems. It was a matter of someone, whom they perceived to be the right man, arriving in the right place at the right time.

***

Christobel Bielenberg described the Germany which she knew in 1932 where one German in five was out of work (i.e. 6.5 million Germans unemployed, out of a workforce of 30 million)[1] and there was great social unrest.

> Every weekend political marches took place in Hamburg, and the Nazis used to march through the communist districts. The communists then answered by coming into the other parts of the town and there were fights, deaths, and shooting practically every weekend.

'People said, "It can't go on like this",' said Emil Klein (Nazi Party member 1921–45). 'Then the debate began about the need for a strong man, and the call for a strong man became louder and louder, because democracy achieved nothing.'[2] His sentiments were echoed by Christobel Bielenberg. The political situation was such that,

> People wished that some strong man would clean up the place. We've got to get out of what we're in. Anything is better than this situation that we're in at the moment.[3]

'In this situation,' said Jutta Rudiger (Nazi Party member 1931–45), 'Hitler seemed to be the bringer of salvation. He said, "I will get you out of this misery if you all join in". And everyone understood.'[4]

***

So how did Hitler set about his task of winning over the German people? First, he made it clear that he absolutely identified with them in their view of the Treaty of Versailles as an 'instrument of unrestricted oppression'.[5] (This was followed by hyperinflation and economic depression which compounded Germany's problems even further.) In the early 1920s Emil Klein declared that he once paid 4 billion Reichsmarks for a sausage and bread. 'It really was a collapse.' Jutta Rudiger described the, 'desperation and poverty caused by the mass unemployment .... It was really terrible....'[6]

***

Emergence of the 'Strong Man'

'Whoever wishes to win over the masses,' said Hitler,

> must know the key that will open the door to their hearts. It is not objectivity, which is a feckless attitude, but a determined will, backed up by force, when necessary.[7] The soul of the masses can be won only if those who lead the movement for that purpose are determined not merely to carry through the positive struggle for their own aims, but are also determined to destroy the enemy that opposes them.[8] The masses are but a part of Nature herself .... Their wish is to see the stronger side win and the weaker wiped out, or subjected unconditionally to the will of the stronger.[9]

In July 1932 in an election speech, Hitler made no secret of the fact that his Nazi Party intended to impose a dictatorship. He asked,

> Is it typically German, to have thirty [political] parties? We are intolerant. I have given myself one goal – to sweep these thirty political parties out of Germany. We have one aim and we will follow it fanatically and ruthlessly to the grave.[10]

As for his German National Socialist Labour Party (GNSLP), 'It was imperative from the start to introduce rigid discipline into our meetings and to establish the authority of the chairman absolutely,'[11] because only by violence and terror could, 'a new regime be created by means of constructive work.'[12] In the chambers or senate, said Hitler, envisaging the situation that would pertain should his party come to power, 'the right of decision belongs exclusively to the president, who must be entirely responsible for the matter under discussion.'[13] He then went on to describe, with unconcealed delight, how his Storm Troops had launched an attack on their opponents.[14] (In fact, in *Mein Kampf*, Hitler devoted a whole chapter to the 'Nature and Organisation of the Storm Troops'.)

However, apart from stressing the need for obedience, Hitler was deliberately vague about his party's policies. When he was asked, 'What is your detailed programme?' his reply was,

> I can only answer: after a government with your [i.e. the Weimar coalition's] kind of economy, with your kind of administration, your decay, the German people have to be rebuilt from top to bottom. We do not want to lie, we do not want to cheat. Therefore I have refused ever to appear in front of these people and make cheap promises.[15]

As far as Hitler was concerned, rhetoric would have to suffice.

Speech and Propaganda

Hitler quickly realised that by his words, he was able to influence people; so much so that he made a deliberate study of what is now referred to as 'body language', in order to achieve maximum effect. As Emil Klein observed: '...face to face with Hitler, I was never that enthusiastic about him and his moustache. But he could enthuse me through the power of his speeches. He also convinced me – and everyone else.'

'At a mass meeting,' Hitler cried:

> Thought is eliminated. And because this is the state of mind I require, because it secures to me the best sounding-board for my speeches, I order everyone to attend the meetings, where they become part of a mass, whether they like it or not....[16] I am conscious that I have no equal in the art of swaying the masses, not even [including] Goebbels.[17]

Hitler encouraged his audiences to take a pride in themselves.

> The German people is no longer a people of dishonour, a people of shame, of self-destruction, of faint-heartedness, and lack of faith. No Lord, the German people has become strong again, in its spirit, strong in its will, strong in its persistence, strong in endurance of every sacrifice. Lord, we will not desert you. Now bless our struggle and our freedom, and thus our German people and fatherland.[18]

'Humiliation' was a word which Hitler often used in his appeals to the German people to follow him as leader, and this was an appeal from the heart, because, having come into contact with the poor and underprivileged, he had seen what humiliation and degradation can do at first hand, not only to himself, but also to others.

It is true that, to the majority of his listeners, Hitler had a mesmerising effect: the clenched or shaking fist, the contortions of the face in an agonised way to indicate that the same problems which concerned them, his audience, concerned him. The shrewd observer noticed afterwards however, that despite all the rhetoric, there was a distinct absence of originality, substance or deep intellectual thought contained therein.

It is now known that Hitler's powers of oratory were not entirely spontaneous. Paul Devrient, born in 1890 in Wandsbeck, was a successful German operatic tenor. In his book, *Mein Schuler Adolf Hitler*, published in 2003, he reveals that from 1929–33 he acted as tutor to Hitler. In the year 1932 in particular, Devrient accompanied Hitler on his Nazi Party campaign trail, which took them to more than a hundred German towns, in the course of which the former gave the latter lessons in oratory (paid for by Hitler at his own expense).

The careful observer would also realise that Hitler used the same speeches over and over again; delivered in a hostile, snarling voice such as might be heard from a dog trapped in a corner by a hostile adversary, or with agonised hand-wringing and breast-beating. His vocabulary was limited and his speeches were strong on rhetoric, but lacked substance. For example, '...and we know before us lies Germany, within us marches Germany, and behind us comes Germany;'[19] or, when he addressed the first Party rally at Nürnberg: 'The most precious possession we have is our people, and for our people, and on behalf of our people, we want to struggle, and we want to fight, and never weaken, and never weary, and never doubt, and never despair. Long live our Movement! Long live the German nation!'

In the creation of his new regime, said Hitler, propaganda would be of the utmost importance,[20] and no fewer than fourteen pages were devoted by him to this subject in his book, *Mein Kampf*.

The function of propaganda, he said,

> does not lie in the scientific training of the individual, but in calling the masses' attention to certain facts, processes, necessities, etc., whose significance is thus for the first time placed within their field of vision. The whole art consists in doing this so skilfully that everyone will be convinced that the fact is real, the process necessary, the necessity correct, etc. But since propaganda is not, and cannot be the necessity in itself ... its effect for the most part, must be aimed at the emotions and only to a very limited degree at the so-called intellect ....[21]

An example of this is Hitler's attempt to convince the German people that they had not really lost the war.

> As far as England is concerned, the war was really won when Germany was destroyed as a colonial and commercial power, and was reduced to the rank of a second-class state.[22] The stigma of shame incurred by a cowardly submission can never be effaced.[23] (Here, he was quoting the Prussian general and author, Karl Philip Gottlieb von Clausewitz.)

Hitler now offered the German people a solution to their problems:

> Today you must stand before the world, with me, and behind me, and solidly declare, we want nothing but peace, we want nothing but calm, we want only to devote ourselves to our duties, we also want nothing but equal rights, and we will not allow anyone to take away our honour.

Although it is clear with hindsight that Hitler was being disingenuous when he spoke of wanting nothing but peace and calm, this was a message with which the war-weary German people readily identified.[24]

Pageantry

As a devotee of the late composer Richard Wagner, Hitler was conscious of the power which drama and pageantry could exert over an audience. Those who attended the Nürnberg Party Rallies of the mid to late 1930s can scarcely deny that Hitler held his enthralled audiences in the palm of his hand, so to speak, and that they would have followed him, probably without exception, to the very ends of the earth.

The rallies were best described by Sir Nevile Henderson, the then British Ambassador to Germany:

> ... the hypnotic effect of thousands of men marching in perfect order, the music of the mass bands, the forest of standards and flags, the vast perspectives of the stadium, the smoking torches, the dome of searchlights. [The 'dome' effect was achieved by making the beams of the searchlights intersect high up in the sky, giving the auditorium a cathedral-like appearance.] The sense of power, of force and unity was irresistible, and all converged with a mounting crescendo of excitement on the supreme moment when the Führer himself made his entry. Paradoxically, the man who was most affected by such spectacles was their originator, Hitler himself, and, as Alfred Rosenberg, German Nazi politician, remarks in his memoirs, they played an indispensable part in the process of his self-intoxication.[25]

Since early 1920, Hitler had been concerned with the design of a flag for his Party (the NSDAP).

> I, as leader, was unwilling to make public my own design, as it was possible that someone else could come forward with a design just as good, if not better, than my own. As a matter of fact, a dental surgeon from Starnberg submitted a good design very similar to mine, with only one mistake, in that his swastika with curved corners was set upon a white background. After innumerable trials, I decided upon a final form – a flag of red material with a white disc, bearing in its centre a black swastika.... The new flag appeared

in public in the mid-summer of 1920.[26] (Although Hitler did not mention him by name, the dentist referred to was a Doctor Friedrich Krohn.)

A ritual, first established in the July 1926 Nazi Party Rally held at Weimar, was the Blood Banner ceremony, where Hitler consecrated in excess of 300 huge flags by touching each one with the tattered remnants of a bullet-ridden, blood-stained Party banner which had been held by a dying Nazi during the failed 'Putsch' of 1923. In the four days between 31 August and 3 September at the 1938 Party Rally held at Nürnberg, Hitler took the salute of a million men, and addressed some 60,000 or so Hitler Youth.

Appearances, however, were deceptive, because behind the serried ranks and precision marching of the Storm Troopers lay a disorganised system of government in which Hitler, for his part, often delegated the same tasks to two or more of his minions at the same time. Confusion was compounded by his obsequious henchmen, whose principal desire was to please him, rather than to act for the benefit of their country.

The Nazis were anxious to connect Germany to its past, to the glorious days of the Teutonic knights. With this in mind, Hitler and his Party attempted to recreate this 'medieval era' by staging elaborate pageants, with knights on horseback wearing chain mail, and flamboyant swastikas emblazoned on their breast, and with comely maidens attired in long, white, flowing dresses.

With God's Help…

Hitler, in his speeches, often invoked the imagery of Christianity: 'The German people have become strong again. May the Lord God bless our struggle and our German people and Fatherland,'[27] said Hitler in *Mein Kampf*:

> Everybody who has the right kind of feeling for his country, is solemnly bound, each within his own denomination, to see that he is not constantly talking about the Will of God merely from the lips, but that in actual fact he fulfils the Will of God and does not allow God's handiwork to be debased. For it was by the Will of God that men were made of a certain bodily shape, were given their natures and their faculties. Whoever destroys His work wages war against God's Creation and God's Will. Therefore, everyone should endeavour, each in his own denomination of course, and should consider it his first and most solemn duty to hinder any and everyone whose conduct tends, either by word or deed, to go outside his own religious body and pick a quarrel with those of another denomination.[28]

As for his Nazi Party, it was to be, 'the selecting ground for German political leaders. It's doctrine will be unchangeable. Its organisation will be as hard as steel. Its total image however, will be like a holy order.'[29]

The 'Volk'

Since Hitler was anxious for the people of the countryside not to feel excluded from the activities of his Nazi Party, he arranged for his Brownshirts to attend the annual harvest celebrations, where country people recreated the image of the 'Volk' (community of pure blood and race), by dressing in national costume. In this, Hitler displayed a certain cynicism, in that while he would have approved of the idea of the German 'Volk' as a means of maintaining German culture and identity, for him, the celebration of past glories would have been seen as parochial and an irrelevance for one whose agenda was soon to involve a far wider world.

The Hitler Youth

Hitler was anxious to extend his Party's appeal to young people. 'We believe that the German youth must be lean and agile; fleet as a greyhound, tough as leather, and as hard as Krupps steel,' he said.[30]

In 1931 24-year-old Baldur von Schirach, son of a director/manager of a theatre, became Reich Youth Leader. Two years later, the Nazis took over all Germany's youth organisations. 10-year-old boys were conscripted into the organisation of young German people. At 14 they joined the Hitler Youth (which Schirach had founded and become leader of in the same year), and at 18 they joined the Nazi Party. Girls joined the League of German Girls (BDM), which taught domestic skills (rather than encouraging intellectual pursuits). At the Nürnberg Party Rallies the Hitler Youth were obliged to swear their allegiance to Hitler.

Although membership of the Hitler Youth and BDM was ostensibly voluntary, in practice, any child who opted out would find him or herself disadvantaged when it came to choosing a school or later, to choosing a career.

Addressing the Hitler Youth, Hitler said: 'We want our people to be peace-loving but also courageous. You must be peace-loving.'[31] [*Remarks that were utterly mendacious, in the light of what was to follow.*] 'We can look proudly on our German youth. You are our life blood ..., our own flesh.' However, he added the rider: 'Nothing is possible unless one will commands ... and the others visibly obey. German boys and German girls, we want our people to be obedient. You must practise obedience.'[32]

In fact, as far as peace was concerned, the reality was quite different. In the words of Hans Fruhwirth (ex Hitler Youth): 'Now there was paramilitary training ... small bore rifle shooting, and marches using a map and compass.'[33] With hindsight, the inference was obvious: when the time came, Schirach would be able to deliver his willing recruits directly to the armed forces.

(Later, SS Reichsführer Heinrich Himmler came to an agreement with Schirach, whereby the Death's Head units of the SS would recruit directly from the Hitler Youth. Wearing their black uniforms they would be trained to be willing executioners. The Hitler Youth therefore, had become in essence a pre-military training unit.)

Hitler's Appeal to Women

Hitler no doubt realised that his appeal to women was greater as a single man than it would have been had he been married (although because of his sexual proclivities, he appears to have ruled marriage out right from the start).

As for women, those who were not married were encouraged to attend elite bridal schools, of which there were five. Here they were trained to become 'perfect housewives' – i.e. to manage a household, become proficient in cookery and learn about motherhood. At the end of such a course at bridal school, the woman would be presented with a diploma indicating that she had now qualified as a 'master housewife'.

Underpinning this, however, was the concept of the pure master race. It was a woman's duty to increase the birth rate, and to have as many children as possible, for which, according to the results of her labours, she would receive the Motherhood Cross in either gold, silver or bronze! However, before she was given permission to marry, proof of her racial and medical purity was required, and the couple were required to confirm this on their marriage certificate. She must be fit, in every sense, to breed.

Nonetheless, women were excluded, not only from the annual Nürnberg Rallies, but also from certain professions: if they were married, from the Civil Service and other positions of power and authority. It was made clear to them that their duty was in the home, looking after the husband and children. This had the added virtue of helping to reduce unemployment. However, for women there were cross country runs and communal physical training to foster a sense of community spirit.

Hitler summed up his idea of the contented woman. 'Charm, grace, and rhythm unite to form a happy picture and a positive approach to life. They [women] have no longing for public office or the parliament. A happy man, and a host of happy children are dearer to them.'[34]

Putting Germany back to Work

When Hitler became Chancellor on 30 January 1933 the first action of the Reichsbank was to inject the sum of 1 billion Marks into the housing and construction industries; then to finance the first of the 'autobahns' (2,500 miles of superhighway linking the major cities), which would cost another 600 million Marks. (Although Hitler claimed credit for the 'autobahns', they had actually been planned long before he came to power.) There now commenced a crash programme of public works and covert re-armament; so that Hitler was soon able to say with justification, that during his first year in power, over 2.7 million unemployed had been brought back into the labour force.[35]

Germany and her Neighbours

In October 1930 Hitler re-emphasised his desire for Germany to live in peaceful coexistence with her neighbours:

> I think I can assure you, that there is no one in Germany who will not with all his heart approve any honest attempt at an improvement of relations between Germany and France. My own feelings force me to take the same attitude ... the German people has the solemn intention of living in peace and friendship with all civilised nations and powers ... and I regard the maintenance of peace in Europe as especially desirable and at the same time secure, if France and Germany, on the basis of equal sharing of natural human rights, arrive at a real inner understanding ... the young Germany that is led by me and that finds its expression in the National Socialist Movement, has only the most heartfelt desire for an understanding with other European nations.[36]

During the 1930s Hitler continued to tell a pack of outrageous lies in respect of his future intentions towards his fellow European countries, while all the time he was tightening his grip on his own country, and covertly building up, with hostile intentions, a massive war machine.

> Our boundless love for, and loyalty to our own national traditions makes us respect the national claims of others and makes us desire from the bottoms of our hearts to live with them in peace and friendship.[37] Before the entire world I declare: we are ready to offer the French people a hand of reconciliation.[38]
>
> The world must know that my love of peace is a longing for peace of the entire German people.[39] When did the German people ever break its word?[40] The German government is ready at any time to participate in the system of collective cooperation for safeguarding European peace ....[41]
>
> The assertion that it is the intention of the German Reich to coerce the Austrian state is absurd and cannot in any way be substantiated or proved .... Germany neither intends nor wishes to interfere in the internal affairs of Austria, to annexe Austria, or to unite Austria.[42] It is my wish to solve the great differences among the nations in precisely the same way in which I solved our domestic problems – according to the principles of justice, fairness, and understanding.[43]
>
> The German government has assured Belgium and Holland that it is ready to recognise and to guarantee these states as neutral regions in perpetuity.[44] Without taking the past into account, Germany has concluded a non-aggression pact with Poland [reference to the German-Polish Pact of 26 Jan. 1934]. This is more than a valuable contribution to European peace, and we shall adhere to it unconditionally.[45] Germany had no intention of attacking other peoples.[46] None of the Scandinavian statesmen, for example, can contend that the German government or that German public opin-

ion has ever made a demand which was incompatible with the sovereignty and integrity of their state.[47]

And the most classic lie of all: 'We have no territorial demands to make in Europe'![48]

***

Not everyone was taken in by Hitler's rhetoric. Those of the intellectual elite who left Germany following Hitler's accession included tenor Richard Tauber (born in Austria), and German novelist and Nobel Prize winner Thomas Mann. German Jewish mathematical scientist Albert Einstein also left the country.

Dr Hjalmar Schacht, President of the Reichsbank, was forthright in his opinion when he heard in September 1938 that British Prime Minister Neville Chamberlain was about to visit Berlin. He said, 'Imagine! The Prime Minister of this world power [Britain] comes to visit this gangster! [Hitler][49]

Notes

1. Weitz, John, *Hitler's Banker*, p. 11.
2. *The Nazis: A Warning from History, Part 1.
3. *World at War: Hitler's Germany: the Only Hope, 1933–1936.
4. *The Nazis: A Warning from History, Part 1.
5. Hitler, Adolf, *Mein Kampf*, p. 347.
6. *The Nazis: A Warning from History, Part 1.
7. Hitler, op. cit., p. 191.
8. Ibid, p. 192.
9. Ibid.
10. *The Nazis: A Warning from History, Part 1.
11. Hitler, op. cit., p. 269.
12. Ibid, p. 254.
13. Ibid, p. 252.
14. Ibid, p. 280–1.
15. *The Nazis: A Warning from History, Part 2.
16. Rauschning, Hermann, *Hitler Speaks*, p. 211.
17. Ibid, p. 210.
18. *Hitler: a Profile. The Blackmailer.
19. *The Nazis: A Warning from History, Part 2.
20. Hitler, op. cit., pp. 306–18.
21. Ibid, Vol.1, pp. 106–11 and 187–210.
22. Ibid, p. 370.
23. Ibid, p. 368.
24. *Hitler: a Profile: The Blackmailer.

25. Henderson, Sir Nevile, 1940. *Failure of a Mission*. London, p. 71.
26. Hitler, op. cit., p. 276.
27. *Nazis: The Occult Conspiracy*.
28. Hitler, op. cit., p. 310.
29. *Nazis: The Occult Conspiracy*.
30. *Hitler's Henchmen: Schirach, the Corrupter of Youth*.
31. *Hitler: a Profile: The Seducer*.
32. Ibid.
33. Ibid.
34. *Hitler's Women*.
35. *World at War: Hitler's Germany: the Only Hope, 1933–1936, Part 1*.
36. *Der Volkischer Beobachter*, 26 October 1930.
37. Prange, Gordon W (ed.), *Hitler's Words*, 17 May 1933, Berlin, p. 161.
38. Ibid, 24 Oct. 1933, p. 191.
39. Ibid, 26 Oct. 1933, Köln, p. 159
40. Ibid, 11 Nov. 1933, Berlin, p. 179.
41. Ibid, 21 May 1935, Berlin, p. 183.
42. Ibid, 21 May 1935, Berlin, p. 184.
43. Ibid, 12 March 1936, Karlsruhe, p. 167
44. Ibid, 30 Jan. 1937, Berlin, p. 186.
45. Ibid, 30 Jan. 1939, Berlin, p. 189.
46. Ibid, 1 April 1939, Berlin, p. 182.
47. Ibid, 28 April 1939, Berlin, p. 185.
48. Ibid, p. 181.
49. Gisevius, Hans Bernd, *Bis zum Bitteren Ende*, p. 356.

CHAPTER XIII

The Path to Power

Hitler's rise to power must be seen against a backdrop of a depressed economy and high unemployment.

In 1923 the value of Germany's currency fell, and as it did so, the government responded by printing more and more paper money in order that employers and factories could meet their obligations to their workers, and to their suppliers. However, this merely served to increase the upward spiral of inflation. Soon a situation arose where the banks successively overprinted say, a one Reichsmark banknote, first with the number 10, then 1,000 and finally, 1,000,000 or more. In other words the currency was rendered virtually valueless; savings accounts became worthless, and foreigners were able to purchase German land, property and businesses at knock-down prices.

On 22 December 1923 46-year-old Dr Hjalmar Schacht (formerly head of the German National Bank) was appointed President of the Reichsbank (even though he was not a member of the Nazi Party). Of Danish descent, Schacht had been brought up in New York City, where his father was a merchant. He now proceeded to establish a gold reserve and travelled to London in order to peg the Mark to a gold standard.

On 21 January 1924 Schacht declared that German reparations could be paid only through German exports. However, French Prime Minister Raymond Poincaré insisted that they be paid in cash. Nevertheless, in that year the German economy recovered to the extent that inflation was reduced to single figures. The Weimar government had achieved this by borrowing money from the Americans and using it to pay the French and British the reparations due to them under the terms of the Treaty of Versailles. In other words, the recovery was based on short-term credit.

Under a plan put forward by an Allied committee led by American Charles Dawes (and ratified by the Reichstag on 29 August 1924), Germany achieved some amelioration of the harsh terms of the Treaty of Versailles. Also, the French agreed to end their occupation of the Ruhr. Germany now came to the attention of Americans anxious to invest in the German State, and in every possible German business and municipality.

In accordance with their notion of a world Jewish conspiracy, the Nazis declared that when they came to power they would strip German Jews of their citizenship and even expel them from the country. In Hitler's words, 'Men dispossess one another, and one perceives that at the end of it all it is always the strongest who triumphs, the stronger exerts his will.'[1] However, by 1924 the Nazis had as yet failed to make any significant impact on the German political scene. Not only that, but a potential rival to Hitler had emerged in the form of Captain Ernst Röhm, Commander of the SA, whose ambition it was to be the army's commander in chief with his men taking over the army's role.

On 26 April 1925 Field Marshal Paul von Hindenburg was elected President of the Republic, following the death of Friedrich Ebert. On 16 October the Treaty of Locarno (or so-called Rhineland Security Pact signed in London) guaranteed Germany's existing frontiers with France and Belgium. The following year, Germany was admitted to the League of Nations and normal relations with the Western Powers were restored.

Meanwhile Hitler, on his (early) release from prison in December 1925, set about reforming the SS (which had originally been created to form his personal bodyguard), enlarging it to include in each German city a core of Nazis whose loyalty to himself would be total and unquestioning.

***

In the 1928 election, the Nazis won only twelve seats in the Reichstag (seat of the democratic German government) with just 2.6 per cent of the vote. At the same time a sudden drop in agricultural prices brought poverty to the countryside.

At an international conference held in February 1929 in Paris under Owen D Young (American lawyer and Chairman of the General Electric Company), the question of German reparations was again discussed. The result was that on 7 June the Young Plan was accepted by the Germans: a new Bank for International Settlements would be opened in Basel in Switzerland into which Germany would be required to pay reparations until the year 1988. Payments would increase annually for the first thirty-six years, but annual instalments would never exceed 660 million Marks. For Germany this was another considerable improvement.

On 29 October of that year, the New York Stock Market crashed. This was followed by the Great Depression of 1929–30 in which many businesses were destroyed as numerous American investors in Germany went bankrupt, and America withdrew its short-term loans.

On 7 March 1930 a discouraged Hjalmar Schacht resigned as President of the Reichsbank. He now embarked on a lecture tour of America where he argued that Germany was unable to pay her reparations under the Young Plan, and that these reparations should therefore be suspended for fear of there being a, 'menace to world peace and stability'.[2]

On 27 March 1930 following the collapse of Germany's so-called 'Great Coalition Government', a minority government of centre and right-wing parties was formed under Heinrich Brüning. However, national elections called by Brüning on 14 September left the Great Coalition unable to form a majority, and Brüning was forced to rely upon President Hindenburg's powers of rule by emergency decree.

In that year, Heinrich Himmler (Nazi Party member from 1923) was made head of the SS, which, under his leadership, effectively became the Party's police force. In the September elections, the Nazis increased their percentage of the vote, winning 170 seats (compared with the communists' seventy-seven, and the coalitions of middle parties which held the remainder) out of a total of 560 seats.

In 1931 the five major German banks crashed, more than 20,000 German businesses failed, and the unemployment figure rose to 5.5 million. Increasingly desperate Germans now turned to the Nazi Party. However, the communists also gained support and there followed a period of civil unrest.

Reinhard Heydrich now joined the SS, and proceeded to use that organisation to gather intelligence on Hitler's rivals. Soon, this organisation would become a vehicle for the perpetration of state terror as a means of achieving total political and social control of the country through its network of informants in every walk of life.

Throughout that summer, the German press contained stories of homosexual behaviour and sleaze among the higher echelons of the Nazi Party. This applied particularly to the SA, whose leader Ernst Röhm, was openly homosexual. At first, Röhm and his henchman were tolerated by the Nazis, Hitler stating that as far as SA leaders were concerned, 'Their private lives cannot be an object of scrutiny, unless it runs counter to vital principles of National Socialist ideology.' However, to the Nazis, the excesses of the SA were soon to become an embarrassment.

In the election of July 1932 the Nazis captured 37.3% of the vote, making them (with 230 seats) the largest party in the Reichstag, even though they still lacked an overall majority. On 13 August Hitler demanded of President von Hindenberg, that he (Hitler) be made chancellor. The 85-year-old was horrified. Was democracy in Germany to be snuffed out after a mere fourteen years? However, a group of businessmen, together with Hjalmar Schacht (President of the Reichsbank from 1923–30), argued that Hitler should receive the chancellorship for the good of Germany.

In another election held in November 1932 the Nazi vote fell back slightly, to 33.1%. The Party was also in some difficulty, being acutely short of funds. Now, former Chancellor Franz von Papen proposed that Hitler could become Chancellor provided that he, von Pappen, was appointed Vice-Chancellor, and that the number of National Socialist (Nazi) Party members in the cabinet was restricted to two.

This was accepted, and on 30 January 1933 Hitler was duly sworn in (by President von Hindenberg) as chancellor of a coalition government (at 43, the youngest Chancellor in Germany's history). That same evening, the Nazis held a torchlight celebration parade through the streets of Berlin.

**

Meanwhile, across the English Channel from the continent of Europe, there were those who welcomed the advent of Hitler with the same fervour and anticipation as that of his Nazi followers back in Germany.

Notes

1. *The Nazis: A Warning from History, Part 1.*
2. Weitz, John, *Hitler's Banker*, p. 114.

CHAPTER XIV

A View from Britain:
The Anglo–German Association

Hampshire's Isle of Wight, situated off the south coast of England, sixty miles across the sea from France was, and still is, an area of outstanding natural beauty: rolling hills and downs with little fields and isolated farmsteads, breath-taking views, and elegant 'watering places' such as Ventnor, Sandown and Shanklin. A visitor to the island in the early to mid 1930s would have had little idea of the mayhem which was shortly to come, for at that time, relationships with Germany were cordial, even friendly. Yet within a decade, the island's radar facilities would play a pivotal role in protecting England against the Luftwaffe in the so-called 'Battle of Britain' (August–November 1940).

One summer's day in 1936 for example, St Lawrence Hall, situated on the south side of the island and home of Lady Constance, widow of the late Admiral Earl Jellicoe, received an important visitor. Jellicoe, who had died in the December of the previous year, had commanded the British fleet at the Battle of Jutland, and had subsequently been a vice-president of the Anglo–German Association, which was dedicated to forging stronger post-war links with Germany.

Who was the visitor? He was none other than Prince Friedrich, grandson of the German Kaiser Wilhelm II, who had taken a liking to the Jellicoes' daughter Prudence, and in the parlance of the times, was 'paying court' to her.

Also indicative of the relaxed atmosphere between Britain and Germany was the fact that within three miles of St Lawrence was a youth hostel (now the Hermitage Hotel) where the Hitler Youth stayed regularly in the holidays.

The Isle of Wight County Press (newspaper) edition of 4 April 1936 reported a speech by the chairman of the local Conservative Association, Sir Henry Sweetman JP, in which he referred to the 'irreparable loss' his country had sustained by the death of its beloved sovereign King George, who had died on 20 January at the age of 70. Sir Henry recognised what a splendid monarch he had been, and how he had sacrificed himself at all times to carry out the duties of his great office, and offered Queen Mary (his widow) his sincere and humble sympathy in her 'very great bereavement'.

The same edition of the newspaper made reference to the fact that, 'German liners will be bringing large parties of tourists to the island again this summer. The Hamburg/America and Hamburg/South America lines have included visits to the island in three of their pleasure cruises. Passengers from the liners "Milwaukee", "Monta Rosa" and "Monta Pascoal" will tour the island on 2 June, 22 June and 13 July respectively.'

It was in such an atmosphere as this that, back in 1932, the Anglo–German Association had been formed. It should also be said that among the more enlightened members of that society, there was a certain sympathy for the plight of post-war Germany, which they believed had been treated unfairly by the terms of the Treaty of Versailles.

***

The Anglo–German Association (AGA) was based in Hampstead in north London. Under the presidency of the Most Honourable the Marquess of Reading, its membership was restricted to '100 gentlemen being natural born British subjects'. They included: members of parliament, high ranking ministers and civil servants, barristers, newspaper editors and journalists, directors of banks, authors, university lecturers, and the warden of an Oxford college.

The AGA's officers and committee were to be elected annually in April at the General Meeting of the Association at the House of Commons Committee Room. Some of the committee members had strong links with Germany, for example, Group Captain M G Christie, formerly Air Attaché in Berlin, who had 'an enormous circle of German friends, as well as being able to speak the language with great fluency'.[1]

The aims of the AGA were to promote, 'a good understanding between Germany and Britain …;' also to, 'cooperate in particular with the corresponding German society in Berlin … (namely, the 'Deutsche-Englische Gesellschaft' – DEG),' and to, 'study such international questions as are relevant to the association's aims.'

The leading light in the AGA was General Sir Ian Standish Monteith Hamilton (1853–1947), who had fought in both the First and the Second Boer Wars, and in the Sudan. In 1915 he had been General Officer commanding the Mediterranean Expeditionary Force at Gallipoli. He retired from the army in 1920.

President of the German DEG (one of whose members bore the same aristocratic surname as Count Claus von Stauffenberg, who would one day attempt to assassinate Hitler) was Dr Wilhelm Cuno. In the early years, the relationship between the AGA and the DEG was cordial. However, as the years passed, tensions would arise over events that were taking place in Germany.

In June 1931 Dr Heinrich Brüning (Chancellor of Germany's Weimar Republic) and Dr Julius Curtius (former Minister of Economics) were guests of the AGA in London. In November Hamilton wrote to committee member Major General Sir Robert Hutchison on the subject of a possible visit to London by Adolf Hitler at the invitation of the AGA. Hutchison admitted that he was, 'curious to see the man [Hitler], as several of my old friends, ex-officers in the German army, have written to me so often about this magnetic power'.

However, having consulted, 'very quietly one or two important personages, as to the wisdom or otherwise of such a step' (i.e. offering to entertain Hitler), Hamilton was advised that this,

> would be very dangerous ... it would alienate some of our best friends on both sides; it might put a spoke in the wheel of Brüning's government, and it would scare the French just when these critical financial negotiations are opening. [This presumably was a reference to Germany's repayment of war reparations.][2]

The decision was therefore taken not to invite Hitler to London.

On 27 April 1932 Herr von Kardoff, Vice President of the Reichstag, took lunch with the AGA at the House of Commons, and in early October, members of the AGA paid a visit to Germany.

On 5 April 1933 Count Gottfried von Bismarck, Honorary Secretary of the DEG and a member of the Reichstag, spoke in the House of Commons on the subject of the Nazi Party (the Nazis having seized power in Germany with Hitler as Chancellor three months previously, on 30 January).[3]

In May 1933 Hamilton came under pressure from the British government to put the AGA, 'into cold storage for a little time', even though it was his opinion that the, 'mass of propaganda in our press at present' about the situation in Germany was mostly false.[4]

In June 1933 Hamilton decided that it would be, 'unwise at present to offer our membership to any Jewish gentleman'. This apparently, because he was fearful of offending his German counterparts in the DEG.

In January 1934 Hamilton visited Berlin, to be received by President Paul von Hindenburg at 12 noon on the 31st, and to spend the evening with General Werner von Blomberg, the German Minister for War. Another evening was passed in the company of Minister of Foreign Affairs Baron Konstantin von Neurath; the DGA also invited him for luncheon.[5]

In November 1934 AGA Secretary Morgan, who had recently returned from a visit to Berlin, told Hamilton that the Nazi authorities had informed him that the German DEG had been dissolved the previous month. Nonetheless, the Hamburg branch of the DEG appeared still to be extant, because Hamilton was invited to address it. 'With great reluctance' he declined.

In his letter of apology to Dr Arnold Koster, Hamilton stated that, 'There are dark forces in the world driving Germany and England towards death and destruction ...' even though, 'in truth, they [the two countries] are first cousins belonging to the same family ....' Hamilton recalled with gratitude how, during the occupation of the Rhine[land], when British soldiers went into German billets, 'as [soon as] they came back from manoeuvres they would find that the lady of the house had put slippers by the stove to make them comfortable ....' However, public opinion (in England) was, 'so sharply divided that any strong partisan speech in favour of remembering the blood tie between Germany and ourselves would certainly provoke a violent reaction ....'[6]

In March 1935 it was clear that the AGA was coming under pressure (presumably from the Nazi regime in Germany) to purge Jews from its list of members. Hamilton however, resisted. The AGA's,

> Jews, and strong Jewish sympathisers would naturally … feel it rather an affront if we were to reconstitute [the organisation] on a fresh basis which would automatically exclude Jews. Therefore, they [the committee of the AGA] would prefer to smash up the whole concern [AGA] in as open a way as possible, part of their wish being that this should be a slight to Herr Hitler and the present regime [in Germany].[7]

In any event, since the German DEG had already been dissolved it was considered that the legal position had to be that the British branch must likewise cease to exist.

On 19 March 1935 Colonel R Meinertzhagen of London announced that he was resigning from the AGA (which he described as 'moribund') as he, 'did not agree with the negative policy pursued', and regarded, 'the majority of members unsympathetic with Germany ….' Now, with a group of influential businessmen and others, he proposed to form a new group which would be called the Anglo–German Fellowship (AGF).[8] However, when he invited Hamilton to join his AGF the latter declined.[9]

On the evening of 13 May 1937 Hamilton and his wife Jean dined with His Excellency the German Ambassador Joachim von Ribbentrop and his wife Annelies at the German Embassy. However, he declined an invitation to attend the Annual Congress of the National Socialist (Nazi) Party at Nürnberg, to be held that September.[10]

On 16 December 1937 Leo Geyr, Commander of the Third German Panzer Division, sent Hamilton, 'very sincere wishes for Christmas and a happy New Year'.[11]

On 21 July 1938, in a letter to Consul General Karlowa of the German Embassy in London, Hamilton referred to a forthcoming tour of Germany, starting in Köln and ending in Berlin, which he was due to make as head of a delegation from the British Legion in London.[12]

On this tour, Hamilton dined and spent a night at the 'Berghof' (Hitler's mountain retreat) as Hitler's guest, having been flown from Berlin to München by Deputy Führer Rudolf Hess in his private aircraft. On Hamilton's return from Germany, *The Daily Telegraph* carried a photograph of the two men, Hamilton looking benign and relaxed; Hitler on the other hand, appeared grim-faced with arms folded across the chest in a defensive manner.

Britain's *Sunday Chronicle* of 7 August 1938 displayed a photograph depicting Austrian Nazi sympathisers humiliating Jews. Its caption read,

> Jew Purge – this remarkable picture, smuggled out of Austria and the first of its kind to be published in Britain, shows elderly Jews on their knees scrubbing one of the main streets of Vienna. The young Nazis watching them are obviously enjoying the sight.

On 8 August 1938 one Henry Dexter wrote to Hamilton concerning British newspaper reports which quoted him (Hamilton) as saying, 'I am sure that Hitler's attitude is strongly for peace.' 'In that case,' said Dexter, 'Why does *Mein Kampf* still circulate in millions of copies in Germany? If Hitler were to have the book re-printed, deleting the obnoxious passages … it would be a step towards peace.' In his reply, Hamilton said that the Führer,

> is the one man standing now between Germany and war. Let me assure you, if Hitler were to die within the next few days, August would not be over before the troops – German – began to march. Of course, if you don't believe that the man is an idealist with a strong vein of poetry in his composition, you will not be able to follow me.[13]

On 9 August 1938 Hamilton, in a letter to one Ezra Lloyd, went even further, describing Hitler as, 'a sympathetic and lonely man faced with the awful responsibility of guiding his nation along the crest of a precipice at the bottom of which lies war'.[14]

On the same day Hamilton, in a letter to E Baker (a former rifleman in the Fourth Royal Scots) explained that his [Hamilton's] invitation to visit Hitler, had come as he was returning to Berlin to lay a wreath on the tomb of the Unknown Warrior.

> This [laying of the wreath] I had to drop and go and pay my respects to one I consider at present, the most interesting figure on Earth [i.e. Hitler]. He [Hitler] has indeed a horror of war and shrinks from the idea of what he (I am sure truly) believes would be the end of civilisation.[15]

In other words, Hamilton had been completely duped by the German leader.

On the other hand, Lord Londonderry, Secretary of State for Air, made it clear that he himself was in no doubt about the situation in Germany: 'The continued effort [by the Nazis] to exterminate the Jews is the part of their policy which I cannot understand, and this is turning world opinion against them ….' He had spoken with Göring about it and with Ribbentrop and Himmler and, 'their replies are not convincing at all'.[16]

Also, on the same day the British newspaper, *The News Chronicle*, gave even grimmer details of Nazi activities:

> More than 80 Jews died in Buchenwald concentration camp, near Weimar … during the month of July, according to reliable information reaching London. They were transported thither from towns throughout the Reich on trumped up charges. This information is supported by documentary evidence. The youngest Jew, Erich Löwenberg was 21 years old, and the oldest Ludwig Kahn, is understood to have been a septuagenarian. The cause of death was the kind of work to which they were subjected, and the inhuman treatment meted out to them.

Again on 9 August 1938 Sidney Salomon, captain in the Eighth Manchester Regiment, commented sarcastically in a letter to Hamilton:

> It must indeed have been an honour when you shook Herr Hitler by the hand …, [for this was a man] who has deprived Jewish blinded soldiers from the right to a free radio licence (which every other blinded soldier possesses) [and who] has ordered that in future no Jewish name must be placed on war memorials …. I suppose you regard with indifference the 7,000 suicides in Vienna that followed the 'Anschluss', the hundreds of deaths that are taking place in the concentration camps at Dachau and Buchenwald, and even hail with approbation the decision to deprive Jewish doctors of their right to practise, so that a few more hundred may be driven to self-destruction.

It was Salomon's opinion that Hamilton's attitude was,

> a deadly insult to the thousands of soldiers of the Jewish faith who laid down their lives, not only for this country, but for Germany, for you may not be aware that no less than 12,000 German Jews died for their one-time fatherland, that no less than 1,500 German Jewish soldiers received the Iron Cross of the First Class, that 35,000 were promoted for gallantry in the field ….

For barbarism of this magnitude, said Salomon, one had to go back, 'to the Dark Ages'.[17]

Hamilton however (by now an elderly gentleman of 85), was not to be deflected, and declared his intention to entertain, 'on the 20th September … a large body of German ex-servicemen here in my house.'[18] Even now, he still could not bring himself to recognise the truth.

Salomon was incensed. 'Peace,' he said, 'can be obtained by other means than kowtowing to scoundrels and bullies …. There is only one way to treat a bully (and what are the Germans but bullies of the most disgusting and nauseous type) and that is by showing that you are not afraid of them.' [19]

On 22 August 1938 Hamilton received an invitation from the German Chargé d'Affaires in London, Theodor Kordt, inviting him and his wife to visit Germany and to attend the Annual Congress of the German National Socialist Party at Nürnberg the following month, as honorary guests.[20]

On 10 September 1938 Hamilton wrote, full of confidence, to Company Sergeant Major Jay Mason, formerly of the Fifth Lincolnshire Regiment, 'I have seen Hitler and you have not …. He is permitting 800 of his old frontline fighters to come and drink a glass of beer in my house in London on 24th, and I don't think he is likely to declare war before that comes off.'[21]

However, by 27 September 1938 a telegram sent by Hamilton to Hitler in München, showed that the light was beginning to dawn:

Zero hour – as an admirer of Your Excellency and your Army and as a Scottish soldier who, fighting [having fought] in the Dardanelles, has shed no German blood, I implore you in the name of those about to die to pause before you cry havoc and let loose the dogs of war.

Alas, Hamilton's plea was to no avail.

Notes

1. Hamilton, Sir Ian, Duke of, *The Hamilton Papers*, E Bernard Morgan to Hamilton, 26 May 1931.
2. Hamilton to Hutchison, 24 Nov. 1931.
3. E Bernard Morgan, 28 March 1933.
4. Hamilton to Morgan, 12 May 1933.
5. Simson to Morgan, 17 Jan. 1934.
6. Hamilton to Dr Koster, 29 Jan. 1935.
7. Hamilton to Thorne, 3 March 1935.
8. Colonel R Meinertzhagen to Hamilton, 19 March 1935.
9. Hamilton to Meinertzhagen, 22 March 1935.
10. Hamilton to Woermann, 27 August 1937.
11. Geyr to Hamilton, 16 Dec. 1937.
12. Hamilton to Karlowa, 21 July 1938.
13. Hamilton to Dexter, 9 Aug. 1938.
14. Hamilton to Lloyd, 9 Aug. 1938.
15. Hamilton to E Baker, 9 Aug. 1938.
16. Londonderry to Hamilton, 9 Aug. 1938.
17. Salomon to Hamilton, 9 Aug. 1938.
18. Hamilton to Admiral Algernon Walker-Heneage-Vivian, 9 Aug. 1938.
19. Salomon to Hamilton, 12 Aug. 1938.
20. Kordt to Hamilton, 22 Aug. 1938.
21. Hamilton to Mason, 10 Sept. 1938.

CHAPTER XV

Edward, Prince of Wales

Edward, born on 23 June 1894, was the eldest child of King George V and Queen Mary. As a child, he learnt German and French, and later became fluent in Spanish. He began by hating the Germans and ended up admiring the Nazis. The German people were not alone in coming under the spell of Adolf Hitler!

Educated at the Royal Naval College Dartmouth, Edward was created Prince of Wales in 1910 on his 16th birthday. The investiture, which took place on 13 July 1912 at Caernarvon Castle, was followed by a tour of Wales in which Edward expressed concern for the poor and unemployed people of that principality. In the same year, he went up to Magdalen College Oxford, taking the opportunity to visit Germany twice during the university vacations.

When World War I broke out in 1914 Edward was astonished and appalled. 'England at war with Germany? That seems a sentence which will appear nowhere but in a mad novel,' he told his brother George ('Bertie').[1]

Determined to have a fighting role, Edward was commissioned into the Grenadier Guards. However, Lord Kitchener, Secretary for War, apprehensive that Edward might be captured by the enemy, forbade him to fight on the Front Line. Instead, the Prince was posted to the staff of the British Expeditionary Force's Commander in France. Nevertheless, on at least one occasion, he visited the troops on the front line.

Of Edward's hostile attitude to the Germans, at this time, there is no doubt. Referring to a gas attack made by them he commented: 'One can't be surprised at anything those German buggers do. One really can't believe we're fighting European Christians. I am a great advocate of taking no prisoners, or as few as possible!'[2]

World War I ended with the signing of the Armistice on 11 November 1918. Even so, Edward's strong feelings against the former enemy were still very much in evidence. He bewailed the fact that, 'we are not making these Huns feel they are beaten. The infantry, and in fact all the men, still loathe the Huns and despise them.'[3] Edward now travelled widely throughout the world, and would soon visit virtually every major nation, except for Soviet Russia.

In 1921 Edward expressed his concern for the ordinary people of Britain: 'It is a very sad and depressing thought that there are so many desperately sad and sordid homes this Christmas ... destitute men (thousands of them ex-service men), and consequently still more starving women and children,' he said.[4] This was no empty gesture, for in that year Edward founded the National Relief Fund, and in the words of Sir George Arthur, formerly an official in the War Office, 'stumped up nearly £4,000 for wages of the clerical staff'.[5] Edward also moved some of the London tenants of the Duchy of Cornwall (of which he was Duke) into better housing, and was instrumental in improving the standard of farm workers' dwellings on the Duchy estates in the West Country.

Edward's concern for the poor was ongoing. In 1927 he became Patron of the National Council of Social Service, an umbrella organisation for the multitude of voluntary bodies concerned with welfare. In 1929 he visited the depressed coal mining regions of the counties of Durham and Northumberland, and remarked upon the, 'squalor and distress which exists', and upon the, 'amazing bravery and friendliness' of the people, 'despite the ghastly times they are existing through'.[6]

In the early 1930s Edward toured Tyneside, the Midlands, Lancashire, Yorkshire, Scotland and Wales, where unemployment had reached calamitous proportions, and acquainted himself with the most underprivileged slum areas. Nevertheless, he was realistic about his limitations in being able to make a significant inroad into these problems. '... I had the feeling that, empty as was my mission, my appearance among them [the poor] was in large measure appreciated and taken as a sign that the monarchy had not forsaken them in their misfortune.'[7]

On 10 January 1931 Thelma, Lady Furness, one of his former mistresses, introduced Edward to a friend of hers, Wallis Simpson, an event which would change his life for ever.

***

Bessie Wallis Warfield, born on 19 June 1896 at Blue Ridge Summit, Pennsylvania, USA, and brought up in Baltimore, Maryland, was two years younger than the Prince of Wales. They soon became partners, and attended social functions together including in 1932 being entertained by the German Ambassador Leopold von Hoesch. When Hitler came to power in March 1933 he employed as his emissary, Karl Eduard, Duke of Saxe-Coburg-Gotha, who was not only a friend of Edward, but also his first cousin.

It was at a dinner given by society hostess Emerald Cunard that Edward and Wallis first met Hitler's advisor on Foreign Affairs, Joachim von Ribbentrop.[8] Having met Wallis, von Ribbentrop was in the habit of periodically sending her a gift of seventeen roses, presumably in order to ingratiate himself with her.

Edward, in an address to the annual conference of the British Legion in June 1935, showed that any antipathy he might have felt towards the former enemy was definitely a thing of the past: 'I feel that there could be no more suitable body or organisation of men to stretch forth the hand of friendship to the Germans than we ex-servicemen who fought them and have now forgotten all about it and the Great War,' he told his assembled audience of British war veterans. And as far as that country was concerned, Edward made it quite clear that his policy was one of non-intervention. For this, the Prince was severely reprimanded by his father King George V, who considered his speech to be too pro-German.[9]

Between August and October 1935 while they were cruising together in the Mediterranean, the Prince and Wallis made the decision to marry. There was a huge impediment to the match however, for Wallis was a twice-divorced woman: both of her former husbands were still living. In addition, King George V strongly disapproved of his son having a relationship with Wallis and banned her from appearing at court.

When Edward dined in Paris with Albert Gregoire, who had previously acted for Wallis in a libel suit, he may or may not have known that Gregoire was a Nazi agent who, as a Paris banker, was responsible for channelling funds to British fascist leader Sir Oswald Mosley on behalf of Hitler and the Italian dictator, Benito Mussolini.

When Mussolini's Italy invaded Abyssinia on 2 October 1935 Edward's father, King George V, was adamant that he was not prepared to confront the Italian dictator. Neither did Conservative Prime Minister Stanley Baldwin, now 68 years of age, nor his government have any wish to quarrel with either Italy or Germany.

Under the terms of the Hoare-Laval Pact of 9 December 1935 signed by French Premier Pierre Laval and British Foreign Secretary Samuel Hoare, Lord Templewood, a large portion of Abyssinia was ceded to Italy. Edward gave the pact his full support, but by meddling in politics, he served only to worsen his already deteriorating relationship with his father, the King. Not only that; both he and Wallis, as suspected fascist sympathisers, had now been placed under regular surveillance by the Special Branch of the Metropolitan Police.

Now, a British security agent reported that London based Russian emigrée Anna Wolkoff (a member of the Right Club and a Nazi spy), was using her position as a close personal friend of Wallis, to spy on Edward, and that these two women might be involved in passing state secrets to the German government. Wolkoff, the daughter of a former Russian admiral who had once been the tsar's naval attaché in London, had been recruited by Nazi intelligence through her membership of white Russian (i.e. anti-Bolshevik) organisations. She was highly regarded by the Nazis and was known to be in close contact with such leading figures as Nazi politicians Hans Frank and Konrad Henlein, and with Deputy 'Führer' Rudolph Hess. She was also acquainted with William Joyce. According to MI5 agent Joan Miller, Wolkoff's primary occupation was dressmaking, and the Duchess of Windsor was one of her best clients.[10]

When King George V died on 20 January 1936 Hitler, in order to show solidarity with the new King Edward VIII (now aged 41), organised an elaborate memorial service in Berlin, where Crown Princess Cecilie, Heinrich Himmler, Josef Goebbels and Hermann Göring were among those present. The King should 'tell these plutocrats and Marxists' that nothing would prevent him from marrying 'a girl of the people,' said Hitler.[12]

That same month, two hundred men from the impoverished area of Jarrow-on-Tyne in the north-east of England set out to march to London to present a petition of their grievances to the Bar of the House of Commons. When the march terminated in London's Mall leading to Buckingham Palace on the 31st of that month, Edward was there to meet it. He was cheered by the marchers who felt that he had their interests at heart. It was not only the German people who were suffering.

When, contrary to the terms of the Treaty of Versailles, German troops invaded the demilitarised Rhineland on 7 March 1936, Ribbentrop reported that King Edward VIII, had issued, 'a directive to the government … that no matter how the details of the affair are dealt with, complications of a serious nature are in no circumstances to be allowed to develop'.[11] In other words, there was to be no intervention by Britain.

Wallis's decree nisi was granted on 27 October 1936. In late 1936 Edward returned to South Wales, which was still in the grip of the Depression, and again he expressed his concern for the suffering of the long-term unemployed. His last public engagement as King was on 11 November 1936 when he attended the Remembrance Day ceremony at Whitehall and laid a wreath at the Cenotaph.

Edward and Prime Minister Baldwin met at Buckingham Palace on 16 November 1936 when the former announced his intention to marry Mrs Simpson. If the government opposed the marriage, Edward said, then in the circumstances he was, 'prepared to go'. On 10 December he signed the instrument of abdication. From now on he would be known as 'His Royal Highness, the Duke of Windsor'. The title of 'Her Royal Highness' would, however, be denied his wife Wallis. For the German Ambassador von Ribbentrop, Edward's abdication was an enormous setback.

Edward immediately sailed from Portsmouth to Boulogne on the destroyer HMS *Fury*, and then travelled to Vienna to spend five months as guest of Baron and Baroness Eugene de Rothschild. Meanwhile, his brother George, Duke of York, who would succeed Edward as King George VI, made it clear that Edward would not be welcome at his forthcoming coronation. Edward's brother was duly crowned King on 12 May 1937 in Westminster Abbey.

On 3 June 1937 Edward and Wallis were married by a Church of England parson in a simple ceremony at the Château de Conde, near Tours in France. The Royal Family boycotted the ceremony at which only a few friends were in attendance. After their honeymoon, the Windsors occupied an apartment in Paris. They had always assumed that they would be permitted to return to England; however, this was not to be the case.

In August 1937 war began in the Far East when the Japanese armies of Emperor Hirohito invaded the Chinese mainland. Nevertheless, this did not prevent the Windsors from travelling to Berlin (where they arrived on 11 October) as guests of the Nazi government. The reason Edward gave for the visit to Germany was so that he could, '… see for myself what National Socialism was doing in housing and welfare for the workers ….'[13]

In the circumstances one might have expected Hitler to have lost interest in Edward, but this was far from the case, and they (Edward and Wallis) were fêted by the German leaders. To greet them was a full reception with Union flags, Nazi swastikas, a brass band, and a host of German officials at the head of which was Dr Robert Ley, the Nazi Minister of Labour. Afterwards they were accommodated in luxury at the Kaiserhof hotel.

At a party for the Duke and Duchess hosted by Dr Ley, there were present: Ribbentrop, SS leader Heinrich Himmler, Deputy Führer Rudolf Hess and his wife Ilse, and Josef Goebbels, Minister of Propaganda and his wife Magda. Edward inspected an elite division of the SS, as well as a Nazi youth camp. The Duke and Duchess also met with Hermann Göring, Commander of the Luftwaffe and his wife Emmy. Emmy Göring, perhaps echoing her husband's thoughts and those of his Nazi henchmen, would later write that she, 'could not help thinking that this woman [the Duchess] would certainly have cut a good figure on the throne of England'.[14]

On 22 October 1937 the couple were entertained to tea by Hitler at the Berghof. According to abdication papers released to the Public Record Office in Kew (Surrey, England) in 2003 Edward had a long conversation with Hitler, 'during which the Duke made no contentious statements, nor offered any support for Nazism ....'

By the autumn of 1937 refugees fleeing from Nazi Germany were describing the horrific state-sponsored brutality that was being perpetrated by the Nazi regime. It was therefore difficult to believe that Edward and Wallis were ignorant of what was going on behind the scenes in that country.

On 20 June 1939 (by which time the Germans, who had broken through French lines, were threatening Paris), the Windsors left France and three days later arrived in Spain, a country whose fascist government, led by General Franco, had received help from both the Germans and the Italians during the Spanish Civil War.

Although it suited Ribbentrop to have the Windsors installed in Spain on a permanent basis, where he could keep an eye on them, so to speak, it was not to be, and on 3 July the Windsors left for the Portuguese capital Lisbon, to stay at the villa of a wealthy pro-German banker, Ricardo Espirito Santo Silva.

Now Ribbentrop went so far as to attempt to mount an operation to return the Duke to Spain by force if necessary, but his plans were thwarted when, on 4 August 1939 the Windsors left Lisbon for Bermuda, where Edward was to take up the post of Governor.

On 25 August 1939 Edward telegraphed Hitler: 'Remembering your courtesy and our meeting two years ago, I address to you my entirely personal, simple, though very earnest appeal for your utmost influence towards a peaceful solution to the present problem.'[15] To this Hitler replied:

You may rest assured that my attitude towards Britain and my desire to avoid another war between our two peoples remains unchanged. It depends on Britain however, whether my wishes for the future development of German–British relations can be realised.[16]

***

The best that can be said about Edward is that he was deceived by Hitler and was merely flirting with Nazism, a philosophy that he had no intention of embracing. The worst is that he was deliberately positioning himself, in the hope that by ingratiating himself with the Nazis, this would enable him to regain his throne in the event of a Nazi invasion of Britain. In this way, Hitler would have taken control not only of Britain, but also of her Empire (which he so admired), with Edward, now the puppet king, as its figurehead.

As for Wallis, an avid Nazi sympathiser – judging by the kind of company she liked to keep – she would undoubtedly have, 'gone with the flow', as it were.

Notes

1. RA (*Royal Archives*) GV (*King George V*) EE (*King Edward VIII*) 13/2, 5 Aug. 1914.
2. Ibid, RA GV EE 8/112, Edward to W E Houston-Boswell, 7 May 1915.
3. RA DW (Royal Archives, Duke of Windsor's Papers) 2207, 14 Dec. 1918.
4. Edward to Queen Mary, 31 Dec. 1921. RA GV EE 3.
5. Ziegler, Philip, *King Edward VIII, the Official Biography*, p. 182.
6. Baldwin Papers, 31 Jan. 1929, 177/45.
7. Windsor, Duke of, *A King's Story*, p. 248.
8. Schmidt, Dr Paul, 1951, *Statist auf Diplomatischer Bühne, 1923–1945*. Bonn: Athenaeum. p. 315.
9. King, Greg, *The Duchess of Windsor*, p. 130.
10. Archibald Ramsay, www.spartacus.schoolnet.co.uk. P RramsayA2.htm.
11. *Documents on German Foreign Policy, 1918–1945*, Ser. C, vol.4, 1962. Document No. 531. London. HMSO, 1957–1966.
12. Schwarz, Dr Paul, *This Man Ribbentrop*, p. 99.
13. *New York Daily News*, 13 Dec. 1966.
14. Göring, Emmy, 1967, *An der Seite meines Manne. Begebenheiten und Bekenntrisse*, Göttingen. Shutz.
15. 27 Aug. 1939. RA DW Trunk 2. RA. DW papers.
16. *Captured German Documents*, Vol X. Series D.

CHAPTER XVI

Sir Oswald Mosley

Oswald Ernald Mosley, born on 16 November 1896, was educated at Winchester College, where he excelled at boxing and fencing.

When Britain declared war on Germany on 4 August 1914, Mosley was at the Royal Military College, Sandhurst, training to become an officer. Having been gazetted into the Sixteenth Lancers, he became impatient with the inactivity and so, quickly transferred to the Royal Flying Corp's Sixth Squadron. Within weeks, the 18 year old was flying over German lines in the capacity of observer.

It was whilst Mosley was undergoing further training at the flying school at Shoreham near Brighton, that he crashed his aeroplane and injured both his legs, one of them severely. This left him with a chronic limp, and venous phlebitis. Although he rejoined his regiment and spent the winter of 1915–16 in the trenches, Mosley, because of ongoing problems with the veins of his leg, was sent back to London to spend the remainder of the war in the Ministry of Munitions and at the Foreign Office.

Mosley's political life was one of chop and change. In December 1918 he was elected to Parliament as Conservative MP for Harrow, and thus became, at the age of 22, the youngest member of the British House of Commons. He had grave doubts, however, about parliamentary democracy in its current format.

According to his son Nicholas, Mosley once said:

> What is the point of a parliamentary system where you pay the prime minister and the government an enormous sum of money to get the job done, and you pay an opposition an enormous sum of money to stop them getting the job done? We do not propose dictatorship, said Mosley, but we do propose a drastic revision of the parliamentary machine in order that the will of the people may be carried out.[1]

In May 1920 Mosley married Lady Cynthia Blanche Curzon, daughter of Conservative politician George Nathaniel Curzon (formerly Viceroy of India), who was of American-Jewish descent. Meanwhile, Mosley voiced his dissatisfaction with the Conservative government over its Irish policy.

In 1914 a bill granting Home Rule for Ireland had been passed into law, but it was shelved for the duration of the war. In 1916 however, Irish Nationalists, impatient with the lack of progress, rebelled. When in 1918 seventy-three Sinn Fein MPs (political party whose aim was a united Republican Ireland) were elected to Westminster, they declared themselves to be a separate parliament and Ireland to be an independent republic. The Irish Republican Army, with which Sinn Fein was closely associated, then proceeded to take control of much of Ireland by force. Prime Minister David Lloyd George was finally obliged to act, and terrorism on one side was met with savage reprisals on the other.

The 'Black and Tans' were an irregular force attached to the depleted Irish police force and recruited mainly from unemployed English ex-soldiers, whose purpose was to maintain order among the Irish population. Mosley, however, objected to the fact that they were also employed to carry out reprisals against the guerrilla Irish Republican Army and the local population which sustained it. 'The name of Britain was being disgraced,' he said. 'Every rule of good soldierly conduct [is] disregarded, and every decent instinct of humanity outraged.' Finally, on 3 November 1920 a disgusted Mosley crossed the floor of the House and joined the opposition.

In 1922 when the coalition government collapsed and was replaced by the Conservatives, Mosley forsook the Conservative Party, stood as an Independent, and retained his seat at Harrow with a healthy majority.

In January 1924 shortly after Labour came to power for the first time, under Prime Minister Ramsay Macdonald, Mosley again changed sides and joined the Labour Party. However, that October, the Conservatives were restored to power under Stanley Baldwin and Mosley lost his seat. In December 1926 Mosley was returned to Parliament as Labour MP for Smethwick. In 1928 he succeeded to the baronetcy on the death of his father.

When, in May 1929 Ramsay Macdonald's Labour Party once again defeated the Conservatives, Mosley was returned a second time as MP for Smethwick and joined the Cabinet as Chancellor of the Duchy of Lancaster. He thus became the youngest person for fifty years to hold ministerial rank. That October brought the Wall Street Crash, and with it a worldwide slump in trade.

On 20 May 1930 Mosley resigned from the Cabinet, having become disillusioned after his 'Memorandum' (in which he made radical recommendations for economic reform and the alleviation of the current high levels of unemployment resulting from the Wall Street Crash) was narrowly rejected by the Labour Party.

On 1 March 1931 Mosley launched his left-wing 'New Party', and hoped that other MPs from all sides would join him. However, in that October's General Election (in which the National Coalition government under Ramsay MacDonald came into being), the New Party failed to have a single one of its twenty-four candidates elected, including Mosley himself.

With the eclipse of his New Party, Mosley, on 6 January 1932 visited Italy, where he had what would be the first of several meetings with leader Benito Mussolini, that country being the first to embrace fascism.

He returned fired with enthusiasm for the way Italy's fascists had constructed new factories, launched employment schemes, provided child welfare, youth training, and holidays for poor children; established clubs for workers, and so forth. He would later describe Mussolini as, 'a modern man imposing modern solutions'.[2] Mosley was now determined to establish a fascist party of his own, modelled on the Italian system.

In his first published book entitled *The Greater Britain*, Mosley set out his plans for the economic, social and political reconstruction of Britain, which, with her Empire, he envisaged would become an economically completely self-sufficient trading bloc, insulated from the competition of cheap labour from elsewhere in the world.

***

Sir Oswald Mosley first met Diana Guinness (née Mitford) in July 1932 at a ball given by herself and her husband Bryan Guinness (heir to the brewing empire of the same name). Mosley, married with three children of his own, was then aged 35. Diana, daughter of 2nd Baron Redesdale, had just celebrated her 22nd birthday.

Impatient at what he perceived as parliamentary democracy's failure to solve the country's economic and social ills, the tireless Mosley founded, on 1 October 1932 the British Union of Fascists (BUF) with himself – moustached, with hair oiled and smarmed back – as its leader. Diana Guinness, for her part, became the head of the women's section. Party members, like their Italian 'Blackshirt' counterparts, wore black uniforms and jackboots, and practised the 'Nazi salute'. Diana's younger sister Unity (also a member of the BUF) was also overtly pro-Nazi, and in the habit of driving around with a swastika pennant flying from her car.

In the early days, the BUF, with its particularly strong following in the East End of London, had the support of newspaper proprietor Lord Rothermere's *Daily Mail*. Modelled on the German and Italian fascist parties, the BUF established its own so-called 'Defence Force', which would be there to deter trouble makers at its future public meetings, the first of which was held in Trafalgar Square on 15 October.

That autumn, Mosley visited Mussolini for a second time, where, standing on a podium with the dictator, he and 'Il Duce' ('The Leader') reviewed a march past of Italian troops.

In early January 1933 Diana left her husband Bryan and took up residence at Eaton Square, near Mosley's Ebury Street flat. In February, the BUF's weekly publication *The Blackshirt* went into production. An editorial on 1 April 1933 pronounced that as far as the BUF was concerned, anti-Semitism was forbidden, and membership was open to all British subjects of whatever race, colour or creed.

At the end of April 1933 Mosley, accompanied by his wife Cynthia, paid another visit to Italy, where he attended Mussolini's International Fascist Exhibition. (Mussolini was now financing Mosley to the tune of approximately £60,000 per year.) On 8 May however, Cynthia suffered an attack of acute appendicitis, underwent surgery, but died of peritonitis a few days later.

In the summer of 1933 Diana was introduced to a German by the name of Putzi Hanfstaengl who was Hitler's Foreign Press Secretary. Hanfstaengl had helped to finance the Nazi Party from its earliest days with American dollars brought into Germany by the family business (his father being a München art dealer). Hanfstaengl had also provided the funds which had enabled Hitler to buy the newspaper *Der Volkischer Beobachter*, and it was his wife Helene who, after the failed 'Putsch' of 1923, had taken Hitler in, given him sanctuary, and hidden him from the police.

Having regaled Diana and Unity with the wonders of the new Nazi State and its leader, Hanfstaengl now invited them to come to Germany to witness the true situation for themselves, as a counterbalance to what he considered to be the false impression of the Nazis being depicted in the British press.

The two sisters duly arrived in Munich where Hanfstaengl, now ensconced in the impressive new Nazi Party headquarters at the Brown House, provided them with accommodation and an invitation to what was to be the first September Nürnberg Party Rally of the Nazi era.

Referring to the rally, Diana wrote:

The gigantic parades went without a hitch. A feeling of excited triumph was in the air, and when Hitler appeared an almost electric shock passed through the multitude .... It was a thanksgiving by revolutionaries for the success of their revolution. They felt the black years since their defeat in the war were now over, and they looked forward to a better life .... By a strange chance ... I witnessed this demonstration of hope in a nation that had known collective despair.[3]

Having witnessed this impressive spectacle, Diana's sister Unity, who had been unable to understand Hitler's speeches which were of course in German, was desperate to return to München and acquaint herself with that language. To this end, she enlisted the help of her German teacher Fräulein Baum.

Unity also made it her business to find out where Hitler was wont to dine whenever he was in München: it was the 'Osteria Bavaria' restaurant, situated not far from the Nazi Party headquarters. Here she would wait, day after day, hoping that the Führer would come in and notice her. Not to be outdone, Diana also set out to learn German, realising that in this way she would be able to cultivate her friendships with the Nazi leaders which could only be beneficial to Mosley and his BUF.

In 1934 membership of the BUF peaked to approximately 40,000, of whom 10,000 were active members. Mosley now founded the January Club, through which he hoped to persuade businessmen and former military officers to embrace fascism.

On 7 June 1934 Mosley held a huge rally at Olympia with all the pageantry and paraphernalia of a paramilitary display. This ended up in a violent confrontation between the BUF and the Communist Party whose Stepney contingent contained a large proportion of Jews. Up until now, Mosley and his Party had refrained from indulging in anti-Semitism to any great extent, but he now regarded the Jews as his adversaries. When Lord Rothermere withdrew the support of his *Daily Mail* newspaper for the BUF, Mosley believed that this was because of pressure put upon him by Jewish advertisers, and there is no doubt that the Olympia episode undermined the image of respectability that Mosley was striving to create.

Three weeks later on 30 June 1934 came the notorious Night of the Long Knives, Hitler's bloody purge of Ernst Röhm and his SA (Storm Troopers), after which public opinion shifted even more against Mosley.

The diaries of Goebbels, together with records in German archives, confirm that the BUF was financed with Nazi money, the principal condition being that its stance must be openly anti-Semitic. This was reflected in the fact that in July 1934, the BUF made the decision not to accept Jews as members. Confrontations between the BUF and its opponents now became much more violent and more targeted towards the Jews.

The autumn of 1934 found Diana and Unity (whose activities had now come to the attention of the British security services) once again attending the Nürnberg Party Rally, which had grown in size to accommodate approximately 700,000 people. The sisters were apparently unmoved by the brutality which Hitler had displayed during the Night of the Long Knives; on the contrary, Diana's sympathies lay with Hitler. 'I am so terribly sorry for the Führer – you know Röhm was his oldest friend and comrade … It must have been so terrible for Hitler when he arrested Röhm himself and tore off his decorations ….'

There appeared in the 2 November 1934 issue of the magazine *Blackshirt* (official organ of the BUF) the headlines: 'Refugees take [i.e. are taking] Your Boys' Jobs.' This was a reference to the arrival of Jewish and other refugees from Nazi Germany, most of whom joined the pre-existing Jewish community in the East End of London.

***

In early 1935 Mosley met Edward, then Prince of Wales, at the London home of society hostess Lady Emerald Cunard. According to the Special Branch, the Prince of Wales, 'questioned Mosley regarding [the] strength and policy of [the] British Union of Fascists …' which Mosley explained to him at some length.[4]

On 9 February 1935 Unity, who had just 'come out' (entered society) and was attending art classes in München, finally achieved her ambition when she was introduced to Hitler at the 'Osteria' restaurant. Following this meeting with Hitler, Unity decided to stay in Germany, from where she wrote to her sister Diana, telling her that she simply must come over and meet this 'marvellous man' [i.e. Hitler].[5] The outcome was that on 11 March Diana accompanied Unity to the 'Osteria' where she met Hitler. In early June their brother Tom Mitford, an ardent Germanophile, was also introduced to the Führer.

In April 1935 Mosley's words appeared to mirror those of Hitler: 'I openly and publicly challenge the Jewish interest in this Country, commanding commerce, commanding the press, commanding the cinema, commanding the city of London, commanding sweatshops.'[6] Meanwhile in Germany, this was music to the ears of the Nazi press. However, in Britain, Mosley's influence was waning, for by now the BUF, without Lord Rothermere's support, was in increasing financial difficulty.

Hitler clearly delighted in the company of the two Mitford sisters, and between 1935 and 1939 Unity met with him on no less than 140 occasions, often with her sister Diana, either for a meal at the 'Osteria Bavaria', or at his flat for lunch and tea. As his guests, the sisters attended every Bayreuth Festival and every Party rally during that period. Occasionally, Unity was invited to Hitler's Berghof retreat in the Obersalzberg, but never to stay overnight.

On 25 April 1935 Mosley himself visited Germany and met Hitler for the first time, for lunch and afterwards at his München apartment (conversing through an interpreter, as Mosley did not speak German). Also present were Ribbentrop, the Goebbels, Winifred Wagner, the Duchess of Brunswick (daughter of the Kaiser and great grand-daughter of Queen Victoria), and Unity Mitford. Diana, however, was not present, being in Paris at the time.

According to Mosley, Hitler said that he,

did not desire war with Russia because his aims were limited to the union of the German peoples in Europe, but he wanted assurances from England and Western Europe that they would not jump on his back in the event of a clash between Germany and Russia, would not intervene against him during a life and death struggle with communism.

If I had been responsible for British government, I would certainly have granted this wish [of Hitler's] because, while I detest all war, I certainly thought war between national socialism and communism a lesser evil than war between Britain and Germany. In return he (Hitler) would have been ready to offer all possible guarantees for the support of the British Empire ....[7]

Hitler, however, was being totally disingenuous when he told Mosley that he did not desire a war with Russia because, with hindsight, it is clear that this was his intention all along.

***

In June 1935 Unity demonstrated that she had fallen completely for Hitler's web of lies and deceit, when in a letter to the German newspaper *Der Sturmer*, she wrote: 'The English have no notion of the Jewish danger .... We think with joy of the day when we shall be able to say with might and authority: England for the English! Out with the Jews! I want everyone to know that I am a Jew hater.'[8]

That summer, Mosley visited Mussolini once again, but without Diana who was recuperating after a road traffic accident. However, by July Diana had recovered sufficiently to attend the Bayreuth Festival with Unity as Hitler's guests. Others present on this occasion included their brother, Tom, and author Henry Williamson. Here, at the opera, they met Hitler's mistress Eva Braun for the first time. Sir Oswald Mosley, however, was not present.

By the autumn of 1935 when Italy was threatening war with Abyssinia (a member of The League of Nations), Mosley, whose new-found anti-Semitism appeared to pervade all his thoughts wrote 'Rise the stink of oil, and stronger than even the stink of the oil is the stink of the Jew.'[9] Sure enough, on 2 October Italy duly invaded Abyssinia in an imperialistic adventure designed to boost Mussolini's vision of Italy as a world power.

***

In 1936 the BUF, now heavily influenced by Nazism, changed its name to the British Union of Fascists and National Socialists. However, it was commonly referred to as the BU.

According to Hitler's Propaganda Minister Dr Joseph Goebbels, when Diana and Unity visited Hitler on 19 June 1936 he (Goebbels, in response to a request from Diana) managed to secure £10,000, to be supplied secretly to Mosley and his BU. However, the sum fell far short of what had been asked for. (By this time, Mosley was already in receipt of substantial sums of money from Mussolini.)

The outbreak of the three year long Spanish Civil War on 18 July 1936 in which Nationalists (fascists), led by General Francisco Franco (who was aided by some 25,000 Germans and 75,000 Italians), were pitted against Republicans (communists and socialists, aided by international brigades and the USSR) made people in Britain, who had already witnessed Mussolini's invasion of Abyssinia in 1935 increasingly nervous about Mosley and his party. This, despite the fact that Mosley supported the British government's policy of non-intervention. Mosley and his BU now found it difficult to gain a foothold anywhere in the country outside the East End of London.

On 1 August 1936 the Olympic Games commenced in Berlin and were attended by both Diana and Unity, who were accommodated by the Goebbels family at their country house just outside Berlin. Sir Oswald Mosley was however conspicuous by his absence. The Games provided the Nazis with a golden opportunity to extol the virtues of Nazism, while at the same time they hoped to deceive the spectators and competitors by covering up all traces of the heinous nature of their regime; for the time being, at any rate.

To Hitler, Unity and Diana, both of them tall and blond, seemed to be the very epitome of his vision of perfect 'Aryans'. He described Diana as an 'angel', and she in turn recalled that the 'Führer' had, 'extraordinary mesmeric eyes'. As for Diana's sister Unity, Hitler called her 'Valkyrie' (goddess of Scandinavian mythology), and referred to her as his, 'ideal of the Germanic woman'.[10] He was equally impressed by the fact that their grandfather, the 1st Baron Redesdale, was a devotee of the author and diplomat Houston Stewart Chamberlain, whom Hitler admired enormously.

Hitler was also gratified to learn that Redesdale was a friend of the family of the late German composer Richard Wagner, someone to whom he (Hitler) was equally devoted. The sisters Unity and Diana would become close friends of the Wagners and regular visitors to their München home 'Haus Wahnfried'.

The sisters were again present at the September Party Rally, as was their mother, Lady Redesdale, who was there as a guest of Prince Bismarck, the former Chargé d'Affaires in London. When Goebbels' wife Magda learned from Diana, whom she was entertaining to dinner, that she and Mosley planned to marry, she suggested that the wedding be held in Berlin. Also present at the rally were several British Members of Parliament, and BU sympathisers, such as Sir Harry Brittain, Lord Mount Temple, Admiral Sir Barry Domvile, Sir Frank and Lady Newnes, and Lord Rennel who would afterwards describe Hitler as, 'That remarkable man of vision who directs the destinies of Germany.'

Others were equally fulsome in their praise. Writer Beverly Nichols, in the The Sunday Chronicle, spoke of the 'moral strength' of the new nation:

> ... there is so much in the new Germany that is beautiful, so much that is fine and great, and all the time in this country we are being trained to believe that the Germans are a nation of wild beasts who vary their time between roasting Jews, and teaching babies to present arms. It is simply not true.

Former British Prime Minister David Lloyd George, having visited Hitler at the Berghof in the summer of 1936, declared in an interview with The News Chronicle on 21 September that the Führer was an 'unquestionably great leader .... The Germans have definitely made up their minds never to quarrel with us again.'[11]

On 5 October 1936 there occurred the Cable Street riots when between 2,000 and 3,000 BU supporters attempted to march through London's East End, but were stopped by the police who feared a confrontation between them and their socialist, communist and Jewish opponents.

The following day, Mosley and Diana were duly married in secret in Berlin, in the drawing room of the Goebbels' home. Hitler was one of the guests. His wedding present to the couple was a large photograph of himself in a heavy silver frame, embossed with the double-headed German eagle. The occasion gave Diana – now Lady Mosley – the opportunity to acquaint Goebbels with the abdication crisis, and with the difficulty in which King Edward VIII found himself in his desire to marry Wallis Simpson.

Although the Mosleys' wedding was supposed to have been a secret affair, the head of the British Intelligence Service MI6, in Berlin, was told of it almost immediately by Unity, who, 'couldn't understand why it had to be kept a secret'.[12] As for Diana, according to MI5 files, 'there is little doubt that she acted as a courier between her husband and the Nazi government'.

Had Diana but known it, her conversations were being covertly relayed on a regular basis to MI5 by the governess of her two sons by her previous marriage to Bryan Guinness. For example, in regard to the new Messerschmitt fighter, details of which had not yet been made public, Diana, 'boasted of their [the aircrafts'] invincibility' but was 'disappointed at their performance ....' According to the governess, Diana is also alleged once to have said: 'We are revolutionaries and we would kill.'[13]

Mosley, in his 'Stand by the King' campaign, did everything he could to dissuade Edward from abdicating, and at a BU rally on 4 December 1936 in London's East End, referring to the looming abdication crisis, he spoke in defence of King Edward VIII's right to marry whom he chose. However, to the King, Mosley had become an embarrassment on account of the rioting which had accompanied his rallies, and the attacks on the homes and businesses of Jews by his BU supporters.

For two years, Diana campaigned on her husband's behalf, for a radio licence to be issued by Germany so that broadcasts could be made into Britain from that country. Mosley described the scheme as a purely commercial venture in which light music would be transmitted, and the money thus generated would go to benefit the BU. It seems far more likely that Mosley's real purpose was to include a political message in the broadcasts. With the outbreak of war, however, negotiations finally collapsed.

Diana continued to visit Berlin, where she stayed at the 'Kaiserhof' hotel situated opposite the Reich Chancellery. Here, she would receive telephone messages from Hitler asking her to join him for a meal, and perhaps watch a film. These meetings were, and remained, purely platonic.

Following a visit to Germany by Diana in August 1937 Goebbels expressed his dissatisfaction with the poor performance of Mosley's BU Party. He (Mosley) was, 'spending a fortune and getting nowhere .... I think he's a busted flush,' he said.[14] This was borne out when financial difficulties forced the BU to lay off 100 of its staff of 130.

As usual, the sisters attended the 1937 Party Rally, as did their brother Tom. The following year, Diana would visit Germany on at least seven occasions. In August 1938 Unity became seriously ill with pneumonia in Bayreuth, where she had been Hitler's guest at the festival. Hitler responded by sending her flowers.

Mosley made it clear that he saw the Munich Agreement of September 1938 undertaken by British Prime Minister Neville Chamberlain as, 'an act of courage and common sense', but he (Mosley) seemed curiously unconcerned about Germany's plans to incorporate the Czech Sudetenland (German-speaking region) into the Reich. 'Has the British Empire sunk so low that we have to shut up shop if another ten million Germans enter their fatherland?' he said. 'If not, what is the fuss about?'[15] Mosley's reaction to 'Kristallnacht', the systematic destruction of Jewish shops, homes and synagogues on 9–10 November 1938, was to excuse it by complaining that, 'Jewish finance controlled the press and political system of Britain.'[16]

From 1939 the British pro-Nazi organisations, the BU, the Link, the Nordic League, and the Right Club began to hold secret meetings with one another. Mosley appeared to be positioning himself favourably in the event of a future Nazi invasion. The intelligence services even suspected that he was plotting some kind of coup.

In June 1939 Unity, who had been staying at the home of Ernst Hanfstaengl (German–American Harvard graduate and financial benefactor of the Nazis), moved into a modern apartment in München, provided by Hitler. 'It [the flat] belongs to a young Jewish couple who are going abroad,' Unity told her sister Diana, even though she must have known full well that its former owners would have been forcibly driven out by the Nazis.

In July Mosley held a rally at Earls Court where he made a speech on the theme that war would be a mistake, and a disaster for Britain which would lose her empire, and that Britain's best option was to seek a peaceful solution with Germany. However, even though 15,000 supporters were in attendance, this proved to be the BU's swansong.

In August Diana and Unity, as Hitler's guests, again attended the Wagner Festival at Bayreuth, where they socialised with the Wagner family and other Nazi leaders. On the final day, 2 August, Hitler and the sisters attended a performance of Wagner's *Götterdämmerung* (*Twilight* – or ultimate defeat by evil – *of the Gods'*). To Diana this was a bad omen. 'Never had the glorious music seemed so doom laden,' she wrote. 'I had a strong feeling ... that I should never see Hitler again, that the whole world was crumbling, that the future held only tragedy and war.'[17] In all three respects, it has to be said, she was right!

According to Nicholas Mosley (the elder son of Mosley by his first marriage), Unity told everyone that, '... if there is war between England and Germany, I'm going to go and shoot myself.'[18]

Notes

1. *Betrayal: Oswald Mosley, the English Führer.*
2. Ibid.
3. Dalley, Jan, *Diana Mosley: A Life*, p. 150.
4. Guardian Unlimited. *Fear that the Windsors would 'flit' to Germany.* www.guardian.co.uk/Freedom/Story.
5. *Betrayal: Oswald Mosley*, op. cit.
6. Dalley, op. cit., p. 186.
7. Mosley, Sir Oswald, *My Life*, p. 365.
8. Dalley, op. cit., p. 188.
9. Ibid, p. 187.
10. *Hitler's Women.*
11. Dalley, op. cit., p. 211.
12. *The Daily Telegraph*, 14 November 2003.
13. *The Times*, Editorial, 14 November 2003.
14. *Goebbels' Diaries*, 14 August 1937, in David Irving's *Goebbels: Mastermind of the Third Reich*, Focal Point Publications, 1996, p. 220.
15. Dalley, op. cit., p. 234.
16. Ibid, p. 235.
17. Ibid, p. 236.
18. *Betrayal: Oswald Mosley*, op. cit.

CHAPTER XVII
Other British Nazi Admirers

The British Union

Sir Oswald Mosley's British Union (BU) could boast of having many notable people in its ranks. One example was Josslyn Hay, 22nd Earl of Errol and one of Scotland's senior aristocrats.

The BU's Director of Publications was John Beckett, a former Labour left-wing MP and reformer (whose mother incidentally, was Jewish). J F C Fuller, a former army officer and one of the first to develop the theory of tank warfare, was a prominent member of the BU's Policy Committee; he was also an anti-Semite and a dabbler in the occult. Henry Williamson, a World War I veteran, Aryan mysticist, virulent anti-Semite, naturalist, and author of the best-selling book *Tarka the Otter* (1927), was an active member of the BU and contributed several articles to its newspaper *Action*. AK Chesterton was the editor of *Action*, although he resigned in 1936 because of what he perceived to be the party's over-intimate links with the Nazis, and the untruthfulness of its propaganda.

The Anglo–German Fellowship (AGF)

The following were members of the AGF: Charles Stewart Henry, Lord Londonderry, who was a close friend of German Ambassador to Great Britain Joachim von Ribbentrop, and attended the 1937 Nürnberg Party Rally. When Hitler annexed Austria, Londonderry blamed Britain. The latter he said had, 'failed to hold out the hand of friendship'.

Admiral Sir Barry Domvile, a former head of Naval Intelligence and President of the Royal Naval College, who until 1934 was noted for his eccentric theories on 'race'. He later founded *Link*, a pre-war, pro-German magazine. In 1937 at the invitation of Heinrich Himmler, he attended the Nürnberg rally, and was also given a tour of the Dachau concentration camp. [*Therefore for anyone to suggest that people in Britain were ignorant of what was going on in Germany under the Nazis is frankly ludicrous.*] According to MI5, Domvile told ex-servicemen living in a British residential home that Hitler 'would soon be in this country, but that there was no reason to worry about it, because he would bring the Duke of Windsor over as King and conditions generally would be much improved.'[1]

Alan Ronald Nall-Cain, Lord Brockett, born into an English brewing family, was educated at Eton and Oxford, who worked as a barrister in London before becoming a Conservative MP. An enthusiastic Nazi sympathiser, he was also a close friend of Ribbentrop, and in 1939 accepted an invitation to attend Hitler's birthday celebrations in Germany.

Others

There were other prominent Nazi admirers who were not members of the BU, the AGA or the AGF.

Captain Archibald Maule Ramsay, son of Lt Colonel Henry Ramsay, was born in Scotland on 4 May 1894. Educated at Eton College and at Sandhurst Military College, he joined the Coldstream Guards in 1913, serving as a captain in France during the Great War. Having been invalided out in 1916 he worked from 1917–18 at the War Office.

An MI5 agent, who attended a meeting of Ramsay's 'Militant Christian Patriots' at Caxton Hall on 23 May 1929 quoted Ramsay as saying 'The Jewish menace is a real menace. The time at our disposal is getting short. Take with you … a resolution in your hearts to remove the Jew menace from our land.' In 1931 Ramsay became a Conservative Member of Parliament.[2]

When in 1935 the Nordic League (an upper-middle class fascist organisation, as opposed to the BU, whose appeal was mainly to the working classes) was established by two secret agents from Nazi Germany, Ramsay would swiftly emerge as its leader. The League, many of whose members also belonged to the BU, was controlled directly from Berlin. It described itself as, 'an association of race-conscious Britons', whose purpose was to assist 'those patriotic bodies known to be engaged in exposing and frustrating the Jewish stranglehold on our Nordic realms'.[3]

Fred Pateman, writing in *The Daily Worker* in July 1939, described a meeting of the Nordic League. 'The audience of rabid Jew-baiters was addressed by Captain A Ramsay, MP … who spoke of the alleged Jewish control of the Press …. We must change the present state of things, and if we don't do it constitutionally, we'll do it with steel (wild applause).'[4]

In 1937 Ramsay, a deeply religious man, created the United Christian Front whose intention it was, 'to confront the widespread attack upon the Christian verities which emanates from Moscow …'.

Ramsay was strongly opposed to having Jews in the government, and to this end he attempted in 1938 to have Leslie Hore-Belisha, a Jew, dismissed as Secretary for War. Hore-Belisha, he stated on 27 April, 'will lead us to war with our blood-brothers of the Nordic race in order to make way for a bolshevised Europe'.

Following Kristallnacht (9–10 November 1938 – a Nazi orgy of murder and destruction of Jews and their property), Ramsay was unmoved. He remained convinced that the Jews were orchestrating a confrontation between Britain and Germany which he strongly opposed.

On 13 January 1939 Ramsay, in a letter to the *Peeblesshire and South Midlothian Advertiser*, wrote:

> There was not the smallest doubt that there was an international group of Jews who were behind world revolution in every single country at the present time .... People, did not agree in this country [Britain] with Hitler's methods with regard to the Jews, but he [Hitler] must have his reasons for what he did. Did it not strike them that a man of Hitler's ability would not turn out [i.e. expel] an enormous section of the people from his country, and have half of Europe howling at him unless he had some reason for doing so?[5] [This of course, was a rhetorical argument.]

In May 1939 Ramsay founded the secret organisation called the Right Club, charged with the task in his words of, 'co-ordinating the work of all the patriotic societies' in Britain. 'The main object of the Right Club was to oppose and expose the activities of organised Jewry .... Our first objective was to clear the Conservative Party of Jewish influence .... Our hope was to avoid war, which we considered to be mainly the work of Jewish influence centred in New York.'[6] Unbeknown to Ramsay, however, MI5 agents had infiltrated the Right Club.

Members of the Right Club had their names recorded in the so-called *Red Book*: there were 135 names on the men's list, and 100 names on the women's. They included peers, Members of Parliament, aristocrats, academics, civil servants, clerics and other leading figures in society. The vehemence of their anti-Jewish sentiments is revealed in a hymn, to be sung to the tune of 'Land of Hope and Glory', which was entered in the book in Ramsay's handwriting:

Land of Dope and Jewry,
Land that once was free,
All the Jew boys praise thee,
While they Plunder thee.

Poorer still and poorer, Grow the true-
born sons,
Faster still and faster,
They're sent to feed the guns.

Land of Jewish Finance,
Fooled by Jewish lies,
In Press and books and movies,
While our birthright dies.

1. A watercolour painting by the Führer from the year 1914: Courtyard of the Palace of the Old Residence, Munich.

2. A drawing by Hitler (a soldier at the Front): A military store in Fournes, France.

3. *Far left:* In custody in 1924, in the Fortress of Landsberg.

4. *Left:* Reichs President von Hindenburg and Reich Chancellor Hitler.

5. The Führer's journey through the Hartz Mountains, where even he could have a happy time.

6. Meeting between Adolf Hitler and Benito Mussolini in Venice, June 1934.

7. Visiting the Fortress of Landsberg, 1934.

8. *Top:* The Führer receives a Japanese naval delegation, 1934.

9. *Above left:* November 1934 in Munich. The Führer addresses those of the Hitler Youth and the League of German Girls who have newly joined the Party, in the Feldherrnhalle.

10. *Above right:* The morning of January 15, 1935: the Führer thanks Gauleiter Burckel on the occasion of the victory of the Saar (return of the Saar territory to Germany).

11. *Right:* The Führer leaves his studio in the Academy of the Arts in Munich.

12. *Far right:* 9 November 1935 in Munich. The Führer talks to a member of the Party, the widow of one of the fallen of 9 November 1923. The Brown House (Nazi Party National Headquarters) is in the background.

13. The Führer at the Rally for Freedom. Inspection of a guard of honour formed by the Company of his Personal Bodyguard.

14. The Führer consecrating the Banners at the Rally for Freedom.

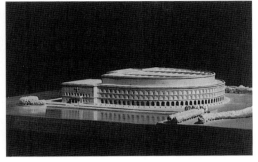

Clockwise from top left:

15. Reich Party Rally, 1935. Consecration of the Banners and the Conferring of Honour on the Dead.

16. Army Day, 1935: the Führer and his commanders in chief. From left to right: the Commander in Chief of the Luftwaffe, Supreme General Hermann Göring; of the Armed Forces, General Field Marshal Werner von Blomberg; of the Army, General Baron Werner von Fritsch; of the Fleet, General Admiral Dr Erich Raeder.

17. Model for the proposed Convention Hall of the Reich Party in Nuremberg.

18. The Führer and Rudolf Hess viewing progress at the construction site of the 'Führer houses' in Munich.

19. English ex-servicemen meet the Führer.

20. Meeting at Obersalzberg.

21. After the New Year's Diplomats' Reception, 1936.

22. An historic meeting: Britain's Anthony Eden, Lord Privy Seal, and Sir John Simon, Foreign Secretary, with the Führer, 6 March 1935.

23. Minister President Göring visits the Führer at the Obersalzberg.

24. *Right:* The Führer on his 47th birthday, 20 April 1936.

25. *Far Right:* Day of Rest. The Führer and a small girl, Helga Goebbels.

26. The Führer, Professor Leonhard Gall and Architect Albert Speer witnessing the construction of German Fine Art in Munich.

27. Good News.

Clockwise from top left:

28. The opening of the first part of the Autobahn from Munich to the border with Austria.

29. The Führer surrounded by children: on the right is Baldur von Schirach.

30. The Hitler Youth on a visit to Obersalzberg.

31. The opening of the Autobahn Frankfurt-Darmstadt, with left to right: Reichs Minister of War, Werner von Blomberg; the Führer; General Inspector, Dr Fritz Todt; President of the Reichs Bank, Dr Hjalmar Schacht; General Director of Reich Transport, Dr Julius Dorpmuller; Reichs Minister, Dr Goebbels.

32. On board a warship: the Führer visiting a Norwegian fjord.

Longer still and longer,
Is the rope they get,
But by the God of Battles,
T'will serve to hang them yet.

***

Winston Churchill, as a Conservative Member of Parliament, visited Germany in September 1932, where he was told that Hitler would be very glad to meet him. Churchill declined the offer, but later said:

> I had no national prejudices against Hitler at this time. I knew little of his doctrine or his record and nothing of his character. I admire men who stand up for their country in defeat, even though I was on the other side. He had a perfect right to be a patriotic German if he chose.

However, Churchill disagreed with Hitler's virulent opposition to the Jews saying: 'What is the sense of being against a man simply because of his birth?'[7]

On 9 February 1933 the Oxford Union Debating Society voted by almost two to one in favour of a motion, 'that this House declines to fight for King and Country', a result which must have angered Churchill intensely.

> My mind turns across the narrow waters of the Channel and the North Sea, where great nations stand determined to defend their national glories or national existence with their lives. I think of Germany with its splendid clear-eyed youth, marching forward on the road of the Reich, singing their ancient songs, demanding to be conscripted into an army; eagerly seeking the most terrible weapons of war; burning to suffer and die for their fatherland.[8]

However, Churchill was not slow to observe the increasingly 'odious conditions' which pertained in Germany with the threat of, 'persecution and pogrom of Jews'.[9]

Edward Doran, the violently anti-Semitic, pro-Nazi MP for Tottenham North, having been defeated in an election for the post of Sheriff of the City of London (by Councillor Isidore Jacobs, a Jew), expostulated in a speech made outside the Palace of Westminster 'We have lost London to the Jews, and we will have to make war on them like Germany.'[10] Both Doran and Arthur Bateman, the anti-Semitic and pro-Nazi MP for North Camberwell, lost their seats in the 1935 parliamentary election.

Arnold Leese had worked as a veterinary surgeon in India and Africa for twenty years, and was the world's leading authority on camels. A fanatical anti-Semite, his anti-Semitism was based in part on his disapproval of the 'Kosher' method practised by the Jews to slaughter animals. In 1928 he founded the extreme Imperial Fascist League.

In 1936 Leese was convicted of having libelled Jews in the League's monthly newspaper *The Fascist*, and was imprisoned for six months.[11] Leese rejected the idea of amalgamating with Oswald Mosley's BU, on the grounds that Mosley's first wife was part Jew.

A K Chesterton (a cousin of the author G K Chesterton) became prominent in British fascist circles in the 1920s, speaking at BUF meetings and writing a biography of Sir Oswald Mosley entitled *Portrait of a Leader*.[12]

Britain's pro-Nazi Propagandists

Others, not content with admiring Nazism from afar, decided to take positive action against Britain via use of the airwaves.

William Joyce was born on 24 April 1906 in New York, of an Irish father and an English mother. When he was aged 3, his father returned to Ireland with the family and purchased a public house near Westport in County Mayo. Here, Joyce was educated at a convent school.

As a youth, Joyce joined the notorious pro-British 'Black and Tan' gangs which terrorised the Irish population, and he thus became a target for the Irish Republican Army, one of whose 'hit men' was given the task of murdering the 15 year old on his way home from school – but he failed.

The Anglo–Irish Treaty of 1921 gave Ireland dominion status as the Irish Free State (subject to the right of the North to opt out). Now the Joyce family, who would have much preferred the continuing union of Southern Ireland with Britain, were forced to flee to England. Joyce enlisted in the British Army, but was discharged when it was discovered that he had lied about his age.

In 1923 when he was aged 17, Joyce joined the British Fascist Party, a movement based on its larger Italian counterpart. During a subsequent fracas with left-wing agitators, he received a razor slash (which left a scar running from mouth to ear). Joyce laid the blame for this on what he described as 'Jewish communists' whom he referred to as 'the enemy', and whom he claimed were behind the 'troubles in Ireland'. He went on to study at London University's Birkbeck College where he met his wife-to-be Hazel, a fellow student.

In 1925 Joyce left the British Fascist Party and joined the Conservative Party, with the ambition of becoming its parliamentary candidate for Chelsea – but was ejected for seducing a young party assistant.

When Sir Oswald Mosley created the British Union of Fascists in October 1932 Joyce was one of its first members, and between 1933 and 1937, served as its Deputy Leader. Joyce said of Mosley, 'There is no greater man that God ever created.'[13]

In 1934 Joyce (who was intensely anti-Semitic and described the Jews as, 'Aliens from Palestine, hairy troglodytes who crept out of the ghettos of Germany' and, 'Men with prehensile toes'),[14] was made the BUF's Director of Propaganda. He also became a member of the Nordic League, and of the Right Club.

When, in April 1937 the BU (formerly the BUF) through lack of funds, was obliged to make considerable reductions in its staff, Joyce fell victim to the cuts and was dismissed.

Thoroughly frustrated in his ambitions, Joyce (with John Beckett) now created the British National Socialist League (BNSL), and much to Mosley's chagrin, took approximately sixty of the BU's members with him. Although the membership of the BNSL subsequently shrank to about twenty, the organisation gained a reputation for rowdiness and street fighting.

In the 1920s Joyce had worked for MI5, and he now received a warning from a former contact in the service. This enabled him to escape arrest and internment under the emergency powers, and on 26 August 1939, eight days before the outbreak of war, he and his family fled to Berlin from where he would make Nazi propaganda broadcasts back to Britain on the programme 'Germany Calling'. In Britain, he was dubbed 'Lord Haw Haw'.

James Clark moved from England to Germany with his mother just before the war, and like Joyce, broadcast Nazi propaganda back to Britain. Asked why he did it, he said it was 'out of love' (presumably for the Nazis).[15]

***

Would Britain's Nazi admirers have behaved in the way they did, had they known what Hitler was currently planning for Britain?

Dr Franz Six was a former journalist, who with the collusion of the Nazis, was appointed Dean of the Economic Faculty of Berlin University. Having joined Heydrich's SD, he was made responsible for setting up the death squads ('Einsatzgruppen'), by which British freemasons, Marxists, Liberals and Jews would be eliminated, following Hitler's proposed invasion. Their names were contained in the so-called *Black Book* (a rare copy of which exists in The Imperial War Museum, London). On its cover is the word 'Geheim' ('Secret'), and inside are the names of 2,820 individuals, classed as enemies of the Reich, who were to be eliminated. This included all members of the British government and Civil Service, European émigrés who had fled from Nazi persecution, and the cream of Britain's intellectual elite.[16]

Notes

1. *The Daily Telegraph*, October 12, 2004. Ben Felton (on release of new material from the National Archives).
2, 3. *Archibald Ramsay*, www.spartacus.schoolnet.co.uk. PRramsayA2.htm.
4. www.spartacus.schoolnet.co.uk/2WWfifthC.htm.
5. *Archibald Ramsay*, op. cit.
6. Ramsay, Archibald, *The Nameless War*.
7. Churchill, Winston S, *Second World War*, vol.1, p. 65.

8. Gilbert, *Winston S. Churchill*, vol.V, p. 456.
9. Jenkins, Roy, *Churchill: A Biography*, p. 470.
10. Griffiths, Richard, *Patriotism Perverted: Captain Ramsay, the Right Club and British Anti-Semitism 1939–40*, p. 81.
11, 12. National Archives. KV2/1365–7 and KV3/60–3.
13. Lewis, Peter, *Daily Mail*, 12 Dec. 2003. *A Very Twisted Patriot*.
14. Ibid.
15 *The Brits who fought for Hitler.*
16. *Hitler's Britain.*

CHAPTER XVIII

How the Allies Helped to Build the Nazi War Machine

The size of the post-World War I German army had been limited to 100,000 men by international agreement, namely the 1919 Treaty of Versailles. Despite this however, on 16 March 1935 the German government openly refuted the disarmament clauses contained in the treaty. Hitler introduced universal conscription with the aim of building up an army of thirty-six divisions – the 'Wehrmacht' (amounting to approximately 550,000 personnel, over five times the permitted number), as well as a powerful air force and navy. Members of the armed services were now required to swear an oath of allegiance to the Führer in person: 'I pledge to you, Adolf Hitler, my obedience unto death, so help me God.'[1] Soon afterwards, Hitler announced that he intended to occupy (remilitarise) the Rhineland.

In 1937 Dr Hjalmar Schacht, President of the Reichsbank and Minister of Economics, told Hitler that the economy was overheating, and that armament production should therefore be scaled down. As a result, he was relieved of his position as Minister of Economics and replaced by Hermann Göring.

In May 1938 Schacht was instrumental in helping to float a massive public loan of 1.6 billion Marks. Later that year, the German government attempted to raise money for the financing of armaments by issuing bonds, but this met with only limited success.

On 7 January 1939 Hitler received a memorandum from the Board of Governors of the Reichsbank and its President Hjalmar Schacht: 'The currency is severely threatened by the uncontrolled expenditure of those who govern …,' it said. To which Hitler retorted: 'This is mutiny!'[2] Schacht was now dismissed by Hitler from the presidency of the Reichsbank. Schacht however, as Minister without Portfolio, remained a member of the Cabinet.

Just how much the exercise had cost was revealed in a statement by the Führer himself:

I've worked for over six years at building up the Wehrmacht. During this time, over 90 billion Marks have been spent on building up these armed forces. Belief in victory is unshakeable. Now I do not want to be anything other than the foremost soldier of the German Reich. Therefore, I've again put on the uniform which for me has always been the most revered. *I will only take it off after victory, or I will not live to see the end.*[3]

Soviet Russia

In 1926 the Treaty of Berlin (an extension of the 1922 Treaty of Rapallo) was signed. In it, the Soviet Union agreed to offer facilities to Germany for training and weapons development on its territory, and also for the testing of the new generation of German fighters and bombers. This was done in secret, it being contrary to the terms of the Treaty of Versailles.

The German Junkers Corporation was granted a concession to manufacture aircraft engines in a Moscow suburb. The company Bersol commenced the manufacture of poison gas in the Samara district province. The Germans trained their tank officers at a test centre near Kazan. Meanwhile, German instructors trained a squadron of the Red Air Force (whose pilots were solely German), and German technicians helped the Russians to establish three ammunition manufacturing plants in Russia.

Japan

Although Germany was banned from producing aircraft and submarines by the Treaty of Versailles, German designers such as Ernst Heinkel continued to develop aircraft in secret, with the help of the Japanese, who duly ordered a number of such secretly produced Heinkel torpedo bombers. In another covert operation, German engineers also assisted Japan in building a fleet of submarines.

Britain

In May 1935 during the British Royal Family's Silver Jubilee celebration, Hitler sent Joachim von Ribbentrop, his 'special envoy and plenipotentiary', to London with the object of reaching agreement with Britain on the size of a proposed new German navy. The result was that on 18 June Britain (unilaterally, and without consulting her ally France) and Germany signed a naval agreement, whereby Britain would allow Germany to fix her naval tonnage at 35% of her own fleet, and would also concede a 45% ratio for submarines. As it transpired, this was to be the first step taken in a prolonged campaign to contain Hitler by the policy of 'appeasement' [*for which Britain would pay dearly in the years to come!*].

The USA

Hitler had nothing good to say about American President Franklin D Roosevelt, and accused him of being a 'criminal'.[4] Even worse, Roosevelt himself had, 'boasted recently that he had "noble" Jewish blood in his veins' – or so said the Führer in July 1942.[5] Be this as it may, much of Germany's military hardware and technology was exported to that country from the USA, not only prior to, but also throughout the course of World War II.

William E Dodd (US Ambassador to Germany, 1937) declared that,

A clique of US industrialists is hell-bent to bring a fascist state to supplant our democratic government, and is working closely with the fascist regime in Germany and Italy. I have had plenty of opportunity in my post in Berlin to witness how close some of our American ruling families are to the Nazi regime …. Certain American industrialists had a great deal to do with bringing fascist regimes into being in both Germany and Italy. They extended aid to help fascism occupy the seat of power, and they are helping to keep it there.[6]

George Seldes in his book, *Facts and Fascism* (published in 1943), declared that the Aluminum Corporation of America (ALCOA) was, 'largely responsible for the fact that America did not have the aluminum with which to build airplanes before and after Pearl Harbor; while Germany had an unlimited supply.'[7]

Charles Higham in his book, *Trading With The Enemy: An Expose of the Nazi-American Money Plot, 1933–49*, declared that, 'General Motors (GM), under the control of the Dupont family of Delaware, played a part in collaboration' (i.e. with the Nazis). Higham states that, 'Between 1932 and 1939, bosses of General Motors poured 30 million Dollars into I G Farben Plants ….' (the giant Nazi chemical cartel).[8]

According to Morton Mintz and Jerry S Cohen in their book *Power, Inc.*, 'In 1929, GM acquired the largest automobile company in Germany, [namely] Adam Opel, A G'. In a report presented to the US Senate Sub-committee on Anti-trust and Monopoly in February 1974, Bradford C Snell, an assistant sub-committee counsel wrote:

G M's participation in Germany's preparation for war began in 1935. That year its Opel subsidiary cooperated with the Reich in locating a new, heavy truck facility at Brandenburg [Germany], which military officials advised would be less vulnerable to enemy air attack. During the succeeding years, G M supplied the Wehrmacht with Opel 'Blitz' trucks from the Brandenburg complex. For these, and other contributions to the Nazis' wartime preparations, G M's Chief Executive for Overseas Operations [James Mooney] was awarded the 'Order of the German Eagle (First Class)' by Adolf Hitler.

Snell described how,

G M and the Standard Oil Company of New Jersey [now Exxon] formed a joint subsidiary with I G Farben, [which] provided the mechanised German armies with synthetic tetraethyl fuel [leaded gas]. Without lead-tetraethyl, the present method of warfare would be unthinkable ... because Germany's scarce petroleum reserves would not satisfy war demands.[9]

According to author Charles Higham, on 27 February 1942 Thurman Arnold, Assistant District Attorney of the United States, told Standard Oil of New Jersey that, 'By continuing to favour Hitler in rubber deals and patent arrangements,' the company, 'had acted against the interests of the American government ....'[10] In fact, according to authors Mark Aarons and John Loftus, 'Before the war, Standard of New Jersey had forged a synthetic oil and rubber cartel with the Nazi-controlled I G Farben,' which, 'worked well until the United States joined the war in 1941 ....' Amongst other things, Standard had 'provided Farben with its synthetic rubber patents and technical knowledge ....'[11]

Higham states that as late as 1940 the Ford Motor Company, 'refused to build aircraft engines for England, and instead built supplies for the 5 ton military trucks for the backbone of German army military transportation.'[12] Also, that even after the Japanese attack on Pearl Harbor on 7 December 1941 the International Telephone and Telegraphic Company [ITT] was still supplying the German army, navy and air force under contract with, 'switchboards, telephones, alarm gongs, buoys, air raid warning devices, radar equipment and 30,000 fuses per month for artillery shells, used to kill British and American troops.' ITT also, 'supplied ingredients for the rocket bombs [V1 and V2] that fell on London,' without which, 'it would have been impossible for the German air force to kill American and British troops; for the German army to fight the Allies in Africa, Italy, France and Germany; for England to have been bombed, or for allied ships to have been attacked at sea.'[13]

Researcher and author Jim Hougan reports that in 1938,

following a series of meetings with 'Luftwaffe' chief, Herman Göring, Sosthenef Behn [ITT founder and chairman] encouraged ITT's Lorenz subsidiary to purchase 28% of the Focke-Wulf firm, manufacturer of the bombers that were to sink so many Allied ships during the war.[14]

Allen Dulles worked for the US Office of Strategic Services (wartime intelligence and special operations organisation, or 'OSS') in World War II, and later became Director of the Central Intelligence Agency. Authors Aarons and Loftus said:

In the beginning, moving money into the Third Reich was quite legal. Lawyers saw to that. Allen and his brother John Foster [Dulles] were not just any lawyers. They were international finance specialists for the powerful Wall Street firm of Sullivan and Cromwell .... The Dulles brothers were the ones who convinced American businessmen to avoid US government regulation by investing in Germany. It began with the Versailles Treaty in which they played no small role. After World War I, the defeated German government promised to pay war reparations to the Allies in gold, but Germany had no gold. She had to borrow the gold from Sullivan and Cromwell's clients in the United States. Nearly 70% of the money that flowed into Germany during the 1930s came from investors in the United States, many of them Sullivan and Cromwell clients .... Foster Dulles, as a member of the board of IG Farben, seems to have had little difficulty in getting along with whoever was in charge [i.e. of Nazi Germany].[15]

***

Therefore, strange as it may seem, it is true to say that the three major powers – USA, Britain and Soviet Russia – who would soon be engaged together on the Allied side against Nazi Germany, were instrumental in facilitating the build-up of the Nazi war machine.

Notes

1. *Hitler: a Profile: The Dictator.*
2. Weitz, John, *Joachim von Ribbentrop: Hitler's Diplomat*, p. 244.
3. *Hitler: a Profile: The Commander.*
4. Trevor-Roper, H R (ed.), *Hitler's Secret Conversations, 1941–1944*, p. 400.
5. Ibid, p. 510.
6. Seldes, George, *Facts and Fascism*, p. 122 and Higham, Charles, *Trading With The Enemy*, p. 167.
7. Seldes, op. cit., p. 68.
8. Higham, op. cit, p. 166.
9. Mintz, Morton and Jerry S Cohen, *Power, Inc.*, pp. 497–9.
10. Higham, op. cit., pp. 45–6.
11. Aarons, Mark and John Loftus, *The Secret War Against the Jews*, pp. 44–65.
12. Higham, op. cit., pp. 154–6.
13. Ibid. p. 99.
14. Hougan, Jim, *Spooks*, pp. 423–4.
15. Aarons and Loftus, op. cit., pp. 55–60.

CHAPTER IXX

Nazism in Practice: Echoes of Ostara

Germany and her Neighbours

With Hitler now in power, who would Germany chose as her allies, and who would she see as her enemies? An indication was given by Hitler in his book, *Mein Kampf*, written almost a decade earlier, in 1924. Prior to World War I, Hitler had,

> thought it would have been better if Germany had abandoned her sense-less colonial policy and her naval policy, and had joined England in an alliance against Russia, therewith renouncing her weak world policy for a determined European policy with the idea of acquiring new territory on the Continent.
>
> The Russia of today, deprived of its Germanic ruling class [a reference to the fact that since the days of Tsar Peter the Great 1672–1725, the princes of some of Germany's lesser reigning Houses, such as Hesse-Homburg, had served in the Russian administration][1] is not a possible ally in the struggle for German liberty ....
>
> From the purely military viewpoint, a Russo-German coalition, waging war against Western Europe, and probably against the whole world on that account, would be catastrophic for us [because] the struggle would have to be fought out, not on Russian, but on German territory ....[2]

France, Hitler described as,

> The mortal enemy of our nation [who] deprives us ... by holding us in her grip and pitilessly robbing us of our strength. Therefore we must stop at no sacrifice in our effort to destroy the French striving towards hegemony over Europe.[3]

At that time, he considered, 'England and Italy as the only countries with which it would be worth while for us to strive to form a close alliance ....'[4] Whereas King

Edward VIII of the United Kingdom had, 'succeeded partly against interests that were of their nature opposed to his work,' they, the Germans, 'must and will succeed'.[5] And as for Italy, Hitler, referring to that country's leader Benito Mussolini, declared that he had, 'conceived a profound admiration for the great man beyond the Alps, whose ardent love for his people inspired him not to bargain with Italy's internal enemies, but to use all possible ways and means in an effort to wipe them out'. What placed Mussolini, 'in the ranks of the world's great' was, 'his decision not to share Italy with the Marxists, but to redeem his country from Marxism by destroying internationalism [i.e. International Communism]'.[6] 'The colossal Empire in the East [i.e. Russia],' said Hitler, indicating that he had set his sights firmly on war with Russia, 'is ripe for dissolution.'[7]

***

By February 1933 Hitler's National Socialists included no fewer than 400,000 SA Storm Troopers (their numbers would soon rise to 3 million) who would swear an oath of allegiance to their leader Ernst Röhm, rather than to Hitler. The smaller SS, on the other hand, was a better disciplined force commanded by Heinrich Himmler.

On the night of 27 February 1933 the German parliament building – 'Reichstag' – was partially destroyed by fire. Hitler immediately announced that this was part of a communist plot and issued an emergency decree which President von Hindenberg countersigned, giving him the authority to crush the communists. This decree also enabled Hitler to suppress newspapers, search premises without a warrant, and imprison people without trial, and he was not accountable to anyone except von Hindenberg. In fact, according to Hermann Rauschning (politician and president of the Danzig Senate, who became disillusioned with the Nazis, resigned in 1934 and fled to Switzerland), it was Hermann Göring, 'who ordered the "Reichstag" building to be burnt at Hitler's command'.[8]

In a new election called by Hitler on 5 March 1933 the Nazis achieved 43.9% of the vote. Together with the Nationalists, they were now able to form a majority in government, the communist deputies (officials) having been either arrested or forced underground.

21 March 1933 saw the state opening of Parliament, which Hitler proclaimed as a 'day of national unity'. Now came a torrent of propaganda (orchestrated by Joseph Goebbels, Reichsminister for Propaganda), terror and intimidation. Storm Troopers began incarcerating so-called enemies of the state in concentration camps, the first at Oranienburg near Berlin; another, Dachau, was opened near München. These so-called enemies included communists, social democrats, liberals, religious dissidents and Jews. After a year, most were released after suffering beatings and psychological torture. The first step had been taken to identify and isolate those whom Hitler's mentor, Lanz von Liebenfels, had already identified as being enemies of the state.

On 23 March 1933 the passing of the 'Enabling Act' granted Hitler's cabinet full legislative powers without its having to obtain the consent of the Reichstag.

Now, all political parties, other than the Nazis, were forcibly disbanded and censorship was imposed. Although Hitler proclaimed 1 May 'Labour Day', trade unions had no place in the German society which he envisaged, and they would therefore be abolished.

In April 1933 Hermann Göring founded the Gestapo, the political police force of the Third Reich, which he based on the Prussian Secret State Police Force. On 10 May students at universities throughout Germany lit bonfires to destroy tens of thousands of books which the Nazis considered to be 'un-German'. On 21 May a non-aggression pact was agreed between Britain, Italy, Germany and France.

In the summer of 1933 the Nazis superimposed on the Federation of German Sovereign States (which had constituted the old Weimar Republic) regional Nazi Party leaders – 'Gauleiters' – who received their instructions directly from Berlin. This was precisely the administrative structure advocated by Guido von List, whose works (as previously stated), were known to be familiar to Hitler.

A new, supreme 'People's Court' was created against which there was no appeal, except to Adolf Hitler himself. This too was dominated by the Nazis. All political parties were abolished, apart from the National Socialist Party.

On 20 July 1933 Reichschancellor Franz von Papen, a Roman Catholic, made a treaty with the Vatican under the terms of which it was agreed that if the Nazis refrained from interfering with the Church, then the Church in turn would not complain about the way in which the country was being run.

Now there developed a power struggle between Hitler, big business, the army, Heinrich Himmler (head of the SS) on the one hand, and Captain Ernst Röhm, head of the SA on the other.

Röhm wanted his Storm Troopers to be integrated into the regular German army, but the army saw this as an attempt by Röhm to take over the armed forces and become their minister. Hitler, however, realised that the expertise of the armed forces would be vital for the future battles in which he planned to engage. So a deal was struck: in return for Hitler eliminating Röhm, each and every member of the armed forces would undertake to swear an oath of allegiance to Hitler: 'I swear by God, this Holy Oath, to the Führer of the German Reich and the German people, Adolf Hitler.'[9]

Hitler now decided to stage his National Socialist ('Nazi') Party Rallies in Nürnberg (instead of Weimar as hitherto), where vast complexes of stadia would be built for the purpose. The rallies would hereafter be held every September.

On 14 October 1933 Germany withdrew from the League of Nations, also from the Geneva Disarmament Conference. Both were events of great significance, in the light of what is now known about Hitler's warlike intentions.

In the elections of 12 November 1933 the Nazis won 92% of the seats, and the votes of those who dissented were declared invalid. By the end of the year, unemployment had decreased by about 2 million.

In order to fund the government contracts for armaments (estimated to be worth approximately 21 billion Marks), Hjalmar Schacht, President of the Reichsbank, founded the Metallurgical Research Company – MEFO – confining its bond issues in equal parts to Germany's four leading industrial companies, namely: Krupp, Rheinstahl (steel), Gutehoffnungshutte (coal) and Siemens.

As for Hitler, he did not trouble himself with the minutiae of economic detail:

I have never had a conference with Schacht to find out what means are at our disposal. I restricted myself to saying, 'This is what I require and this is what I must have.'

On 6 January 1934 in what transpired to be a supreme irony, the Nazis signed a non-aggression pact with Poland. [*Such pacts were for Hitler temporary expediencies, to be reneged upon and discarded at the very moment when it suited his purpose.*]

By the spring of 1934 the Hitler Youth and BDM movements (Bund Deutscher Mädel – League for German Girls) were well established, with communal singing, night hiking, organised games, and parades and marches, all intended to engender a new spirit of community and hope. Soon their numbers would rise to 3.5 million.

At the so-called Transfer Conference, convened in Berlin in April 1934, Schacht told Germany's foreign creditors that on 1 July, the country would have to declare itself bankrupt unless they accepted more of Germany's exports.

In April Himmler, commander of the SS, took over from Göring both the control of the Gestapo ('Geheime Staatspolizei' – or State Secret Police), and the supervision of the concentration camps.

When it was reported that Ernst Röhm, head of the SA and its 3 million Storm Troopers, was planning a 'massive insurrection',[10] Hitler decided to make his move, taking personal charge of the operation in order to avoid any subsequent split in the Nazi Party.

First, he persuaded Röhm to take a holiday. Then, on 30 June 1934 in an operation code named 'Hummingbird', he employed his SS to imprison and summarily shoot leaders of the SA throughout Germany, eighty-five in all. This was the so-called 'Night of the Long Knives'. Hitler personally arrested Röhm, by bursting into his hotel room brandishing a pistol and screaming: 'You are a traitor!'

Röhm was imprisoned in München; it was only after two days of intense pressure from Himmler that Hitler finally agreed to Röhm's execution by the SS (Röhm had previously been offered a pistol and given the opportunity to commit suicide). By then, dozens of SA leaders had been arrested, tortured and executed.

Himmler's SS was now given orders to crush all Hitler's opponents. They included Gustav von Kahr (who had put down Hitler's beer hall 'Putsch'). He was murdered in the vicinity of Dachau (a concentration camp established by the Nazis near München in Bavaria); General Kurt von Schleicher, the last Chancellor of the democratically elected Weimar Republic, was likewise murdered, along with his wife; Gregor Strasser, an early rival of Hitler's for the leadership of the Nazi Party, suffered the same fate; Karl Ernst, Head of the

Berlin Storm Troopers, was murdered whilst on his honeymoon. The death toll ran into hundreds and possibly thousands.

Two weeks after Röhm's death, Hitler addressed the German parliament to tell the members that the Nazi Party had now been purged of these 'degenerate' homosexuals. For his action he received warm applause, even though thirteen of those killed in his purge of the SA had themselves been Members of Parliament. The SS now replaced the SA as the dominant force, its membership by 1939 reaching a quarter of a million. Von Hindenberg and the army generals were both delighted and relieved.

In an effort to eradicate homosexuality from the SS, Himmler now required that all new recruits sign a statement saying that they understood that were they to practise homosexuality, then this would incur the death penalty. The result was that some homosexuals were shot; others were dismissed from their posts or sent for counselling.[11]

According to army officer Ewald von Kleist, many people, including some army generals, were murdered without trial. Their deaths were announced in the newspapers which stated quite openly that the Government had been obliged to shoot each one on the grounds that it was an 'Emergency Case'.

Schacht was relieved when, on 1 July 1934, Britain offered Germany a moratorium on all debts, after which the United States followed suit. Instead, payments were to resume through bonds. By now Schacht had turned the economy round to such an extent that he was able to encourage fifty-one German banks (of which fifteen were still under Jewish management) to float a new German Reichsbond, to be sold abroad at 4% interest.[12]

On 27 July 1934 Hitler invited Schacht to be his economics minister (in addition to being President of the Reichsbank), an appointment which he took up on 2 August. German policy was now to pay for foreign goods with so-called 'blocked' German Marks (i.e. ones that could only be used in turn for the purchase of German goods). Germany soon found, however, that other countries were quick to retaliate with similar forms of financial self-protection. Czechoslovakia decided to cease trading with Germany altogether, thus depriving the 'Fatherland' of a major source of iron ore, machinery, coal, weapons, automobiles and shoes.[13]

2 August 1934, marked the death of President von Hindenburg (at the age of 87), after which the office of 'president' was promptly abolished. Hitler would henceforth be known as 'Führer' and 'Reichschancellor'. On 18 September Soviet Russia was elected to membership of the League of Nations, a reflection of international concerns over Nazi Germany.

In 1935 Himmler was given overall charge of the SS, into which the Gestapo had now been absorbed. When, on 2 October 1935 Mussolini invaded Abyssinia (Ethiopia), the Führer lent him his full support, the quid pro quo being that the Italian dictator would withdraw his protective hand from Austria – now a target for Hitler's expansionist plans.

***

In order to guarantee the success of the 'Aryan' race as many Aryan babies as possible had to be born, and to this end Heinrich Himmler, in December 1935 created an organisation known as the 'Lebensborn' ('Spring of life'). This provided homes where unmarried German mothers could give birth to pure, Aryan children; also, any foreign children believed to be racially pure could be imported into the Reich.

Himmler encouraged the practice of eugenics (defined as: 'pertaining to race improvement by judicious mating ... [thereby] helping the better stock to prevail').[14] 'No longer shall it be left to chance that healthy people make the correct and successful choice of spouse,' said Himmler, 'so help your own race as best you can and then you shall belong to the best race.'[15]

SS men were encouraged to be promiscuous and to indulge in premarital sexual intercourse. They were ordered to have at least four children, in or out of wedlock, and preferably sons. SS bachelors were encouraged to marry, and childless SS men were paid less. This order was enshrined in writing, but was to be kept secret. (However, in the face of opposition from the SS, many of whose members were Roman Catholics, the order was revoked on Hitler's command.) These policies of Lebensborn and eugenics were a copybook reproduction of the doctrine put forward by Liebenfels in *Ostara*.

Later, in 1941 Himmler would demand that any strong, healthy, blond orphans found in Poland were to be sent to the Reich for forcible adoption and 'Germanisation'. The children were separated into groups, for example: ultra-Aryan 'Group 1A' children were only allowed to be adopted by Nazi Party members who had a university degree. Eye colour and skull shape was meticulously measured, and checks were made of their general health. Finally, children not only from Poland, but also from Russia and the Ukraine were imported into Germany, over 200,000 of whom were adopted by German families.[16]

***

In 1936 Himmler was appointed Reich Chief of Police. Now, in addition to the SS and the Gestapo, he commanded the SS's own Security Service (the SD), the Criminal Police, and the ordinary uniformed police of town and country. In the same year, the SS created an autonomous combat unit known as the 'Waffen SS' ('Waffen' meaning 'armed'.)

By now, two million girls aged from 15 to 21 had joined the BDM (League of German Girls), thereby dedicating themselves to, 'comradeship, service, and physical fitness for motherhood'.

On 7 March 1936 Hitler repudiated the demilitarisation clauses of the Treaties of Versailles and Locarno by marching his troops into the demilitarised Rhineland, and as he had calculated, the Allies took no action.

That summer Hitler's Foreign Affairs Advisor Joachim von Ribbentrop, who had negotiated the Anglo–German Naval Agreement, was sent to Britain to replace German Ambassador Leopold von Hoesch, who had died in London on 10 April. Hitler hoped that Ribbentrop would bring the same techniques of persuasion to bear on Britain as he had done on his customers in his former life as a champagne salesman, and improve Germany's relationship with Britain with a view to creating a formal Anglo–German Alliance.

However, the new ambassador was not regarded as a gentleman, and he would later commit a serious faux pas by giving a Nazi salute to King George VI. Such behaviour led to him being referred to, not as 'Herr Ribbentrop', but as 'Herr Brick-en-drop'!

Ribbentrop's objective in England was to organise a formal naval agreement. Hitler believed that in the absence of Germany's control of the seas, it was undesirable for the nation to acquire overseas colonies. Therefore, he would not interfere with Britain and her Empire provided that Britain, in turn, gave him a free hand on the continent of Europe.

On 17 July 1936 civil war broke out in Spain (a republic since 1931) between supporters of Spain's Second Republic (moderates, socialists, communists, and Catalan and Basque regionalists) on the one hand, and nationalist insurgents (monarchists, conservative Catholics, and Falangists – fascists), led by General Franciso Franco, on the other.

Although Hitler sent no service personnel to assist Franco, he did send aircraft, tanks and technicians, and also the Condor Legion of the Luftwaffe, whose aircraft provided transport for Franco's forces. Italy, however, sent 75,000 troops to assist Franco; while Russia, for her part, sent supplies (but no troops) to support the Republic.

Hitler now, as a prelude to his own forthcoming adventures in Europe, would have the satisfaction of helping a fascist dictator overthrow a democratic (albeit corrupt) Spanish government, though the process would take almost three years.

The Olympic Games of 1936 took place in Berlin, where Hitler was aghast to see African–American sprinter Jesse Owens win a total of four gold medals. Meanwhile, only 60km from the city, slave labourers co-opted by the Nazis were demolishing the old Oranienberg concentration camp and replacing it with a new one – to be named Sachsenhausen.

That September, at the Party Rally, Hitler announced a new, four-year plan which would be administered by Hermann Göring. In a programme of autarky (self-sufficiency), Germany would obtain her fuel, textiles, rubber and other industrial necessities through reopening mineral and coal mines inside the Reich's borders, and through new technology.[17] Schact, however, believed that the high cost of raw materials produced in this way would raise prices to such an extent that German products would become uncompetitive. But it was not with world trade that Hitler and Göring were primarily interested, but rather aircraft, tanks and guns for their own particular agenda.

On 25 October 1936 Germany signed a treaty with Italy, thus cementing the 'Rome–Berlin Axis'. Hitler would now give Italy a free hand in Africa and the Mediterranean, in exchange for herself being given a free hand in Central Europe.

On 30 October 1936 Ribbentrop submitted his credentials (as German Ambassador to Great Britain) to the new King, Edward VIII. However, the probability that the King, seen by Germany as potentially a powerful ally, might be forced to abdicate (on account of his love affair with Wallis Simpson, a twice-divorced woman) was deeply troubling to von Ribbentrop.

Japan was under the same pressure as Germany, if not more so, to provide living space for her growing population, and raw materials for her industries. On 25 November 1936 Germany and Japan signed the Anti-Comintern Pact ('Comintern' being an acronym for 'Communist International'), whereby both countries agreed to take steps to combat communism. The Pact also contained a secret protocol, under the terms of which both parties agreed to refrain from making any political treaties with Russia.[18] Hitler made it clear that he would dearly have liked Britain also to join:

> Ribbentrop, bring me England into the Anti-Comintern Pact. That is my greatest wish! However, if all efforts come to nothing, well then I am pre-pared for war, though I'd regret it a lot, but if it has to be … But I believe it would be a short war, and I'd offer generous terms to England, an honour-able, mutually acceptable peace.[19]

On 30 January 1937 Hitler guaranteed the neutrality of Belgium and the Netherlands, a cynical act, bearing in mind what was to come. On 27 April the Spanish market town of Guernica, near Bilbao, which was of no military sig-nificance, was bombed by the German Luftwaffe, an atrocity which cost approxi-mately 1,000 lives.

On 10 March 1937 Hjalmar Schacht's presidency of the Reichsbank was renewed for another four years. However, it now became apparent that Schacht and Hermann Göring were not seeing eye to eye over the economy, and on 6 October Schacht was summoned to the Berghof by Hitler in an attempt to iron out the difficulties. Interference from Göring was making life impossible, said Schacht and he tendered his resignation as Minister of Economics. This came into effect on 26 November.

At a secret meeting in early November 1937 Hitler informed his generals that Germany must expand to survive, that its problems could only be solved by the use of force, and that Austria and Czechoslovakia were to be the first targets.[20] On 9 November Japan invaded China.

On 4 February 1938 Joachim von Ribbentrop replaced Konstantin von Neurath as Germany's Foreign Minister, putting an end to the Nazi-Conservative alliance. On the same day, Hitler dismissed two of his top military commanders, Defence Minister Field Marshal Werner von Blomberg, and Commander in Chief of the German Army General Werner von Fritsch, both of whom had voiced objections to his expansionist plans.

In January 1939 in a speech to the Reichstag, Hitler declared that:

> Amongst the accusations which are directed against Germany in the so-called democracies is the charge that the National Socialist state is hostile to religion. In answer to that charge I should like to make before the German people the following declaration: '*No one in Germany has in the past been*

persecuted because of his religious views, nor will anyone in the future be so persecuted ....[21]

Germany's Catholic bishops took a different view; two years earlier, on 22 January 1937, they had complained, in a pastoral letter, of Nazi Party interference in the conduct of church affairs. German theologian and resistance figure Martin Niemoller, for example, who was arrested in 1937, spent a total of eight years in concentration camps and it is estimated that subsequently, as many as 4,000 priests, mainly German, were murdered by the Nazis.[22]

Within two years, however, Hitler's rhetoric would change completely with statements such as:

National socialism and religion cannot exist together .... The heaviest blow that ever struck humanity was the coming of Christianity. Bolshevism is Christianity's illegitimate child. Both are inventions of the Jews.[23] The reason why the ancient world was so pure, light and serene was that it knew nothing of the two great scourges: the pox and Christianity. [24]

'The Party,' said Hitler, 'must be an Order, that is what it has to be – an Order, the hierarchical order of a secular priesthood.'[25]

[Surely this was Hitler echoing Liebenfels' 'Order of New Templars'.]

Notes

1. Vorres, Ian, *The Last Grand-Duchess*, p. 85.
2. Hitler, Adolf, *Mein Kampf*, pp. 361, 363.
3. Ibid, p. 367.
4. Ibid, p. 366.
5. Ibid.
6. Ibid, p. 374.
7. Ibid, p. 361.
8. Rauschning, Hermann, *Hitler Speaks*, p. 85.
9. *The Nazis: A Warning from History, Part 2*.
10. Weitz, John, *Hitler's Banker*, p. 165.
11. *The Last Nazi Secret*.
12. Weitz, op. cit., p. 163.
13. Muhlen, Norbert, *Schacht: Hitler's Magician*, p. 118.
14. Chambers English Dictionary.
15. *The SS: Himmler's Madness*.
16. Ibid.
17. Weitz, op. cit., p. 208.
18. Shirer, William L, *The Rise and Fall of the Third Reich*, p. 299.

19. Michalka, Wolfgang, 1980, *Ribbentrop und die deutsche Weltpolitik, 1933–1940*. München. Wilhelm Fink. p. 155.
20. Toland, John, *Adolf Hitler*, p. 421.
21. Speech in Reichstag, 30 Jan. 1939.
22. Fourier, *Lexikon der Papiste*.
23. Trevor-Roper, H R (ed.), *Hitler's Secret Conversations, 1941–1944*, Speech, 11/12 July, 1941.
24. Ibid, Speech, 19 Oct. 1941.
25. Rauschning, op. cit., p. 237.

CHAPTER XX

Hitler's Private Life

Late in the summer of 1906 Hitler began taking piano lessons (from the same teacher who was tutoring a friend of his, August Kubizek, the son of an upholsterer). However, these lessons were discontinued in January 1907 when Hitler's widowed mother Klara became ill and the family was obliged to reduce its financial outgoings.

The family doctor who attended Klara was Dr Eduard Bloch, a Jew (who was affectionately known as the 'poor people's doctor') and it is to him that posterity is indebted for supplying some vital information about Hitler's early life.

According to the doctor, the reason for the Hitler family moving from their home town of Braunau to Linz in 1903 was that there were some, 'good schools there', where Hitler's father Alois believed that, 'his son would have the education which had been denied him; an education which would secure him a good government job'.[1] To this end, Alois (who by this time had retired from his post as customs inspector) purchased a small farm in Leonding, a suburb of Linz. However, 'the family had barely settled in[to] their new home outside of Linz when Alois, the father, died suddenly from an apoplectic stroke'.[2]

As it was now apparent that Adolf was, 'too young and altogether too frail to become a farmer', his mother Klara decided to sell the farm and rent a small apartment in a two-storey house, Number 9 Bluetenstrasse, situated, 'across the Danube from the main portion of Linz'.

At this time, said Dr Bloch, Hitler, 'read extensively and was particularly fascinated by stories about American Indians. He devoured the books of James Fenimore Cooper, and the German writer Karl May [who wrote about the native Indians of America, even though he had never visited that country, let alone seen an Indian!].

Dr Bloch describes the young Hitler as, 'a quiet, well mannered and neatly dressed' youth who, 'like any well-bred boy of 14 or 15 ... would bow and thank me courteously', whenever he was treated by the doctor for a minor illness. 'While he was not a "mother's boy" in the usual sense, I have never witnessed a closer attachment,' said Bloch.

It was in the year 1908 that Dr Bloch was obliged to summon the Hitler children to his office to tell them the sad news that their mother had an extensive tumour of the breast. Said Dr Bloch:

Adolf Hitler's reaction to this news was touching. His long, sallow face was contorted. Tears flowed from his eyes. Did his mother, he asked, have no chance? Only then I realised the magnitude of the attachment that existed between mother and son.[3]

Early in the summer of 1908 Klara entered the Hospital of the Sisters of Mercy in Linz, to be operated on by Dr Karl Urban, Chief of the Surgical Staff, in the presence of Dr Bloch, who stated that:

As weeks and months passed after the operation, Frau Hitler's strength began visibly to fail. At most she could be out of bed for an hour or two a day. During this period Adolf spent most of his time around the house, to which his mother had returned. He slept in the tiny bedroom adjoining that of his mother so that he could be summoned at any time during the night. During the day he hovered about the large bed in which she lay.

Klara, having received numerous home visits from Dr Bloch, died during the night of 20/21 December 1908 at the age of 47. Said Dr Bloch:

Adolf, his face showing the weariness of a sleepless night, sat beside his mother. In order to preserve a last impression, he had sketched her as she lay on her death-bed. In all my career I had never seen anyone so prostrate with grief as Adolf Hitler.

Klara's funeral took place on Christmas Eve, and she was buried beside her husband in the Catholic cemetery at Leonding.

After the others ... had left, Adolf remained behind; unable to tear himself away from the freshly filled grave. A few days after the funeral the family came to my [Dr Bloch's] office. [When his turn came around, Adolf, who] wore a dark suit and a loosely knotted cravat ... stepped forward and took my hand. Looking into my eyes he said: 'I shall be grateful to you forever.' That was all. Then he bowed.[4]

***

From the summer of 1925 Hitler is known to have stayed at various inns in the Obersalzburg situated in the mountains of upper Bavaria above the little market village of Berchtesgaden. In July 1926 he first rented and then purchased an alpine house there known as 'Haus Wachenfeld'. Soon, this would be turned into a huge complex known as the 'Berghof'.[5]

According to Herbert Döhring, Hitler spent more time on his design plans for the new buildings, which were to grace the Third Reich, than he did on governing the country. 'He always had his building plans in mind, even when he was travelling.'[6] In 1938 a new Reich Chancellery was built.

Hitler's routine at his Obersalzburg retreat was to rise just before lunch, or even after lunch; take an afternoon walk, and watch films in the evenings. He neither smoked, drank, nor ate meat, affirms Hermann Rauschning.[7] According to Herbert Dohring (member of Hitler's SS bodyguard 1936–43), Hitler's admiration for Britain and her Empire was unbounded, his favourite film being *The Lives of the Bengal Lancers* (1935), which was set in India, Britain's so-called 'Jewel in the Crown'. He would talk admiringly about, 'this huge English Empire ...', and how, 'such a relatively small people could establish and manage something like this, and keep it in order'.[8] Hitler also loved English romantic comedies such as *A Hopeless Case* (1939).

***

An intimate insight into Hitler's private life was gained as a result of the activities of the US secret intelligence organisation, the Office of Strategic Services (OSS), which was headed by General 'Wild Bill' Donovan, a veteran of World War I. In 1943 Donovan asked Dr Walter C Langer of Harvard University for his help in attempting to understand the workings of Hitler's mind. Langer was a Freudian psychoanalyst who hoped that Hitler's sexual behaviour would provide clues to his personality.

Langer interviewed refugees, émigrés and high ranking defectors from Nazi Germany, no fewer than 269 people in all, in order to establish his psychological profile of Hitler. One interviewee was American film director Arnold Zeissler, who had made moving pictures in Germany in the early 1930s. Zeissler told Langer that Hitler had often requested that actresses be sent to him at the Reich Chancellery. Hitler would then regale them with stories of medieval torture methods. One, Renate Müller, became a firm favourite of his.

In his report, Langer described what Zeissler had told him about Müller's relationship with the Führer. One morning, Zeissler found Müller, who had spent the previous evening with Hitler, in a troubled state. She,

> had been sure that he [Hitler] was going to have [sexual] intercourse with her; that they had both undressed and were apparently getting ready for bed when Hitler fell on the floor and begged her to kick him. She demurred, but he pleaded with her and condemned himself as unworthy, heaped all kinds of accusations on his own head, and just grovelled in an agonising manner. The scene became intolerable to her, and she finally acceded to his wishes and kicked him. This excited him greatly, and he begged for more and more, always saying that it was even better than he deserved and that he was not worthy to be in the same room with her. He became more and more excited.[9]

Hitler then allegedly masturbated in front of her, and then thanked her.[10] [Needless to say, for a woman this must have been nothing less than a personal insult of devastating proportions.]

***

Ernst Hanfstaengl was a political and personal confidant of Hitler, who would also entertain him on the pianoforte. After a power struggle with Goebbels however, Hanfstaengl fell from grace and in 1937 fled Germany in fear of his life, to Virginia, USA, where he offered his services to Allied intelligence.

In the spring of 1943 Langer visited Hanfstaengl and talked to him at length: 'Hitler is shy when trying to win a woman's affection,' Hanfstaengl told Langer. His favourite phrase is, 'If you go to a woman, don't forget your whip'. [Hitler was in the habit of carrying a riding whip]. Then, they discussed Hitler's affair with his half-niece Geli.

Geli (whose real name was Angela Maria Raubal) was the daughter of Hitler's half-sister Angela. She spent her childhood in a small village in Austria, and according to her school friend Anna Gruebl, she was blond, friendly and beautiful. She was also a fine sports woman and an excellent swimmer.

In 1928 Hitler invited Angela (who had married Leo Raubal, an official in the tax bureau in Linz, but was now a widow) to be housekeeper at his home 'Haus Wachenfeld', in the Obersalzberg. She accepted, and duly arrived bringing her two daughters, Friedl and Geli. (The latter, who was then aged 20, subsequently enrolled as a medical student at the University of München.)

Ernst Hanfstaengl suggested to Langer that Hitler probably beat Geli with his riding whip, and derived sadistic pleasure from it. When Geli fell in love with Hitler's chauffeur Emil Maurice, Hitler was furious and forbade the couple to meet, except in his company. From then on Hitler and Geli became almost inseparable, Hitler persuading her to abandon her medical studies in favour of becoming a singer.[11]

Otto Strasser was another high ranking Nazi defector interviewed by Langer. Strasser told Langer that by 1931 Hitler's relationship with Geli had become obsessional. She told Strasser that Hitler would make her undress, and that he would lie down on the floor. Then, she would have to squat down over his face, where he would examine her at close range and this would make him very excited. When the excitement reached its peak, he demanded that she urinate on him, and that gave him his sexual pleasure. The whole performance was extremely disgusting to her.[12]

Hanfstaengl also told Langer about a scandal that had been hushed up in 1930. The Nazi Party treasurer had been forced to buy someone off for trying to blackmail Hitler. That person had come into possession of a folio of pornographic drawings which Hitler had made: they were, 'depraved, intimate sketches of Geli Raubal with every anatomical detail'.

In the State Archives of München (Munich), capital city of Bavaria, is the suicide register for 1931. It shows that in that year 334 citizens took their own lives. One of these was Hitler's niece, Angela (Geli) Raubal, who had died in the luxury apartment where she and Hitler had been living together for two years. On the night of 18 September 1931 the couple had allegedly had an argument, after which Hitler left to attend the Nürnberg Party Rally. The following morning Geli was found dead, having shot herself through the chest with Hitler's pistol. In a statement to the press, the Nazis claimed that Geli's death was attributable to anxiety over a forthcoming engagement. Hitler's reaction was: how could this have happened to me?

In 1943 however, Hanfstaengl told Langer that he was certain that Geli had been murdered by Hitler in a fit of rage brought on because she wanted to go out with other men. Hanfstaengl's source was Gregor Strasser (brother of Otto), a close associate of Hitler, who was present when Geli's body was found. This would have been impossible, as at the time of Geli's death, Hitler was attending the Party Rally. (Strasser himself met his death during the infamous Night of the Long Knives.) However, it is possible that Hitler had Geli eliminated because of his fear that she might speak out about his sadomasochistic sexual practices in which he had involved her.

Geli was not the first of Hitler's female acquaintances to come to an untimely end. 18 year old Mimi Reiter, Hitler's first acknowledged girlfriend, almost succeeded in hanging herself in 1926; film star Renate Müller jumped to her death from the window of a Berlin clinic shortly after spending an evening with Hitler, and two other women alleged that Hitler had made attempts on their lives.

***

Running in parallel with such sexual adventures was Hitler's relationship with Eva Braun, the daughter of a vocational teacher, whom he met in early October 1929 when Eva's father found her a job as receptionist and model at the studio of Hitler's personal photographer Heinrich Hoffmann. Born in München in 1912 Eva was 23 years younger than the Führer.

In November 1932 Eva, having been ignored for weeks on end by Hitler, shot herself in the neck but sustained no serious injury. On 28 May 1935 she would make another suicide attempt, this time by taking an overdose of tablets.

> How can he [Hitler] have so little understanding as to let me remain here, bowing to strangers …. He has so often told me that he is madly in love with me, but what does that mean when I haven't had a good word from him in three months?

If she did not get an answer to her letters, she would take an overdose of twenty-five pills, 'and gently fall asleep into another world.' Hitler for his part, described Eva Braun as, 'cute, cuddly, and naïve'. As far as marriage was concerned however, it was out of the question. 'I am married to Germany,' he said.

From 1936 Eva resided with Hitler at the Berghof (where she was known as Fräulein Braun), invariably appearing at his insistence, in the same dress and with the same unchanging hairstyle. Hitler kept her and his official life completely separate. She was not permitted to appear at his side in public, nor to accompany him on his many public engagements. Even when he entertained his guests, who were often glamorous film stars, to lavish receptions, Eva was kept out of sight. As far as they and the public were concerned, she was just one of his many secretaries.

Hitler no doubt realised that for him to be seen by the women of Germany as a single man with no wife or family commitments, who could devote himself to serving the nation, was far more attractive than if he were married. Not only that, but it is highly likely that in their imaginations, many German women saw themselves as his potential partner.

On the occasions when Hitler and Eva are in each other's company, his body language is quite revealing. He treats her with the utmost formality; rather than giving her any demonstrable signs of affection. Both are usually seen with arms folded, and Hitler often has his back to her. Even when he speaks to Eva, Hitler usually stands aloof with hands held behind his back. For Eva, her dog and her rabbit gave her more affection than he did; or so it seemed.

However, according to Hitler's telephone operator Rochus Misch, whereas with Hitler, Eva was 'shy and retiring', in Hitler's absence she was full of fun, holding parties for the staff, and going off to dances.[13] She also loved swimming, skiing and cycling.

At the Berghof, although Hitler and Eva had separate accommodation, their rooms were linked by a passageway. However, Herbert Döhring (Administrator of the Berghof and married to Hitler's personal cook Anna), was quite sure that their relationship was not of a sexual nature.

My wife ... often did Hitler's washing, and the first thing she always did was to check if there had been any sexual activity. But there was never any evidence. My wife checked the sheets, but there were no signs of any sexual activity, none.

This fact was confirmed by the other servants.[14]

***

As a result of her unfulfilled relationship with Hitler, Eva Braun continued to suffer considerably. Her cousin Gertraud Weisker described her as, 'a really depressed person. She had to cover up her depression all the time by doing sport, or buying new clothes. She was trying to distract herself from things that depressed her. She could not concentrate on anything either ....'[15] 'I'm just a prisoner in a golden cage,' Eva said pathetically.

Notes

1. Bloch, Dr Eduard, 'My Patient Hitler', in *Colliers*, 1941, Vol. 1, 15 March, pp. 11, 35–9; and 22 March, pp. 69–73.
2. Bloch, op cit, 22 March, pp. 69–73.
3. Ibid.

4. Ibid, p. 39.
5. Shirer, William L, *The Rise and Fall of the Third Reich*, p. 112.
6. *The Nazis: A Warning from History*, Part 3.
7. Rauschning, Hermann, *Hitler Speaks*, p. 66.
8. *The Nazis: A Warning from History*, op. cit.
9. Langer, Walter, *The Mind of Adolf Hitler*, p. 171.
10. *Sex and the Swastika: The Making of Adolf Hitler*.
11. Ibid.
12. Ibid.
13. *Eva Braun*.
14. Ibid.
15. *Hitler's Women*.

CHAPTER XXI

The Jews, Judaism, and What Hitler Chose to Ignore

The Jews and Judaism

Judaism is a monotheistic religion (i.e. it is based on the notion that there is only one god), and it requires that its followers obey a number of laws which were laid down in the *Torah*, given by God in his revelation to Moses on Mount Sinai (and summarised in the five books of Moses). 'According to rabbinic tradition, there are 613 commandments in the Torah ... less than 300 ... [of which] ... are still applicable today.'

Jewish law dictates that a Jew is a person born of a Jewish mother, or converted, in accordance with Jewish law. However, 'Recently, the American Reform and Reconstructionist Movement have included [as Jews] those born of Jewish fathers and gentile mothers, if [provided that] the children are raised practising Judaism only.'[1]

The practice of Judaism requires adherence to traditional customs: for males for example, circumcision. Orthodox Jews adhere, 'to one particular form of Jewish theology based on Maimonides' (Jewish philosopher 1135–1204) thirteen principles of Jewish faith.' Whereas, 'non-Orthodox forms of Judaism hold that these principles have evolved over time, and thus allow more leeway in what individual adherents believe.'

An 'Apostate' is defined as a Jew who does not follow traditional customs. 'A Jew who ceases to practise Judaism is still considered a Jew, as is a Jew who does not accept Jewish principles of faith and becomes an agnostic or an atheist; so too for the Jew who converts to another religion.'

Hitler, however, made no distinction as to whether a Jew practised or did not practise Judaism, or whether he was Orthodox or non-Orthodox. To the Führer's way of thinking, anyone who had a 'Jewish' appearance was automatically condemned, simply by virtue of his birth. Whatever views that Jew may or may not have held, these were considered by the Führer to be irrelevant.

A Childhood Sweetheart

In the autumn of 1905 when Hitler was aged 15 and living with his mother in Linz, he became infatuated with a young lady called Stefanie, whom he admired from afar; never plucking up courage enough to speak to her (possibly because he was unsure about his own sexuality).

Recently, the historian Anton Joachimsthaler has taken the trouble to look up this Stefanie in the Linz City Archive. To his surprise, he discovered that her surname was Isak, *which indicates that she was Jewish.* Hitler may or may not have been aware of this, and if he was, he may have regarded it as of no importance, his anti-Semitic feelings being as yet unborn.[2]

Vienna

'Almost immediately after his mother's funeral in December 1908 Hitler left for Vienna,' stated former family physician Dr Eduard Bloch, 'to attempt once more a career as an artist.' Here, 'he worked as a hod carrier on building-construction jobs until workmen threatened to push him off a scaffold [the reason for this is not recorded] and we know that he shovelled snow and took any other job that he could find.'

> It was during the following three years, during which time Hitler lived in a men's hostel, that the vitriol of hate began to creep through his body. The grim realities of the life he lived encouraged him to hate the government, labour unions, the very men he lived with. But he had not yet begun to hate the Jews.[3]

This is borne out by the fact that,

> during this period he [Hitler] took time out to send me a penny postcard. On the back was a message: 'from Vienna I send you my greetings. Yours, always faithfully Adolf Hitler.' (*This despite the fact that Dr Bloch was a Jew*).

The doctor also described how he received from Hitler a card, depicting, 'a hooded Capuchin monk, hoisting a glass of bubbling champagne', which he had painted himself.

> Under the picture was a caption: 'Prosit Neu Jahr' – A Toast to the New Year. On the reverse side he had written a message: 'The Hitler family sends you the best wishes for a happy New Year. In everlasting thankfulness, Adolf Hitler.'

Hitler never subsequently acknowledged Dr Bloch, though following the annexation of Austria by Germany in 1938 ('Anschluss'), the doctor was afforded preferential treatment, even though he was Jewish. This, no doubt, was on the instructions of Hitler. *Despite his hatred for the Jews, the Führer was apparently unable to banish from his mind the previous kind and devoted attentions of the good doctor to his mother and his family.*

***

During his period in Vienna (1905–7 and 1908–13), Hitler lived in various lodging houses and hostels for homeless men. Here, he came across Czechs, Poles, Hungarians, Italians and others in a similarly wretched state, and of course, Germans and Jews.

According to an acquaintance of his, and fellow inmate Reinhold Hanisch, in the autumn of 1909 Hitler was living in the asylum for the homeless, situated at the rear of Vienna's South railway station. This shelter was a Jewish (charitable) foundation, as was another at Erdberg (also visited by Hitler), which 'had been endowed by the Jewish Baron Königswarter'.[4] Hanisch stated that Hitler 'also received benefits from [Catholic] convents'.[5]

Soon after Christmas 1909 Hitler moved from the asylum to the 'Mannerheim' (men's hostel) in the Meldemannstrasse in the Twentieth District of Vienna, and it was here [according to Hanisch], that he, 'had helpful advisers who were Jews'.[6] For example, Hanisch cites, 'a one-eyed locksmith called Robinsohn who often assisted him, since he [Robinsohn] was a beneficiary of an accident insurance annuity, and was able to spare a few pennies'. There were other Jews in the 'Mannerheim' who often, 'listened to his [Hitler's] political debates'.

'The salesman Neumann [who sold signboards, produced by the inmates],' says Hanisch, 'became a real friend [to Hitler].' At a time when Neumann was working, 'with another Jew who was buying old clothes and peddling them in the streets', he [Neumann] often gave Hitler old clothes including, 'a long coat'. 'Hitler told me once,' said Hanisch, 'that Neumann was a very decent man, because if any of us had small debts, Neumann paid them [even] though he himself was very much in want'.

Hanisch then went on to describe Hitler's personality and habits. As he 'was much too weak for hard physical work,' Hanisch suggested that he paint postcards. Soon after Christmas 1909 Hanisch began to peddle Hitler's postcards, Hitler himself having told Hanisch that, 'he [himself] wouldn't be able to sell them because he wasn't well enough dressed ...'.[7] Hanisch sold these postcards (which were not originals but copies, mainly of views of Vienna) on Hitler's behalf in taverns, to art dealers, furniture stores and upholsterers, 'for in those days divans were made with pictures inserted in their backs'. Said Hanisch,

In those days, Hitler was by no means a Jew-hater. He became one afterward[s]. Hitler often said that it was only with the Jews that one could do business, because only they were willing to take chances. They are really the most efficient businessmen. He [Hitler] also appreciated the charitable spirit of the Jews ... [but he] admired the Jews most for their resistance to all persecutions.[8]

In fact, according to Hanisch, it was, 'almost solely … Jewish dealers' who purchased Hitler's watercolours. They included Jacob Altenberg; a person called Landsberger, who had a shop in the Favoritenstrasse; and one Morgenstern, whose shop was in the Liechtensteinstrasse. The latter often bought from Hitler, and sometimes recommended him to private customers.

Time and again, Hanisch described being driven to despair by, 'bringing in orders [for watercolour postcards] that he [Hitler] simply would not carry out'.[9]

> In the morning he wouldn't even work until he had read several newspapers, and if anyone should come in with another newspaper he would read that too. Meanwhile the orders I brought in weren't carried out.[10] At such laziness I was very angry and resentful.

Hanisch could finally bear it no longer. He moved out of the asylum into private lodgings and 'decided to work independently'. Despite having befriended and supported Hitler, Hanisch was to discover the duplicity of his character when, to his astonishment, he [Hanisch] was taken to the Brigittenau Police Commissariat where he was confronted by Hitler, who accused him of misappropriating a watercolour of his worth 50 Kronen. The result was that Hanisch was sentenced to a term of seven days' imprisonment.

In 1936 Hanisch committed his memories of Hitler to paper and attempted to find a publisher for his work. He was promptly charged by the Nazi regime and imprisoned for tampering with and falsifying some watercolour paintings made by Hitler during their time together in the men's hostel. The official report stated that Hanisch had died in prison after a sudden attack of pleurisy which had lasted for three days.[11]

War

On 21 October 1914 (Britain having declared war on Germany on 4 August following that country's invasion of Belgium), Hitler entered the frontline as a volunteer corporal in the Sixteenth Bavarian Reserve Infantry Regiment. Here, he fulfilled the function of 'Meldeganger' (despatch runner), who relays messages between his company and the regimental headquarters.

On 7 October 1916 he was wounded in the leg and sent back to hospital in Germany. He returned to the Front in March 1917 and was promoted to the rank of lance-corporal. On the night of 13/14 October 1918 Hitler was gassed during a British attack near Werwick, south of Ypres. He was invalided back to the military hospital at Basewalk in Pomerania (Baltic region) where he remained until the war ended on 11 November 1918.

During the war, Hitler received the decorations Iron Cross, Second Class (December 1914), and Iron Cross, First Class (4 August 1918). For the second award, it was a *Jewish officer*, Lieutenant Hugo Gutmann, whom Hitler had to thank for his nomination.[12] It was also true to say that Hitler would have encountered other Jews as members of Germany's armed forces, who were fighting alongside him. In fact, during the course of World War I, approximately 100,000 German Jews fought for the German Kaiser, of whom about 12,000 lost their lives and 30,000 were decorated for bravery. Nevertheless, despite all evidence to the contrary, Hitler preferred to believe that all Jews, without exception, were trying to undermine the German war effort.

Politics

Hitler acknowledged that, 'Jews have been ready to help me in my political struggle' and that, 'At the outset of our movement some Jews actually gave me financial assistance.'[13]

Notes

1. 'Judaism'. wordiQ.com. in www.msn.co.uk.
2. SAS.
3. Bloch, Dr Eduard, *My Patient Hitler*, Vol. 1, 15 March, pp. 11, 35–9; and 22 March, pp. 69–73.
4. Hanisch, Reinhold, *I was Hitler's Buddy*, 5 April, 1939, pp. 239–42 (I); 12 April, pp. 270–2 (II); 19 April, 1939, pp. 297–300 (III). Hanisch I.
5. Ibid, II.
6. Ibid.
7. Ibid, I.
8. Ibid, II.
9. Ibid, I.
10. Ibid, III.
11. Ibid, I.
12. Wiedemann, Fritz, *Der Mann, der Feldherr werden wollte*, pp. 25–6.
13. Rauschning, Hermann, *Hitler Speaks*, p. 234.

CHAPTER XXII

Creating the Greater German Reich

In 1924 Hitler wrote,

> The annual increase of population in Germany amounts to almost 900,000 souls. The difficulties of providing for this army of new citizens must grow from year to year and must finally lead to a catastrophe, unless ways and means are found which will forestall the danger of misery and hunger.[1]

Hitler decided therefore, that in order to create more living space – 'Lebensraum' – Germany needed to expand her frontiers. (He had considered another alternative, which was to artificially restrict the number of births – following the French example – but had rejected this on the grounds that such a policy 'robs the nation of its future').[2]

***

Swedish Professor Rudolf Kjellen (1864–1922) was the first to use the term 'geopolitics', which is concerned with the relationship between the geographical morphology of a particular country and its politics.

Friedrich Ratzel (1844–1904) was a graduate of Heidelberg University who in 1880 became Professor of Geography at München's Technical High School. Ratzel became particularly interested in the reasons why human populations tend to become distributed in the ways they do, influenced as they were by the physical topography of the areas in which they found themselves – mountains, lakes etc. – as well as by religion, language and ethnicity.

It was Ratzel who, in 1897 in his work *Politische Geographie*, developed the concept of 'Lebensraum'. Whereas Darwin's 'Theory of Evolution by Natural Selection' referred to living organisms, Ratzel, for his part, regarded the nation as a living thing, and subject to the same Darwinist pressures as living creatures, in its quest for survival. Hence the expression 'social Darwinism'. Nations have dynamics of their own; they were born, they grew and matured, but they could also die. If they were to survive, they would require the land and space to do so.

Ratzel believed that it was natural for the state to seek to increase its size, and inevitable that if the state's neighbours were weak, a strong state would expand at their expense. However, in order to achieve this, Ratzel was in favour of colonisation rather than piecemeal takeovers such as the Nazis were shortly to inflict on their neighbours.[3]

As for 'racism', Ratzel was opposed to it, being quick to point out the *advantages* of the admixing of people of different origins, and the extra vitality which this would bring as exemplified by countries such as the USA. He also believed that what moulded a nation was its peoples' relationship with the land and the space it occupied, rather than genetic factors.

What the Nazi regime failed to appreciate was that their attempts to create a genetically 'pure' race (if that were ever possible) would preclude the possibility of genetic diversity (on which evolution itself depends).

***

From the very beginning, it was Hitler's intention to implement the policy of 'Lebensraum' and acquire more territories in the east. First however, his homeland, Austria, must be incorporated into the Fatherland. Even though he was by birth an Austrian, Hitler always harked back to the time when Austria was part of the German Empire. Hence his choosing to champion the cause of a greater German Reich.

Austria

Prior to the 'Anschluss' (the incorporation by Hitler of his Austrian homeland into a greater Germany), Austrian Nazis, funded by the SS, conducted a campaign of terror directed at such strategic targets as railways and power stations.

When Engelbert Dollfuss became Chancellor of Austria in 1932 he was faced with having to deal with violence between the socialists and the Nazis. He responded by raising a private army and ruling as a dictator. This deprived him of the support of those who might later have supported him against the Nazis.

On 25 July 1934 in a 'Putsch' code-named 'Operation Summer Festival', a force of 150 Austrian Nazis, attired in the uniforms of the Austrian army, forced their way into the Austrian Chancellery and shot Dollfuss in the throat. They then announced over the radio that the Chancellor had 'resigned'. Meanwhile, back in Berlin, the German News Bureau (DNB) declared: 'The inevitable has happened. The German people in Austria have risen against their oppressors, gaolers and torturers.'[4] Despite this however, the 'Putsch' was quelled.

In 1935 when Mussolini invaded Abyssinia, Hitler gave the Italian dictator his tacit support. Now in return, Mussolini would himself turn a blind eye to Hitler's annexation of Austria.

The French hoped to contain Germany in the east by forming an anti-Nazi block to include Poland, the USSR and Czechoslovakia. To this end, on 2 May 1935 France and the Soviet Union signed a mutual assistance pact.

Hitler, however, at a conference with his military chiefs on 5 November 1937 declared that his first objective was to seize Czechoslovakia and Austria, as a means of securing his eastern and southern flanks. Not only would this ensure abundant food supplies for the Reich, but it would also mean 'shorter and better frontiers' and 'the freeing of forces for other purposes'.[5]

On 11 February 1938 Austrian Chancellor Kurt von Schuschnigg (who had replaced the murdered Dollfuss) travelled to the Berghof to meet Hitler, who warned him: 'Perhaps you will wake up one morning in Vienna to find us [the Germans] there – just like a spring storm.' However, the Führer, 'would very much like to save Austria from such a fate, because such an action would mean blood.'[6] When Schuschnigg protested that such an invasion of his country would probably lead to war, Hitler declared that in his opinion, nobody – neither Italy, England nor France – would lift a finger to save Austria.

Then Ribbentrop showed Schuschnigg a prepared draft agreement: Germany would support Austria's sovereignty, provided that all Austrian National Socialists, including those who had been imprisoned for the assassination of the former Chancellor Dollfuss, were set free, and all those National Socialist officials who had been dismissed were reinstated. Furthermore, Aurtur Seyff-Inquart, leader of Austria's Pan-German faction, was to be appointed Minister of the Interior with complete control of the nation's police forces; another Austrian Nazi was to be made the new Minister of Defence.

When Schuschnigg refused to sign what was in effect an ultimatum, Hitler sent for General Keitel, Chief of the High Command of the armed forces. Faced with such intimidation, Schuschnigg gave way.

But Hitler still was not content. On 20 February, in a speech to the Reichstag, he accused Austria of mistreating its 'German minority'. It was, 'intolerable for a self-conscious world power to know that at its side are co-racials, who are subjected to continuous suffering because of their sympathy and unity with the whole German race and its ideology'.[7] This was seen by the Austrian Nazis as a green light to commence demonstrations throughout the country.

Hitler now made further demands on Schuschnigg: a Nazi was to be appointed as Minister of Economics; the ban on the Nazi newspaper *Der Volkischer Beobachter* was to be lifted; within three weeks National Socialism was to be recognised and legalised. By this time there was turmoil throughout the country with frequent clashes between the Nazis and the State Police.

Schuschnigg responded by declaring that a plebiscite would be held whereby the nation would be asked the question: 'Are you in favour of a free and German, independent and social, a Christian and united Austria?' This was the last thing that Hitler wanted, and it forced his hand. 'I am now determined to restore law and order in my homeland and enable the people to decide their own fate, according to their judgement, in an unmistakeable, clear and open manner,' he said, in a letter to Mussolini.[8] On 11 March 1938 Schuschnigg resigned as Chancellor of Austria. Hitler for once kept his word, and in the Austrian elections held on 9 April 1938 99.02% of the population voted in favour of the union of Austria with Germany.

On 12 March 1938 Hitler issued a proclamation:

Since early this morning, soldiers of the German armed forces have been marching across the Austro-German frontiers. Mechanised troops and infantry, German airplanes in the blue sky, summoned by the new Nationalist Socialist Government in Vienna, are the guarantors [that] the Austrian nation shall, at an early date, be given the opportunity to decide its own future by a genuine plebiscite.[9]

In the event, the Nazis encountered no resistance. Mussolini telegrammed to Hitler, 'I congratulate you on the way you have solved the Austrian problem.'[10]

On the same day, Hitler's entourage crossed the border at his birthplace, Braunau-am-Inn, for a triumphal procession into Austria which included a visit to Linz, his former home town. Dr Eduard Bloch, who had not seen Hitler for thirty years, remembers the Führer's motorcade passing along the street beneath the windows of his consulting rooms; the very rooms where 'he [Hitler] had gone as a boy to have his minor ailments attended to'.[11]

At the time of the Anschluss there were, according to Dr Bloch, 700 Jews residing in Linz. The, 'homes, shops and offices of all these people were marked with the yellow, paper banners, now visible throughout Germany – JUDE – JEW.' However, after the evacuation order there were but seven members of this race left in Linz. This meant that after thirty-seven years of active work, Dr Bloch's practice was at an end. He, however, would receive favourable treatment at the hands of the Nazis, presumably because of his previous connections with Hitler. Dr Bloch believed that he was the only Jew in all of Austria who was allowed to keep his passport. He was, 'even given a ration card for clothes – something generally denied Jews'. Finally, Dr Bloch was allowed to leave Linz for America. He knew that, 'It would be impossible for me to take my savings with me. But the Gestapo had one more favour for me. I was to be allowed to take 16 Marks from the country, instead of the customary 10!'[12]

***

To the Austrians, Hitler said: 'If Providence once called me forth from this town to lead the Reich, then it must have given me a mission. That mission can only have been to restore my dear homeland to the German Reich.'[13] By this, he was presumably referring to the First Reich, or Holy Roman Empire (800–1806 AD); the Second Reich referred to the unified, post-1871 Germany; and the Third Reich to the enlarged Germany envisaged by Hitler. 'This country and this people are not entering the Reich in a humiliating role,' declared the Führer. 'I myself am leading you there.'

With the occupation of Austria, Hitler secured 60 million pounds of gold, and access to the Erzberg – a mountain rich in iron-ore. The new Reich now contained over 80 million citizens (of whom by this time, 9 million had joined the Hitler Youth movement). In April 1938 Britain formally recognised Italian sovereignty over Abyssinia – yet another milestone on the road of appeasement of the Axis powers.

Czechoslovakia

Three million Germans lived in the adjacent Sudeten region of Czechoslovakia, a country that was to be Hitler's next target.

> I would rather have the war when I'm 50, than when I'm 55 or 60. Ahead of us is the last problem which must and will be solved. [and the most notorious lie of all] *It (the Sudetenland) is the last territorial demand I have in Europe....*[14]

For three years prior to 1938 Hitler had been secretly supporting the Sudeten Nazi Party of Konrad Henlein whom, in March 1938 Hitler named as his personal representative. Having discussed the invasion of Czechoslovakia with Mussolini, Hitler, on 19/20 May, began mobilising his troops on the Czech borders. This prompted Czech President Eduard Beneš to order a 'partial mobilisation' of his own forces, which promptly moved in to protect the Sudetenland.

On 28 May 1938 Hitler told his military leaders, 'It is my unshakeable will to wipe Czechoslovakia off the map ....'[15] This would eliminate any threat which Czechoslovakia might be to the rear, when Hitler's forces made their drive to the east to implement his policy of 'Lebensraum'.

Just as he had done previously in Austria, Hitler now portrayed the German Czechs as an oppressed minority, and gave vent to his feelings in a speech he made on 12 September 1938 at the Nürnberg Rally. 'The Germans in Czechoslovakia are neither defenceless, nor are they deserted, and people should take notice of that fact.'[16] True to form, the Sudeten Germans took this as a signal to commence demonstrations, and the death toll quickly rose to twenty-one. The Sudeten Germans now went on strike and refused to pay their taxes, whereupon the Czech government declared martial law, and further lives were lost as it continued forcibly to put down the rebellion.

On 15 September 1938 British Prime Minister Neville Chamberlain went to Germany for a meeting with Hitler at the Berghof: now aged 69, this was the first time he had flown in an aircraft. After a three-hour discussion, Hitler agreed to give Chamberlain time to consult with his colleagues back in England over the Sudeten question.

On 18 September Premier Edouard Daladier, who was visiting England as head of a French delegation, agreed with Chamberlain that 'friendly pressure' might persuade the Czechs to surrender some portions of Sudeten territory to Germany.[17]

Czech President Beneš, having been informed of the Anglo-French decision, was now assured by Moscow that the Soviets would support Czechoslovakia in the event of an attack by Hitler. Despite this however, Beneš received an ultimatum from Foreign Secretary Lord Halifax, to the effect that he must accept the proposal, 'without reserve and without further delay, failing which His Majesty's Government will take no further interest in the fate of the country [i.e. Czechoslovakia]'.[18] Benes therefore had no choice but to agree.

On 21 September 1938 Chamberlain again left for Germany, this time to meet Hitler at Bad Godesberg on the Rhine. To Chamberlain's surprise however, Hitler told him 'I am exceedingly sorry Mr Chamberlain, but I can no longer discuss these matters. This solution [to the Sudeten question], after the developments of the last few days, is no longer practicable.' He then demanded that the British and French accept forthwith his proposal to occupy the Sudetenland.[19] On the 23rd Hitler upped the anti, by demanding the withdrawal of all Czech forces and the ceding of the Sudetenland to Germany; this to take place within the space of five days! The Czechs responded by mobilising 1 million men, and the French themselves mobilised in support of the Czechs.

Chamberlain had refused Hitler's request that he, President Benes, be presented with a document stating these fresh Nazi demands. To please Chamberlain however, Hitler would make a small concession and, 'agree to 1 October as the date for evacuation'.[20] Chamberlain now flew back to England to discuss matters with his Cabinet. 'Herr Hitler,' he said, 'would not deliberately deceive a man [i.e. Chamberlain] whom he respected and with whom he had been in negotiation.' It would therefore be a tragedy if, 'the opportunity of reaching an understanding with Germany on all points of difference between the two countries' were to be lost.

When the French delegation arrived back in England its leader, Deladier, declared that France did not recognise Hitler's right to seize the Sudetenland. By this time France had already ordered a partial mobilisation of forces.

Chamberlain now decided to write Hitler a personal letter, suggesting that a joint commission be appointed to determine how the proposals already accepted by the Czechs were to be put into effect. 'If the letter fails to secure any response from Herr Hitler,' said Chamberlain, 'then Sir Horace Wilson [Chamberlain's confidential advisor] should be authorised to give a personal message from me to the effect that, if this appeal was refused France would go to war, and if that happened, it seemed certain that we should be drawn in.'[21]

When Sir Horace duly presented Hitler with Chamberlain's letter, the Führer flew into a rage. 'He now holds the decision in his hand,' said Hitler, in reference to Benes. 'Peace or war! Either he will now accept this offer and at last give Germans their freedom, or we will take this freedom for ourselves!'[22]

In a press statement, Chamberlain said that Britain's guarantee that the Czechs keep their promise to evacuate the Sudetenland was conditional on the Germans abstaining from the use of force. However, as Sir Horace told Hitler (through a translator), 'If France, in fulfilment of her treaty obligations, should become actively involved in hostilities against Germany, the United Kingdom would deem itself obliged to support France.'[23] As for Mussolini, he declared that although fascist Italy stood behind Hitler, nevertheless he was, 'of the opinion that it would be wise to accept the British proposal, and begs you [Hitler] to refrain from mobilisation'.[24]

Hitler responded by inviting Chamberlain, Mussolini and Deladier to München for a meeting which took place on 29 September 1938. When Chamberlain enquired as to how the Czechs were to be compensated for losing their property in the Sudetenland, Hitler said angrily: 'Our time is too valuable to be wasted on such trivialities!'[25] At 1.30 the following morning, it was formally agreed that the evacuation of the Sudetenland by the Czechs would begin on 1 October. As for the Czech representatives, they had not been included in the discussions during which the fate of their country was being decided.

Chamberlain returned to England where, to cheering crowds outside No. 10 Downing Street, he said: 'Here is a piece of paper which bears his [i.e. Hitler's] name upon it as well as mine. I believe it is peace in our time.'[26] At this, there was wild applause.

Shortly afterwards, according to Manfred von Schroeder (German diplomat and Nazi party member 1933–45), Hitler was heard to say, 'They have cheated me out of my war.'[27] This was confirmed by Schact who later reported Hitler as saying: 'That damned Chamberlain had spoiled my parade into Prague.'[28] After this so-called 'München Agreement', Czech President Eduard Beneš resigned and went into exile. He was replaced by General Jan Syrovy.

On 1 October 1938 German forces duly moved into the Sudetenland and within twenty-four hours, Hitler himself was paying a triumphant visit to the Czech capital. The region would supply ample quantities of 'brown' coal from which Hitler was able to produce synthetic petrol for his air force and motorised armies.

On 21 January 1939 Hitler increased his pressure on Czechoslovakia when he informed that country's Foreign Minister, Frantisek Chvalkovsky, that Germany would not give guarantees to a state which did not eliminate its Jews.[29] In February 1939 Goebbels launched a propaganda campaign against the Czechs, declaring that ethnic German citizens were being terrorised, and that Czech troops were massing along the Sudeten border. In an all too familiar scenario, Slovak nationalists now demanded their independence.

On 9 March 1939 British Ambassador to Germany, Sir Nevile Henderson, showed just how much he had been taken in by Hitler when, in a letter to Halifax, he said:

Hitler himself fought in the [First] World War, and his dislike of bloodshed, or anyway of dead Germans, is intense. I can find no justification for the theory that he is mad, or even verging on madness. I am of the opinion that he is not thinking today in terms of war.[30]

That evening Emil Hacha, the new President of Czechoslovakia, gave Hitler the excuse he was waiting for by dismissing the Slovak government, ordering his troops to prepare to move into that region, and declaring martial law. Meanwhile, Stalin was telling his Eighteenth Party Congress that although his country was an ally of Czechoslovakia, their Soviet–Czech Mutual Assistance Pact, signed in 1935, required them to act against Germany only after France had intervened against Germany first.

Hitler now increased his campaign of intimidation when, accompanied by five German generals, he crossed the Danube river and disrupted a meeting of the Slovak cabinet, at their regional capital Bratislava, and ordered it to proclaim the independence of Slovakia. It was in the interest of the Nazis to detach Slovakia (eastern Czechoslovakia) from Prague, with a view to using that region as a base for operations against the Soviets.

Karol Sidor (named by Hacha as the new premier of the autonomous Slovak government, in place of Josef Tiso) declared that before doing so, he would first have to discuss the situation with the government in Prague. Tiso was now invited to meet Hitler in Berlin, where on 13 March Hitler announced: 'Tomorrow at midday, I shall begin military action against the Czechs .... Germany does not intend to take Slovakia into her "Lebensraum", and that is why you must either immediately proclaim the independence of Slovakia, or I will disinterest myself in her fate.'[31] In the face of this bullying, the Slovakian parliament was forced to accept a declaration of independence (drafted by Ribbentrop), whereby a new Slovakia came into existence.

On 14 March 1939 the ageing Czechoslovakian President Hacha was invited to Berlin for talks. Having kept Hacha waiting until 1.15 a.m., Hitler informed him that his country would now be invaded by German troops. The order for Czechoslovakia to be incorporated into the Third Reich had already been given, and the army would enter Czechoslovakia at 6 a.m. on 15 March. Hacha was now asked to sign a document which placed the fate of the Czech people in the hands of the Führer. In the event of a refusal, Hitler envisaged the annihilation of Czechoslovakia whose capital, Prague, would be destroyed by bombing within a few hours. Hacha had no choice but to sign.

Tiso now sent a telegram to Berlin proclaiming Slovak independence and requesting German protection. Hitler's troops duly moved into Slovakia to guarantee its newly won independence. The province of Ruthenia however, being of no interest to the Nazis, was ceded to Hungary (whom Hitler wished to appease). On 16 March 1939 Hitler, now in Prague, laid claim to the Czech provinces of Bohemia and Moravia which became a Reich protectorate. The Nazi occupation of Czechoslovakia was complete.

Meanwhile, back in Britain the patience of Prime Minister Chamberlain had run out. It would be a great mistake, he said, for Germany to suppose that Great Britain, 'had so lost its fibre that it would not take part to the uttermost of its power in resisting such a challenge [i.e. an invasion of Poland], if it were made'. Hitler had unilaterally broken the München Agreement. He was, therefore, not to be trusted; there would be no more appeasement.

On 31 March 1939 Britain together with France, gave military guarantees to Poland, Romania, Greece and Turkey, and initiated political and military talks with the USSR.

Poland

Following World War I, the Allies, with the aim of weakening any future German aggressive potential, had allowed the Poles to incorporate the larger portion of the German territories of West Prussia and Posen into their country. Also, in order to give Poland access to a seaport, namely Danzig (a city populated almost entirely by Germans), the Allies had sanctioned the establishment of the so-called 'Polish Corridor'. On 25 January 1932 Poland signed a treaty of non-aggression with the Soviet Union. On 26 January 1934 Hitler, in his typically disingenuous way, signed a ten-year non-aggression pact with Poland.

Following the München Agreement of September 1938 however, Germany requested that Danzig be returned to her, and that Germany be permitted her own corridor – to link East Prussia with the larger part of the Reich. In return, the Poles would be allowed to use Danzig as a free port and their existing borders would be guaranteed.

In the spring of 1939 the Nazis reverted to their usual tactics of accusing the Poles of persecuting the German minority in that country. In other words, blaming the victims of the aggression for the aggression itself. Polish Foreign Minister Colonel Josef Beck now warned the Germans that any action which 'clearly threatens Polish independence' would be resisted.

On 31 March 1939 Chamberlain gave an undertaking to Poland that if its independence was threatened then, 'His Majesty's [i.e. King George VI's] and the French government would at once lend them [the Poles] all the support in their power', and in a speech to the House of Commons he warned Hitler: 'If an attempt were made to change the situation by force in such a way as to threaten Polish independence, why then that would inevitably start a general conflagration in which this country would be involved.'[32] A fortnight later, similar guarantees were given to Romania and Greece.

On 3 April 1939 Hitler issued his senior commanders with a 'Most Secret' war directive: 'Since the situation on Germany's eastern frontier has become intolerable, and all political possibilities of peaceful settlement have been exhausted, I have decided upon a solution by force.' On 28 April Hitler declared that the 1932 Polish–German Non-aggression Pact was to be cancelled, since it had been, 'unilaterally infringed' by the Poles.

Time and again, Hitler indicated that he had no quarrel with England. For example: when Romania's Foreign Minister called on him at the Reich Chancellery on 19 April 1939 Hitler warned that a war with England would be one of 'unimaginable destructiveness' and asked, 'How could the English picture a modern war, when they can't even put two fully equipped divisions in [to] the field?'[33]

On 23 August 1939 German Foreign Minister Ribbentrop was in Moscow signing the 'Nazi-Soviet Pact' with Soviet Commissar for Foreign Affairs, Vyacheslav Molotov. The pact declared that each would observe a benevolent neutrality towards the other in the event of either one being attacked. In this way, Hitler hoped he would avoid having to fight a future war on two fronts. The pact contained a secret protocol, whereby the two countries agreed that in the event of war between

Germany and Poland, then Finland, the Baltic States and Bessarabia would fall within the Russian sphere of influence. It was also agreed that Soviet leader Josef Stalin would have a share in the spoils once Hitler had invaded Poland, which was his intention. However, in retrospect it is clear that Hitler's objective was to lull the Soviets into a false sense of security prior to his invasion of their country.

At the time the pact was being signed in Moscow, Hitler was standing on the terrace of the Berghof staring out at the mountains. A Hungarian woman member of his entourage said to him: 'My Führer, this augers nothing good. It means blood, blood, blood and again blood. Destruction and terrible suffering, blood and again blood', to which Hitler replied, 'If it has to be, then let it be now.'[34]

***

In order to make the Poles appear responsible for the German invasion, Hitler arranged for German SD ('Sicherheitsdienst' – 'Security Service') elements, disguised as Polish soldiers, to create disturbances in the border areas the night before the invasion. To prove that a skirmish had taken place, bodies would be scattered on the ground, but unbeknown to the outside world, these bodies were not those of Germans or Poles; they were those of the murdered inmates of concentration camps.

On 1 September 1939 Hitler declared: 'Last night Poland opened fire on our own territory using regular army troops for the first time. Since 5.45 a.m., we have been returning fire.'[35] The Nazis now invaded Poland – a country rich in coal and agricultural products – with a force of 1.25 million men. [*Just prior to this, the hypocritical Hitler had sent Ribbentrop to Warsaw to lay a wreath in memory of the dead of the First World War, and to reassure the Poles that there would be no attack.*] Two days later, Britain and France declared war on Germany.

***

Meanwhile, Hitler could derive encouragement from the success which the nationalist insurgents were having against the incumbent Spanish Republican regime. On 28 March 1939 Spain's capital city Madrid fell to the Nationalist forces of General Franco. The Spanish Civil War had given Hitler the opportunity to test his military equipment and to improve his military capabilities. This he would have seen as a dress rehearsal for what was shortly to come.

To Hitler's satisfaction, Franco now established a fascist dictatorship in Spain, replacing approximately 50,000 school teachers with 'Falangists' (a Spanish fascist group), whose job it would be to inculcate in their pupils the values that, 'will create the new empire which the people want'.

Under the Franco regime, Spanish children were taught how Spain had seven enemies, namely: liberalism, democracy, Judaism, masonry, Marxism, capitalism and separatism, which had all been 'defeated in the Great Crusade, although not annihilated. They hide like venomous insects, continuing to poison the air from the shadows.'

From newly revised text books, the children also learned that, 'Jews drank Christian blood' and were, 'spies, political conspirators who lived in secret friendship with the Moors,' and that human liberty leads to anarchy. [36]

NOTES

1. Hitler, Adolf, *Mein Kampf*, p. 82.
2. Ibid, p. 83.
3. Mills, Wallace G, Hist. 203, 16, *Fascism Part II*. http://husky1.stmarys.ca/-mills/course203/16_Fascism_2.html.
4. Toland, John, *Adolf Hitler*, p. 353.
5. Ibid, p. 421.
6. Ibid, p. 434.
7. Ibid, p. 437.
8. Ibid, p. 443.
9. Ibid, p. 450.
10. Ibid, p. 453.
11. Bloch, Dr Eduard, *My Patient Hitler*, Vol. 1, 15 March, pp. 11, 35–9; and 22 March, pp. 69–73.
12. Ibid. p. 72.
13. *Hitler: a Profile: The Betrayer.*
14. *Hitler: a Profile: The Blackmailer.*
15. Toland, op. cit.,p. 464.
16. Ibid, p. 473.
17. Ibid, p. 476.
18. Ibid, p. 477.
19. Ibid, p. 479.
20. Ibid, p. 482.
21. Ibid, p. 483.
22. Ibid, p. 484.
23 Ibid, p. 485.
24. Ibid, p. 487.
25. Ibid, p. 490.
26. *Churchill, Part.1. Renegade and Turncoat.*
27. *The Nazis: A Warning from History, Part.1.*
28. Fest, Joachim, *Hitler*, p. 840.
29. Toland, op. cit., p. 510.
30. Ibid, p. 513.
31. Ibid, p. 514.
32. *Hitler's Henchmen: Ribbentrop, the Puppet.*
33. Toland, op. cit., p. 527.
34. *The Nazis: A Warning from History, Part 3.*
35. *Hitler: a Profile: The Seducer.*
36. Foca Ediciones. *La Historia Que Nos Ensenaron, 1937–1975. (The History They Taught Us, 1937–1975.)*

CHAPTER XXIII

The Origins of Communism

According to Hitler in *Mein Kampf*, it was during his time in Vienna (1907–13) that he said he realised the, 'terrible significance for the existence of the German people' of 'Marxism and Judaism'.[1]

However, it is more likely that it was Lanz von Liebenfels who was the source of Hitler's ideas, and that statements by Hitler such as: 'Bolshevism is the mortal enemy of the National Socialist German people. Germany must fight this corrupt world view. This struggle demands ruthless and energetic action against Bolshevik rabble rousers, irregulars, saboteurs, Jews, and the complete removal of all active and passive resistance,' were simply an example of the Führer mimicking what he had read in Liebenfels' journal *Ostara*. Nevertheless, Hitler added his own particular brand of hatred to the mix. He declared:

> The originators of barbaric Asiatic methods of fighting are the political commissars: thus action must be taken against them at once and with the utmost ferocity. Therefore, if they are captured in battle or in resistance they are in principle to be shot immediately.[2]

The Führer promised that whoever [of his service personnel] broke the law in this pursuit would not be punished, even if their [mis] deeds were military crimes or offences.[3]

***

Hitler was shortly to embark on militaristic adventures which would cost the world somewhere in excess of 35 million lives. It is therefore pertinent to enquire whether or not his portrayal of the Jews and the Bolsheviks had any basis in fact.

In order to establish the credibility of Hitler as a witness, the first question to be asked is: was Soviet Russia a real and potent threat to Germany as he claimed, not in the 1910s, 1920s or 1930s, but prior to his invasion of that country in June 1941 in 'Operation Barbarossa'? Or was this merely a smokescreen used by Hitler for turning the Slavs into slaves, and implementing his policy of 'Lebensraum'

– the acquisition of more living space for the German people? *In order to discover the truth of the matter, it is necessary to return to the time of the tsars, and thereby discover how Soviet Russia came into existence. One thing is certain: revolution in Russia was in the air long before Marxism was even invented.*

***

Prior to World War I (1914–18), discontent had been brewing in tsarist Russia for almost a century. The intensity of this discontent is reflected in a poem written by the great Russian poet Alexander Pushkin (1799–1837), who predicted that the, 'heavy chains will fall, the dungeons crumble at a word, and freedom will greet you at the gate, and brothers will give you back the sword.'[4]

The typical tsarist state, 'was characterised by the personification in the ruler of a semi-sacrosanct authority, unlimited by clear legal checks, by an emphasis on the service owed to him by all subjects ... by the idea that all institutions within the state [except the Church] derived from it and had no independent standing of their own ..., and [by] the development of a huge bureaucracy ....'[5]

On 14 December 1825 the day that Tsar Nicholas I took power, there was a rebellion by the so-called 'Decemberists' who demanded a constitution for Russia. After all, the French Revolution had occurred no less than thirty-six years earlier, with the creation of progressive social, political and economic measures, the 'Declaration of Rights of Man and Citizen', and the setting up of a constitutional government. So why should this not happen in Russia? Alas, it was not to be; the 'Decemberist' ring leaders were hanged and their supporters were exiled to Siberia.

A glimmer of light appeared when, in 1848, popular revolutions spread throughout Europe, during the course of which the Austrian Emperor Ferdinand I abdicated in favour of his son, Franz Joseph. However, hopes were quickly dashed when the Russians moved to restore the Hapsburgs to power.

In 1853 the forces of Tsar Nicholas I attacked Turkey's Black Sea ports, provoking Britain and France to oppose Russia in the Crimean War (1854–6) – the Russian imperial forces were defeated.

Hopes were again raised in 1855 when Nicholas I died and his son Alexander II became tsar. Alexander understood the need for change in Russia, a country left behind by the Industrial Revolution which had occurred in the West. Amongst his forward-looking actions were: to relax censorship, pardon the Decemberists, institute trial by jury, and commence the construction of a rail network.

According to the official *History of the Communist Party*,[6] prior to the 1860s, 'Manorial estates based on serfdom constituted the prevailing form of economy.' However because, 'The involuntary [i.e. forced] labour of the serfs in agriculture was of low productivity' therefore, 'the whole course of economic development made the abolition of serfdom imperative.'

***

In March 1861 Alexander II moved to remedy the situation by granting emancipation to the serfs who he declared, 'would receive in time the full rights of free rural inhabitants'. However, because of the extortionate price that the serfs were subsequently charged by the landowners for their land, they were now worse off than they had been before. As agricultural production plummeted, there were fresh demands by radicals for elections and the free distribution of land. Finally in that year, the tsarist government, 'weakened by defeat in the Crimean War, and frightened by the peasant revolts against the landlords, was compelled to abolish serfdom.'[7]

But for the serfs this was not the end of their troubles because, '... even after serfdom had been abolished, the landlords continued their oppression' by 'inclosing' that is, 'cutting off considerable portions of land previously used by the serfs' who were now, 'compelled to pay about 2,000,000,000 roubles to the landlords as the redemption price for their "emancipation".'[8] Moreover, the peasant was, 'obliged to rent land from the landlords on [the] most onerous terms...;' was, 'often compelled by the landlord to cultivate without remuneration a definite portion of his land with their own implements and horses ...;' and in most cases was, 'obliged to pay the landlord rent in kind in the amount of one-half of their harvests'.[9]

According to the 1879 census of population, about five-sixths of the total population were (then) engaged in agriculture. However, 'The landlords bled the backward peasants white by various methods of extortion (rent, fines),' as a result of which, '... the bulk of the peasantry were unable to improve their farms. Hence the extreme backwardness in agriculture in pre-revolutionary Russia, which led to frequent crop failures and famine.'

Having been thus reduced to 'pauperism', the peasants were forced, 'to quit their villages' and seek work in the mills and factories. To make matters worse,

> Over the workers and peasants stood a veritable army of sheriffs, deputy sheriffs, gendarmes, constables, [and] rural police, who protected the tsar, the capitalists and the landlords from the toiling and exploited people. Corporal punishment existed right up until 1903 [and] the peasants were flogged for the slightest offence and for the non-payment of taxes.[10]

On 1 March 1881 revolutionaries expressed their discontent when they succeeded, after several attempts,in assassinating Tsar Alexander II, even though he had shown some flexibility in proposing a new legislative council in which he would share power with the people.

However, the accession of Alexander II's son, Alexander III, served only to bring about a new round of oppression. The Jews were held responsible for the death of the tsar, and the so-called 'Pale' (the land of Russia in which they were confined to live) was now restricted to what had been Eastern Poland, plus part of south-west Russia.

With the abolition of serfdom, the industrialisation of Russia proceeded swiftly and, 'During the 20–25 years 1865–90, the number of workers employed in large mills and factories, and on the railways doubled from 706,000 to 1,433,000.'[11] However, 'progress' came at a price for, '... the working day in the mills and factories was not less that 12.5 hours, and in the textile industry reached 14–15 hours .... Wages were inordinately low .... Housing conditions were appalling.'[12] Therefore, the plight of those working people who had migrated to Russia's emerging industrial cities was just as miserable in its way as it had been in the countryside.

Strikes by the workers, in this and in the preceding decade, 'were usually provoked by excessive fines, cheating and swindling of the workers [by their employers] over wages, and reductions in the rates of pay .... The more advanced workers began to realise that if they were to be successful in their struggle against the capitalists, they needed organisation.'[13] To this end, the South Russian Workers' Union was formed in Odessa in 1875 and in 1878 the Northern Union of Russian Workers was formed in St Petersburg.

In 1887, after an attempt on Tsar Alexander III's life, one of the would-be assassins, Alexander Ilyich Ulyanov, was hanged. This was to have profound repercussions, because Alexander's brother, Vladimir, also a radical (whose revolutionary 'nom de guerre' was 'Lenin') would soon be instrumental in changing the face of that entire continent.

Although the revolution would not come for another four decades, the impetus for it would be provided by Karl Marx.

***

Karl Marx (1818–83)

Born in Trier in Germany in 1818, Karl Marx was the son of a lawyer, and the grandson of a Jewish rabbi named Mordeccai. Having studied history and philosophy at the universities of Bonn and Berlin, he was influenced initially in his political beliefs by a Communist-Zionist named Moses Hess, founder and editor of the newspaper *Die Rheinische Zeitung*, which was the main vehicle of leftist thought in Germany.

In 1843 Marx and his wife Jenny moved to Paris, where the following year he met German philosopher Friedrich Engels (whom Moses Hess had previously converted to communism). Engels was the son of a wealthy textiles magnate who was later to subsidise Marx from the profits from his factories in Britain and Germany. In 1845 Marx removed to Brussels, having been expelled from France for his political activities.

In 1848 Marx returned to Germany with Engels, and took part in the unsuccessful revolutionary uprisings in the Rhineland. This was the year in which he would write his famous *Communist Manifesto*. In it, Marx declared:

The proletariat [poorest labouring class], during its contest with the bourgeoisie [middle class], is compelled by the force of circumstances, to organise itself as a class… by means of a revolution, it makes itself the ruling class, and, as such, sweeps away by force the old conditions of production.[14]

The proletariat will use its political supremacy to wrest, by degrees, all capital from the bourgeoisie, to centralise all instruments of production in the hands of the state, i.e., of the proletariat organised as the ruling class; and to increase the total of productive forces as rapidly as possible.[15]

After the Paris revolution of 1848 (which established the Second Republic), Marx transferred to Köln to resume editorship of *Die Rheinische Zeitung*, but when the newspaper closed the following year, he moved to London (where he would remain for the rest of his life).

Marx was a leading figure in the creation in London in 1864 of the 'First International' (an abbreviation for 'International Working Men's Association'), whose objective was to promote international cooperation between socialist, communist and revolutionary groups.

In 1867 Volume 1 of Marx's magnum opus, *Das Kapital*, was published. As for Engels, he would devote the remainder of his life to editing and translating the works of Marx (including Volumes 2 and 3 of *Das Kapital* published in 1885 and 1894 respectively, after his death). The volumes were 'printed abroad, and circulated … secretly in Russia.'[16]

Marx died in London in March 1883 and is buried in Highgate cemetery. In the same year, the first Russian Marxist organisation, the 'Emancipation of Labour' group, was created in Geneva by G V Plekhanov who, 'had been obliged to take refuge from the persecution of the tsarist government for his revolutionary activities.'[17]

***

There is no doubt that Karl Marx saw the replacement of the 'bourgeoisie' by 'a new, classless, communist society' as being applicable to all countries, and not just Russia. Hence the statement with which he ended his *Communist Manifesto* of 1848: 'The workers have nothing to lose but their chains. They have a world to win. Workers of all lands, unite!'

So Hitler was correct in believing that Communism, as advocated by Karl Marx, was a philosophy which knew no boundaries; that it was Marx's vision that communist regimes should replace those of the capitalists wherever they were to be found, and by force if necessary.

The question now was, would 'International Communism' advance or recede as the new century dawned? The answer would lie in the hands of the person to whom the baton of Marxism would now pass: a man some fifty-two years younger than Marx, namely Vladimir Ilyich Ulyanov, otherwise known as Lenin.

Notes

1. Hitler, Adolf, *Mein Kampf*, p. 22.
2. **Hitler: a Profile: The Commander.*
3. Ibid.
4. **Russia: Land of the Tsars.*
5. Roberts, J M, *History of the World*. BCA. 1992. London. p. 490.
6. Commission of the C.C. of the CPSU (B) (ed.) *History of the Communist Party of the Soviet Union: Bolsheviks*, p. 3.
7. Ibid.
8. Ibid.
9. Ibid.
10. Ibid, p.4.
11. Ibid, p. 5.
12. Ibid, p. 6.
13. Ibid, p. 7.
14, 15. Marx, Karl, *The Communist Manifesto: Selected Works*, Eng. edn., vol. 1, pp. 227–8.
16. Commission of the C.C. of the CPSU, op. cit., p. 9.
17. Ibid, p. 8.

CHAPTER XXIV

Lenin and the Revolution

Vladimir Ilyich Ulyanov (known as Lenin) was born in 1870 into a middle-class family in Simbirsk in Russia. His father was a provincial school superintendent; his mother was the daughter of a doctor. Having graduated from Kazan University, he practised as a lawyer from 1892 in Kuybyshev in southern Russia. It was Lenin who, using the teachings of Marx, would provide the impetus for the Russian Revolution.

In the 1890s railroad construction in Russia continued apace, fuelling the demand for metal, coal and oil, with the result that a so-called 'modern industrial proletariat' of '2,792,000 persons' was created.[1] Nevertheless, '... as in all capitalist countries, periods of industrial boom alternated with industrial crisis and stagnation which severely affected the working class, and condemned hundreds of thousands of workers to unemployment and poverty'.[2] In 1894 Tsar Alexander III died and was succeeded by his son Nicholas II.

In that year, Lenin moved to St Petersburg (renamed Leningrad in 1924), where he organised the illegal and revolutionary 'Union for the Liberation of the Working Class', and wrote a book entitled *What the Friends of the People are*. In it, 'for the first time' he, 'advanced the idea of a revolutionary alliance of the workers and peasants as the principal means of overthrowing tsardom, the landlords, and the bourgeoisie'.[3] To this end, between 1894 and 1900 Marxist organisations were created in Moscow, Siberia and Transcaucasia[4] and, 'in October 1897, the Jewish General Social Democratic Union – known as the "Bund" – was founded in the western provinces of Russia'.[5]

In 1895 Lenin, '... united all the Marxist workers' circles in St Petersburg [there were already about twenty of them] into a single "League of Struggle for the Emancipation of the Working Class"', and thus, 'prepared the way for the founding of a revolutionary Marxist workers' party'.[6] The aims of the League were: 'improvement of working conditions, shorter hours and higher wages – with the political struggle against tsardom.'[7]

In November 1895 Lenin wrote a leaflet aimed at fomenting political agitation amongst 500 striking textile workers at a factory in St Petersburg. The secret police now clamped down on clandestine cells in the country, and the following month, Lenin was arrested by the tsarist government and exiled to Siberia for three years, along with fellow revolutionary Nadezhda Krupskaya, whom he subsequently married. He then fled to the West.

In 1898 'several of the "Leagues of Struggle"... together with the "Bund"... summoned the First Congress of the Russian Social Democratic Labour Party (RSDLP), which was held in Minsk in March 1898'. Nine persons were in attendance, but Lenin was not one of them. He was still living in exile in Siberia. Shortly afterwards, members of the Central Committee of the Party, who had been elected at the Congress, were arrested.[8]

On 19 January 1900 Lenin was moved from Siberia to complete his exile in Pskov, 170 miles from St Petersburg. His wife, Nadezhda, remained behind to serve out the remainder of her sentence.

On his release in the same year, Lenin moved to neutral Switzerland where, with Russian revolutionary and Marxist philosopher Georgi Plekhanov, he created an underground Social Democratic Party, the aim of which was to fan the flames of revolution and lead the working classes in a revolution against Tsar Nicholas II. Lenin also edited the political revolutionary newspaper *Iskra* (*The Spark*). In August 1900 Lenin and his wife moved to München in southern Germany, a place chosen for its ease of communication with the main industrial centres of Russia.

In 1903 in a pamphlet entitled *To the Village Poor*, Lenin pointed out how disadvantaged the peasants were as compared to the 'kulaks' (wealthy peasants). He said:

> Of the 10 million or so households in Russia, no less than 3.5 million contained peasants possessing no horses. On the other hand, 1.5 rich kulak households concentrated in their hands half the total sown area of the peasants. This peasant bourgeoisie was growing rich by grinding down the poor and middle peasantry, and profiting from the toil of agricultural labourers, and was developing into rural capitalists.[9] [Therefore] Far from growing as a class, the peasantry was splitting up more and more into bourgeois (kulaks) and poor peasants (proletarians and semi-proletarians).[10]

In February 1904 Russia became involved in another disastrous war, this time with Japan. It culminated in May 1905 with the destruction by the Japanese of two thirds of Tsar Nicholas' fleet of three hundred ships. Confidence in the tsar was at an all time low, and the capital, St Petersburg, was now in open revolt. That winter saw soaring inflation with hunger and hardship.

When, on 22 January 1905, striking demonstrators marched to the tsar's winter palace demanding a representative government, workers' rights and peace with Japan, there was a massacre in which some 500 people were shot and many injured, despite the demonstration being a peaceful one.

That summer saw strikes and mutinies by the armed services, forcing Nicholas to sign (reluctantly) the 'October Manifesto', granting his people basic civil rights and a new, elected assembly – the 'Dumas'. When, in May 1906, the 'Dumas' demanded more radical reform however, Nicholas responded by dissolving it. Four years passed before it was reinstated.

In 1907 Lenin relocated to Finland, a country subject to Russian imperial control since 1809 and which, in consequence, detested tsarism. By now he had decided that when the time came, councils of workers, soldiers and peasants – known as 'soviets' – were to be the organisers of total revolution.

The year 1912 found Lenin in Poland in the company of sympathetic Marxist revolutionaries led by Polish Jew Rosa Luxemburg and Leo Jogiches. The following year, there were celebrations to mark 300 years of Romanov rule in Russia, making this the longest serving dynasty in Europe.

In the summer of 1914, following a dispute between Austro-Hungary and Serbia (an ally of Russia), the Russian empire clashed with both the German and with the Austro-Hungarian empires. This temporarily united the Russian people – 15 million of whom now fought for their country in World War I, with over half of that number being killed, wounded or captured within the next two and a half years. With the advance of the Russian imperial armies, Lenin was obliged to leave Poland and return to Switzerland. In the summer of 1915 Tsar Nicholas left the capital to lead his troops from the Front.

By early 1917 inflation had made the Russian rouble all but worthless, and there were food queues and starvation. On 23 February there were riots – the so-called February revolution (March by the Western calendar) – and regiments of the army mutinied. By now, Nicholas had lost the support of army, police and educated society.

The tsar now received an ultimatum from the 'Dumas' demanding that he abdicate and hand over all power, which he did on 16 March. One month later Lenin, after twenty years in exile, returned home to Russia from Zürich. Now the First Provisional Government was established under Russian politician Prince Georgi Lvov, but he was replaced in July by Russian revolutionary leader Aleksandr Kerensky.

Lenin's Bolshevik Party took the view that, '... as long as the power was in the hands of the bourgeois Provisional Government [i.e. that of Kerensky], and as long as the soviets were dominated by the compromisers – the Mensheviks and Social Revolutionaries – the people would secure neither peace, nor land, nor bread ...'.[11]

However, in July 1917 a Bolshevik uprising was crushed by Kerensky, who was persuaded by the western powers to continue the war with Germany. Further defeats only led to more unrest.

***

Lenin was careful not to advertise the fact that his revolutionary activities were financed substantially by capitalists, a group which he affected to despise.

An article entitled *America's Unknown Enemy: Beyond Conspiracy* by the editorial staff of the American Institute for Economic Research (2004) concluded that, 'corroborating evidence from a variety of sources' indicates, that Wall Street bankers helped to finance the Bolshevik Revolution.

It points to author Antony C Sutton's account of how,

Jacob Schiff – son of a rabbi, former manager of the Deutsche Bank in Hamburg, and senior partner in the firm Kuhn, Loeb and Company of New York [Abraham Kuhn and Solomon Loeb being German émigré Jews who had come to New York in the 1850s] provided an approximately 20 million dollar loan to the Bolsheviks. Sutton also offers documentation showing that a consortium of banking interests including inter alia: the Morgan Group [i.e. 'J P Morgan', founded by John Pierpont Morgan with huge interests in steel production and railroads] and the Rockefeller-Standard Oil Group [the Standard Oil Co. was founded by John D Rockefeller and his brother William in 1870], were involved in providing financial support for the new (Bolshevik) regime.

Paul Moritz Warburg and his brother Felix (of the banking house M M Warburg and Co. of Frankfurt, Hamburg and Amsterdam) came to the USA from Frankfurt in 1902 and bought into the partnership of Kuhn Loeb and Co. (In fact, Paul married Solomon Loeb's daughter Nina, and Felix married Jacob Schiff's daughter Frieda.) Paul's and Felix's older brother Max was Chief Intelligence Officer in Germany's Secret Service, and also ran the Hamburg bank (until 1938 when the Nazis took it over). According to author Gary Allen, Lenin, 'took some 5 to 6 million dollars in gold' into Russia through a deal, 'arranged by the German High Command and Max Warburg'.[12]

According to the Institute, however, 'such financial deals are not necessarily evidence that the bankers were communists, or even that they wanted the Bolsheviks to triumph'. So what were the motives of the Jewish-American bankers who supported the Bolshevik Revolution? Was it, 'In the hope that such aid might contribute to the emancipation of Russian Jewry?' Also that, 'As Jews [i.e. Jewish-American bankers] they might get preferential treatment should Jewish bankers attain positions of influence in the new [post-revolutionary] regime.'

Another advantage for the Jewish-American bankers was, as Antony Sutton points out, 'The totalitarian, socialist state is a perfect captive market for monopoly capitalists, if an alliance can be made with the socialist power brokers [of that state].'[13]

However, this support for the Bolsheviks was by no means an exclusively Jewish phenomenon, since international American bankers John D Rockefeller and J P Morgan, neither of whom was a Jew, were also conducting business with that regime.[14]

***

The night of 25 October 1917 (7 November by the western calendar) proved to be a turning point in the history of Russia when, 'revolutionary workers, soldiers and sailors took St Petersburg's Winter Palace by storm and arrested the Provisional Government [which had taken refuge there]'.[15] When the Second

All-Russian Congress of Soviets opened that same evening, 'The Bolsheviks secured an overwhelming majority ... the Mensheviks [anti-tsar, pro-middle class, liberal reformists], Bundists, and Right Socialist Revolutionaries, seeing that their day was done, left the Congress, announcing that they refused to take any part in its labours.'[16] For Lenin, the first step had been taken towards the fulfilment of Karl Marx's dream – in Russia, at any rate.

***

Without question, Lenin wished to expand Soviet influence even further: 'Without a world revolution,' he said, 'we will not pull through.'[17]

Lenin's intentions were not to go unnoticed. In a January 1918 dispatch to Washington, David R Francis, United States Ambassador to Russia, warned, 'The Bolshevik leaders here [i.e. in Russia], most of whom are Jews, and 90% of whom are returned exiles, care little for Russia or any other country, but are internationalists and they are trying to start a worldwide social[ist] revolution.'[18]

In the same year Mr Oudendyke, Dutch Consul in St Petersburg, reported,

> I consider that the immediate suppression of Bolshevism is the greatest issue now before the world, not even excluding the war which is still raging, and unless Bolshevism is nipped in the bud, it is bound to spread in one form or another over Europe and the whole world, as it is organised and worked by Jews who have no nationality, and whose one object is to destroy for their own ends the existing order of things.[19]

However, whatever Lenin's dreams for the 'internationalisation' of communism may have been after the Russian Revolution, they were soon to be tempered with harsh reality.

Notes

1. Commission of the C.C. of the CPSU (B) (ed.) History *of the Communist Party of the Soviet Union: Bolsheviks*, p. 5.
2. Ibid.
3. Ibid, p. 20.
4. Ibid, p. 18.
5. Ibid, p. 21.
6. Ibid, p. 16.
7. Ibid, p. 17.
8. Ibid, p. 20–1.
9. Ibid, p. 6.
10. Ibid, p. 13.

11. Ibid, p. 130.
12. Rivera, David, *The Federal Reserve Act: Final Warning: A History of the New World Order*. www.viewfromthethewall.com.
13. *America's Unknown Enemy: Beyond Conspiracy*. www.cooperativeindividualism.org/aier_on_conspiracy_05.html. 27/7/04.
14. Sutton, Antony C, *Wall Street and the Bolshevik Revolution*, pp. 194–5.
15. Commission of the C.C. of the CPSU, op. cit. p. 208.
16. Ibid, pp. 208–9.
17. Uldricks, T J, Russia and Europe: 'Diplomacy, Revolution and Economic Development in the 1920s', *International History Review*, 1, 1979, p. 58.
18. 'The Jewish Role in the Bolshevik Revolution and Russia's Early Soviet Regime'. [This essay appeared in the Jan-Feb. 1994 issue of the *Journal of Historical Review*, published by the Institute for Historical Review.] www.ihr.org/jhr/v14/v14n1p-4Weber.html.
19. *Bolshevism*, British Government White Paper on, issued April 1919. Russian, No. 1.

CHAPTER XXV

The Role of the Jews

Hitler described Bolshevism as 'the invention of the Jew'.[1] 'In Russian Bolshevism,' he said, 'we ought to recognise the kind of attempt which is being made by the Jew in the Twentieth Century to secure dominion over the world.'[2] Was either of these statements true?

Karl Marx was a Jew whose family had converted to Protestantism. However, despite his Jewish ancestry, Marx would later display, in correspondence with his colleague Friedrich Engels, a surprisingly virulent anti-Semitism. (In fact Marx had no time for any religions, Christianity included.) For example, the German revolutionary and political writer Ferdinand Lassalle, was described variously as, 'the yid; wily Ephraim; izzy and the Jewish nigger'.[3] In his essay *On the Jewish Question*, Marx scornfully described 'the secular basis of Judaism' as being characterised by 'practical need' and 'self interest'. The 'secular cult' of the Jew was 'haggling', and his 'secular god' was 'money', he said.

> We therefore recognise in Judaism, the presence of a universal and contemporary anti-social element whose historical evolution – eagerly nurtured by the Jews in its harmful aspects – had arrived at its present peak, a peak at which it will inevitably disintegrate. The emancipation of the Jews is, in the last analysis, the emancipation of mankind from Judaism.

In other words it was Marx's view that the Jews would be better off if they totally abandoned their historical faith.

Marx also made derogatory remarks about Moses Levy, editor of London's *Daily Telegraph* newspaper, whose nose 'provides conversation [i.e was the butt of jokes] throughout the year in the City of London ....'[4] Nevertheless, at the same time Marx saw no reason why Jews should be denied the same status as any other citizens.[5]

Marx had a rival in the First International in Russian exile Michael Bakunin, an anarchist. Whereas Marx's wish was for the Jews to be freed from the tyranny of Judaism, Bakunin demanded no less than their entire annihilation. 'In all countries the people detest the Jews,' he wrote. 'They detest them so much that every popular revolution is accompanied by a massacre of Jews: a natural consequence ....' Marx countered by issuing in June 1872 a pamphlet entitled *The*

Fictitious Splits in the International, which he admitted was 'undergoing the most serious crisis since its foundation'. He accused Bakunin of inciting 'racial war' and organising secret societies as part of his anarchistic master plan to wreck the working class movement. Marx now forced the expulsion of Bakunin from the First International.[6]

***

There had been pogroms (manifestations of hatred, often involving beatings, stonings, and massacres, and the burning of businesses and properties) against Jews in Europe since time immemorial, but particularly during the period of the Crusades (11th and 12th centuries) when, mainly at the instigation of the Catholic Church, Jews were expelled from countries such as England, France, Spain, various Germanic states, Portugal, Lithuania and the Ukraine. (Only in 1965 did the Vatican revise its teaching, by exonerating the Jews for the murder of Christ and accepting the legitimacy of their religion.) The murder of Russian Tsar Alexander II in 1881, which was blamed on the Jews, resulted in pogroms throughout Eastern Europe which lasted into the early 20th century.

The Jews in Russia lived mainly in 'shtetls' (small-town communities) in which they secluded themselves from their neighbours; maintained their own way of life; spoke their own language, Yiddish; married within the community; had their own educational system, and practised their own religion. They therefore tended not to become assimilated into the culture of the country in which they found themselves living.

Tsar Nicholas II contributed to the further isolation of the Jews by issuing anti-Semitic decrees, such as the May Laws of 1882, which restricted their right to settle in the cities and to practise their religion. (Instead, it was his wish that they convert to the Russian Orthodox faith.) Now, Jews were forced to sell their businesses and their homes, and move into a specially designated quarter of Russia's western province, known as the 'Jewish Pale'.

Lenin (like his predecessor Marx) was also partly Jewish, his maternal grandfather being Israel Blak, a Ukranian Jew who was later baptised into the Russian Orthodox Church.[7] However, far from being an anti-Semite, Lenin, according to Maria Ilinichna, was proud of his Jewish ancestry and of the political, scientific and artistic achievements of the Jews, which were out of all proportion to the smallness of their numbers. He also admired the Jews for helping to create a Western European-style culture in Russia.

Russian novelist Maxim Gorky also confirmed that Lenin was fulsome in his praise of the Jews. 'We [the Russians] are a predominantly talented people, but we have a lazy mentality. A bright Russian is almost always a Jew or a person with an admixture of Jewish blood.'[8]

Lenin pointed out to his sister Anna that Jewish activists constituted about half the total of revolutionaries in the southern regions of the Russian Empire. Also, several members of the editorial board of Lenin's Marxist newspaper *Iskra* (a voice for the Russian Social Democratic Labour Party RSDLP) had Jewish backgrounds namely, Pavel Axelrod, Julius Martov and Leon Trotsky. However, all of them had abandoned Judaism in favour of Marxism.

At the Second Party Congress of the RSDLP held on 29 July 1903 in London, one of the questions to be decided concerned the Jewish 'Bund' (Federation), whose Party members, recruited on a purely ethnic basis, were numerous in the western borderlands of the Russian Empire. The complaint of the Bund was that it had been allocated only five of the forty-three places at the Congress. However, finding itself unable to persuade the other delegates to increase its representation, the Bund responded by demanding autonomy for itself within the Party, but was again thwarted when the Congress again refused its request.[9]

In 1911 the USA cancelled its economic treaty with Russia, on the basis that Jews were denied their basic civil rights throughout the Russian Empire.

In 1914 Lenin again showed his support for the Jews by referring, disapprovingly, to the fact that in the ranks of the Russian Imperial armies, which were now fighting the Germans, were to be found so-called 'Black Hundred' gangs – reactionary thugs, who in pre-war days, had organised pogroms of Jews throughout the Russian Empire.

It was not until September 1916 that Tsar Nicholas and his Minister of the Interior, Alexander Protopopov, finally gave their endorsement to full civil rights for the Jews. This was welcomed by progressive members of the Duma, and described by Prime Minister Alexsandr Kerensky as one of the few positive actions taken by the government.

However, right-wing elements, the army, and even the Tsar's own family, were opposed to the granting of such freedom to the Jews. For example, Alexander Mikhailovich Romanov (husband of the Tsar's sister Ksenia), in a letter to his brother Sergei, describes how he told 'N' and 'A' (abbreviations for Nicholas and his wife Alexandra), 'that concessions or new rights for the Jews were unthinkable, that we could not afford to be merciful to a race which the Russian people hate even more now because of their negative attitude towards the war and [their] outright treason ....'[10]

So what made Nicholas II, despite opposition from his family, change his mind and decide to grant civil rights to the Jews? It seems that he was influenced in this by a petition he and his wife received concerning a Russian Jew who had returned from America to fight for Russia in World War I, and who, having been severely wounded, was refused permission to live in Moscow simply on the grounds of his being a Jew.[11] It was this incident which brought home to Nicholas the absurdity of the laws regarding the 'Pale of Settlement' (the area to which the Jewish population was confined). It seems ironic that, after centuries of persecution of the Jews by the Romanovs, one of the reasons for Tsar Nicholas' current unpopularity was his (belated) support for Jewish civil rights.

**

In view of the widespread anti-Semitism prevalent in Russia in the days of the tsars, it is not surprising that, like the rest of the Russian population, and perhaps especially the Jews were actively involved both in the October 1917 revolution, and in its aftermath. It must also be remembered that the Jews had no country which they could call their own (and would not have until the state of Israel was created in 1948). They were also born leaders, who tended to rise to the very top of whatever profession or trade they chose to indulge in, and the idea of participating in a movement which saw no boundaries, but was truly 'international' (i.e. communism), must have seemed an attractive proposition to them.

It is, therefore, perhaps also not surprising that following the Bolshevik take-over, most of the people who assumed positions of power were Jews. For example, Leon Trotsky (Head of the Red Army and Chief of Soviet Foreign Affairs), Yakov Sverdlov (the Bolshevik Party's Executive Secretary, Chairman of the Central Executive Committee, and Head of the Soviet Government), Grigori Zinoviev (Head of the Communist International – or Comintern – the agency responsible for spreading revolution abroad), Karl Radek (Press Commissar), Maxim Litvinov (Foreign Affairs Commissar), Lev Kamenev (Chairman of the Central Executive Committee of the All Russian Congress of Soviets), and Moisei Uritsky (Head of the Secret Police – or 'Cheka'). Interestingly, many, if not all of these persons had exchanged their Jewish surnames for Russian names.

British journalist and author Robert Wilton, in his *Les Derniers Jours des Romanovs*, states that at the time of the assassination of the imperial family, of the sixty-one members of the Bolshevik Party's Central Committee, no fewer than forty-one were Jews; the Extraordinary Commission of Moscow ('Cheka') consisted of thirty-six members, of whom twenty-three were Jews; in the Council of the People's Commissars (the Soviet Government), Jews provided seventeen of the twenty-two members, and as regards the func-tionaries of the Bolshevik State 1918–19, Jews occupied 457 of 556 important positions.

According to Wilton, by 1918 the Central Commission of the Bolshevik Party, which effectively governed the country, was reduced to twelve members of whom nine were of Jewish origin, the remaining three being Russian.

As for the other Russian socialist parties including Mensheviks, Communists of the People, Social Revolutionaries (both right-wing and left-wing), Committee of the Anarchists of Moscow, 'out of sixty-one individuals at the head of these parties, there are six Russians and fifty-five Jews. No matter what may be the name adopted, a revolutionary government will be Jewish.'[12]

A few months after taking power, the new Soviet Government reflected the views of its leader Lenin, by making anti-Semitism a crime in Russia. In a letter to Stalin, Lenin's sister Anna would later assert that Lenin's Jewish origins were, 'further confirmation of the exceptional abilities of the Semitic tribe...', and according to Dmitri Volkoganov (Director of the Institute for Military History in the USSR), this claim by Anna explains why Lenin frequently recommended giving foreigners, especially Jews, intellectually demanding tasks, and leaving the elementary work to the 'Russian fools'.[13]

In another letter to Stalin, Anna declared:

Ilyich [Lenin] himself rated their [the Jews'] revolutionary qualities highly: contrasting them with the more sluggish and unstable character of the Russians. He often pointed out that the great [attributes of] organisation, and the strength of the revolutionary bodies in the south and west of Russia arose precisely from the fact that 50 per cent of their members were of that nationality [i.e. Jewish].[14]

Anti-Semitism means spreading enmity towards the Jews [Lenin would later affirm]. When the accursed tsarist monarchy was living its last days it tried to incite ignorant workers and peasants against the Jews. The tsarist police, in alliance with landlords and capitalists, organised pogroms against the Jews. The landowners and capitalists tried to divert the hatred of the workers and peasants, who were tortured by want, against the Jews. In other countries too, we often see the capitalists fomenting hatred against the Jews in order to blind the workers, to divert their attention from the real enemy of the working people, [which is] capital … [i.e. accumulated wealth]. It is not the Jews who are the enemy of the working people. The enemies of the workers are the capitalists of all countries. Among the Jews there are working people and they form the majority. They are our brothers who, like us, are oppressed by capital; they are our comrades in the struggle for socialism. Among the Jews there are 'kulaks' (that small minority of the peasantry who are rich – 'bourgeois' – rural capitalists), exploiters, and capitalists, just as there are among the Russians and among people of all nations. The capitalists strive to sow and to foment hatred between workers of different faiths, different nations, and different races. Those who do not work are kept in power by the power and strength of capital.[15]

***

In Lenin's words, no one was more guilty than Hitler of 'spreading enmity towards the Jews' (the latter's diatribes against them being so contemptible as to be scarcely worthy of a response). However, to take just one of his statements, 'the Jews have not the creative abilities which are necessary to the founding of a civilisation.'[16] The validity of this can easily be put to the test by a simple perusal of Nobel Prize winners in the 20th century. (This is most convenient, since the first Nobel Prizes were awarded in the year 1901 under the terms of the will of Swedish chemist Alfred B Nobel.) The prizes are awarded to those persons who have made the greatest contributions in five different fields.

The results, from 1901 up until the outbreak of World War II in 1939 are as follows: literature 2; world peace 2; chemistry 5; medicine 7; physics 6 (where the recipients included Albert Einstein and Niels Bohr). In the years subsequent to this and up to the end of the Millennium, Jews would go on to win astonishingly, a further 129 Nobel Prizes including: 19 for chemistry, 8 for literature, 18 for economics, 36 for physics, and an almost incredible 41 for medicine.

The corollary to this is that, had Hitler succeeded in his desire to exterminate the entire Jewish population of the world, the loss to humanity would have been incalculable.

Hitler also said: 'The Jews are a people of robbers .... Everything that he [the Jew] has is stolen.'[17] But is it true that the Jews were in reality, any more likely to commit crime than other ethnic groups? The evidence indicates not.

According to statistics compiled by Dr Leo Goldhammer, whereas Jews in Vienna in 1910 (the period when Hitler was resident in that city) accounted for 8.63% of the population, in the following two years only 6.38% of committed crimes were attributable to them. This indicates that they were in fact LESS likely to commit crime than other ethnic groups.[18]

Notes

1. Commission of the C.C. of the CPSU (B) (ed.) *History of the Communist Party of the Soviet Union: Bolsheviks*, p. 37.
2. Hitler, Adolf, *Mein Kampf*, p. 364.
3. Wheen, Francis, *Karl Marx*, p. 54.
4. Ibid, p. 243.
5. Ibid, p. 57.
6. Ibid, p. 341.
7. 'The Jewish Role in the Bolshevik Revolution and Russia's Early Soviet Regime'. [This essay appeared in the Jan.-Feb. 1994 issue of the *Journal of Historical Review*, published by the Institute for Historical Review.] www.ihr.org/jhr/v14/v14n1p-4Weber.html.
8. Gor'kii, M. *Vladimir Lenin*, Russkii sovrenennik, No. 1 1924, page 241. (in Service, p. 29).
9. Service, Robert, *Lenin: a Biography*, p. 153.
10, 11. *Alexander Palace Time Machine*. www.alexanderpalace.
12. 'The Jewish Role in the Bolshevik Revolution and Russia's Early Soviet Regime', op. cit.
13, 14. Volkoganov, Dmitri A, 1994, *Lenin Politicheskii portret*, vols. 1–2. Moscow.
15. Workers' Liberty,' # 59, December 1999.
16. Hitler, op. cit., p. 171.
17. *Der Volkischer Beobachter*, 16 August 1922, in Prange, Gordon W (ed.), *Hitler's Words*, p. 75.
18. Goldhammer, Leo, 1927. *Die Juden Wiens*, Vienna and Leipzig.

CHAPTER XXVI

Post-Revolutionary Russia

The question was, did Lenin have the capacity on the one hand to govern his vast country, while still on the other retain the energy, drive and capability to promote communism worldwide?

World War I had left Russia exhausted, that country having lost a total of 7 million dead, missing or wounded. Furthermore, because the majority of soldiers were peasants who had left the land to fight for their country, there was a shortage of manpower, which in turn led to a shortage of food.

To add to her woes, Russia was now to experience the added trauma of a civil war, in which the military interference of outside powers made the Bolsheviks feel even more isolated and oppressed. There was also the problem of governing a massive country containing a myriad of ethnic groupings, and Lenin was soon to be embroiled in, and preoccupied with, endless arguments and confrontations with his political opponents. For example, the emergence of a middle-class of peasants – the 'kulaks' – whose philosophy was more akin to capitalism than communism, was a problem that had not been foreseen.

However, only a quarter of a century later, Russia would become involved in another conflict with Germany, one in which the tectonic plate of Bolshevism would collide with that of Nazism; the resulting earthquake would be felt right around the world.

As this world was soon to be engulfed in a conflict which would cost the lives of approximately 40 million people, it is important to establish Hitler's role in this, and to ascertain whether or not the Bolsheviks were the threat to Germany that he claimed they were.

***

The Second Congress of Soviets now 'called upon the belligerent countries of World War I [principally Great Britain, France, and Germany] to conclude an immediate armistice ....' At the same time, the 'Decree on Land' edict declared that: 'landlord ownership of land is abolished forthwith without compensation'.[1] The peasantry on the other hand, were granted in excess of 150,000,000 dessiatins (i.e. over 400 million acres) that had formerly belonged to the landlords, the bourgeoisie, the tsar's family, the monasteries and the churches, and moreover, they were released from paying rent to the landlords which had amounted to about 500,000,000 gold roubles annually. 'All mineral resources, forests and waters became the property of the people,' and finally, 'the All-Russian Congress of Soviets formed the first Soviet Government [or "Council of People's Commissars"], which was made up entirely of Bolsheviks', with Lenin as its elected chairman.[2]

Lenin now set out his ideas for a new workers' state, which would be, 'based on the extension of democracy to such an overwhelming majority of the population, that the need for a special machine of suppression [presumably a reference to a secret police force, such as that which was operational under the tsars] would begin to disappear.'[3] Furthermore, the cornerstone of the new state would be the 'soviet' – or workers' council – of which there would be about 2,000 in all, spread right across Russia. Together with their delegates, who were to be democratically elected, the soviets would become the decision-making bodies of the country.

On 17 November 1917 the Constituent Assembly was elected on the basis of proportional representation. However, for Lenin this proved to be problematic, in that the Socialist Revolutionary Party, led by Victor Chernov, won 380 of the 703 seats, whereas Lenin's Bolsheviks won only 168.

On 5 December that same year, an armistice was signed between Russia and Germany, by which time the central powers (Germany and Austro-Hungary) had overrun Russian Poland, most of Lithuania, Serbia, Albania and Romania.

That same month, anti-Bolshevik 'white' forces, commanded principally by former tsarist generals, and supported by forces from Britain, France, the United States, Japan, Canada and others, began to oppose the Bosheviks, thus beginning a civil war which would last for three years. For the Bolsheviks, Leon Trotsky (Minister for Foreign Affairs from 1917–18) was appointed Commissar for War and it was he who created the so-called 'Red Army'. Meanwhile, the RSDLP faced continuing opposition from political opponents including 'Mensheviks', 'Economists' and 'Bukharinites'.

In January 1918 the Constituent Assembly met with Lenin hoping that it would legitimise his new government. However, when it failed to do so he immediately dissolved it. Lenin had no qualms about his action saying it was, 'The complete and public liquidation of formal democracy in the name of the revolutionary dictatorship.' Svetlana Alliluyeva, daughter of Russia's future leader Josef Stalin, would later state that democracy, having only just been born in Russia was 'murdered in the crib' by the October Revolution which she said 'never brought to Russia anything that was promised'.[4] It would be another seventy years before democracy returned to Russia.

In that same month, the fragile armistice between Russia and Germany failed and German troops swept into Russia threatening the former tsarist capital Petrograd (known as St Petersburg prior to 1914 and renamed Leningrad in 1924); whereupon the Russians were forced, on 3 March to accept the harsh terms of the Treaty of Brest-Litovsk: in return for the cessation of hostilities, Germany now demanded that Russia surrender Russian Poland, the Baltic States (Estonia, Lithuania, and Latvia) and part of the Ukraine. The blow to Russia was enormous. She had now lost 32% of her arable land, 27% of her railways, 54% of her industry, and 89%

of her coal mines;[5] she would also be required to pay Germany an indemnity. In response to the increasing threat from Germany, Russia now declared Moscow (a city strategically less vulnerable than Petrograd) to be its new capital.

At the Seventh Congress held in March 1918 the name of the Party was changed from the 'Russian Soviet Federative Socialist Republic' (RSFSR) to the 'Russian Communist Party (Bolsheviks)' (or RCP-B).

When the 'kulaks' began, 'seizing the lands confiscated from the landlords', 'fought the proletarian government' and 'refused to sell grain to it at fixed prices', it was done to starve the Soviet state into renouncing soviet measures. The Party responded by sending detachments of industrial workers into the countryside, 'with the object of organising the poor peasants and ensuring the success of the struggle against the "kulaks", who were holding back their grain surpluses'.[6]

In addition, by a decree issued on 11 July there was a redistribution of, '50 million hectares of "kulak" land [which] passed into the hands of the poor and middle peasants'. The peasants were also supplied with agricultural implements, and food surpluses collected from the 'kulaks' were distributed to 'working class centres and [to] the Red Army'.[7]

Meanwhile, the Romanov dynasty came to an abrupt end when, on the night of 16/17 July 1918 (on Lenin's orders), Tsar Nicholas II, his wife Alexandra, and their four daughters and 14 year-old son Alexei were shot to death by the Red Army in the cellar of the house at Ekaterinburg in the Ural Mountains, where they had been held prisoner.[8]

Lenin now decided to act more decisively against the intransigent 'kulaks', not all of whom had submitted meekly to his programme of land redistribution. To the Bolsheviks of the Russian town of Penza, he announced on 11 August:

Comrades! The insurrection of five 'kulak' districts should be pitilessly suppressed. The interests of the whole revolution require this because the last decisive battle with the 'kulaks' is now underway everywhere. An example must be demonstrated.

No fewer than 100 known 'kulaks', described as 'rich men, bloodsuckers', were to be hanged in full view of the people. All their grain was to be seized. Hostages were to be 'designated' in 'such a fashion that for hundreds of kilometres around the people might see, tremble, know, shout: they are strangling and will strangle to death the bloodsucking "kulaks".'[9]

***

It was therefore only with great difficulty, and it has to be said, brutality, that Lenin was able to stamp out once and for all the capitalistic ambitions of the 'kulaks'. However, the task of creating a democratic Russia had proved to be totally beyond him.

***

In August 1918 there was an assassination attempt against Lenin, and an attempted coup in Moscow. His response was to initiate the so-called 'Red Terror'. A new state security agency, the 'Cheka', was created (Stalin being a member of the committee that supervised its activities). Press censorship and the death penalty, having previously been abolished, were now reinstated. Lenin's attitude had hardened.

Lenin then turned his attention to promoting a far-left socialist seizure of power in Germany, which in alliance with Russia, would result in the formation of a gigantic geopolitical 'block', which could never be overthrown. 'The absolute truth,' said Lenin prophetically, 'is that without a revolution in Germany, we shall perish.'[10] However, prior to the founding of the Communist Party of Germany in late 1918 Lenin was obliged to operate through the Spartacus League, headed by Karl Liebknecht and Rosa Luxemburg. On 9 November the Spartacists attempted to overthrow the socialist government in Berlin; the uprising was ruthlessly suppressed.

In the same year, in a civil war in Finland (an independent republic since 1917), 'International Communism' received another setback when the 'Reds', supported by Russia's Bolsheviks, were defeated by the 'Whites', led by Finnish soldier Baron Carl Mannerheim and supported by Germany. On 11 November the armistice was signed which ended World War I.

***

The 'International' (an abbreviation for 'International Working Men's Association') was the name given to successive organisations whose aim was to foster socialist, communist and revolutionary groups worldwide. The First International was held in London in 1864; the Second in Paris in 1889; the Third International (or 'Comintern') was founded by Lenin in Moscow in 1919 by which time it represented mainly communist parties.

The First Congress of Communist Parties (at which the 'Comintern' was founded), undeterred by previous setbacks in Germany and Finland, 'adopted a manifesto to the proletariat of all countries, calling upon them to wage a determined struggle for the dictatorship of the proletariat and for the triumph of soviets all over the world.'[11]

Workers everywhere were exhorted to, 'wipe out boundaries between states, and transform the whole world into one co-operative commonwealth'. 'It will not be long,' said Lenin until, 'we shall see the victory of communism in the entire world ....'[12] Soviet joy at the situation in Hungary (where in its capital, Budapest, a communist revolution occurred in March 1919) was however to be short lived, as it was overthrown by counter-revolutionaries after only four months.

In April 1919 a similar uprising occurred in München, which again was swiftly crushed with the aid of government troops.

***

So was Hitler correct in seeing post-revolutionary Russia as a potential threat, and not only to Germany, but to the wider world? The answer in 1919 was a definite 'YES'. However, in Russia the situation was soon to change, with that country's leaders having their work cut out, so to speak, simply to govern themselves, while at the same time being obliged to look on in dismay as communism failed to take permanent root with their neighbours. As so often with Hitler however, once an idea had become embedded in his mind, there was to be no changing it; even though the rest of the world had moved on.

***

Although by 1920 the civil war had been largely won by the Bolsheviks, the disruption caused by the fighting meant that there were further food shortages. Famine now forced the peasants from their villages. The state responded by requisitioning grain. When the peasants rose in revolt, there was bloodshed.

In April 1920 the Poles, believing that a union of Poland and the Ukraine would ensure their security, invaded the Ukraine and captured Kiev. At the same time, former tsarist general P N Wrangel launched an attack on the Soviet Republic from the Crimea. Now came yet another blow to the prestige of Soviet forces, when between 16 and 20 August 1920 the Poles defeated the Red Army on the Vistula river on the outskirts of Warsaw. 100,000 Soviet troops were encircled and taken prisoner, with another 40,000 fleeing to Germany. On 21 August in a cavalry battle at Komarov (Poland), the Red Army was again routed by the Poles. Lenin was left with no choice but to sue for peace. This setback led to a pause in the Red Army being used as an instrument for the promotion of 'revolutionary war'.

Finally, on 12 October 1920 the Armistice of Riga (Latvia) was signed, whereby Poland retained Galicia and part of Belorussia. The following month, Wrangel was defeated by the 'Red' forces.

In a letter to Ottoline Morrell (hostess, patron of the arts and member of the 'Bloomsbury' literary group) written in June 1920, Bertrand Russell (English philosopher, mathematician and writer) expressed his opinion about Russia, following a visit he had made to that country in the same year.

> My time in Russia was infinitely painful to me, in spite of it being one of the most interesting things I have ever done. Bolshevism is a close tyrannical bureaucracy, with a spy system more elaborate and terrible than the Tsar's, and an aristocracy as insolent and unfeeling, composed of americanised Jews. No vestige of liberty remains, in thought, speech or action. I was stifled and oppressed by the weight of the machine as by a cope of leads.[13]

This statement by Russell would appear to be a contradiction in terms. If Russia's aristocratic Jews were 'americanised', this implies that they would have been in favour of democracy, freedom of speech, and the rights of the individual (which Lenin had now realised was nothing more than an unattainable dream).[14]

***

In 1921 Lenin proposed a New Economic Policy (NEP), to replace the former centralised and inflexible policy of so-called 'War Communism'. Now, small-scale businesses would be privatised; major parts of industry decentralised, and foreign investment encouraged. The state would keep control of finance, heavy industry, transport and foreign trade, and the peasants would be permitted to sell their surplus produce on the open market. The results of the implementation of the NEP were initially encouraging: agriculture recovered, as did small businesses (three quarters of which were in the hands of members of the Party).

Lenin now began to intensify his grip on government when, on 8 March 1921 the Tenth Party Congress 'ordered the immediate dissolution of all factional groups ...'[15]. He followed this up by ordering that the Party be thoroughly cleansed, 'of rascals, bureaucrats, dishonest or wavering communists, and of Mensheviks who have repainted their "façade", but who have remained Mensheviks at heart.'[16] In other words, despite having formerly been an advocate of democracy, Lenin now destroyed the last remnants of opposition within his own Party. In the years from 1919–24 it is estimated that the 'Cheka' (political police, which had its headquarters in Moscow in a building called the Lubianka) carried out in excess of 200,000 executions.[17] Lenin, as he had already demonstrated, was not averse to using force if necessary, to achieve his ends.

The Party also voted to turn away from 'War Communism', which Trotsky had defined in 1920 as a class war which could be fought and won only by force (rather than by employing the process of democracy).

On 16 March 1921 an Anglo-Soviet trade agreement was signed with the British insisting on the proviso that the Soviet authorities must desist from engaging in subversive activities in the territories of the British Empire. Two days later a peace treaty was signed with Poland.

On 16 April 1922 Germany and Russia signed a treaty of friendship and neutrality – the Treaty of Rapallo – by which the two countries agreed to cooperate, both economically and militarily. In October 'Vladivostok, the last piece of Soviet territory to remain in the hands of the invaders [i.e. those foreign powers who had supported the 'Whites' in the civil war], was wrested by the Red Army and the Far Eastern Partisans from the hands of the Japanese.'[18]

Lenin's rhetoric changed. Instead of seeing his country as a threat to the outside world, he now saw Russia as an 'oasis of Soviet power in the middle of the raging imperialist sea'.[19] Now it was Lenin who felt threatened: 'We must remember,' he said, 'that we are at all times but a hair's breadth from any manner of invasion.'[20]

In December 1922 it was declared that all the Soviet republics had, 'now united in a single union of Soviet states – the "Union of Soviet Socialist Republics" (USSR) – on a voluntary and equal basis; each of them being reserved the right of freely seceding from the Soviet Union.' The states included Russia, Ukraine, Transcaucasia, Belorussia, Uzbek, Turkmen and Tadjik.[21]

***

The failure of communism to take root in Germany and Hungary was a bitter pill for Lenin to swallow, and the invasion of Russia by Poland, followed by the subsequent defeat of the Red Army, was the last straw.

Therefore, although at the time of his death it is true to say that Lenin's policy of 'internationalising' communism was entirely in accordance with Karl Marx's vision, and he had worked tirelessly to achieve this end, nevertheless, in practical terms, very little progress on this front had been made; in fact, he had suffered one reverse after another.

***

Stalin

Josef Dzhugashvili was the son of a peasant woman and a cobbler father. Born in Tiflis (now Tblisi), Georgia (then part of the Empire of the Tsars of Russia) in 1879 he had adopted the name 'Stalin' ('Man of Steel') in 1910. Like Hitler, his junior by ten years, Stalin had considered becoming a priest, but he was expelled from the Tiflis Theological Seminary, allegedly for disseminating Marxist propaganda.

In 1902 Stalin married Ekaterina Svanidze, but she died young. 'With her died my last warm feelings for people,' said Stalin.[22] In the same year he was arrested and imprisoned by the tsarist police for secretly helping to produce revolutionary publications. Two years later, Stalin escaped from Siberia where he was living in exile, and made his way back to Georgia – a distance of over 3,000 miles. Astonishingly, having been recaptured he would perform this feat again no fewer than five more times!

Having (illegally) attended several Party conferences in cities outside Russia, Stalin came to the notice of Lenin, who co-opted him on to the Party's Central Committee and sent him to Russia as one of a group of four men who were organising the Party's activities there. However, in the Bolshevik Revolution of 1917 Stalin did not play a major role, but as a member of the government, he was appointed Commissar of Nationalities, and in May 1918 became Director of Food Supplies in southern Russia.

In 1922 Stalin became General Secretary of the Communist Party. Now Lenin, whose health had deteriorated, sent him to Georgia (which, since the Revolution, had behaved like an autonomous region), in order to achieve its further integration with the Bolshevik state. Stalin however, instead of looking on his homeland with affection, behaved as a Russian conqueror, and sent the Red Army in to invade and annex Georgia by force.

At the 1923 Party Congress, which he was unable to attend because of ill health, Lenin, who by now had begun to have grave misgivings about Stalin, appealed to Trotsky for his support. Trotsky however, demurred, choosing not to confront Stalin over the Georgian issue, but instead, presenting his own programme for economic recovery.

***

Lenin died in January 1924. In his testament (will), which was read out at the Thirteenth Party Congress, he declared it to be his wish, that after his death, there should be a collective leadership, comprising Grigori Zinoviev and Lev Kamonev, two senior figures who were former colleagues of Lenin, and Nikolai Bukharin and Leon Trotsky (although the influence of the latter was now waning).

The testament also expressed Lenin's desire that Stalin be removed. However, in this his wishes would be thwarted. Instead, according to Boris Bazhanov (Stalin's Secretariat 1923–26), the following statement was read out: 'Comrades, you know we are sworn to carry out Lenin's will and so we shall, but we are happy to say [that] his fears about our General Secretary [i.e. Stalin] ... have turned out to be unfounded. [During] These last months he has worked with the Central Committee excellently ... and without friction.'[23] A vote was then taken and the outcome was that Stalin remained General Secretary.

Stalin established a countrywide network of Party leaders whose appointments he controlled. According to Nadezhda Ioffe (described as, 'daughter of Old Bolshevik'), 'As General Secretary, he [Stalin] managed to install his own people ... i.e. regional Party secretaries and such like ... [who were] already loyal to him [and] who suited him.'[24] He also moved swiftly to eliminate any potential rivals. His rule was to be marked by purges, exiles, 'gulags' (corrective labour camps), and great show trials, which were intended to make an example of anyone whom he saw as a potential threat.

***

By the mid-1920s many of the peasants had organised themselves into cooperatives, using their new prosperity to purchase tractors, improve the roads, build schools and hospitals, and have electricity installed in their domestic dwellings.

However, at the Fourteenth Party Conference held in April 1925 it was regretfully pointed out, that the USSR was, 'as yet the only socialist country, all the other countries remaining capitalist', and that it, 'continued to be encircled by a capitalist world'. The question arose therefore, as to what was to be the relationship between 'the Soviet people' on the one hand and 'the international bourgeoisie, which hated the Soviet system and was seeking the chance to start armed intervention once again in the Soviet Union ...' on the other. In the circumstances, it was decided that although the Red Army,

> would be able to beat off a new foreign capitalist intervention, just as they had beaten off the first capitalist intervention of 1918–20... this would not mean that the danger of a new capitalist intervention would be eliminated. It followed from this that the matter of promoting the proletarian revolution in the capitalist countries was a matter of vital concern to the working people of the USSR.[25]

***

Tensions still existed between the advocates of 'Communism in one country' (i.e. the USSR) and the advocates of 'permanent revolution' (whereby it was envisaged that revolution in Russia would spread throughout the countries of Europe, and eventually throughout the world). At the heart of the faction in favour of 'permanent revolution' was Leon Trotsky.

Trotsky

Born in the Ukraine, the son of a Jewish farmer, Trotsky joined the Social Democrats and in 1898, at the age of 19, was arrested as a Marxist and exiled to Siberia. Four years later he escaped to England. In London he met Lenin, and collaborated with him on the publication of the journal *Iskra*. In 1903 Trotsky broke with Lenin and became leader of the Menshevik wing of the Social Democratic Party.

In the abortive revolution in St Petersburg in 1905 he became President of the city's soviet. Exiled again to Siberia, he escaped once more, and fled to the West where he joined other Russian émigrés, becoming a revolutionary journalist. Trotsky returned to Russia in 1917, joined the Bolshevik Party, and played a major part in the revolution. In the ensuing civil war, he was military commander of the Bolshevik forces.

Trotsky, however, was to be disappointed in his aspirations, for with Stalin's rise to power, the Comintern distanced itself from his concept of 'permanent revolution', and instead was content to promote the interests of Soviet communism only. In November 1927 Trotsky, now portrayed as someone, 'ready to spy, sabotage, commit acts of terrorism and diversion, and to work for the defeat of the USSR in order to restore capitalism', was expelled from the Party and exiled to Alma Ata in Kazakhstan.[26]

At the Fifteenth Party Congress, held in December 1927, Stalin achieved final victory. All 'deviation' was now condemned, and enemies were purged or exiled.

***

From 1928 in place of Lenin's New Economic Policy (NEP), Stalin substituted a series of Five Year Plans with rapid industrialisation and collectivisation in which land was seized from the peasants to form collective farms. (This resulted in the disappearance of some 5 million 'kulaks'.)

In April 1929 the Party held its Sixteenth Conference, with the First Five Year Plan as the main item on the agenda. 19.5 billion roubles were to be invested in industrial and electric power development; 10 billion in transport development; 23.2 billion in agriculture.[27] In this way, steel output was increased from 4 million to 18 million tons; oil production from 11 million to 28 million tons; aircraft production from 1,000 to over 10,000 per year, and tank production from 170 to almost 5,000. In the same year, Leon Trotsky was expelled from the USSR. He finally found refuge in Mexico.

***

Stalin was conscious that in military terms Russia had been a continual loser. She had been beaten, 'by the Mongol khans ... by the Turkish beys ... by the Swedish feudal lords ... by the Polish and Lithuanian gentries ... by the British and French capitalists ... [and] by the Japanese barons,' he said in 1931. The reason for this was her military, cultural, political, industrial and agricultural backwardness. 'We are fifty years behind the advanced countries. We must make good the distance in ten years. Either we do it, or they crush us.'[28]

In that year, Stalin's fears of external aggression were heightened when Japan (with a view to acquiring colonies, and with them the prestige which was attached to other great colonial powers such as Britain, France and Germany) invaded the Chinese province of Manchuria, and thus acquired a common border with the USSR.

The failure of the Allies to intervene against Japanese aggression gave Hitler the confidence to ignore the Versailles Treaty and commence rearmament. Ties between Germany and Japan were strengthened by a five-month visit to Berlin by General Tamayuti Yamoshita, Head of the Japanese Army Air Force.

When, in February 1933 Germany's Communist Party – the largest in Europe – was destroyed by the Nazi SA in a reign of terror, military cooperation between the USSR and Hitler came to an abrupt end.

Thanks to the First Five Year Plan, the USSR could boast that, whereas in the great world economic crisis of 1930–33 industrial output in the USA and Europe had slumped, in the USSR it had 'more than doubled ... to 201 per cent of the 1929 output'. Now in 1933 the Second Five Year Plan was put into operation.[29]

Meanwhile, the philosophy of the Comintern had changed in that, whereas even as late as 1933, its members were being sent on 'manoeuvres' to teach revolutionaries how to use explosives and so forth, by 1934 these tactics were abandoned in favour of cooperation with parties (such as the 'Popular Front' of communists, socialists, and radicals, created in Paris in July 1935) which were opposed to the, 'terroristic dictatorship[s]' as practised by the fascists. [30]

**

The signing by Germany of a pact with Poland in 1934 served to exacerbate relationships between that country and the USSR, by whom the Poles, who had defeated the Red Army in August 1920, were seen as a hated enemy.

That September the USSR joined the League of Nations, 'in the knowledge that the League, in spite of its weakness, might nevertheless serve as a place where aggressors can be exposed', and because the League was an, 'instrument of peace, however feeble, that might hinder the outbreak of war'.[31]

The murder of the popular Leningrad Party chief and Secretary of the Central Committee, Sergei Kirov, on 1 December (presumably at the instigation of Stalin) marked the start of a great terror campaign on his part, which lasted for several years. There were purges of the opposition (with, for example, as many as 1,500 to 2,000, 'enemies of the people' being shot in a single day in the summer of

1937). Unrest among the peasants was suppressed and they were herded into collective farms. Nationalists, religious leaders, critical intellectuals and internal Party opponents were arrested and imprisoned.

In May 1935 the USSR signed a treaty of mutual assistance with both France and Czechoslovakia 'against possible attack by aggressors'. In 1936 when the new so-called Stalin Constitution came into being, Stalin asserted that, 'the export of revolution is nonsense'.[32] That March the USSR signed a similar treaty with the Mongolian People's Republic. In August 1937 the USSR signed a pact of non-aggression with the People's Republic of China.

The Third Five Year Plan (1938–41, which would be curtailed by the Nazi invasion), succeeded in completing the collectivisation of agriculture, and further industrialising the USSR – a fact that was soon to have severe implications for any would-be aggressor, as Nazi Germany was shortly to discover to its cost!

The exclusion of the USSR from the München Agreement of 29–30 September 1938 enhanced that country's feeling of isolation. Stalin now realised that he must face the fact that, 'The Soviet Union will stand alone. Alone and unaided, she will have to wage war against Hitler .... To save our country from this war, I would be prepared to treat with the devil.'[33]

Meanwhile, in his purges Stalin is estimated to have murdered in excess of 40 million of his own citizens, amongst them, some 35,000 of his most senior army officers – hardly the act of a leader who was preparing for war! When the famous Russian neuropathologist, Professor Vladimir Bekhterev, diagnosed him as suffering from paranoia, the professor died soon afterwards. Stalin was believed to have had him poisoned.

On 10 March 1939 Stalin addressed the Eighteenth Party Congress. The USSR would 'continue the policy of peace'; the Party would be 'open, cautious' and we 'would not allow our country to be drawn into conflicts by warmongers who are accustomed to have others pull the chestnuts out of the fire for them'.[34]

In July 1939 hostilities broke out between the USSR and Japan along the Soviet-Manchurian border with Mongolia. However, the Japanese were pre-empted by Stalin's General Georgi Zhukhov who, in a surprise attack, secured a total victory in which over 20,000 soldiers of the Japanese Imperial Army were killed. (This would prompt Japan on 27 September 1940 to join the tripartite 'Axis' pact with Germany and Italy.)

That August Britain and France made a half-hearted attempt to come to some accord with the USSR, but the talks petered out in an atmosphere of mutual mistrust. This left the door open for Germany to sign a non-aggression pact with the USSR, in which the lands lost by the latter country to Poland would be restored, and henceforth the Baltic States and Finland would be regarded as coming under the Soviet sphere of influence. Germany would grant the USSR credit of 200 million Reichsmarks, at an interest rate of 5%, to be used to finance Soviet orders of machine tools and industrial plant from Germany; also a limited quantity of optical instruments and armour plate. In return the Soviets would supply the Germans with raw materials.[35]

This agreement gave the Soviets a much needed breathing space, which they used to expand their army by a factor of 2.5, and to produce, in the two years from June 1939, 7,000 tanks and 81,000 artillery pieces[36]

***

Karl Marx had urged the workers to free themselves from their chains. Lenin had created a more egalitarian society, but at a cost, and he failed to realise his dream of turning Russia into a democratic society. However, he did acknowledge the role Russia's Jews had played in helping to overthrow the autocratic tsar.

When Stalin came to power, he quickly realised Russia's weakness – both militarily, and in her failure to spread communism worldwide. His industrialisation of that country would, however, stand Russia in good stead when war with Germany – which he neither envisaged nor wanted – finally came. So the fact was that by the mid-1930s it was Stalin who felt threatened, both by capitalist countries on his western borders, and by militaristic Japan in the east.

For Hitler to pretend that the USSR was any kind of a threat to Germany, *was a complete travesty of the truth*; nevertheless, this is *precisely what he was shortly to do*. 'We had no conception of the gigantic preparations of this enemy against Germany and Europe,' said Hitler in June 1941, 'of how tremendously great this danger really was, and how very narrowly we escaped this time the annihilation not only of Germany, but of all Europe.'[37]

Notes

1. Commission of the C.C. of the CPSU (B) (ed.) *History of the Communist Party of the Soviet Union: Bolsheviks*, p. 209.
2. Ibid.
3. *Socialism from Below, 5: from Marx to Lenin*. www.ann.edn.au/polsci/marx/contem/pamsetc/socfrombel/stb_5.htm 06/03/2004.
4. *Stalin.
5. Bullock, Alan, *Hitler: A Study in Tyranny*, p. 69.
6. Commission of the C.C. of the CPSU, op. cit., p. 222.
7. Ibid.
8. *Russia: Land of the Tsars.
9. *Komsomol'skaya Pravda*. 12 February 1992.
10. *Socialism from Below*, op. cit.
11. Commission of the C.C. of the CPSU,. op. cit., p. 232.
12. Goodman, E R, 1960. *The Soviet Design for a World State*. New York. pp. 30–2.
13. Bertrand Russell to Ottoline Morrell, Stockholm. 25 June 1920.
14. *The Autobiography of Bertrand Russell: 1914–1944*, Vol.2.
15. Commission of the C.C. of the CPSU, op. cit., p. 254.
16. Ibid, p. 259.
17. Bullock, Alan, op. cit., p. 67
18. Commission of the C.C. of the CPSU, op. cit., p. 260.
19. Ulam, A, 1968. *Expansion and Co-existence: a History of Soviet Foreign Policy, 1917–67*. London. p. 79.

20. Stalin, J, 1947. *Problems of Leninism*, Speech to the First All-Union Conference of Managers, February 4, 1931. p. 160.
21. Commission of the C.C. of the CPSU, op. cit., p. 261.
22. *Stalin.
23. Ibid.
24. Ibid.
25. Commission of the C.C. of the CPSU, op. cit., pp. 274–5.
26. Ibid, p. 330.
27. Ibid, p. 296.
28. Stalin, J, op. cit., p. 356.
29. Commission of the C.C. of the CPSU, op. cit., p. 300.
30. McKenzie, K E, 1964, in *Comintern and World Revolution*, New York. pp. 143–5.
31. Commission of the C.C. of the CPSU, op. cit., p. 335.
32. Overy, Richard, *The Road to War*, p. 199.
33. Haslam, J, 1984. *The Soviet Union and the Struggle for Collective Security, 1933–1939*, London. pp. 196–7.
34. Stalin, J, *Problems of Leninism*, Report to the 18th Congress of the CPSU. 10 March 1939, p. 606.
35. Toland, John, *Adolf Hitler*, p. 541.
36. Zhukov, G, 1971, *The Memoirs of Marshal Zhukov*. London. pp. 197–201.
37. Prange, Gordon W (ed.), *Hitler's Words*, Berlin. 3 October 1941, p. 271.

* Film documentary.

CHAPTER XXVII

War

As World War II progressed, Hitler's leadership of it (as commander-in-chief of Germany's armed forces) provides a further valuable insight into his character. It would present him with two golden opportunities, firstly at Dunkerque where he could, had he so wished, have crushed the Allied forces and thus nullified any meaningful future resistance on his Western Front. This he conspicuously failed to do. The second opportunity for winning the war in the east would come later in 'Operation Barbarossa' – the invasion of Soviet Russia.

Poland

At 4 a.m. on 17 September 1939 (seventeen days after Germany had invaded that country from the west), the Red Army invaded Poland from the east. Ten days later, on 27 September Ribbentrop arrived once more in Moscow for the signing of the Soviet-German Boundary and Friendship Treaty. Western Poland, including the Polish capital Warsaw, would now come under the German sphere of influence; whereas eastern Poland (including the strategically important oilfields of Borislav-Drohbysz) and the Baltic States would come under Soviet control.

Norway and Denmark

On 9 April 1940 Hitler launched a simultaneous attack on Denmark and Norway. This, he said, was to have, 'the character of a peaceful occupation, designed to protect by force of arms the neutrality of the northern countries; however, any resistance would be broken by all means available.'[1] The inference being that it was the Soviet Union rather than Germany, which posed a threat to these two countries.

As Nordic peoples, the Norwegians were, in Hitler's view, akin to the Aryans and therefore he was not particularly antagonistic towards them. In the end the Norwegians were able to put up only a limited resistance to Hitler, and the Danes even less. On the down side however, the German navy sustained heavy losses, when off the Norwegian coast (and particularly off Narvik), there was damage and destruction to nineteen vessels including: two battle cruisers, two heavy cruisers and one pocket battleship – caused by the British Royal Navy.

Holland, Belgium and Luxembourg

Hitler decided that when Holland, Belgium and Luxembourg were invaded on 10 May 1940 there would be no bombing by the Luftwaffe of the cities of those countries. However, the Luftwaffe did inadvertently drop ninety-eight tons of high explosive bombs (which were intended to destroy the Dutch Resistance) onto the centre of the city of Rotterdam.

Dunkerque

When, by May 1940, the forces of Generals Fedor von Bock and Gerd von Rundstedt had broken through the Belgian and Dutch lines (by-passing the French Maginot Line), the expectation was that the Allied forces (consisting of the British Expeditionary Force, three French armies, and the remnants of the Belgian Army), now trapped between the Germans and the sea, would be destroyed. However, this was not to be the case.

To the astonishment of German commanders on the ground, at 12.45 p.m. on 24 May 1940 their Fourth Army was ordered to halt. (It should be noted that Hitler had previously postponed the date for the invasion of France on numerous occasions.) Also, Hitler's Chief Lieutenant, Hermann Göring, who was anxious to demonstrate the prowess of his Luftwaffe, had intervened with the Führer, to assure him that further ground fighting was unnecessary; his Luftwaffe would destroy the remaining Allied forces from the air.

The result was that by the time Hitler finally gave the order for the advance on Dunkerque, no fewer than 338, 226 British and Allied troops had, between 26 May and 4 June 1940, been ferried back to England by boat, Göring's Luftwaffe having failed to achieve its objective.

Hitler's remarks to Frau Gerdy Troost (wife of German architect Professor Paul Ludwig Troost), indicate that he would have taken no pleasure in seeing the British army destroyed. 'The blood of every single Englishman is too valuable to be shed,' he said. 'Our two peoples belong together, racially and traditionally; this is and always has been my aim, even if our generals can't grasp it'.[2] However, in view of Hitler's subsequent behaviour, and in particular his instructions to Göring concerning the bombing of British cities, these remarks should be viewed with some scepticism.

There appears to be no doubt that Hitler was in a position to deliver the knockout blow to Allied forces at Dunkerque. *Why therefore, did he choose not to do so?* He had only to give the order to his generals. Instead, his failure to act decisively left them bemused and exasperated. Was he hoping against hope that, even at this late stage, Britain would throw in the towel, as it were? *Or were the reasons more to do with what was going on inside the mind of Hitler himself, rather than with any external factors or influences?* The answer to this question would become clearer with the passing of time.

***

As the Germans advanced on all fronts, Hitler, instead of paying visits to the Front (which he did only rarely), and to the concentration camps (which he did not at all), preferred to live in an escapist world of glamorous women and motion pictures, spending as much time as possible at his idyllic retreat, the Berghof, where he dreamed up and made drawings of the architectural buildings which he hoped would one day grace his new German Reich, and in particular 'Germania', which would be the capital city of the whole world.

Summer 1940

Although in the pre-war years Stalin had been careful to avoid direct conflict with Germany, now that the war had begun and German forces were engaged against Britain and France in the west, the wily Soviet leader was not averse to exploiting the difficult situation in which Hitler now found himself. To this end, in early August 1940 the Soviet Union annexed the Baltic states of Lithuania, Latvia and Estonia.

On 28 June 1940, five days after the French had capitulated, Soviet troops occupied the Romanian regions of Bessarabia (acquired by Romania from Russia at the end of the First World War) and Bucovina. Fortunately for Hitler, however, this did not include that part of the country which contained the rich resources of oil upon which his military machine depended (since supplies from elsewhere had been curtailed by the British naval blockade of Germany).

Astonishingly, even now, with the war in progress, Stalin was still entirely ignorant of Hitler's real intentions. This is demonstrated in an exchange of views between Stalin and Sir Stafford Cripps, British Ambassador to the Soviet Union (the contents of which were leaked in turn to the German Ambassador in a written memorandum):

> The British government was convinced that Germany was striving for hegemony in Europe. This was dangerous to the Soviet Union as well as [to] England. Therefore, both countries ought to agree on a common policy of self protection against Germany, and on the re-establishment of the European balance of power ….

Stalin's answer was as follows:

> He did not see any danger of the hegemony of any one country in Europe, and still less the danger that Europe might be engulfed by Germany. Stalin

observed the policy of Germany and knew several leading German statesmen well. He had not discovered any desire on their part to engulf European
countries. Stalin was not of the opinion that German military successes
menaced the Soviet Union and her friendly relations with Germany.[3]

With the fall of France in June 1940 Hitler travelled personally to Compiègne
where, in the same railway carriage (now an item in a museum) in which French
Marshal Ferdinand Foch had accepted Germany's surrender on 11 November
1918, he now presented the French with Germany's terms for armistice.

When Hitler visited Paris and Napoleon's tomb at Les Invalides, he singularly
failed to learn from the catastrophic mistake which the late French emperor
had made when he decided to invade Russia in 1812. Instead, Hitler preferred
to focus optimistically on the World War I Battle of Tannenburg (26–30 August
1914) in which the Russian army was routed by the Germans. In *Mein Kampf*,
Hitler described the 'interminable columns of Russian war prisoners' which
'poured into Germany ...' after this battle. A stream, which he thought would
never end for, 'as soon as one [Russian] army was defeated and routed, another
would take its place. The supply of soldiers which the gigantic [Russian] Empire
placed at the disposal of the Tsar seemed inexhaustible ....'[4]

The Problem of Britain

By the end of July 1940 Hitler had come to the conclusion that given the strength
of the British navy, an invasion of that country was impracticable. He told his
generals:

> England mainly puts her hopes in Russia. If Russia is crushed, England's
> last hopes will have gone. Germany will be the master of Europe and the
> Balkans. Decision: Russia will have to be finished off. Date [proposed]:
> Spring 1941.[5]

Between July and mid-September, more than half of Germany's divisions in the
west were transferred to the east for a proposed attack on the Soviet Union.

From material (which included 8mm cine film) smuggled out of Moscow by
the German Military Attaché there, Lieutenant General Ernst Koestring, Hitler
was aware of the growing strength of the Red Army and of the new tanks which
Russia was producing. '...we have to hurry up and beat them to it,' he said.[6]

On 13 August 1940, a fortnight after Hitler's Berghof conference with his
generals (so-called 'Eagle Day'), Hitler held, 'a number of conferences with
Göring and his Luftwaffe.' According to Herbert Döhring (a member of Hitler's
household staff), he then came to the conclusion that Germany would now have
to launch intensive air raids (against Britain) for two or three weeks. 'They [the
Nazis] didn't have military intentions, but political ones,' he said. 'They hoped
that politicians like Lloyd George would somehow rise up together with the

English people. That was the aim of this bombardment.'[7] In other words, British leader Winston Churchill was seen as an impediment to peace.

By the end of August, when the British retaliated by bombing Berlin, Hitler's attitude to Britain hardened.

If the British Air Force drops two, three, or four thousand kilos of bombs, then we will drop 150,000 or 180,000; 230,000; 300,000; 400,000 kilograms in one night. When they say they will mount large scale attacks on our cities, then we will eradicate theirs.[8]

On 7 September 1940 Hitler ordered a massive bombing raid on London, which would be the first of seventy consecutive night raids on the British capital. Finally, by September 15, the Germans had lost so many bombers that they realised the attacks could not be sustained.

On 28 October 1940 Italy invaded Greece, by which time Hitler had already sent troops into Romania. For the two Axis leaders there was now resentment on both sides; for each had acted without the full consent and backing of the other.

Hitler, whose forces were infiltrating ever more eastwards, now gave Romania a guarantee of her new frontiers against foreign attack, that country being immensely valuable to him on account of its Ploesti oilfields. When Germany invaded the Soviet Union, Romanian forces would be at her side.

On 3 November 1940 the British opened a second front in Greece. This had the crucial effect of delaying 'Operation Barbarossa' (Hitler's proposed invasion of the Soviet Union), and would force Hitler's armies to do what every general dreaded, namely fight a war on Soviet soil in winter time.

Now that Stalin had tasted success, he decided to pressurise Germany even further. On 12 November 1940 the two foreign ministers Ribbentrop and Vyacheslav Molotov met in Berlin. On 26 November Molotov, now back in Moscow, informed the German Ambassador of the Soviet Union's terms for joining the Axis Pact. They were as follows: German troops to be withdrawn from Finland; a mutual assistance pact to be signed between the USSR and Bulgaria; the granting to the Soviets of control over the Arabian and Persian oil fields, and over the Dardanelles; the renunciation by Japan of her rights to concessions for coal and oil in the Soviet province of Northern Sakhalin.[9] Stalin was now playing Hitler at his own game.

In the same month (November 1940), Molotov visited Hitler in Berlin, where much to Hitler's embarrassment their meeting happened to coincide with a British bombing raid on the city, forcing the leaders to retreat into an air raid shelter. Far from improving relationships between the two countries, the visit was a dismal failure, the Russians being only too well aware of the build up of German forces along their border.

As for Hitler, the Soviet proposals were totally unacceptable. He was now convinced that,

sooner or later, Stalin will abandon us and go over to the enemy [the enemy being Britain and France].[10] The Third Reich, defender and protector of

Europe, could not have sacrificed these friendly countries on the altar of communism. Such behaviour would have been dishonourable .... War with Russia had become inevitable whatever we did .... I therefore decided, as soon as Molotov departed, that I would settle accounts with Russia as soon as fair weather permitted.[11]

The Curious Exploit of Rudolph Hess

Following the outbreak of war on 1 September 1939 Douglas Douglas-Hamilton, Fourteenth Duke of Hamilton and Brandon (who happened to be a distant relation of General Sir Ian Hamilton of the Anglo–German Association) was to become involved in an extraordinary incident which concerned Hitler's deputy, Rudolf Hess.

Hess was born in Alexandria, Egypt, into a wealthy German family of colonial traders. His father kept a large picture of German Emperor Wilhelm II in his office, and regularly toasted the health of the Kaiser on the occasion of that person's birthday. During the First World War, Hess served as a lieutenant on the Western Front.

Germany's post-war, socialist revolution was regarded by Hess as a stab in the back. Like Hitler, he blamed the Jews and became a convert to anti-Semitism. While a student of economics at the University of München, he became acquainted with General Karl Haushofer, Professor of Geopolitics, or the study of the relationship between a country's geographical features and its politics; the Nazis would later develop this theme to justify their policy of 'Lebensraum' (the acquisition by Germany of more living space for her people).

When Hess, who had joined the counter-revolution (opposed to the communist takeover of München, 4 April–1 May 1919) first heard Adolf Hitler describe the new German Reich which he (Hitler) foresaw, he was so impressed that his life was transformed for ever.

Hess recruited members to the SA (Stormtroopers) and actively participated in the so-called München 'Beer Hall Putsch' of November 1923 after which he fled to Austria. However, having heard that Hitler had been subsequently imprisoned for his crime in the fortress of Landsberg, Hess chose voluntarily to surrender to the authorities in order to join him there. In the annual ceremony marking the deaths of those who died in the 1923 'Putsch', Hess was regularly to be seen with Hitler at the front of the procession.

Following the abortive 'Putsch', the relationship between Hitler and Hess became a close one, Hitler becoming godfather to Hess's son, and Hess being appointed the Party's Deputy Leader from April 1933, with Martin Bormann as his Chief of Staff. It was Hess who approved the Nürnberg Laws of September 1935, depriving Jews of their rights as citizens.

***

Even when war was imminent, Hess was convinced that what his Führer really wanted was peace.

> The Führer has often stressed Germany's commitment to peace. It makes us happy to see that this plea for peace did not go unheard in other countries. The soldiers of other nations have raised their voices too. I am convinced that these voices were not raised in vain. [This may have been a reference to a previous goodwill visit made by General Sir Ian Hamilton and ex-soldiers' British Legion to Berlin.][12]

Shortly after the invasion of Poland on 1 September 1939 Hitler made the somewhat surprising decision that, should anything untoward happen to him, then Hermann Göring (Reich War Minister), and not Hess, was to be his successor.

At the time of Dunkerque (26 May–4 June 1940) Hitler said 'I have offered England friendship again and again. But love cannot be offered by one side alone.'[13] According to Rochus Misch, a soldier on Hitler's staff, it was while Hitler was having dinner, with Hess as his guest, that Press Officer Dr Otto Dietrich, came with a message saying: 'My Führer, the English don't agree' [to a truce with Germany]. To which Hitler replied: '*My God what else can I do? After all I can't fly there and get down on my knee.*' According to Rochus Misch, this gave Hess the idea for the action which he was now about to take.[14]

In the summer of 1940 Rudolf Hess and his former tutor, Professor Karl Haushofer, met in the Grünwalder Forest. Hess was opposed to the notion of Germany fighting a war on two fronts, and was anxious to discover a way in which peace with Britain might be negotiated. The two men discussed the possibility of approaching either 'the old [General Sir] Ian Hamilton, or the other [Duke of] Hamilton [then Marquis of Clydesdale].'[15]

Hess, with Hitler's approval, subsequently met with Albrecht Haushofer, the professor's eldest son, who was an official in the German Foreign Office. It was Albrecht who suggested the Duke of Hamilton as being the more appropriate person for Hess to meet, on account of his having, 'access at all times to all important persons in London, even to Churchill and the king'.[16]

Hess's mind was now made up. On 10 May 1941 at 17.45 hours (British Double Summer Time), he took off from the Messerschmitt works at Augsburg, and by 22.08 hours his aircraft, a Messerschmitt BF110, was detected by British radar as he approached the north-east coast of England. He now crossed from England into Scotland with a British Defiant night fighter aircraft in pursuit. Having crossed Scotland from east to west, Hess found himself unable to locate his destination, namely Dungavel House, the Duke of Hamilton's home in South Lanarkshire, where there happened to be a private airstrip. He doubled back, but ran short of fuel and was forced to bail out over Boynton Moor, about ten miles from Glasgow's city centre.[17]

Shortly after 23.00 hours, 45 year-old Scottish ploughman David McLean heard an explosion and saw a parachutist land in the meadow of Floors Farm, near Eaglesham. Beside a crashed and burning aircraft was an injured German officer, who was none other than Hitler's deputy, Rudolf Hess. On landing he had sustained minor injuries to his ankle. Astonishingly, Hess had made the 900-mile journey from Germany to Scotland single-handed: no mean feat, even for an experienced flier such as himself, who had won the 1934 annual air race around the Zugspitze, Germany's highest peak. Hamilton was himself an aviator of some note, having in 1933 been the first man to fly an aircraft over Mount Everest. By a strange coincidence, Hamilton was currently serving as Station Commander at RAF Turnhouse, situated to the west of Edinburgh. Hess was now taken away as a prisoner for interrogation and treatment to his ankle.

When Hamilton visited Hess, Hitler's deputy explained who he was, and claimed to have met the Duke in Berlin at the Olympic Games, and that the Duke had lunched at his house.[18] Hess stated: 'I am here on a personal, unauthorised mission of humanity.'[19] According to Sir Ivone Kirkpatrick, British Foreign Office expert on Germany, Hess stated that he had come to Britain without Hitler's permission in order to,

> convince responsible persons that since England could not win the war, the wisest course was to make peace now. The solution was that England should give Germany a free hand in Europe, and Germany give England a completely free hand in the Empire, with the sole reservation that we should return Germany's ex-colonies which she required as a source of raw materials.[20]

According to historian James Douglas-Hamilton (eldest son of the late Duke): 'When Hamilton told Churchill what had happened that evening, Churchill said, "Do you mean to tell me that the Deputy Führer of Germany is in our hands?" He looked at my father as though he was having hallucinations.'[21] The following day there was a massive German air raid on London in which the Houses of Parliament were hit.

Had Hitler the slightest inkling that his deputy was in Britain on a peace mission, it is unthinkable that he would have bombed London the evening after Hess's arrival – unless of course, this was the 'stick', to counterbalance the 'carrot' which Hess was offering. The outcome was that Hess's offer to Hamilton was rejected.

It is not known if Hitler was privy to Hess's clandestine activities. However, the Führer now disowned his deputy, and in a statement made on the radio declared: 'On Saturday 10 May, Comrade Hess took off on a flight from which he has not returned. A letter he left behind shows signs of mental derangement, and we fear that Hess was suffering from hallucinations.'

Rochus Misch believed that all Hess's servants, who were suspected of being involved in the 'plot', were subsequently sent to concentration camps. As for Hess, he was not officially replaced as Deputy Führer, but Martin Bormann effectively filled his place. According to Albert Speer, 'Hitler said that in a peace treaty [with Britain] he would demand Hess's return. He [Hess] would then be tried and executed for treason.'[22]

Hess remained in prison for the duration of the war where, realising that he had failed in his mission, he made three separate suicide attempts. Had Hess been successful in persuading Britain to cease hostilities against Germany, there is no doubt that Hitler would have been delighted, as he would have then been able to concentrate solely on his battles in the east. However, having failed in his mission, Hess had become nothing but an embarrassment, and for both sides. Were they to get to hear about it, Hitler's Axis partners would take a dim view of Hess's unilateral negotiations with the British (even though they were apparently unsanctioned by the Nazi regime), and worse than that, how could Hitler be sure that Hess would not reveal the secret of 'Operation Barbarossa' – the forthcoming invasion of Russia? As for Churchill, he would face a similar problem, were his ally Stalin to suspect that secret negotiations were going on between Britain and Germany.

In Hitler's mind, there was no doubt who was to blame for Hess's action, namely the astrologers who had given Hess incorrect advice. Now, by an edict entitled 'Action Hess', the public practice of any occult sciences including astrology was forbidden, and all prominent astrologers were arrested.

Greece and Yugoslavia

With the defeat of Mussolini's Italian troops in Albania and Greece, Hitler realised that before he launched 'Operation Barbarossa' against the Soviet Union, it was essential for Greece to be occupied and subdued. Between Germany and Greece however, lay four countries: Hungary, Romania, Bulgaria and Yugoslavia. The first two of these were already under German occupation, while the third, Bulgaria, had in March 1941 joined the Axis 'Tripartite Pact'. Therefore, only Yugoslavia, a country hostile to both German and Russian occupation of the Balkans, remained as an obstacle to Hitler's ambitions. Furthermore, Hitler calculated, were he to invade Greece, then Yugoslavia would be sure to intervene against him.

Having decided to invade Yugoslavia, Hitler agreed to appease the Hungarians once more, and in return for that country's collaboration, Hungary would be permitted to regain territory lost to its neighbours in 1920 (under the Treaty of Trianon).

Hitler now invited Prince Paul, Regent of Yugoslavia, to the Berghof for discussions. However, although the Prince's Crown Council agreed to sign the Axis Pact, such was the opposition that by 27 March 1941 pro-Allied army officers had overthrown the government, and replaced Paul with his nephew Peter. The Soviet Union instantly recognised King Peter and his new government, and signed a pact with Yugoslavia on 5 April. Faced with this setback, Hitler declared: 'Now I intend to make a clean sweep of the Balkans ....'[23] Hitler issued a directive, whereby Yugoslavia and Greece were to be attacked simultaneously. First, the Yugoslav forces were overwhelmed in a devastating 'Blitzkrieg-type' attack.

On 12 April 1941 German and Hungarian troops marched into Belgrade, and ten days later German tanks entered the Greek capital Athens. However, in order to achieve this goal, Hitler had been forced to employ no fewer than twenty-nine German divisions. This had a knock on effect, in that it delayed 'Operation Barbarossa', a delay which was to have the most profound repercussions for Germany in the very near future.

Notes

1. Toland, John, *Adolf Hitler*, p. 599.
2. Ibid, p. 611.
3. *Documents on German Foreign Policy*, Files of the German Foreign Office, pp. 207–8.
4. Hitler, Adolf, *Mein Kampf*, p. 116.
5. **Hitler's Britain.*
6. Ibid.
7. Ibid.
8. Ibid.
9. *Nazi-Soviet Relations* Dispatch of Schulenburg. Nov. 26, 1940, NSR. pp. 258–9.
10. Toland, op. cit., p. 646.
11. Ibid.
12. **Hitler's Henchmen: Hess, The Deputy.*
13. Ibid.
14. Ibid.
15. Douglas-Hamilton, James, *The Truth about Rudolf Hess*, pp. 117, 119.
16. Ibid, p. 121.
17. Ibid, p. 11.
18. Ibid, p. 144.
19 **Hitler's Henchmen: Hess, The Deputy.*
20. Kirkpatrick, Sir Ivone, 1959, *The Inner Circle*. London. in Douglas-Hamilton, op. cit., p. 155.
21. **Hitler's Henchmen: Hess, The Deputy.*
22. Ibid.
23. Toland, op. cit., p. 653.

CHAPTER XXVIII
'Operation Barbarossa'

Up until now, Hitler's armed forces had carried all before them, albeit having thus far been up against fairly modest opposition. Now his commanders were to present him with a golden opportunity of striking a decisive blow against the Soviets. However, as with the debacle of Dunkerque Hitler, by his indecisiveness, would nullify their efforts and therefore create a second debacle at his eastern front.

The race war, advocated by Lanz von Liebenfels in his *Ostara* journals, was now to be made reality by Hitler, as he waged his battle of attrition against the Slavs. Genocide, also advocated by Liebenfels, would be another potent tool in Hitler's armoury.

***

In the spring of 1941 Hitler invited the new Japanese Ambassador General Hiroshi Oshima, to a secret briefing at which he outlined his plan for a global war to be fought by Germany and Japan, with a view to conquering the world – 'Operation Orient'. The proposal was for one German force to sweep across north Africa, Egypt, Iraq and Iran; for another to cross the Soviet Union into the oil-rich Caucasus. Then, having joined up, the forces would move to attack India, the 'Jewel in the Crown' of the British Empire. Meanwhile, Japan would conquer Europe's colonies in the east before joining with the Germans in India.

That March Hitler issued the so-called 'Commissar Order' by which, following the invasion of the Soviet Union, the entire Soviet leadership, both military and civilian, was to be eliminated. However, so that Hitler should not personally be implicated in the decision, nothing was put in writing.

On 20 March 1941 Yosuke Matsuoka, the Japanese Foreign Minister, arrived in Berlin, where he urged the Führer to make peace with Stalin, and with him, help create a joint German-Soviet-Japanese alliance. This, however, was not in accordance with Hitler's long-standing ambition to invade Russia. The Germans now urged the Japanese to attack the Russians in the east; the Japanese responded by massing their troops in Manchuria.

On 13 April 1941, greatly to the annoyance of Hitler, Japan, in order to secure her northern flank, signed a neutrality pact with the Soviet Union. This would be of immense help to Stalin in the months to come, as it would allow him to transfer many of his eastern divisions to his Western Front.

***

'I had always maintained that we ought, at all costs, to avoid waging war on two fronts,' Hitler told Martin Bormann, Head of the Party Chancellery. 'And you may rest assured that I pondered long and anxiously over Napoleon, and his experiences in Russia.'[1] So why did Hitler decide to invade the Soviet Union?

The answer is that from an early stage, he had convinced himself that his mission in life was to destroy Bolshevism. However, time was now working against him; the Battle of Britain had dashed any hopes he had of invading England, and he feared (rightly as it transpired) that America was soon to play a potentially decisive role.

By May 1941 the Soviets had supplied Germany with approximately 1.5 million tons of grain, 100,000 tons of cotton, 2 million tons of petroleum products, 1.5 million tons of timber, 140,000 tons of manganese and 25,000 tons of chromium.[2] This was hardly the action of a country which was expecting imminent invasion by the recipient of all these commodities!

Meanwhile, owing to the failure of the Italians (who had invaded Greece on 28 October of the previous year) to subdue their opponents, Hitler was obliged to divert valuable forces to the Grecian campaign, which had the effect of delaying 'Operation Barbarossa'. Instead of commencing on 15 May it now began on 22 June.

***

Such was the disarray of the Soviet Union in its unpreparedness for an attack by Germany, that by the time Stalin had finally consented to Soviet Commander Marshal Zhukhov putting the frontier forces on the alert, it was too late for them to take effective action. As for the Red Air Force, the majority of its aircraft were destroyed on the ground before they even had the chance to take off.

The previous December, in 'Directive No. 21', marked 'Top Secret', Hitler had outlined his plan. 'Barbarossa' was to be a multi-pronged attack, involving not only German forces, but also those of Finland, Italy, Romania and Hungary. The three main units concerned were Army Group North (AGN), under Field Marshal Wilhelm von Leeb: it would advance towards Leningrad – which the Finns would also attack from the north, cutting off Soviet forces in the Baltic States in the process; Army Group Centre (AGC), under Field Marshal Feodor von Bock, which would drive directly towards Moscow; Army Group South (AGS), under General Gerd von Rundstedt, which would drive towards the Ukraine, overrun that region's industrial centres, capture the town of Rostov and the Crimea, then finally, the valuable oilfields of the Caucasus. Farther south still, German and Romanian troops would advance towards Odessa and the Black Sea.

***

On 22 June 1941 (Day 1 of 'Operation Barbarossa') German Ambassador Count Friedrich von der Schulenburg went to the Kremlin to accuse the Soviet Union of being 'about to fall on Germany's back'. He told Soviet Foreign Affairs Commissar Molotov that the Führer had therefore ordered the Wehrmacht 'to oppose this threat with all the means at its disposal'; to which Molotov retorted: 'It is war! Your aircraft have just bombarded some ten [Russian] "villages". Do you believe that we deserve that?'[3] Meanwhile, Propaganda Minister Goebbels declared: 'Now that the Führer has unmasked the treachery of the Bolshevik rulers, National Socialism, and hence the German people, are reverting to the principles which impelled them – the struggle against plutocracy and Bolshevism.'[4]

As the German forces advanced, they were followed by four SS 'Einsatzgruppen' (Special Groups – a euphemism for murder squads), each consisting of 3,000 men whose aim was to eliminate Bolshevik leaders, Jews, gypsies, and the mentally and physically sick. Hitler now transferred his headquarters to the 'Wolfsschanze' ('Wolf's Lair'), near Rastenburg in East Prussia.

The Jews, instead of acting in a way consistent with how Hitler liked to portray them, i.e. people opposed to the Germans, and anxious to spread Bolshevism throughout the world, instead welcomed the Germans as liberators. Their reward was to be rounded up and despatched to concentration camps and killing centres. In the words of Obergruppenführer von dem Bach-Zelewski, Senior SS and Police Commander for Central Russia: 'Never before has a people [i.e. the Jews] gone as unsuspectingly to its disaster.'[5]

The primary initial objective of 'Barbarossa' was to destroy the Red Army and at first all went brilliantly well. In huge pincer movements German forces cut off their Soviet counterparts: at Minsk (9 July 1941 290,000 captured); at Smolensk (12 July 300,000 trapped); at Umlan (4 August 100,000 prisoners taken). The Germans' greatest success however, was at Kiev (19 October), when 665,000 Soviet troops surrendered.

By 14 July 1941 AGN had reached Leningrad and was in occupation of its suburbs. The city, invested as it was to the north by the Finns, was now only able to hold out by being supplied across Lake Lagoda. AGC encountered serious Soviet resistance at the Battle of Smolensk (10 July–10 September), but continued nevertheless with the drive on Moscow.

On 2 October 1941 Hitler said:

Only when the entire German people becomes a single community of sacrifice can we hope and expect that providence will stand by us in the future. Almighty God never helped a lazy man. Nor does He help a coward.[6]

However, the fatal flaw in Hitler's directive was to become apparent. Whereas he had envisaged that after the initial onslaught, AGC would divert to support AGN, rather than press on to Moscow, Field Marshal Walther von Brauchitsch and General Franz Halder, Chief of the General Staff, believed that the attack on Moscow, centre of Russian communications and armament production, should be the primary objective. Against the advice of his generals, Hitler ordered that armoured units of AGC were to be diverted, some to be sent north to AGN, to facilitate the capture of Leningrad, and others to the south to AGS, to assist with the drive into the Ukraine. 'My generals understand nothing of the war economy,' he said.[7]

Finally, on 5 September 1941 Hitler, at the urging of Brauchitsch, changed his mind once again and ordered that the focus be once more switched to Moscow, which on 2 October was attacked with seventy-seven divisions in 'Operation Typhoon'. This, despite warnings from Field Marshal Feodor von Bock that the season was too far gone to risk an attack.

Further catastrophes befell the Soviets, when at Bryansk and Vyazma another 650,000 prisoners were taken. By October, when the Germans were barely fifty miles from Moscow, around 3 million Soviet troops had been killed, captured or wounded.

Halder, in his response to Hitler's statement that the Russians were 'finished', told his Führer that the army's own intelligence showed that this was far from the case.

Hitler's decisions had ceased to have anything in common with the principles of strategy and operations as they have been recognised for generations past. *They were the product of a violent nature following its momentary impulses, which recognise no limits to possibility, and which made its wish-dreams the father of its acts....*[8] You didn't have to have the gift of a profit, to see what would happen when Stalin unleashed those million and a half troops against Stalingrad and the Don flank. I pointed this out to Hitler very clearly.

The result was the dismissal of the Chief of the Army General Staff.[9]

Heavy rains caused the German Mark IV tanks to flounder in the mud. Not only that, but the Luftwaffe, which would have supported their attacks by Blitzkrieg, could not fly owing to the poor visibility. The attack had come too late. Even worse, the Germans now found themselves facing a new and able Russian Commander, General Georgi Zhukov.

When, in November 1941, Colonel General Heinz Guderian, Commander of the Second Panzer Army, informed Bock that he could 'see no way of carrying them [i.e. Bock's orders] out', because of the poor condition of his men, Bock ignored him and ordered another assault on Moscow (the domes of whose buildings were clearly visible to the Germans) to commence on 15 November. Now came snow, ice and temperatures of minus 40 degrees Celsius, for which the German troops were ill prepared, due to an earlier edict by Hitler which prohibited the making ready of winter clothing for the men. On 5 December Guderian was forced to halt his attack on Moscow. AGC's losses alone had by now amounted to 55,000 dead, and 100,000 wounded or suffering from frostbite.

On 6 December 1941 Hitler, after a huge Russian counter-attack on a 200-mile front, confessed to Colonel General Alfred Jodl, Chief of OKW's Operations ('Obercommando der Wehrmacht') that, 'Victory could no longer be achieved.'[10]

Meanwhile, on 7 December Japan, anxious to prevent America from intervening in her plan to conquer Europe's Far Eastern colonies, attacked the American Fleet at Pearl Harbor. Japanese forces went on to capture Singapore, Hong Kong, Malaya and Dutch Indonesia.

On 11 December 1941 Hitler (together with Italy) declared war on America (the first and only time that the Führer declared war on a country before attacking it); *an act of crass stupidity, given the fact that there was in the USA a substantial anti-war lobby – a fact which President Roosevelt was well aware of.* Now, however, the decision had been taken out of Roosevelt's hands.

By 13 December 1941 it was clear that Hitler's attempt to surround Moscow had failed. His response? To dismiss Brauchitsch and assume personal command of the army. Now, instead of sanctioning a retreat he gave the order: 'Stand fast: not one step back!' and with an air of supreme arrogance, which was totally misplaced in view of the situation on the ground, declared:

> This little affair of operational command is something anybody can do. The commander-in-chief's job is to train the army in the National Socialist Idea, and I know of no general who could do that as I want it done. For that reason, I have taken over control of the army myself.[11]

Between December 1941 and January 1942, Hitler dismissed not only the commanders of the army groups which had embarked on 'Operation Barbarossa', but thirty-five other generals as well.[12] In the words of Ulrich de Maizière (of Hitler's General Staff):

> *One of Hitler's greatest weaknesses as a commander was that, in that mood, any feelings for logistics deserted him. Thus the operational aims he set, and his decisions, became more and more unreal ... further and further from reality.*[13]

Stalingrad

On 28 May 1942 AGS captured Kharkov, and on 24 July Rostov on the Don river. In the far south, the Germans reached the Crimea, where the newly formed XI Army, under General Fritz Erich von Manstein, sealed off the fortress of Sevastopol.

The events at Stalingrad during the winter of 1942–3 would, however, provide a graphic demonstration, not only of Hitler's incompetence as a commander, but also of his utter lack of concern for the well-being of his armed forces.

***

At first, for the Germans, all went well. On 12 May 1942, Soviet Marshal Semyon Timoshenko's forces attacked the Germans at Kharkov, and were routed, with 600 tanks lost and 250,000 troops taken prisoner.

'Fall Blau' (or 'Case Blue') was an operation designed by Hitler to drive through the Caucasus to the Caspian Sea, capturing the oilfields of Grozny and Maikop on the way. On 28 June 1942 Army Group South, commanded by Field Marshal Feodor von Bock, duly launched the attack, but failed to encircle and destroy the Soviets in the customary classic pincer movement, which hitherto had been so successful.

On 13 July 1942 Hitler dismissed Bock, and divided his forces into Army Group 'A' (AGA) under Field Marshal Wilhelm von List, and Army Group 'B' (AGB) under Field Marshal Maximilian von Weichs. List's AGA, in 'Operation Edelweiss', was to continue the drive to the Caucasus; Weichs' AGB, in 'Operation Siegfried', was to drive towards Stalingrad, an industrial city situated on a great bend in the Volga river. (In this operation Italian, Hungarian and Romanian forces would also be involved on the German side.)

Hitler also ordered the XI Army to withdraw from the south and instead travel north to join the attack on Leningrad; this had the effect of extending the German southern front from 500 to 3,000 miles. In another bizarre move, Hitler transferred General Hermann Hoth's IV Panzer Army from General Friedrich von Paulus' VI Army (Paulus was Deputy Chief of the Army General Staff under General Franz Halder, and the VI Army was the main element of AGB) to the south, to the command of AGA. This weakened Paulus' offensive capability, and thereby retarded his advance on Stalingrad.

Although List's AGA captured Rostov on 23 July 1942, by the time it reached the Caucasus it found the mountain passes had been blocked by the Soviets.

At the end of August 1942 Paulus, whose supply line stretched 1, 200 miles back to Berlin, commenced his attack on Stalingrad, much of which was reduced to rubble by German artillery fire and bombing. However, the Soviets capital-ised on this by using the ruins as defensive fortifications. By early October the Germans, in hand-to-hand fighting, managed to occupy roughly 70% of the city and had pinned the Russian Sixty-second Army with its back to the Volga river.

The Russian winter found the German soldiers much less adequately clothed than their Russian counterparts; nor was their equipment designed to deal with the sub-zero temperatures which pertained. In the words of Kurt Sametreiter (SS 'Liebstandarte' – 'bodyguard' – Adolf Hitler), the temperature fell to minus 46 degrees Celsius. 'I saw how my fellow soldiers [frozen] ears fell off,' he said, 'so we got some rope and tied our ears to our heads, and that's how we coped.' In the absence of overcoats, the only way for the German soldiers to obtain them was from dead or captured Russians.[14]

By early November 1942 90% of Stalingrad was in the hands of the Germans. Nevertheless, in a holding operation of unsurpassed tenacity, heroism and improvi-sation, the Red Army under General Vasili Chuikov (whose overall commander, General Georgi Zhukov, had organised and directed the successful counter-offen-sive before Moscow) was reinforced from across the river and managed to hold on.

Now, it was Zhukov's turn to take the offensive. On 19 November 1942 he launched 'Operation Uran', a counter-attack made simultaneously on three fronts. (Prior to this, General Kurt Zeitzler, the new Chief of Army General Staff

– Halder having been replaced by Hitler – had flown back to Hitler's headquarters to request permission to withdraw his forces before the Russian counter-offensive began: the Führer had declined.)

Zeitzler now urged Hitler to give permission for the VI Army to withdraw from Stalingrad to the Don bend, in order that the front line, now fractured by the Soviets, could be restored. Hitler responded: 'I won't leave the Volga! I won't go back from the Volga!'[15] Meanwhile, Paulus' army of 250,000 men was encircled by the Soviets.

On the evening of 22 November 1942 General Friedrich Paulus, Commander of the VI Army (which consisted of twenty German and two Romanian divisions), signalled by wireless message that his troops were surrounded. Hitler's response was that the VI Army would be supplied by Göring's Luftwaffe, until it could be relieved. Paulus declared that he would need a minimum of 750 tons of supplies per day to be flown in. In the thick fog and freezing conditions, this proved to be well beyond the capability of the Luftwaffe.

On 25 November 1942 Hitler hastily ordered Field Marshal von Manstein back from the Leningrad Front, and gave him command of Army Group Don (newly improvised from part of the AGA), with the task of relieving the VI Army from the south-west. Manstein believed that the only chance of success would be for the VI Army to break out of Stalingrad, while he made his own assault against the intervening Russian armies. However, once again Hitler refused to countenance a withdrawal from Stalingrad.

Manstein commenced his attack on Stalingrad on 12 December 1942 in 'Operation Winter Tempest', and advanced to within thirty miles of the southern perimeter of the city from where Paulus' besieged army could see the signal flares of their would-be rescuers. Had the VI Army chosen this moment to break out from Stalingrad, they would almost certainly have met with success, but Paulus stubbornly obeyed Hitler's orders to stand and fight to the last. By now, the Volga river had frozen over, thus facilitating the relief of the city by the Soviets.

In his only concession, made on 21 December 1942, Hitler gave Paulus permission to break out, but only provided that he also held on to Stalingrad! Said Chief of Staff Zeitzler:

> I begged Hitler to authorise the breakout. I pointed out that this was abso-lutely our last chance to save the 200,000 men of Paulus' army. However, Hitler would not give way. In vain I described to him conditions inside the so-called fortress [of Stalingrad]: the despair of the starving soldiers, their loss of confidence in the Supreme Command, the wounded expiring for lack of proper attention, while thousands froze to death. *He remained as impervious to arguments of this sort as to those others which I had advanced.*[16]

On 8 January 1943 General Konstantin Rokossovski, Commander of Soviet Forces on the Don front, offered General Paulus terms for surrender. When Hitler yet again turned down Paulus' request that he be permitted to comply with Rokossovski's demand, the Soviets, on 10 January, began what would be their final assault on the city. Meanwhile, many Germans soldiers began to commit suicide.

On 24 January 1943 the Soviets again offered Paulus the chance to surrender. 'Troops [are] without ammunition or food,' said Paulus in a wireless message to Hitler. 'Effective command no longer possible …. 18,000 wounded without any supplies or dressings or drugs …. Further defence senseless. Collapse inevitable. Army requests immediate permission to surrender in order to save lives of Romanian troops.' To which the reply came back from the Führer:

> Surrender is forbidden. VI Army will hold their positions to the last man and the last round, and by their heroic endurance, will make an unforgettable contribution towards the establishment of a defensive front and the salvation of the western world.[17] *One must cut off one's own lines of retreat; then one fights more easily and with greater determination.*

In other words, there must be no way out for Paulus, however dire his situation. On 30 January 1943, with supreme irony, Hitler promoted General Paulus to the rank of field marshal.

The following day Paulus' army surrendered, by which time, of his 285,000 soldiers, only 91,000 remained alive, together with 20,000 Romanians. Awaiting them now were the prisoner of war camps of Siberia, places of such harshness that only 5,000 would ever see their fatherland again.[18] For the Germans, the only positive outcome of Stalingrad was that by tying down seven Soviet armies, this had successfully enabled them to evacuate their own armies from the Caucasus.

Hitler was seemingly indifferent as to whether a single soldier was lost, or a whole army. This is commensurate with the notion that he was at heart a gambler. His adjutant Reinhard Spitzy said of him, 'Hitler always wanted to gamble. He risked everything. Before the war Göring said, "We should stop risking everything." To which Hitler replied, "We've always risked everything and I always will risk everything."'[19] Otto Gritschneder went further:

> *What he [Hitler] called BRAVELY was really the 'all or nothing' PSYCHOSIS OF A MADMAN.* There are people who take the greatest risks, so as to feel the joy and thrill of adventure. He certainly wasn't a realist.[20]

In retrospect, Gritschneder was nearer the truth than perhaps he realised, as will shortly be demonstrated.

'For me,' said Count Johann Adolf Kielmansegg of Hitler's General Staff, 'it [the experience of Stalingrad] destroyed [not only] any respect [I had] for Hitler as a commander, but also as a man, as a leader.' Vincenz Griesemer (soldier at Stalingrad) said, 'For us, Hitler was, by this stage, our grave-digger.'[21]

***

Following the German defeat at Stalingrad on 2 February 1943 Hitler promoted Martin Bormann to the post of Secretary to the Führer, in charge of all the affairs of state.

Bormann, the son of a postal worker, failed to gain his high school diploma. A mediocre student, he fought as an artilleryman in the Great War. Having been released in 1927 following his imprisonment for the murder (when he was serving in the Freikorps) of a former school teacher, Bormann joined the German National Socialist Workers' Party, and finally the staff at Nazi Party Headquarters in München. In 1933 Hitler appointed him Head of the Office of Deputy Führer Rudolf Hess.

Not surprisingly, Bormann was viewed with contempt by senior members of the armed services. They saw him as an uneducated person, and as someone who restricted their access to the Führer.

***

The defeat of Nazi forces at Stalingrad would prove to be the turning point of the war, and yet Hitler seemed strangely unmoved by it all, preferring to blame his generals for yet another debacle. To them, and to his party officials and close acquaintances, it must have seemed that Hitler was working to a different agenda, one to which they were not privy, and which they were unable to comprehend. This again begs the question, as to whether the Führer, who was willing to sacrifice his troops on a massive scale and seemingly without compunction, *was suffering from some derangement of the mind*.

***

Hitler once more displayed his intransigence when in February 1943 following a Soviet counter-attack, Rundstedt realised that his position in the town of Rostov was untenable, and that he must withdraw. When Hitler duly and predictably ordered him to remain where he was, Rundstedt replied: 'It is MADNESS to attempt to hold. First the troops cannot do it, and second, if they do not retreat, they will be destroyed. I repeat that this order must be rescinded, or that you find someone else [to command].'[22] ('Madness' was a word which was being used *more and more frequently* in relation to the Führer.) To this Hitler replied: 'I am acceding to your request. Please give up your command.' Rundstedt was now replaced by Field Marshal von Reichenau. Rostov fell to the Red Army on 14 February 1943.

***

Hermann Rauschning described how Hitler's acolytes (metaphorically) '... threw sand in Hitler's eyes ....

The German people, once the most objective and scientific of peoples, now went to unbelievable extremes of lying servility. Hitler was never told the uncomfortable truth. By favourably coloured reports, he was pushed ever farther along the road to ruin.[23]

Hitler subsequently made it clear where in his opinion the blame for the defeat, both at Stalingrad and elsewhere, lay – not of course, with himself, but with his fellow countrymen. *'If many people are shattered by this trial of will, then I shall shed no tears for them. They deserve this fate. They have forged their own destiny. They do not deserve any better.'*[24] By the end of 1944 more than two thirds of German towns and cities had been bombed, but Hitler did not take the trouble to visit them.

Newsreels and press reports designed for homeland consumption revealed nothing of Germany's defeat at Stalingrad and the huge losses sustained by her forces, nor of the untold atrocities committed by the Nazis, and in particular by the Waffen SS (which by now was so short of manpower that, among others, Balkan Muslims and Ukranian Slavs were recruited into its ranks). They included the SS massacre at the Russian military hospital at Kharkov in March 1943 and the destruction of the village of Oradour-sur-Glane in south-west France on 10 June 1944 when its men folk were shot to death in a barn, and its women and children locked in a church which was then set on fire, to name but two.

***

Given the fact that Hitler had a long-standing intention to invade the Soviet Union, he might well have learned a lesson not only from the bitter experience of French Emperor Napoleon I, but also from his own country's experiences in World War I, when the retreating Russians had employed a 'scorched earth' policy, and where Austro-Hungary had been fought to a standstill by Italy (then on the Allied side) over a period of three years, in the mountainous Alpine region.

***

In 1944 dissatisfied with the existing German legal system, Hitler set up the euphemistically named 'People's Court'. This became a means whereby opponents of his could be swiftly incarcerated. 'Intensive interrogation', a phrase used by the Gestapo, was a euphemism for torture, where those who did not confess to the court were beaten. Even those acquitted were still sent to concentration camps. When students of München University's White Rose Society denounced Hitler as a mass murderer, they were sentenced to death.

General Kurt von Schleicher, former Reich Chancellor, who was seen as an obstacle to the Nazis, was shot to death, along with his wife. When civil servants working in Secretary of State Roland Freisler's Reich Ministry of Justice prepared a document describing this as a 'political murder', Freisler (according to Otto Gritschneider, Counsel for the Defence, at the Nürnberg War Crimes Tribunal) ordered the document to be destroyed saying, 'That was no political murder, that was suicide.'[25]

The capture by American soldiers of Gestapo files in the town of Würzburg gave an insight into how the Gestapo (State Secret Police) actually operated: mainly by relying on German citizens to denounce their friends and neighbours, even for such seemingly innocuous pastimes as consorting with Jews, having homosexual or lesbian tendencies, or failing to give the Nazi salute, 'Heil Hitler!'.

In an atmosphere where nobody trusted their neighbours, who might at any time denounce them, thousands of Germans left the country and became émigrés. Was there no end in sight to the terror and misery which Hitler was perpetrating, not only on others, but also on his own people?

It was felt by some that if Hitler could be assassinated, then the Home Guard could take over power in Germany and end the war. On 20 July 1944 German Army Colonel Klaus von Stauffenberg placed a bomb under a table where Hitler was holding a conference. Although the bomb exploded, Hitler sustained only minor injuries. Stauffenberg and his fellow conspirators were arrested (the Gestapo having discovered lists of their names), and they were tried at the Supreme Court in Berlin the following month by Freisler (whose vicious shrieking and snarling surpassed even that of Hitler himself), presiding over the proceedings.

General Beck was given the opportunity to commit suicide. Stauffenberg and General Friedrich Olbricht, together with their two adjutants, were sentenced to death for high treason, and executed by firing squad. Other prisoners included Field Marshal Erwin von Witzleben, Generals Erich Hoepner, Helmuth Stieff and Paul von Hase. Colonel Mertz von Quirheim and Lt Werner von Haeften suffered a slow and agonising death by being hanged with piano wire from meat hooks.

It is believed that approximately 5,000 men and women suspected of having been involved in the uprising of 20 July, 1944 were executed by the Nazis. One of the accused, Count Peter Yorck von Wartenburg, a cousin of Stauffenberg, was brave enough to express his views before being shouted down by Freisler. 'Why didn't you join the Nazi Party?' Freisler enquired. 'Because I am not, and never could be, a Nazi.' When Freisler asked the Count whether he agreed with the 'National Socialist conception of justice, say, in regard to rooting out the Jews', Yorck replied, 'What is important, what brings together all these questions, is the totalitarian claim of the State on the individual which forces him to renounce his moral and religious obligations to God.'[26] On 3 February 1945 the court building, where trials were still in progress, received a direct hit from an American bomber. Freisler was killed instantly as the building collapsed.

Notes

1. Toland, John, *Adolf Hitler*, p. 650.
2. Ibid, p. 667.
3. Ibid, pp. 671–2.

4. Ibid, p. 673.
5. Ibid, p. 676.
6. Ibid, p. 685.
7. *Hitler: a Profile: The Commander.*
8. Halder, Franz, 1949, *Hitler als Feldherr*, München, p. 50.
9. Shirer, William L, *The Rise and Fall of the Third Reich*, p. 917.
10. Toland, op. cit., p. 690.
11. Ibid, p. 697.
12. Campbell, Christy, *The World War II Fact Book*, p. 102.
13. *Hitler: a Profile: The Commander.*
14. *The SS: Himmler's Madness.*
15. Zeitzler, General Kurt, 'The Fatal Decisions', Essay on Stalingrad in Freidin, 1956, New York.
16. Shirer, op. cit., p .927.
17. Ibid, p. 930.
18. Ibid, p. 932.
19. *Hitler: a Profile: The Blackmailer.*
20. Ibid.
21. *Hitler: a Profile: The Commander.*
22. Toland, op. cit., p. 689.
23. Rauschning, Hermann, *Hitler Speaks*, p. 204
24. *Hitler's War: Air War over Germany.*
25. *Hitler's Henchmen: Freisler: the Executioner.*
26. Shirer, op. cit., p. 1071.

CHAPTER XXIX

The 'Final Solution'

Hitler never met Liebenfels, nor did he acknowledge his work, or ever disclose that the *Ostara* magazines (and probably other of Liebenfels' works) were the source of his core beliefs. The relationship between the two men was that of puppeteer and puppet, and it was undoubtedly Liebenfels who pulled the strings, as it were. Now, in 'The Final Solution', the puppet was about to transform the puppeteer's notions into reality.

The full implications of The Final Solution – 'Holocaust' – would be felt not only in Germany but throughout all the countries occupied by the Nazis. Its seeds, however, had been sown long before Adolf Hitler arrived on the scene.

During the Christmas period of the year 1920 the Nazi Party's message, carried to its readers on the front page of its newspaper *Der Volkischer Beobachter*, was as follows: 'Germans! Buy your Christmas presents at German stores, but not from Jews or in Jewish stores.'[1]

However, when the Nazis came to power in 1933 Eugene Levine (German Communist Youth 1930–3) said that because a substantial number of the storm troopers had Jewish girlfriends, many German Jews thought, 'It's not going to be so bad .... They can't hate us all.'[2] In fact, life for the Jews got worse.

On 1 April 1933 the Nazi Party organised a boycott of all Jewish shops for a period of one day. On 10 May outside Berlin's opera house, there was a great bonfire of books, perceived to contain un-German or pro-Jewish sentiments.

Jews, gypsies, Slavs and those with hereditary disabilities, physical or mental, could clearly play no part in the production of an Aryan master race. Thus from 1933 onward, it was the duty of nurses and doctors to report them to the health authority where a 'eugenics committee' would decide who was, and who was not worthy to procreate. Those designated as unworthy were labelled 'a-socials', and compulsorily sterilised. The message was reinforced by propaganda films demanding that women should question whether the genes of their forebears were worthy to be passed on.

One of Propaganda Minister Dr Josef Goebbels' films showed two scorpions fighting with each other, illustrating the theory of the survival of the fittest. The 'professor', who was commentating on the film declared: 'All animals live in a permanent struggle, whereby the weak is destroyed.'[3]

On 27 July 1934 Hitler offered Hjalmar Schact, President of the Reich Bank, the additional post of Economics Minister. However, 'Before I accept,' said Schacht, who as it transpired was one of the very few people courageous enough to stand up to Hitler, 'I want to know how you wish me to handle the Jewish question.' To this Hitler replied: 'In matters which concern the economy, Jews can participate as they did in the past.'[4]

As far as international trade was concerned, and particularly that with America, Schacht held that, 'Jews should not be molested in commerce, since any hampering of Jewish operated trade brings unemployment for German employees.'[5]

Pressure continued to mount on the Jews of Germany when the Nürnberg 'Blood Laws' of 15 September 1935, 'For the protection of German blood and German honour', came into effect. Now, Germans with Jewish ancestry were categorised as being 'non-Aryans', who were either 'full', 'half', or 'quarter-bred'. It was now a criminal offence for pure Germans to marry, or even have sexual intercourse with Jews who were declared to be non-German citizens. Jews also faced prohibitions on residence and employment. According to Johannes Zahn (economist and banker from 1931), 'The general opinion was that the Jews had gone too far in Germany ....' Zahn pointed out that of the 4,800 lawyers in Berlin, 3,600 were Jews, and apart from German orchestral conductor Gustav Furtwangler, '... there was hardly a theatre director who wasn't a Jew'[6]– as if to imply that this was some kind of crime!

Jews were forced to wear 'Stars of David' on armbands or on their jackets as a means of identification, and Jewish children were ejected from the state education system. In München, one of the largest synagogues in Germany was demolished to make way for a car park. Posters appeared in the streets saying: 'BEWARE OF JEWS AND PICKPOCKETS'; 'JEWS ARE NOT WELCOME HERE'; 'JEWS ARE NOT WELCOME IN OUR GERMAN FORESTS'.[7]

Propaganda Minister Goebbels pleased his Führer by announcing that as a result of Nazi activities,

> We have German films, a German press, German literature, German art, and German broadcasting. The objection that was often raised against us in the past, that it was not feasible to remove Jews from the arts and from cultural life because there were too many of them, and that we'd be unable to fill all the vacant positions – all this has brilliantly been proved wrong.[8]

Economics Minister Schacht realised the danger of anti-Semitism to foreign trade, and pointed out at the 1935 Nürnberg Party Rally that instead of 'a display of turbulence in the racial wars', action must be, 'conducted within a legal and controlled framework and co-ordinated with the country's economic necessities'. Hitler's Nazi henchman were infuriated by these remarks, but Hitler himself did not intervene. Now, instead of keeping a low profile, Schacht made a point of attending (Lutheran) religious services, presided over by Pastor Martin Niemoller (a former World War I submarine commander) at his local church in the wealthy Berlin suburb of Dahlem. Niemoller was subsequently arrested by the Nazis; he would spend a total of eight years in various concentration camps.

During the Berlin Olympic Games of 1936 (when German athletes won thirty-three gold medals, more than any other country), all traces of anti-Jewish activity were concealed for a period of three weeks. The ubiquitous banners proclaiming that 'THE JEWS ARE OUR MISFORTUNE', previously to be seen on guest houses and hotels, were temporarily removed.

Meanwhile, visitors to the Games, who had travelled from all parts of the world, would have had no idea that a mere 60km away, slave labourers were demolishing the Oranienburg concentration camp, and replacing it with a new one called Sachsenhausen.

On 1 August 1937 the Buchenwald concentration camp was opened; by the time war broke out there would be a total of six camps holding approximately 50,000 detainees.

When Hitler annexed Austria on 11 March 1938 anti-Jewish pogroms were initiated, and the same anti-Semitic laws applied in Austria as were in force in Germany. The result was that the Jews, having been robbed by the SS of their homes, businesses, capital and possessions, engaged in a mass exodus from Austria.

As for Reich Chief of Police Heinrich Himmler, he chose the picturesque village of Mathausen as the site for a new concentration camp. Gypsies were declared to be 'inveterate criminals' and subject to forced labour and mass sterilisation.[9] In fact, a special section for gypsies was created within Buchenwald concentration camp where, during the holocaust, between a quarter and half a million were exterminated.

Reinhard Heydrich, of the Reich Security Head Office, had a network of informers within the Catholic church in Vienna. Even nuns were not immune from Nazi persecution. Helen Kafka Restituta, for example, had for twenty years been a nurse, working in the operating theatre of a hospital at Modling, a suburb of Vienna. According to her friend Gertrude Jancsy, she had put up crucifixes on her wall and had refused to remove them, having been 'ordered' to do so by the Nazis. 'I will happily put a cross up, but I will certainly not take one down,' she said.

When Sister Restituta disseminated the words of a soldier's song criticising the Nazis, she was denounced by a doctor, and on Ash Wednesday 1942 she was accused of, 'aiding and abetting the enemy in the betrayal of the Fatherland, and for plotting high treason'. The Gestapo forced her to leave the Order, and despite the pleas of her colleagues, she was condemned to death and executed. (She would be beatified by the Pope in 1998.)[10]

In July 1938 at an international conference held at Evian-les-Bains in France, the problem of Jews, who were unable to emigrate from Germany because of restrictive quotas imposed by other countries, was discussed, but no solution was forthcoming.

In November 1938 Schacht requested a meeting with Hitler at which he told him: 'Unless you can assure the Jews that they will be safe, you will have to give them the chance to emigrate.'[11] Schacht then proposed that all Jewish holdings in Germany and Austria be paid into a trust fund. This fund would issue twenty-five year bonds which Jews throughout the world would be expected to purchase. Part of the dividends from these bonds would then be paid to German and Austrian Jews to assist them to emigrate. Somewhat surprisingly, Hitler agreed, but Schacht's scheme for Jewish emigration failed to gain the support of western countries, particular America, where it was felt that this was an attempt by the Germans to extort ransom money for each Jewish life.

In early November 1938 Hitler received a telegram informing him that Ernst Freiher von Rath, Third Secretary to the German Ambassador in Paris, had been assassinated by a 17 year-old Polish Jew named Herschel Grunspan, who was angry about the way his family had been treated by the Nazis. This was Goebbels' opportunity to persuade Hitler to take even more extreme action against the Jews. Reinhard Heydrich now issued a series of statements to the police and SS units across the Reich.

Demonstrations against Jews are expected and must not be prevented. Jewish property may be destroyed but not looted .... As many Jews as possible, for now only healthy males, are to be arrested. All concentration camps are to be alerted to accommodate them.

At that time the Jewish population of Germany numbered about half a million.

The result was that on 9–10 November 1938 some 7,500 Jewish homes, 275 synagogues, and hundreds of businesses were destroyed by the Nazis in 150 towns and villages throughout the Reich; even Jewish hospitals, such as the one for sick children in Laupike, were attacked. Some 26,000 Jews were arrested, of whom ninety were murdered, only a few managing to escape abroad.

This became known as 'Kristallnacht' (literally, 'night of broken glass') – the name deriving from the fact that glass from the shattered windows of Jewish shops littered the streets of Berlin and other towns and villages throughout the Reich. The event was timed to coincide with the anniversary of Hitler's first attempt to seize power in München, fifteen years earlier.

Having perpetrated these horrors on the Jewish population, Goebbels now added insult to injury by extorting 1 billion Reichsmarks from the Jews in order to pay for a clean up of the operation. He also announced ominously that a resolution of the Jewish question would require a 'final solution'.[12]

Schacht was open in his contempt for the way Germany was treating its Jews. At the annual Reichsbank Christmas party of December 1938 he made a speech saying: 'The burning of Jewish synagogues, the destruction and looting of Jewish businesses, the ill treatment of Jewish citizens, was so disgraceful that every decent German must blush with shame ....'[13]

At this time Hitler was in receipt of a letter from a father who sought permission to terminate the life of his mentally disabled child. Hitler, who had already ordered the compulsory sterilisation of the disabled, now approved a secret policy for the selection and murder of disabled infants within a few days of their birth. Within months the remit spread to include disabled children also, and they were given lethal injections of morphine in special children's units. However, the cause of death was recorded as 'measles', or even 'general weakness'.[14]

With the German invasion of Czechoslovakia on 15 March 1939 Heydrich was dispatched to the region of Bohemia/Moravia to effect the 'Germanisation' of the region, and to co-opt the Czechs into supporting the German war effort. Dissidents were sent to Mathausen concentration camp, whereas Jews were incarcerated in the ghetto at Terezin (in German Theresienstadt) before being moved on to death camps farther east. Meanwhile, former Czech President Eduard Benes fled to England, where he became head of the Czech government in exile.

On 13 May 1939 the German liner *St Louis* left Hamburg with 937 wealthy Jews on board, to whom Hitler had given permission to leave the country. Having been rejected by Cuba and the United States however, the ship was forced to land its passengers at Antwerp, Belgium. Some settled there; others made their way to England, France and Holland – countries which also accepted them.

From now on, homosexual men were seen as a threat to the growth of the master race. They did not breed and were therefore of no use and must be eliminated. They were forced to wear an inverted pink triangle on their jackets and over the next decade, 50,000 or so of them would be sent to their deaths in the concentration camps. The same strictures did not apply, however, to lesbian women; the theory being that they could always be impregnated, and so produce children for the Führer.

Following the invasion of Poland by Germany on 1 September 1939 and by the Soviet Union on 17 September that country was divided into three administrative regions: the eastern part came under the control of the Soviets; the western region was annexed to the Reich; the remainder formed the Government-General, under the jurisdiction of Nazi lawyer Hans Frank.

Now, in typical fashion, the Nazis began rounding up all the Polish Jews, a total of about 3 million. In a clumsy attempt to achieve secrecy, Jews were usually abducted from their homes at night and moved into ghettos, which were created in all the major towns and cities in order to facilitate their deportation.

Some ghettos were surrounded by barbed wire; others were deliberately walled up to screen from passing Germans those within who were starving to death (the food requirement for inmates being set by the Nazis at under 200 calories per person day, which was inadequate to sustain life); also to avoid the danger of epidemics caused by poor sanitation spreading to the non-Jewish population. There was inadequate shelter for the large numbers, and in winter time many had no choice but to exist outdoors in the snow. Whatever valuables they still possessed were exchanged for bread; some were even obliged to sell their clothes, and when they had nothing left with which to barter, they began to starve.

It was decided that, rather than let all the Jews in the ghettos perish from starvation and disease, some should be used as slave labourers in the making of textiles, construction of roads, or even the building of palaces for their Nazi masters.

For what would be their final journey (though they did not know it), Jews selected for the death camps were made to purchase their own railway tickets, as they went unknowingly to their deaths, the fare being set at 4 pfennigs per person per kilometre. 'Don't forget to wash your hands. Remember to look where you left your clothes so you can remember to find them afterwards.' Right up until the end they were never told the real truth as to the fate that awaited them.

In the Treblinka concentration camp, situated in a small clearing in the middle of a forest near Warsaw, and built near a hamlet of the same name, every prisoner who arrived was executed within a few hours, in excess of 700,000 Jews in all.[15]

***

The question arises as to whether or not the local Nazi governors were obliged to put Hitler's and his Nazi Party's infamous policies into operation.

The Reichgau Wartheland was the name given by the Nazis to the territory of greater Poland. It was administered by Artur Griser, who attempted to transform his sector into a model Nazi state.[16] Those Poles who were permitted to stay in the areas (which he proceeded to 'Germanise') were treated as slaves; the remainder were deported to other districts. Griser and the SS had a completely free hand and were able to perpetrate their atrocities on the local population at will. Even ethnic Germans who refused to relocate were deported to camps.

In West Prussia (which had been part of Poland since the Treaty of Versailles) on the other hand, a region administered by General Albert Forster, it was a different story. Without bothering to check the ethnic origin of the Poles, he simply declared whole groups of them to be 'German', and instead of deporting them he allowed them to receive an education.

Griser now complained to Heinrich Himmler about Forster's leniency. Himmler responded by ordering Forster to make a detailed, ethnic examination of each and every Pole, and told him, *'You, as an old National Socialist, know that just one drop of false blood that comes into an individual's veins, can never be removed.'*[17] Hitler however, disinclined as ever to trouble himself with practicalities, refused to intervene.

Now, under an earlier agreement with Stalin, ethnic Germans began to arrive in occupied Poland from neighbouring countries, and in order to accommodate these new arrivals the ethnic Poles were simply turned out of their homes into the street. Entire Polish villages were taken over, their occupants deported, and Baltic Germans moved in to replace them.

Within a year, over 700,000 Poles had been deported from the Reichgau Wartheland, many to Hans Frank's Government-General region in the south-east, in filthy and overcrowded railway carriages on a journey which could take up to eight days. In consequence, almost one in five Poles would die during World War II.

The Germans saw the Danes, fellow Nordics, as kinsmen, and after their invasion of that country on 8 April 1940, they were less vigilant than they were elsewhere: a fact which enabled Denmark to evacuate virtually all of their population of some 8,000 Jews to safety in neutral Sweden. In June an official in the German Foreign Office, Hans Rademacher, proposed that the Jews throughout the Reich be resettled on the French island of Madagascar. However, following the outbreak of war, this was no longer a feasible project. (Madagascar might at first seem a strange choice, unless the long arm of Lanz von Liebenfels, who advocated throwing the 'untouchables' out 'into the forest of the monkeys', had somehow influenced Rademacher's decision.)

In July 1941 4,400 Jews were murdered in Lithuania. By August the figure had risen to 38,324. Here, the local population helped the Nazis round up the Jews, and even collaborated in their murder. In the same month Himmler visited the Front Line in the Russian city of Minsk. Here, he witnessed an execution of 100 Jews and partisans, who were ordered to lie face down in a ditch freshly dug outside the city gates. Then, members of the SS 'Einsatzgruppe B' opened fire. (The 'Einsatzgruppen' were special extermination units which followed Germany's fighting troops into the occupied territories.) The scene was described by Himmler's adjutant Karl Wolff:

> It was of course inevitable that Himmler had a look, and from these shots, shots to the head, bits of brains spurted out, and splattered in a high arc on to his coat. He trembled, didn't he? Of course, he was nauseated by what he saw. He then began to stagger and reel.[18] [In fact the shock to Himmler's system was so great that his personal physician had to be called.] From then on, another way had to be found of realising the Führer's goal of exterminating human beings.[19]

When SS Brigadeführer Arthur Nebe, Commander of 'Einsatzgruppe B', complained to an already convinced Himmler that such murders were having an adverse effect on the morale of his men, further experiments were made. They included: gassing the victims with carbon monoxide; using the outlets from the exhausts of automobiles, which were fed into sealed rooms; gassing with prussic acid. However, by a process of trial and error, the most effective gas for the purpose was found to be Zyklon B.

Himmler now announced that not only Jewish men, but also women and children, were all to be executed. This was in accordance with the Nazi belief that all Jews must by definition be Bolshevik supporters. Therefore, every single Jew was seen as a military threat. In September 1941 a secret order from Himmler decreed that all Jews from Germany, Austria and the occupied Czech lands should be transported to camps in the east.

Baldur von Schirach, who had been sent to Vienna and appointed 'Gauleiter' of that city by Hitler, in order to placate its citizens following the Anschluss, described the city as a pearl which he would deliver to Hitler, cleansed of Jews. He was as good as his word. By December 1941 virtually none of Vienna's original complement of 180,000 Jews remained, all having been transported to death camps.

Chief of the Reich Chancellery Hans Lammers described a 'Führer Order' which was, 'transmitted by Göring to Heydrich ...' entitled, 'Final Solution of the Jewish Problem'.[20] (No copy of this order has ever been found, and it was probably never committed to paper). To this end, Heydrich convened a meeting of the SS and SD, at the Berlin suburb of Wannsee on 20 January 1942 to work out details of how all Jews in occupied Europe were to be deported and killed. At this meeting, Heydrich was able to report that there were now only 131,800 Jews left in the original Reich territory, out of an original 250,000. However, in the USSR there were 5 million; in the Ukraine 3 million; in Poland 2¼ million; in France ¾ million (and in England ⅓ million.) Heydrich explained:

> The Jews should now, in the course of the 'Final Solution', be brought to the East ... for use as labour. In big labour gangs with separation of sexes, the Jews capable of work are [to be] brought to these areas and employed in road building, in which task undoubtedly a great part will fall through natural diminution. [And then ominously] The remnant, that finally is able to survive all this – since this is undoubtedly the part with the strongest resistance – must be treated accordingly, since these people representing a natural selection, are to be regarded as the germ cell of a new, Jewish development.[21]

Some 55,000 Jews were deported from Berlin alone, and by the end of 1942 experiments with gas had enabled the Nazis to set up extermination centres at Auschwitz, Birkenau, Belzec, Sobibor, Chelmno, Majdanek and Treblinka. It was now logistically feasible to take and to exterminate Jews from all the territories that Germany occupied.

Jews were deceived, even as they were sent to their deaths in the camps. Above the entrances were cruel and cynical signs: Auschwitz for example, 'ARBEIT MACHT FREI' – 'WORK MAKES YOU FREE'; Buchenwald, 'JEDEM DAS SEINE' – 'EACH TO HIS OWN'. Rudolf Hoess, one time camp commander at Auschwitz, in south-west Poland, described the situation there as he found it. Arrivals from places as far away as France, Holland and Greece were, 'given pretty picture postcards marked "Waldsee", to be signed and sent back home to their relatives, with a printed inscription saying, "We are doing very well here. We have work and we are well treated. We await your arrival".'[22]

From the outside the gas chambers, 'were not sinister looking places at all,' said Hoess. 'In fact it was impossible to make them out for what they were. Over them were well-kept lawns with flower borders; the signs over the entrances merely said: "BATHS".'

> Whilst the selection was being made for the gas chambers, [a] unique musical ensemble played gay tunes from *The Merry Widow* and *Tales of Hoffmann* to the unsuspecting Jews; the orchestra consisting of young and pretty girls

all dressed in white blouses and navy-blue skirts. To such music, recalling as it did happier and more frivolous times, the men, women and children were led into the 'bath houses', where they were told to undress preparatory to taking a 'shower'. Sometimes they were even given towels. Once they were inside the 'shower room' – and perhaps this was the first moment that they may have suspected something was amiss, for as many as 2,000 of them were placed into the chamber, like sardines, making it difficult to take a bath – the massive door was slid shut, locked and hermetically sealed. Up above, where the well-groomed lawn and flowerbeds almost concealed the mushroom-shaped lids of vents that ran up from the hall of death, orderlies stood ready to drop into them (i.e. the chambers) the amethyst blue crystals of hydrogen cyanide, or Zyklon B, which had originally been manufactured as a strong disinfectant and for which, as we have seen, Herr Hoess had with so much pride found a new use.

Through heavy glass portholes the executioners could watch what happened. The naked prisoners below would be looking up at the showers from which no water spouted; or perhaps at the floor wondering why there were no drains. It took some moments for the gas to have much effect. But soon the inmates became aware that it was issuing from the perforations in the vents. It was then that they usually panicked, crowding away from the pipes and finally stampeding towards the huge metal door where, as author Gerald Reitlinger puts it, 'They piled up in one blue, clammy, blood spattered pyramid, clawing and mauling each other, even in death.'[23]

Twenty or thirty minutes later, when the huge mass of naked flesh had ceased to writhe, pumps drew out the poisonous air, the large door was opened and the men of the 'Sonderkommando' took over. These were Jewish male inmates, who were promised their lives and adequate food in return for performing the most ghastly job of all. (However, even these men were regularly sent to their fate in the gas chambers, and were replaced with others; it being the SS's wish that no survivors remained to tell the tale.) Protected with gas masks and rubber boots, and wielding hoses they went to work. Their first task was to remove the blood and defecations, before dragging the clawing dead apart with nooses and hooks, the prelude to the ghastly search for gold and the removal of teeth and hair, which were regarded by the Germans as strategic materials. Then the journey by lift or rail-wagon to the furnaces, the mill that ground the clinker to fine ash, and the truck that scattered the ashes in the stream of the Sola river.

Other 'special prisoners' were simply killed by an injection of benzene. Said Hoess,

Our doctors had orders to write ordinary death certificates, and could put down any reason at all for the cause of death.[24] [In fact what was usually written down was 'heart disease' or, 'cardiac weakness complicated by pneumonia'.][25]

According to camp survivor Samuel Willenberg imprisoned in Treblinka 1942–3 the number of Jews and gypsies (who were also considered racially inferior) murdered at that camp alone numbered about 875,000.[26] Their remains were buried in enormous ditches.

***

When the Nazis came to power, Pope Pius XII's dilemma was that 22 million Germans were Roman Catholics, as were a quarter of the SS. In fact, both Hitler and Himmler had been born into the faith[27] However, the Holy See was neutral, and not only that, Pius regarded Germany as a bastion against communism.

Following the invasion of Poland, when priests and nuns were arrested, tortured and shot, the response of the Catholic church left much to be desired; for even though the Vatican was advised that such atrocities were taking place, it chose to remain silent.

In March 1942 Gerhart Riegner, of the World Jewish Congress in Geneva, prepared a dossier documenting the persecution of the Jews in countries throughout Europe, including the fact that 92,000 Jews had been executed by firing squad. He duly informed Archbishop Philippe Bernardini, the Pope's representative in Switzerland. (In fact, Riegner had discovered that there was a pattern to the persecution; or in other words that the Nazis were systematic in their persecution of the Jews.)

Riegner duly sent a telegram to London and Washington, containing details of a plan emanating from the Führer's headquarters for the extermination of 3.5 to 4 million Jews, possibly using the chemical prussic acid. When the US government sought corroboration of the story from the Vatican, the reply was non-committal.

When, in July 1942 Archbishop Jan de Yong of the Catholic church of Utrecht (in occupied Holland) issued a pastoral letter condemning the persecution of the Jews, the Nazis took immediate reprisals against Jewish Catholic convents, from which ninety-two Jews were deported and murdered, even though they had converted to Catholicism.[28]

By 1943 three quarters of Slovakia's Jews had been deported. Rudolf Vrba, a Jewish Czech (Slovak) deportee and one of the few people to escape from Auschwitz, said that when the Jews complained to the Catholic bishops that they were being beaten by the Germans, the reaction was, 'After having crucified Jesus Christ, you have the arrogance to complain?'. 'That was the mentality [of the bishops]', said Vrba.[29]

President of the new Slovakia, Josef Tiso, had the rare distinction of being not only a Nazi, but also a Catholic priest. However, the Pope failed to apply sanctions against him. 'When the criminal regime of Monsignor Tiso in all his priestly clothes, surrounded by all his bishops, was preaching Nazism on every first [front] page of the newspaper, alternating with pictures of Tiso and Hitler,' said Vrba, 'it was clear where Pius XII stood. Because if he had told them that using his name for clerical, fascist propaganda would lead to excommunication, they would have thought twice.'[30]

On 5 May 1943 a memorandum was prepared for the Vatican Secretary of State Cardinal Luigi Maglioni:

Horrendous situation. In Poland there were before the war about 4.5 million Jews. Now there remain only 100,000. The disappearance of so many is only explicable by death. There are death camps at Lublin and near Bresk-Litovsk. They [the Jews] are put by their hundreds in chambers where they are finished off with gas.

Again this provoked no papal response. However, when the Allies bombed Rome, the Pope was at last moved to speak out: 'That day will be known in history as the most sorrowful for the Eternal City during the Second World War,' he said.[31]

On 25 July 1943 Italian dictator Benito Mussolini was deposed. On 8 September the Italian government surrendered unconditionally to the Allies. By this time, the German forces in Italy amounted to some sixteen divisions, which proceeded to seize control of Rome. On 19 October in an extraordinary volte face, Italy declared war on Germany.

Princess Enza Pignatelli (a resident of Rome), having been informed that the Nazis were abducting Jews from the city and loading them into trucks, went to see the situation for herself. After which she immediately went to the Vatican to protest, demanding to see the Pope. However, although Cardinal Maglioni responded by summoning the German Ambassador Ernst von Weizacker for an explanation, the Pope refused to protest to the Germans about the fate of Rome's Jews, and on 18 October the deportation train left for Auschwitz.

Finally, the Pope decided that, although the convents of Rome were normally closed-orders, they must now open their doors and offer shelter to any Jewish refugees. The Holy See also published notices to be put on the gates of the convents, to inform the Germans that this was the Holy See's territory and that they must not enter. In this way one convent alone saved 138 Jewish men, women and children. In all, several thousand Jews were saved by such institutions throughout Italy.[32]

However, 2,091 of Rome's Jews were deported by the Nazis, of whom only fifteen survived, including one woman Settimia Spizzichino. 'The Pope,' she said, 'was anti-Semitic and pro-German. He didn't take a single risk. When they say the Pope is like Jesus on Earth, this is not true. He did nothing to save even a single child.'[33] The Pope did, however, request that the Allies refrain from using black soldiers to garrison the Vatican after the liberation. So what was the reason for the Pope's failure to speak out?

According to Archbishop Emmanuele Clarizio (Vatican 1939–45), the traditional Catholic view was that the Jews had refused to recognise Christ as the Son of God; had killed him, and had rejected the truth of the New Testament. But as the archbishop pointed out, 'The apostles were all Jews, Jesus was a Jew, the Madonna was a Jew, St Joseph was a Jew.' How therefore, asked Clarizio, could the Church have said such stupid things?[34]

In 1944 there were ¾ million Jews living in Hungary. As yet, the Nazis had largely left them alone, but this was now to change. During the summer of 1944 at Auschwitz an estimated 250,000–300,000 Hungarian Jews alone would be gassed to death.

On 7 April 1944 Rudolf Vrba and Alfred Wetzler, both Slovak Jews, escaped from Auschwitz, and by 21 April they had reached Slovakia. They wrote a report describing the conditions there in great detail, even including a drawing of a new railway line which had been built directly to the gas chambers. They stated that 1,765,000 Jews had already been murdered there. Vrba hoped by this to give warning about what was to befall the remaining Jews in Hungary, but despite a six-hour meeting with a papal diplomat, no action was taken by the Catholic church to publicise his document. It was regarded as a private matter.[35]

The Papal Nuncio (Ambassador), Angelo Rotta, issued a string of protests to the Hungarian authorities saying,

> The whole world knows what this deportation [of Jews] in fact means. The Hungarian government is requested not to continue its war against the Jews. If God has given them life, no one in the world has the right to take it away from them.[36]

On 25 June 1944 the Pope finally sent the Regent of Hungary, Admiral Miklos Horthy, a message: 'We are beseeched to do everything ... [in order that] the sufferings, already so heavy, endured by a large number of unfortunate people because of their nationality or race may not be extended and aggravated. Our Father's heart cannot remain insensitive by virtue of our ministry of charity, which embraces all men.'[37]

In Hungary's capital Budapest, the Papal Nunzio was besieged by Jews seeking protection. He responded by issuing 15,000 letters of safe conduct, and the Vatican itself then acted by taking over whole houses, thus protecting their Jewish occupants.

Many Jews escaped persecution by converting to Catholicism. For example, in Budapest's Parish Church of Terezvàros, where the numbers of pre-war conversions were rare, from 1944 onwards they began to rise (from six in January, to over a thousand in October). However, the Nazis ignored this and continued to deport even those Jews who had converted. For them, a Jew was a Jew, irrespective of his faith. Despite the best efforts of the Nazis, the Pope's representatives did manage to save 5,000 Hungarian Jews, a tiny number in comparison with the half million or so murdered.

Pius XII died in 1958. He has been criticised for the fact that, during all the long years of war, he never once remonstrated with the Nazis directly over their fiendish activities.

***

The search for a way of creating a perfect 'Aryan' race would find its ghastly apotheosis in the works of one Dr Josef Mengele.

Son of a retailer of farm machinery, Mengele was fascinated by the subject of 'eugenics' – the science of genetic breeding – a subject which he studied at München University. Having joined the Nazi Party in 1934 Mengele became a Doctor of Philosophy and studied under Professor Otmar von Verscher, also an ardent Nazi at the University of Frankfurt.

Mengele joined the Waffen SS, an organisation which insisted on the racial purity of its members, and of their brides. Both he and von Verscher were interested in studying twins as a basis for their genetic experiments, and they found them – 250 pairs in all – in the concentration camp at Auschwitz in south-eastern Poland, where Mengele became camp doctor (having been wounded while serving on the Eastern Front).

Hoping to unlock the secret of creating a pure, Aryan race, Mengele sent the results of his researches to von Verscher at the Kaiser Wilhelm Institute for Anthropology in Berlin. His 'research' was flawed however, in that he failed to ensure that his twins were identical, rather than non-identical.

Mengele was an accomplished pianist, and the sound of his piano could be heard throughout the death camp. He did not confine himself to medical research. According to Auschwitz survivor Siegfried Halbreich, Mengele would, 'make his selection of the most beautiful girls, Jewish girls, entertain them all night, and in the morning shoot them'.[38]

On 26 November 1944 Mengele unexpectedly found himself in a position to be able to save lives instead of taking them, when Heinrich Himmler, head of the German SS, telegraphed all camp commandants and ordered them to dismantle the death camps. Mengele, despite this order, sent 461 of the 509 new train arrivals to Auschwitz to instant death.

***

It is distinctly possible that some Germans living in remote areas were ignorant about the fate of the Jews and other 'undesirables'. But for the majority such a notion is patently absurd. The process or rounding up, herding into ghettos, transporting to death and labour camps, and keeping records; to say nothing of the architects, engineers, and camp operatives needed to ensure the whole, ghastly system worked efficiently, would have required the participation of a huge bureaucracy. And for anyone who still had not noticed what was taking place, there would always be the stench of burning human flesh, detectable for miles around.

***

The question arises, could the German people have risen up against Hitler? 'Young people sometimes ask me,' said Countess Marion Donhoff, then a student, 'why we didn't demonstrate.' The answer was, she said, that, 'No one would have come out of any demonstration alive. No. One simply couldn't protest.'[39]

Henriette, wife of Baldur von Schirach ('Gauleiter' of Vienna) said:

I saw Jewish women being taken to a camp in Holland. The German officer said to me, 'When you see Hitler, tell him that what we're doing is madness. We've made enemies of the friendly Dutch. We're locking people up.' I was horrified. I hadn't known about it. I told Hitler I'd heard that we were doing awful things and that the soldiers were ashamed … and … it ended up in a dreadful argument.

Then, according to Hitler's secretary Traudl Junge,

The Führer got up and said, 'That's sentimental nonsense. Don't interfere in things you don't understand.'

He left the room, putting an end to the evening. Mrs von Schirach was never asked back to the Berghof.[40]

**

It is interesting to compare Hitler's despicable treatment of the Jews with that advocated by his arch enemy, the Russian revolutionary and advocate of international communism, Leon Trotsky.

At a press conference in January 1937 in Mexico (where he was living in exile), Trotsky revealed his thoughts about the Jews, of whom he was one by birth (although an atheist by persuasion). Trotsky declared:

During my youth I rather leaned towards the prognosis that the Jews of different countries would be assimilated and that the Jewish question would thus disappear, as it were, automatically. The historical development of the last quarter of a century has not confirmed this view. Decaying capitalism has everywhere swung over to an intensified nationalism, one aspect of which is anti-Semitism. The Jewish question has loomed largest in the most highly developed capitalist country of Europe, Germany.[41]

Trotsky went on to develop his train of thought thus:

Socialism will open the possibility of great migrations …. Not compulsory displacements [that is, the creation of new ghettos for certain nationalities], but displacements freely consented to, or rather demanded by certain nationalities, or parts of nationalities. The dispersed Jews who would want to be reassembled in the same community will find a sufficiently extensive and rich spot under the sun. To work for international socialism means to work also for the solution of the Jewish question.[42]

In June 1937 Mrs Beba Idelson, a Russian-born Jewish socialist Zionist leader in Palestine, visited Trotsky in Mexico. 'A feeling accompanied me all the time,' she said, 'that he [Trotsky] was a Jew, a wandering Jew without a fatherland.' Trotsky asked her, 'How many Jews are there in Palestine? Where do they reside? How do we bring Jews to Palestine and how do they join our Party?' 'I was under the impression,' said Beba Idelson, 'that the subject absorbed his [Trotsky's] thought and heart.'[43]

In 1937 Trotsky was sentenced to death in his absence by a Soviet court. In 1940 he was murdered by the Soviet Secret Police. On 14 May 1948 the independent State of Israel was created.

***

Of the estimated 16 million or so people murdered by the Hitler regime between 1933 and 1945 – in the so-called 'holocaust' – around 6 million were Jews. This represented approximately 67% of the Jewish population of Europe. They met their deaths by shooting, hanging, torture, gassing in the gas chambers – many being burned alive in the incinerators of the concentration camps on occasions when the gas ran out. Many died as a result of ghoulish medical experiments performed by qualified doctors of the Third Reich, who subjected their unfortunate victims to hypothermia, hyperthermia, and deliberate wounding and infection, the idea being to study how best they could treat their own wounded from the battlefield.

The number of labour and extermination camps built by the Nazis in Germany and in occupied Europe ran into hundreds. Not only were the victims imprisoned and murdered in these camps, but in some such as Auschwitz, they were subjected to slave labour. Not only Jews, but gypsies, homosexuals, and anyone deemed unfit or unwanted by the regime were exterminated. Chief architect of the extermination system was Austrian Nazi SS officer Karl Adolf Eichman.

Involved in the holocaust were the prime movers and those who were given the task of effecting the huge logistical operation that it entailed. In mitigation of the latter, it has to be said that because of the reign of terror Hitler had imposed throughout Europe, those who refused to obey orders would without doubt have met the same fate as their victims. It is perhaps easy for others to judge those who were simply obeying Hitler's orders, when they were not faced with that situation themselves.

Notes

1. *Der Volkischer Beobachter*, 25 December 1920.
2. *The Nazis: A Warning from History, Part 1.*
3. Ibid.

4. Schacht, Hjalmar, *76 Jahre meines Lebens*, p. 404.
5. Weitz, John, *Joachim von Ribbentrop: Hitler's Diplomat*, p. 185–6.
6. *The Nazis: A Warning from History*, Part 2
7. *Hitler: a Profile: The Criminal*.
8. *The Nazis: A Warning from History*, Part 2
9. *The Third Reich in Colour*.
10. *The SS: Himmler's Madness*.
11. Schacht, op. cit., p. 842.
12. *Kristallnacht: 9 November 1938*.
13. Schact, op. cit.
14. *The Nazis: A Warning from History*, Part 3.
15. Ibid, *Part 5*.
16. Ibid, *Part 4*.
17. Ibid.
18. *The SS: Himmler's Madness*.
19. Kerten, Andreas (son of Himmler's personal physician), in *The SS: Himmler's Madness*.
20. *A Trial of the Major War Criminals: Nuremberg Documents and Testimony*. TMWC,xi, p. 141
21. Shirer, William L, *The Rise and Fall of the Third Reich*, p. 965–6.
22. Ibid, p. 969.
23. Reitlinger, Gerald, 1953, *The Final Solution: The Attempt to Exterminate the Jews of Europe*, New York.
24. Hoess, Affadavit, NCA (*Nazi Conspiracy and Aggression*), NCA, vol VI, pp. 787–90; ND (Nuremberg Document) 3868-ps.
25. Kogon, *The Theory and Practise of Hell*. p. 218.
26. *The Nazis: A Warning from History*, Part 5.
27. *Pius XII: the Pope, the Jews, and the Nazis*.
28. Ibid.
29. Ibid.
30. Ibid.
31. Ibid.
32. Ibid.
33. Ibid.
34. Ibid.
35. Ibid.
36. Ibid.
37. Ibid.
38. *Josef Mengele: Medical Madman of Auschwitz*.
39. *Hitler: a Profile: The Dictator*.
40. *Hitler's Henchmen: Schirach, the Corrupter of Youth*.
41. Nedava, Joseph, *Trotsky and the Jews*, p. 204.
42. Jewish Telegraphic Agency. 18 January 1937.
43. Ibid, p. 206.

CHAPTER XXX

British Nazi Admirers in Wartime

Edward and Wallis Windsor

On 10 May 1940 the day that Germany invaded the Low Countries, Winston Churchill replaced Neville Chamberlain as head of a coalition government. Two days later, Germany invaded France.

With the fall of France in June 1940 (armistice signed 21 June), the Windsors transferred to Madrid, capital of neutral Spain, where they stayed at the Ritz hotel. Edward was popular in Spain, being related to the Spanish Royal House of Bourbon through his great grandmother Queen Victoria. However, Prime Minister Winston Churchill sent a telegram to Edward urging him to transfer to Lisbon, from there to be taken by flying boat back to England.

Foreign Minister von Ribbentrop would have much preferred Edward to have stayed in Madrid (where he would have been more accessible), and to this end he approached the Spanish authorities asking that the Windsors be detained while their exit visas were being processed. However, on 2 July 1940 Edward left Madrid and arrived in Lisbon.

From Lisbon Edward hoped to visit New York, but the British government put a stop to his plan and instead his ship was diverted to Bermuda, where he had agreed to accept the position of Governor of the Bahamas, based at Nassau.

Continuing where he had left off in post-World War I Britain, Edward, as Governor, took a lively interest in the conditions under which the natives of the Bahamas were living. 'I have personally rarely seen such slums and squalor as exist in most of the native settlements, and many of our Out[er] Islands have no doctor at all,'[1] he said. However, in his view the blacks were in no way to be equated with the whites. While,

> liberal, socialistic ideas of freedom and equality, regardless of race and colour, may sound fine theoretically, the forcing of these theories is, to my way of thinking, both premature and dangerous, so far as the western hemisphere is concerned.[2]

In a speech to the opening session of the Bahamas Legislature in late October 1940 Edward, pursuing one of his favourite themes, made it clear that he was determined to improve working conditions, and tackle the unemployment which beset the black population. (This was a vindication to some degree, of the reason he gave for his visit to Germany in October 1937, when his professed object was to see how the Nazis tackled such problems, and to try to discover whether their methods could be employed in Britain.)

In March 1941 the American magazine *Liberty* published an interview between Edward and the American novelist and broadcaster Fulton Oursler: 'You cannot kill 80m [million] Germans,' said Edward, 'and since they want Hitler, how can you force them into a revolution [presumably against Hitler] they don't want?' The only hope in his view, was for a 'Pax Americana' – in other words, a peace imposed upon Europe by the United States of America. For this, Churchill was quick to rebuke him. 'Edward's words,' he said, would be interpreted as, 'openly defeatist and pro-Nazi, and by implication, approving of an isolationist aim to keep America out of the war.' In future, the Duke should seek advice before making public statements of this nature.[3]

In April 1941 Edward, notwithstanding his indiscretions to the press, was given permission to visit the United States and President Roosevelt.

On 18 June 1943 Adolf Berle, Roosevelt's Assistant Secretary of State, gave his reasons why the letters of both the Duke and Duchess of Windsor should not be exempt from censorship. Once again, the problem appeared to be the dubious company the Windsors were keeping.

Berle observed that, 'Both the Duke and Duchess of Windsor were in contact with Mr James D Mooney' (President of General Motors Overseas Corporation) who was suspected by James B Stewart, American Consul-General in Zürich, of conducting espionage on behalf of Nazi Germany.[4] Also, that the Windsors,

> had maintained correspondence with Bedaux (Charles Bedaux, a French-born American who had invited the couple to stay at his Château de Cambe, at Tours, prior to their wedding, and who had arranged their visit to Germany in 1937), now in prison under charges of trading with the enemy and possibly of treasonous correspondence with the enemy. [Finally] that they [the Windsors] have been in constant contact with Axel Wenner-Gren [Swedish multi-millionaire industrialist and a friend of Bedaux, who had contributed generously to Wallis' charities in Nassau, and had on occasion given the Windsors the use of his yacht], presently on our blacklist for suspicious activity ....[5]

***

Following the cessation of hostilities on 3 May 1945, the Windsors left the Bahamas for France, and lived for most of the remainder of their lives at Neuilly, outside Paris. In August Edward called on President Roosevelt's successor, President Truman. On 4 October, having left Wallis in France, Edward arrived in

London to be reunited with his brother King George VI and his mother Queen Mary. A measure of reconciliation was achieved, and it was agreed that Edward should receive an allowance of ten thousand pounds per annum.

The Windsors now became firm friends of Sir Oswald and Lady Mosley, who were near neighbours of theirs in Paris. To the dismay of Mosley's followers back in Britain, many of whom had sacrificed their all for the British Union cause (BU – formerly British Union of Fascists), their leader had now chosen to retire and live in luxury. In the words of Lady Mosley's sister Nancy, as far as the Windsors and the Mosleys were concerned, nothing had changed:

> They want us all to be governed by the kind, clever, rich Germans and be happy ever after. I wish I knew why they all live in France, and not in outré-Rhein [i.e. beyond the Rhine in Germany].[6]

The Mosleys and the Mitfords

When war broke out on 1 September 1939, Diana was thwarted in that she had hoped to introduce her two sons (by her first marriage) to Hitler, but was now unable to do so. According to their governess, 'the children would have known how to greet the Führer, for they had been taught to give the Nazi salute, and to say, "Heil Hitler".'[7] As for Diana's brother Tom Mitford, now an officer in the Territorial Army, he had shocked his colleagues in the Queen's Westminster Regiment by giving a fascist salute, something which the Press was not slow to notice and to reveal.

It was not until two days later that Unity Mitford received news from the British Consulate that Britain had declared war. Now, she went to see Adolf Wagner, 'Gauleiter' of München, and handed over an envelope containing her Nazi Party badge, a signed photograph of Hitler, and a letter from herself to the Führer. She then went into the Englische Garten (English Garden), sat herself down on a bench, and shot herself in the temple with a small, automatic pistol. With the bullet lodged in her brain she was taken to hospital in München – still alive. Hitler visited her on several occasions, and when her speech returned after six weeks, the Führer gave her the option of staying in Germany, or going back to Britain. She chose the latter.

Unity was met by her parents in neutral Switzerland and brought home to England. By now her father, Lord Redesdale, had become firmly opposed to Hitler, whereas her mother Sydney's main concern was to keep the peace with Unity, who remained dependant on her parents until her death in 1948.

On 11 September 1939 the Nordic League was closed down by MI5. Its ruling council now instructed its members to join the British Union (BU) and henceforth to regard Mosley as their leader. Similar arrangements with the BU were entered into by the Right Club.

A report from an MI5 agent in October, on the activities of the Right Club, stated that it was, centred principally upon the contacting of sympathisers, especially among officers in the armed services, and the spreading, by personal talks, of the Club's ideals. There is talk of a military 'coup d'état', but there seems to be lack of agreement among members on the question of leadership ....[8]

In 1940 BU members were to come to the notice of the authorities for activities which can only be described as treasonable. In January Claude Duvivier and William Crowle, BU members in Devon, were tried for attempting to supply the Nazis with classified information which concerned the movement of British warships. William Swift and Marie Ingram, members of the BU in Portsmouth, were also tried and found guilty of providing classified information to the Abwehr (Intelligence Department of the German Armed Forces), and of recruiting some sixty BU members into the ranks of the local defence volunteers, with the object of, 'obtaining arms and ammunition to assist the planned Nazi invasion of the United Kingdom'.[9]

In April 1940 Nazi agent Anna Wolkoff approached a member of the Right Club, Joan Miller, with a request that the latter deliver a message to William Joyce in Berlin. What Wolkoff did not realise was that Miller was an agent of British Intelligence's MI5, who had been aware of her (Wolkoff's) activities since 1935.[10]

Mosley's fascist sympathies did not prevent him on 9 May 1940 from advising his members in the BU publication *Action*, what should be done were Britain to be invaded:

> In such an event every member of the British Union would be at the disposal of the nation. Every one of us would resist the foreign invader with all that is in us. However rotten the existing government, and however much we detest its policies, we would throw ourselves into the effort of a united nation until the foreigner was driven from our soil.[11]

On 23 May 1940 (three days after Hitler had invaded Belgium), Mosley was detained under an amendment to Defence Regulation 18b, which had been passed the previous day. The Amendment was designed to indict persons, 'who are concerned in the government of, or sympathise with a system of government of, any power with which His Majesty is at war.'[12] [Incidentally, while Mosley was languishing in prison, his son Nicholas was fighting with British forces against the Germans in Italy.]

When it came to the question of whether Mosley's wife Diana should also be arrested, her sister Nancy was very much in favour. In a letter to her lifelong friend Mark Ogilvy-Grant she wrote: 'I am thankful Sir Oswald "Quisling" [a reference to Norwegian fascist leader and traitor Vidkun Quisling] has been jugged [imprisoned] aren't you, but think it quite useless if Lady Q [Quisling] is still at large.' Diana's former father-in-law, Lord Moyne, was also in favour of Diana's arrest, describing her as an 'extremely dangerous character'.[13]

On 29 June 1940 Diana was duly arrested and imprisoned in Holloway. She was permitted to take her youngest son aged 11 weeks into prison with her, but not her three other children, the youngest only 18 months old.

By the summer of 1940 no fewer than 740 of the BU's senior members and sympathisers (100 of whom were women) had also been interned. Besides these, other Nazi sympathisers who were not members of the BU, were also interned including Captain Archibald Ramsay, John Beckett (who had severed all contacts with the BU in 1937), and Admiral Nikolai Wolkoff (father of Anna).

Curiously enough, Mosley's associate Major General J F C Fuller was not included among their numbers; neither was Viscountess Downe, a friend of Queen Mary (wife of King George V), nor Admiral Sir Barry Domvile, former Chief of Naval Intelligence. Author Henry Williamson was interned in 1940 but released after two years on condition that he did nothing to impede the war effort.

Although Mosley had not been charged with any crime, the eminent barrister Norman Birkett, KC (later Lord Birkett) was given the task of interrogating him in the hope of discovering some lawful way of keeping him in custody.

Mosley admitted to Birkett in July 1940 that his grandfather had led the House of Commons in its opposition to Jewish emancipation fifty years earlier. He himself bitterly resented the way in which the international system of money lending and usury (the charging of excessive interest on loans) was controlled by the Jews. Yes, Mosley did admit that he saw the Jews as a problem. 'I think it is partly them, and partly us,' he said, appearing to apportion blame equally to both sides. His solution was to construct,

> a national home for them [the Jews] which would put an end to all this friction ... which is as harmful to the Jews as it is to us. It [by which presumably he meant the Jewish presence in Britain] changes his character into a gangster and arouses in us a certain brutality, and is bad for the Jew and bad for us.

However, he had 'always actually thought' that anti-Semitism was 'the work of cranks'.[14]

Birkett was finally to catch Mosley out when the latter repeatedly denied that he and his BU had received money from foreign sources. However, a letter dated 25 August 1933 from the Foreign Office in Rome to a Count Grandi in London, attests to the payment of the sum of £60,000; the currency deal being negotiated by a trusted friend of Mosley's in Italy, W D E Allen (who, unbeknown to Mosley, was an agent of MI5). In this way, Birkett was able to prove that Mosley had lied, and he used this as grounds for arguing for his continued imprisonment.

Now it was Mosley's wife Diana's turn to be interrogated. 'I am not fond of Jews,' she told Birkett. Was she aware of Nazi atrocities against them? 'I saw the book called the *Brown Book of the Hitler Terror*, but I did not pay much attention to it,' she said.[15] This may have been a reference to Nazi Dr Franz Six's *Black Book*, which contained the names of 2,820 Britons who were to be arrested, and in all likelihood eliminated, following the (intended) invasion of Britain. This *Black Book* was a supplement to a supposedly highly secret handbook called *Informationsheft*, the purpose of which seems to have been to aid the conquerors in looting Britain and stamping out anti-German institutions there.[16]

When Birkett asked Diana if she disapproved of the way the Jews were being bullied in Germany, she replied:

> I always disapproved of bullying … for example, I strongly disapproved of the treatment of black people in the southern states of America, where they had no civil rights and there were frequent lynchings which went unpunished, but … I did not therefore consider Britain should declare war on the United States.[17]

She admitted to being a fascist and to the fact that Mosley had converted her. Yes, she was a friend of Hitler, and admired his achievements. However, both her visits to Rome in 1933 and 1934 were private and non-political. She was not in favour of German invasion of Britain, but would like to see in place in England the German system of government, because of what it had achieved in Germany. From her final conversation with Hitler at Bayreuth in August 1939 she said that it was clear that the Führer was well aware that if he were to invade Poland, war would then be inevitable.

In early September 1940 Mosley reiterated his instructions to his followers: '… do nothing to injure our country, or to help any other power …,' he said. They were, '… to obey orders, and in particular to obey the rules of their service [i.e. the country's armed services].'[18]

That Sir Oswald Mosley was not to be trusted is evident from the fact that he lied to Norman Birkett. He also appears to have been less than honest in his autobiography, *My Life*, in which, while condemning Hitler's treatment of the Jews, he professes to be unaware of their suffering, even though British newspapers, including *The Manchester Guardian*, had been printing articles about the persecution of Germany's Jews since the mid 1930s.

***

Most of those detained under the Defence Regulations were released by the end of 1940, a condition for those of military age being that they joined the armed forces.

During Christmas 1941 Mosley complained that the fetid air of Brixton Prison was detrimental to his health, whereupon he was allowed to join his wife Diana in Holloway (where, at that time, she was the only prisoner). Diana later described this reunion as one of the happiest days of her life! Here, they lived in some style, food being delivered to them regularly from the prestigious department store Fortnum & Mason.

***

In November 1943, when the threat of invasion had ebbed away, Mosley, who was suffering from severe phlebitis in the leg following his injury in the aeroplane accident during World War I, was released from prison on compassionate grounds, as was Diana. However, they remained under house arrest, in the comfort of their own home, for the remainder of the war.

On 4 April 1945 Tom Mitford, Diana's brother who, for all his fascist sympathies, had enlisted in the British armed forces, was killed in action in Burma at the age of 36.

Archibald Ramsay

Following the outbreak of war, Captain Archibald Ramsay, in the House of Commons, had opposed the passing of the Defence Regulation Order which gave the Home Secretary the right to imprison without trial anyone whom he believed likely to 'endanger the safety of the realm'.

On 23 February 1940 Ramsay (who himself had sons serving in the British Army) asked for details of Jews fighting in the British armed forces. On 20 March Ramsay declared in the House of Commons that, 'international Jewish finance and continental freemasonry are pursuing a policy of world domination by wars and revolutions and credit monopoly …'.[19]

During that spring, Ramsay was associating with Russian émigré and Nazi spy Anna Wolkoff, and with Joan Miller (who, unbeknown to him was an agent for MI5). He was also associating with Tyler Kent, a code and cipher clerk at the American Embassy in London, who was a member of Ramsay's Right Club (founded by the latter in May 1939), and of another right-wing organisation, namely the Nordic League. The main meeting place for members of the Right Club was Wolkoff's Russian tea room in South Kensington.

On 20 May 1940 Kent was arrested for spying for the Nazis. It was discovered that he had illegally copied and stored at his flat no fewer than 1,500 US Embassy documents including US military and naval attaché reports detailing statistics of British land, sea and air forces; 'their disposition and reserves, the food and oil stocks held in Britain and the Commonwealth, and the strategic plans for the future'.[20]

Kent's partner in crime was none other than Anna Wolkoff, whose role was to copy the documents which Kent had obtained from the US Embassy, and hand them to friends of hers at the Italian Embassy, who duly passed them on to Berlin via the German Ambassador in Rome.

The prosecution at the trial of Kent and Wolkoff (which commenced on 7 November 1940) stated that Anna Wolkoff had provided the Abwehr with detailed plans for the British invasion of Norway in April 1940 which subsequently enabled the Nazis to defeat the British invading forces. The pair were found guilty. Wolkoff was sentenced to ten years' imprisonment. (She would die in a road traffic accident soon after her release.) Kent received only seven years.

The arrest of Tyler Kent and Anna Wolkoff gave Churchill the excuse to move against the fascists, which he promptly did, and the BU was then dissolved by Home Secretary John (later Sir John) Anderson.

On 23 May 1940 Ramsay was interned in Brixton Prison, where he would remain until 26 September 1944.

A K Chesterton

Chesterton broke with Mosley during World War II because he opposed Mosley's 'Stop the War' policy, believing instead that the way to advance the fascist movement in Britain was to defeat Germany. During the early stages of the war he worked as a transport officer, and later became a journalist.

Arnold Leese

Leese was detained in November 1940 under the Defence Regulations Order. Released in 1943 on the grounds of ill health, he resumed his anti-Semitic activities by writing for example, *The Jewish War of Survival*, which was published privately in the USA. In December 1944 he founded the 'National Front'.[21]

Sir Ian Hamilton

In October 1939, a month after war was declared, the elderly but ever optimistic Hamilton wrote a letter to *The Times* newspaper: 'I look forward to the day when a trusted Germany will again come into her own. That day may be far off, but when it comes, then hostilities could and should, cease.'

William Joyce

When in 1939 William Joyce (then aged 33) left England for Germany with his wife, the Germans were quick to realise how valuable he might be to them for propaganda purposes. He was therefore introduced to Dr Erich Hetzier, Secretary to Germany's Foreign Minister von Ribbentrop. By 6 September Joyce was making radio broadcasts (anonymously) from Germany to Britain, always beginning with the words 'Germany calling!' 'Germany calling!' By talking of the presence of a fifth column in Britain, and by his gratuitous advice on how best to treat wounds sustained from German aerial bombardment, Joyce's purpose was to cause alarm and despondency throughout the British nation.

Although he had hoped to keep his identity a secret, Joyce's cover was blown when his wife in England recognised his voice (he spoke with a characteristic nasal drawl – the result of a broken nose sustained in a fight at school; he also had a somewhat affected accent) and informed the press.

In a broadcast on 30 September 1939 Joyce asked,

> Why has Chamberlain allowed anti-German politicians [in Britain] to make him break faith with the spirit of München? [The München Agreement permitted Germany to annex large areas of western Czechoslovakia.] Why did the British Government not listen to German complaints about Polish brutality, instead of giving Poland that unfortunate guarantee [a reference, presumably, to Britain and France's guarantee to Poland of the integrity of her borders]? Hitler has insisted that Germany has no territorial claims in Western Europe, and as Eastern Europe is now safeguarded by the Soviet-German Agreement, a lasting peace can be established for the benefit of civilisation.[22]

During the Christmas period of 1939–40 no fewer than 9 million British people listened in to Joyce's broadcasts, compared to 16 million who listened to the BBC news. However, the effect of his broadcasts was not altogether what was intended. British *Daily Express* newspaper journalist and radio critic, Jonah Barrington, said of him, 'He speaks English of the Haw-Haw, damn-it, get-out-of-my way variety with gentlemanly indignation.' Hence in Britain, Joyce became a subject of ridicule, and was given the nickname 'Lord Haw Haw'.[23]

On 16 May 1940 Joyce was still bewailing the fact that Britain and Germany were at war. 'Within six weeks of the British Government declaring war on Germany, Hitler offered peace,' he said in a broadcast. 'His terms could easily have been accepted … [even though] they would have left Germany far weaker than she is today ….'[24]

On 21 August 1940 Joyce berated Winston Churchill for taking England to war when the country was not properly equipped for such a venture. Churchill was 'the chief warmonger', 'a traitor to England', and it was thanks to him that the 'engines of destruction' had now, 'descended on their cities, towns, factories, docks and railways'. However, he was sure it would 'not be long before Britain has to yield to the invincible might of German arms …'.[25] By 17 October 1940 Joyce was predicting pestilence, plague, and starvation, 'by the million', for the people of Britain.

Joyce, who continued broadcasting throughout the war, made reference on 24 June 1944 to the V1 rocket projectiles, which for the previous nine days had been descending on London, and implied menacingly in his broadcast,

> that Germany has other new weapons which have as yet not been employed against the enemy. It can reasonably be assumed, that the battle in the East against the Bolshevik foes of civilisation will be hard and fierce, and there is every reason to believe that the battle in the West against the capitalist agents of Jewish international finance will attain a climax of violence, possibly without precedence. But in the closing rounds of this war it will be seen that Germany has conserved her strength to a degree that will confound her enemies.[26]

That September Joyce was awarded the German Cross of War Merit, First Class, together with a certificate signed personally by Adolf Hitler.

As Germany's fortunes worsened Joyce took to drink, and as the Red Army approached Berlin, he moved to Hamburg, making his final broadcast on 30 April 1945 (which incidentally was the day that Hitler committed suicide), in which he pointed out that the war would leave the Russians in control of most of Europe (on which point he was to be proved right). Then he uttered these final words of defiance: 'I say to you these last words: Long Live Germany! Heil Hitler, and farewell!' He escaped from Germany to Denmark, where he was captured by the British. He was tried and executed in London in 1946.

***

The British Free Corps (BFC)

During the war, support for Hitler came from an unexpected source, namely a tiny minority of the 160,000 or so British prisoners of war who had been captured by the Germans.

John Amery, English pro-Nazi adventurer (and son of L S Amery, a member of Churchill's wartime Cabinet) was living in France when it fell to the Germans in 1940. He was an anti-Semite, despite being one quarter Jewish. Now he moved to Berlin and offered his services to Joseph Goebbels and his Ministry of Propaganda.

Amery began producing propaganda pamphlets entitled, 'Why die for Stalin?' 'Why die for the Jews?', but now he produced his plan for, 'the greatest propaganda idea ever ...' namely, his so-called 'Legion of St George', in which he intended to recruit British and Allied prisoners of war to join an English legion of fascist sympathisers who would fight for the Germans. He put this idea to Hitler, who on 28 December 1942 issued the orders for such a legion to be established. It would be attached to the SS (which already included French, Scandinavians, Muslims and other nationalities among its ranks) and would be called 'The British Free Corps'.

In order to induce potential recruits to join, a special 'holiday camp' was set up for British prisoners of war, where they were given free beer, decent food, allowed to play football, and entertained with a band. On the staff of this 'holiday camp', which was next door to and in full view of Gross-Beeren concentration camp (situated near the German town of that name), were British Nazi sympathisers – 'stool pigeons' – whose aim was to persuade their countrymen to change sides. One of these, Quartermaster Sergeant John Brown, was however a double agent working for MI5. The Germans also used prostitutes as bait, and subsequently blackmailed the prisoners of war (who were normally forbidden under German military law from having sexual relationships with German women).

One person recruited in this way was Francis McLardy, a Liverpudlian with fascist sympathies, who, as was customary for the BFC, signed up under a false name 'Frank Wood'. Another was Eric Pleasants, a physical fitness instructor and also a fascist, who said the Germans had assured him that the British recruits 'were only going to fight communism ...' and would not be 'asked to fight any Englishman, or any other thing except (soviets on) the Eastern Front'.[27]

Recruit Thomas Cooper, a Londoner, who had already fought for Germany on the Russian Front, was the only British subject to receive a German war medal as a serving German soldier. Fluent in German, he had also once been a guard in a concentration camp. Yorkshire born Robert Chipchase recalled how Cooper loved to tell him, 'all about the people in the SS, and how he [Cooper] was in the death camps, going out and helping with the work there'.

For those prisoners of war who failed to respond, however, it was a different story: they were stripped and fed on a diet of bread and water. John Eric Wilson, a captured commando, broke down after three days of such ill treatment.

Eric Pleasants probably epitomised the true feelings of most members of the BFC, when he declared that although its members trained with machine guns and rifles, this was 'only to keep out of the way', as they had no intention of fighting.

When the BFC arrived at the Waffen SS Headquarters (established in 1943 in a monastery at Hildesheim, a district in Lower Saxony), the recruits received an SS uniform, on the collar of which were the three lions of England; on the sleeve, beneath the Nazi swastika and German eagle, the union flag and logo 'British Free Corps' written in English.

A total of fifty-nine British prisoners of war joined the BFC (which officially came into existence in 1944 on Hitler's birthday, 20 April). It was commanded by SS Captain Hans Werner Roepke, who had formerly served on the Eastern Front and spoke fluent English. In an attempt to recruit more men into the BFC, twenty-five of its members were sent as ambassadors into the concentration camps, where they met with very little success.

As for the young women of Germany, they regarded it as a status symbol to have a British SS boyfriend. 18 year old Elfride Keuntje, for example, fell in love with Robert Kingsley (real name Hugh Wilson Cowey), a captured private from the Gordon Highlanders.

The BFC was subsequently transferred to Dresden and trained to use explosives and flamethrowers. When that city was bombed on 13 February 1945, BFC recruits were ordered to help with the clean up operation.

In March 1945 the BFC was transferred from Dresden to the Eastern Front, where it witnessed the German army's last stand on the Oder river. By this time the Wehrmacht was so short of manpower that it was conscripting 14 year-old boys from the Hitler Youth, together with amputees and elderly men, to confront the 2 million Russians on the other side of the river.

A month later the BFC was asked to help evacuate civilians, and in this way, it escaped the Russian artillery barrage. As the Russians advanced, BFC members fled west and intermingled with Allied prisoners of war in the hope that they would not be recognised.[28]

***

It is interesting to speculate as to what role Sir Oswald Mosley might have been offered, should the Nazis have succeeded in invading Britain. To be appointed the 'British Führer' perhaps, to govern on behalf of his Nazi master?

This seems unlikely, judging by the modest welcome given to Mosley when he visited Hitler in 1935. This welcome pales into insignificance, when compared with the elaborate 'red carpet' treatment afforded to Edward, Duke of Windsor, in 1937 – even though by that time, Edward was no longer on the throne, having abdicated the previous year.

It appears, therefore, that if anyone was to have a major role to play, it would be the former king, who might well have been offered the chance to reclaim his throne – on certain conditions of course, which are not difficult to guess, judging by what occurred in the other German-occupied territories!

Notes

1. *RA (Royal Archives) DW (Duke of Windsor)* 4737, 28 Jan. 1941.
2. Ibid, Add/165, 10 Nov. 1942.
3. Ibid, 4756, 17 Mar. 1941.
4. Higham, Charles, *Wallis: Secret Lives of the Duchess of Windsor*, p. 273.
5. *National Archives, Washington D.C.*, US State Department File 811.711/4039, 18 June, 1943.
6. Hastings, Selina, 1985, *Nancy Mitford*, London. p. 207.
7. *The Times*, Editorial, 14 November 2003.
8. *Anna Wolkoff*, www.spartacus.schoolnet.co.uk/SSWolkoff.htm
9. Henri, Dr Pauline, 29.10.03, *Verge of Treason*, www.searchlightmagazine.com/stories/mosley/htm.
10. www.spartacus.schoolnet.co.uk/SSwolkoff.htm.
11. Dalley, Jan, *Diana Mosley: A Life*. p. 241.
12. Ibid.
13. Ibid, p. 243.
14. Ibid, p. 252.
15. Ibid, p. 253.
16. Shirer, William L, *The Rise and Fall of the Third Reich*, p. 784.
17. Dalley, op. cit., p. 254.
18. Ibid.
19. *Hansard, Proceedings at House of Commons*, 20 March 1940.
20. www.spartacus.schoolnet.co.uk/2WWfifthc.htm.
21. *Royal Archives: KV (King George V)* 2/1365–7 and KV3/60–3.
22–26.   *Fifth Column*, www.spartacus.schoolnet.co.uk/2wwfifthc.htm.
27. *The Brits who fought for Hitler
28. Ibid.

CHAPTER XXXI

Wonder Weapons: Hitler's Last Hope

As the war drew to its inevitable conclusion, Hitler deceived himself into thinking, long after all hope was gone, that he could still win by using new technology.

Slave labour from the concentration camps was used to build Hitler's so-called 'wonder weapons' as for example, in the Dora-Nordhausen complex, situated in the Hartz Mountains of Germany's Lower Saxony, where from 1943 onwards, 60,000 workers toiled in the twenty kilometres of artificially constructed tunnels. Albert Speer himself visited Dora at the end of 1943 in his capacity as Armaments Minister, and confessed that the conditions he found there were 'barbaric' and 'inhuman'.[1]

By 1944 the German air force, which was suffering serious fuel shortages, was outnumbered by ten to one in the skies over Germany. The race was now on to produce advanced weaponry, which even at this late stage, might turn the tide.

The Messerschmitt Me262 single seater, twin-jet fighter could fly at 560 miles per hour (as compared with the Stuka dive bomber which could only manage 230 miles per hour). It was, therefore, 100 miles per hour faster than any fighter possessed by the Allies. Hitler, however, saw the Me262 as a bomber as well as a fighter, and so work was begun to convert it for this purpose.

Due to problems in the acquisition of the precious metals upon which the engine relied for its construction, only 800 of these Me262 machines were ever handed over to the Luftwaffe, and the first squadron of Me262s did not become operational until early October 1944.

The Messerschmitt Me163 was the world's first rocket powered interceptor fighter, designed to reach the high altitudes at which the Allied bombers were flying. It flew at 700 miles per hour, and was the fastest aircraft of World War II. However, it could only carry enough fuel for seven minutes of powered flight, and had a range of only twenty-five miles, after which it was obliged to glide back to earth. From August 1944 300 of these aircraft would go into frontline service.

In January 1944 a prototype of the Junkers Ju390, 6-engined, propeller-driven bomber flew across the Atlantic to within twelve miles of the US coast (north of New York City), and returned safely to base in Germany after a journey of some 6,000 miles. Had Allied bombing not made further production of this aircraft impossible, the Germans would undoubtedly have bombed cities on the east coast of America.

At Peenemunde, on Germany's Baltic coast, German scientists developed the V1 and V2. The V1 was a pilotless monoplane, powered by a jet engine and carrying a bomb. It had a range of 140 miles. From 13 June 1944 some 18,000 V1s were launched from enemy occupied France against London, but because of their low trajectory and slow speed, half were intercepted before they reached their targets, and others were shot down by anti-aircraft guns.

The V2 – the world's first long range ballistic missile – was a rocket bomb with a preset guidance system. From 8 September 1944 V2s were launched against London, flying fifty miles above the Earth's surface, reaching a speed of 4,000 miles per hour after twenty miles, and from then on gliding towards their target. Each warhead contained about 1,700 pounds of explosive.

By November 1944 all of the rocket launching sites in France had been captured by the invading Allied forces. The Germans were now obliged to withdraw their rocket programme to Germany; London now being out of range, they switched their target to the Belgian port of Antwerp, which was now in Allied hands.

The Nazis also considered the idea of attacking America with submarines, from which the V2 rockets would be launched off the American coast. (With a range of only 250 miles the V2 could not otherwise be deployed against the USA.) The steering of these rockets was effected through gyroscopes, so that any untoward movement could be detected and compensated for accordingly via the steering mechanism. In the event, a V2 rocket was never fired from a submarine, owing to the launching procedures being too complex for this to be possible.

***

For the Nazis, the 'Holy Grail' of weaponry was the Atomic Bomb, and had they been able to produce one in time, this might have been a decisive factor in them winning the war. However, since the time when, following their rise to power in 1933 the Nazis demanded the forced resignation of Jewish professors and scholars (whom they deemed to be 'politically unreliable') from the cradle of nuclear science, namely the University of Gottingen, this was never a realistic proposition. Despite this the fact remains that it was a German, Doctor Otto Hahn, who in 1938 first discovered that if atoms of uranium were bombarded with neutrons, atomic energy would result.

One of those scientists forced to flee Nazi Germany was Albert Einstein (born in Bavaria of Jewish parents, and Director of the Kaiser Wilhelm Physical Institute in Berlin from 1914–33). Allegedly he left with only the clothes he stood up in, and a case containing his violin. In 1939 Einstein warned President Roosevelt that Germany might attempt to make an atomic bomb.

After this self-inflicted 'brain drain', the Nazis made matters worse by failing to give the German atomic bomb project the resources it required, the whole enterprise being marred by Hitler's attitude to nuclear physics, which he described scornfully as 'Jewish physics'. The final blow, however, was yet to come.

In the 1920s and 1930s Germany was pre-eminent in science and technology. Head of atomic research at Germany's Kaiser Wilhelm Institute in Berlin was Werner Heisenberg, who in 1932 had won the Nobel Prize for physics for his discovery of quantum mechanics. He was one of the few non-Jews to be working in the field of atomic research. Heisenberg and his team designed a nuclear reactor which required deuterium oxide (heavy water) to act as a moderator or 'brake' to the nuclear reaction (without which an atomic bomb could not be made to work).

Prior to the outbreak of World War II, heavy water was being manufactured at a factory in Norway – known as the Norsk Hydro – situated at Vermork, near Rjukan to the west of the capital Oslo, in the bleak mountains of the province of Telemark. Following the invasion of Norway on 19 April 1940, the Nazis took charge of this factory.

On 27 February 1943 a team of Norwegian saboteurs (refugees from the Nazis, who were now either serving in the British armed forces, or in the Special Operations Executive – SOE) parachuted into Norway, entered the factory, and destroyed approximately one ton of heavy water. Following a subsequent Allied bombing raid, the Germans attempted to relocate the factory to Germany, but the remaining stock of heavy water was destroyed en route, when a ferry carrying it across a lake was destroyed, also by Norwegian saboteurs working for SOE.

Hitler had miscalculated yet again. Those Jewish scientists who had fled from the Reich to the United Kingdom and the USA as a result of his oppressive Nazi regime (including Otto Frisch, born in Vienna) would now be instrumental in helping the Allies build their own atomic bomb.

Note

1. *Hitler's Henchmen: Speer – the Architect*.

CHAPTER XXXII

Hitler's Personality

Hitler's Friends

It is said that one may know a person by his friends, and it has to be said that those whom Hitler appointed to positions of power within his Nazi Party were arguably as bizarre a group of individuals as ever came together under one roof.

They included Rudolf Hess (Hitler's deputy and leader of the Party), whose inferiority complex led him to undertake single-handedly, a secret mission to Britain in order to conclude a peace treaty; Hermann Göring, Reich Minister without Portfolio, whose brutality as head of the Gestapo was only matched by his greed and self-indulgence, and whose over estimation of the power of his Luftwaffe finally caused Hitler to lose faith in him; Martin Bormann, Hitler's Chief of Staff and Reich leader of the NSDAP, who personally decided what Hitler should and should not be aware of, by screening all his letters and communications; Eva Braun, his mistress and eventually his wife, with whom he was apparently unable to form a normal relationship; Adolf Eichman, who worked in Himmler's SD (Security Service) where he was put in charge of the deportation of Jews to the death camps in all German controlled territories; Heinrich Himmler, Chief of the German police and Reichsführer SS, who attempted to turn the fanciful notions of German folklore, chivalry and the occult, into reality; Joseph Goebbels, the nauseating Propaganda Minister, whom his colleagues nicknamed 'Cuckoo'; Reinhard Heydrich, head of the Reich Main Security Office (RSCHA) who administered the policy for exterminating no fewer than 6 million Jews; Josef Mengele who, as chief doctor at Auschwitz, conducted gruesome scientific experiments on its inmates by day, whilst playing the violin to them by night; Joachim von Ribbentrop, Foreign Minister and former champagne salesman, whose coarseness, crudity and inappropriate 'Heil Hitler' salutes upset the British establishment, and whom the British nicknamed 'Herr Brick-en-Drop'; Alfred Rosenberg, self-styled philosopher, politician, and 'intellectual' whose book *The Myth of the Twentieth Century* (published in 1930) was long, tedious and unoriginal, so much so that his bored Führer failed to complete the reading of it, and it came to be ridiculed, even by the Nazis themselves; Baldour von Schirach, who as Reich Youth Leader supplied Hitler with an inexhaustible supply of cannon fodder for his armed forces; finally, Albert Speer, the architect who was put in charge of designing buildings for Hitler's new Reich, and who later became Minister of Armaments and claimed at the Nürnberg War Crimes Tribunal that he knew nothing of the concentration camps, despite having visited at least one of them personally, and on more than one occasion.

These characters, seemingly so diverse by nature, all shared one thing in common, namely the desire (metaphorically) to jump through hoops and perform somersaults if they thought that by so doing, they would please their Führer.

***

Hermann Rauschning, Nazi Governor of Danzig, also posed the question, 'Is Hitler mad?' and went on to say,

> I think everyone who has met the Führer two or three times must have asked himself this question. Anyone who has seen this man face to face, has met his uncertain glance, without depth or warmth; from eyes that seem hard and remote, and has then seen that gaze grow rigid, will certainly have experienced the uncanny feeling: 'that man is not normal'.
>
> Never was a conversation with Hitler possible. Either he would listen in silence, or he would 'speechify' and not allow one to speak. Or he would walk restlessly up and down, interrupt constantly, and jump from one subject to another as if unable to concentrate.[1]

The Classification of Personality Disorders

Psychiatrists tend to compartmentalise the various types of personality disorder that they describe. However, for a particular patient, the symptoms may not always fall entirely within one category and may overlap into another.

Histrionic Personality Disorder, for example, is described as, 'a pervasive pattern of excessive emotionality and attention seeking, beginning by early adulthood and present in a variety of contexts....' Such a person may be,

> uncomfortable in situations in which he or she is not the centre of attention; display rapidly shifting and shallow expressions of emotion; have a style of speech that is excessively impressionistic and lacking in detail; and show self-dramatisation, theatricality, and exaggerated expression of emotion.[2]

The following symptoms, however, are typical of *Paranoid Personality Disorder*: such a person is 'suspicious', or has 'unfounded suspicions', and 'believes others are plotting against him/her'. Such a person is also likely to bear grudges.[3]

Antisocial (or Dissocial) Personality Disorder may be characterised by callous unconcern for the feelings of others; gross and persistent attitude of irresponsibility and disregard for social norms, rules and obligations; incapacity to maintain enduring relationships ...; very low tolerance to frustration and a low threshold for discharge of aggression, including violence; incapacity to experience guilt and to profit from experience, particularly punishment; marked proneness to blame others, or to offer plausible rationalisations, for the behaviour that has brought the patient into conflict with society.[4]

James Morrison MD, has developed the theme of *Antisocial Personality Disorder* even further, and lists some of its possible features, many of which immediately bring Adolf Hitler (and the Nazis) to mind. They include:

> frequent bullying or threatening (often with the starting of fights) – [viz. Hitler's intimidation of his neighbours prior to invasion]; physical cruelty to people [the Holocaust]; theft [of art treasures from many European capitals occupied by the Nazis]; property destruction (with deliberate setting fire to and causing damage) [The Reichstag and Kristallnacht]; frequent lying [a constant feature throughout Hitler's entire life]; the frequent breaking of promises, for gain or to avoid obligations [Hitler's breaking of treaties].

Continuing with his description of a typical patient with *Antisocial Personality Disorder*, Morrison speaks of,

> serious rule violation – beginning by age 12, frequently staying out at night against parents' wishes – ran away from parents twice or more. [During his childhood Hitler himself is alleged to have run away from home.] Since age 15, the patient has shown disregard for the rights of others in a variety of situations – including is impulsive, or does not plan ahead [Hitler's handling of 'The Battle of Britain' and 'Operation Barbarossa']; irritability and aggression [Hitler in his speeches]; shows irresponsibility by repeated failure to sustain employment [Hitler's early life], or to honour financial obligations [deliberately borrowing money, which he knew he would never be able to pay back, in order to finance his war]; lacks remorse for his own injurious behaviour [witness, Hitler never visited a concentration camp, and dismissed in a peremptory fashion anyone who dared to mention such matters].[5]

It seems that Hitler was therefore suffering from a combination of *Histrionic*, *Paranoid* and *Antisocial Personality Disorders*. However, this is not the end of the story.

Schizophrenia

Posterity is indebted to two people above all, for shedding light on the psychological make-up of the Führer, although neither of them was aware of the full implications of what he wrote concerning the life of Hitler. One was Otto Wagener (1888–1971), who for some years was at the very centre of the Nazi Party; the other was Hermann Rauschning (1887–1961), Nazi Governor (and later President) of Danzig Province. (In 1932 Danzig was an independent city-state, then under the protection of The League of Nations. In 1939 Danzig was annexed by Germany.)

Interestingly, the two men, Wagener and Rauschning, were at opposite ends of the spectrum, for as Henry Ashby Turner Jr points out in his Introduction to Wagener's memoirs (of which he is editor):

> Whereas Rauschning wrote as a renegade Nazi, liberated from all illusions about Hitler and implacably opposed to him, Wagener's faith in the Führer survived even the Third Reich's total defeat in the Second World War.[6]

In the Introduction to Wagener's book, *Hitler – Memoirs of a Confidant* (published in 1978), Turner states that: 'Wagener was born in 1888 in the city of Durlach in Baden, in the south-western corner of the German Empire. He grew up in Karlsruhe, Baden's capital ...'[7] He describes Wagener as 'a prominent official in the Nazi Party, with close ties to Adolf Hitler from the Autumn of 1929 [when Wagener attended the Nazi Party's Nürnberg Congress] until the Summer of 1933.' Turner also states:

> Wagener served as Chief of Staff of the Storm Troop Auxiliary, the SA; headed the Economic Policy Section of the Party's National Executive [Reichsleitung]; worked on special assignment for Hitler in Berlin; headed the Party's Economic Policy Office during the early months of the Third Reich; and briefly served as Commissar for the Economy. [However] Wagener fell into disfavour with Hitler at the end of June 1933. This cost him his posts in the Party and the government .... He retained only his nominal rank as SA Group Leader, and a meaningless seat in the rubber-stamped Nazi legislature the Reichstag, which rarely even convened.[8]
>
> During the Second World War, Wagener ... served in the [German] army. He entered as a captain, and had attained the rank of major general by the end of the war, when he surrendered the remaining German forces to the British on the island of Rhodes. After seven years in British and Italian internment, he returned to Germany in 1952 and settled in Bavaria, where he dabbled in nationalistic politics until his death in 1971 at the age of 83.[9]

The story of Wagener's book, and of how it came to be published, is an extraordinary one.

Wagener wrote his memoirs while interned in the British camp for German officers at Bridgend in Wales during 1946. He filled thirty-six British military exercise notebooks – approximately 2,300 pages – with his narrative. The notebooks contain pages [each] about six by eight inches [in size], and bear the inspection stamps placed upon them by the British camp officials.

Before leaving Wales, he placed the memoirs in a suitcase which he turned over to a representative of the Red Cross with the request that it be sent to his wife in Germany. The 1958 postscript states that after a lengthy period the suitcase reached his wife in damaged condition, but with the notebooks containing the memoirs intact.[10]

In Chapter 25 of Wagener's *Memoirs*, entitled 'Hitler's Thought Processes', 'Wagener reports … on a talk he had with Hitler at the Elephant Hotel in Weimar during one of their political trips'. Hitler stated:

I'm now and then aware, that it is not I who is speaking, but that something speaks through me. On such occasions, I frequently feel as if there were a mistake in human logic or as if it had limits of which it is not aware. Now and then ideas, concepts, views occur to me that I have read nowhere, heard nowhere, and never before thought, nor can I justify them by logic, and they do not even seem to me capable of being logically justified.[11]

The Führer himself realised therefore, that his mind was in the grip of forces which were illogical and beyond his control. He then attempted to explain it.

I owe to [Albert] Einstein [mathematical physicist – Hitler had recently attended a lecture on Einstein's Theory of Relativity] the scientific proof that there are things which, recognised by man's senses, nevertheless cannot be understood and justified, though they are true and could form the basis for a new way of thinking, perhaps even of a new conception of the world. In future, I will know how to console myself when some perception comes to my mind to which I am lacking a logical bridge. I shall nevertheless have the courage to build on it.[12]

When asked by Wagener, 'Do you always know whether such a perception comes from beyond or through the agency of the human senses within this world?' Hitler replied,

In general, at such moments I have a sensation like an inner vibration, as if I were being touched by an invisible charge. Whenever I have seized the impulse, what I said or did as a result of that feeling always turned out to be correct. Whenever I have let it go, almost invariably it turned out later that it would have been right to follow the inner voice.[13]

Wagener was working along the lines that Hitler's peculiar perceptions were the result of some supernatural, superhuman forces. It does not appear to have occurred to him that the defect – if so it may be called – was in the mind of the Führer himself.

In the penultimate page of Wagener's Memoirs, Hitler appears to demand secrecy of him, saying:

> During so many nights we discussed so many things, and I have revealed to you my innermost thoughts and my most fundamental ideas, as I have done perhaps to no one else. Please keep this knowledge to yourself, and thus become the guardian of the grail, whose innermost truth can be disclosed only to the few.[14]

Hermann Rauschning's book *Hitler Speaks*, published in December 1939 and described as 'A Series of Political Conversations with Adolf Hitler on his Real Aims', gives another extraordinary insight into the mind of the Führer. In Chapter 14, entitled, 'A New Social Order, A New Economy', Hitler, in conversation with Rauschning, explains his decision-making process:

> Unless I have the inner, incorruptible conviction, [that] *this is the solution,* I do nothing. Not even if the whole Party tries to drive me to action. I will not act; I will wait, no matter what happens. But if the voice speaks, then I know the time has come to act.[15]

'He [Hitler] seemed to take it for granted that the ideas [which he expounded] were his own,' said Rauschning. 'He had no notion of their actual origin, and considered that he had worked them out himself, and that they were inspirations, the product of his solitude in the mountains.'[16] Again, Hitler is at a loss when attempting to identify the source of his ideas.

In Chapter 18 of *Hitler Speaks*, entitled 'Hitler Himself', Rauschning attempts to explain this in terms of 'mediums' (persons through whom ultra-physical perceptions are revealed to others). Most mediums, said Rauschning, are,

> ordinary, undistinguished persons [who can] suddenly … acquire gifts that carry them far above the common crowd. These qualities [however] have nothing to do with the medium's own personality. They are conveyed to him from without. The medium is possessed by them.[17] In the same way undeniable powers enter into Hitler, genuinely demonic powers, which make men his instruments. The common united with the uncommon – that is what makes Hitler's personality so desperate a puzzle to those who come into contact with him.[18]

In the same chapter, Rauschning describes how Hitler, 'loves solitary walks. He hears voices. I have met him when in this mood. He recognises nobody then: he wants to be alone. There are times when he flees from human society.'[19]

Rauschning appears to have taken Hitler at face value, by attributing his perceptions to demonic powers which enter into Hitler from without. As with Wagener, *it does not appear to have occurred to Rauschning* that he was dealing with an *intrinsically abnormal mind.*

***

As to the credibility of these two crucial witnesses to the life of the Führer, German historian Theodor Schieder had this to say: Rauschning's book is, 'a document of unquestionable value, since it contains views derived from immediate experience'.[20] Henry Ashby Turner, points out:

> One cannot regard the utterances Wagener attributed to Hitler and others as verbatim quotations. On the other hand, Wagener's recollections, like those of Rauschning, come from a person who repeatedly experienced Hitler at first hand.[21]

Turner, in his Introduction to Wagener's *Memoirs*, gives further important information about the latter:

> Theodor Schieder reckoned that Rauschning met with Hitler at most thirteen times, [and] in only about half of those encounters was Rauschning alone with Hitler.[22] [In contrast] Wagener … maintained an office in the same München building which Hitler used as his headquarters, the Brown House. Constantly in the immediate entourage of the Führer, he had many opportunities for confidential talks with him of the sort he recounts in the memoirs. He also accompanied Hitler on the latter's frequent travels through Germany. During his three years as a member of the National Executive of the Nazi Party, he undoubtedly found himself together with Hitler literally hundreds of times, often unaccompanied by others.[23]

In Wagener's *Memoirs*, says Turner,

> Wagener's accounts of public events, his descriptions of organisations, especially those of the Nazi Party, and his identifications of individuals and their positions, provide many opportunities to check the accuracy of his memory. [And he concluded that, in the instances where such checks could be made, Wagener's memory proved highly reliable].[24]

***

Most importantly, both Wagener and Rauschning reported that Hitler heard voices, though neither realised the full significance of this, which is that *the hearing of voices is one of the classic symptoms of schizophrenia.* Given this fact, so much of what has *previously been regarded as inexplicable about the Führer,* can now *more easily be understood.* This will be discussed more fully later.

Hitler's Father

Various accounts indicate that Alois Hitler beat his son Adolf, sometimes severely, yet perhaps too much has been made of the negative aspects of their relationship, and not enough of the positive. For example, in *Mein Kampf,* Hitler describes, 'having the picture of my father constantly before my mind, who had raised himself by his own efforts to the position of civil servant, though he was the poor son of a village shoemaker'.[25]

As already mentioned, Alois relocated his family from Braunau to Linz, specifically in order that Adolf should receive a good education. To Hitler's credit, when his father died in 1903, he refused to accept an allowance from his mother, and 'signed over his minute inheritance [from his father] to his sisters.'[26]

His Mother

Dr Rudolph Binion, of Brandeis University, Massachussets, USA, believed that Hitler's mother, Klara, may have influenced her son, not only during her lifetime, but also after her death. During her final illness, her doctor, Eduard Bloch, had visited her home and seen her at his surgery no fewer than seventy-seven times, and had given her forty-seven treatments: mostly with iodoform (a crystalline compound of iodine, used as an antiseptic). The cost of treatment was considerable, and on Christmas Eve 1907 the doctor duly presented his bill for 359 Kronen (of which 59 had already been paid on account).

'Consciously,' said Dr Binion,

> He [Hitler] loved Bloch like a kind father; unconsciously, he blamed Bloch for his mother's cancer, for the toxic treatment [iodoform, which the doctor prescribed her], and for the huge terminal bill [Dr Bloch's account] paid on Christmas Eve. This blame surfaced after 1918 as a burning rage against *the Jewish profiteer [i.e. Bloch]), the Jewish poison [iodoform] [and] the Jewish cancer.*

Therefore, when, later, during World War I, Hitler,

> emerged from his trance [following his hospitalisation of October–November 1918 for mustard gas poisoning], he resolved on entering politics in order to kill the Jews by way of discharging his mission to undo and reverse Germany's defeat.

Binion's argument rests substantially on his sweeping and unsubstantiated statement that: 'Consciously or unconsciously the bereaved always blame the doctor for the patient's death.'[27] However, Hitler's actions at the time certainly give no indication that he consciously blamed Doctor Bloch for his mother's death, rather the reverse in fact. Did he therefore blame him unconsciously? This notion is, of course, impossible to prove one way or the other but against it is the fact that when Austria's Jews were rounded up by the Nazis following the Anschluss, Dr Bloch was perhaps the only one not to be persecuted – undoubtedly on Hitler's instructions. The virulence of the

> Führer's anti-Semitism being apparently insufficient, on this rare occasion, to overcome the feeling of gratitude which he owed to Dr Bloch for looking after his family, and his mother in particular.

Dr Bloch has provided a fair, unbiased and even charitable portrait of the young Hitler whom he knew. *However, even Bloch felt compelled to describe him as 'this strange boy'.*[28]

Binion dates Hitler's anti-Semitism from this time, and is sceptical of Hitler's statement in *Mein Kampf* that he did not become an anti-Semite until after World War I.[29] However, whatever the truth may be, it is difficult to see how such irrational notions could have taken root in Hitler's mind, unless that mind was itself irrational.

The Gas Attack

Hitler, in *Mein Kampf*, describes how during the autumn of 1918,

> the British opened an attack with gas on the Front, south of Ypres. They used the yellow gas, whose effect was unknown to us, at least from personal experience. I was destined to experience it that very night … [13–14 October]. At about midnight a number of us were put out of action – some forever. Towards morning, I also began to feel pain: it increased with every quarter of an hour, and at about seven o'clock my eyes were scorching as I staggered back and delivered the last despatch I was destined to carry in this war. A few hours later my eyes were like glowing coals and all was darkness around me.[30] … when the waves of poison gas enveloped me and began to penetrate my eyes, the thought of becoming permanently blind unnerved me ….[31] I was sent into hospital at Pasewalk in Pomerania, and there it was that I had to hear of the Revolution.[32]
>
> [By early November] I had begun to feel somewhat better. The burning pain in the eye-sockets had become less severe. Gradually, I was able to distinguish the general outlines of my immediate surroundings. [Then, when news broke that the German army wished to capitulate] darkness surrounded me as I staggered and stumbled back to my ward and buried my aching head between the blankets and pillow.[33]

In view of the depression which followed the gas attack, Professor Edmund Forster, Chief of the Berlin University Nerve Clinic, having been asked to see Hitler, diagnosed his patient as, 'A psychopath with hysterical symptoms.' (These findings of Dr Forster's were reported by Dr Karl Kronor, a former Viennese nerve specialist who had apparently been present at the original medical examination of Hitler at Pasewalk.) Was Dr Forster correct in describing Hitler as a psychopath and an hysteric?

There are many definitions of psychopathy, but one thing they all have in common is that the patient experiences a loss of contact with reality. Can this therefore be said of Hitler? It is arguable to say the least, for there are those who would affirm that the Führer knew EXACTLY what he was doing (the fact that so many of his actions were premeditated being borne out in his book *Mein Kampf*).

Dr Forster defined psychopathy as:

Mental inferiority usually conditioned by hereditary disposition, and distinguished especially by weakness of will and inability to adapt oneself to society. It produces in consequence, a tendency to misdemeanour and crime.[34]

Although this definition would not be accepted today, as far as Hitler was concerned, it proved to be a most perceptive summing up of his mental state.

Possible Long-Term Effects of Mustard Gas Poisoning

The gas to which Hitler was exposed was sulphur mustard (mustard gas, or HD) an agent used deliberately to produce blistering of the skin in chemical warfare. Could it be that such exposure brought on a subsequent change in Hitler's personality?

The major clinical effects of exposure to HD are significant skin, eye and pulmonary lesions, which are usually non-fatal: the length of hospitalisation for these injuries is estimated at forty-six days per casualty during World War I.[35]

Approximately 90% of people with eye injury are disabled for approximately ten days with conjunctivitis, photophobia and minimal corneal swelling.[36] However, psychosis is not known to be either an acute or chronic effect of mustard gas poisoning (although anxiety disorders and post traumatic stress syndrome may result).[37]

Dr Forster was correct when he described Hitler's symptoms as 'hysterical'; 'dominant characteristics' of this condition being 'shallow, labile emotions, manipulative behaviour, a tendency to over dramatise situations, a lack of self-criticism, and a fickle flirtatiousness with little capacity for sustained sexual relationships'.[38]

Education

According to Albert Speer,

Hitler ... had seen nothing of the world and had acquired neither knowledge nor understanding of it. Moreover, the average Party politician lacked higher education: of the fifty 'Reichsleiters' and 'Gauleiters', the elite of the leadership, only ten had completed a university education. A few had attended university classes for a while, and the majority had never gone beyond secondary school. Virtually none of them had distinguished themselves by any notable achievement in any field whatsoever .... Their educational standard certainly did not correspond to what might have been expected of the top leadership of a nation with a traditionally high intellectual level.[39]

Animals and Children

Did Hitler have any redeeming features? He enjoyed being photographed with children, but whether this was for reasons of publicity, or out of genuine affection, is not known.

His love of dogs was revealed when, in 1915 a British one accidentally strayed across the German lines. Hitler adopted it and named it 'Foxl', and when it subsequently went missing, he was distraught. Subsequently, at his Berghof mountain retreat, there were always a number of his canine friends in evidence, in particular an Alsatian called 'Blondi', which he taught to perform tricks. Also, 'He loved his canaries,' said Hermann Rauschning, 'and could cry when one of them sickened and died.'[40]

Women

Hitler's relationship with women gives further insight into his character.

Based on evidence gathered for his report to the US Office of Strategic Services (OSS), Dr Walter Langer concluded that Hitler suffered from, 'an extreme form of masochism in which the individual derives sexual gratification from having a woman urinate or defecate upon him'. Langer believed that this sexual perversion was the manifestation of 'an intense self-loathing, which his subconscious turned into an aggressive hatred of other nations and races'.

Sexual masochism (which comes under the general heading of 'Paraphilia') is defined as intentional participation in an activity in which one is humiliated, beaten, bound, or otherwise abused to experience sexual excitement. Masochistic fantasies tend to begin in childhood ... and,

masochistic activity tends to be ritualised and chronic. Persons may act out their masochistic fantasies themselves, or seek a partner who may be a sexual sadist. Activities with a partner include: bondage …, flagellation, humiliation by means of urination or defecation on person ….

Such, 'arousal patterns' are considered deviant because they are often obligatory for sexual function [i.e. erection or orgasm cannot occur without the stimulus].

In persons with a paraphilia, the capacity for affectionate, reciprocal, emotional and sexual intimacy with a partner is generally impaired or non-existent, and other aspects of personal or emotional adjustment are also impaired. Paraphilias are far more common among males than among females in most cultures.[41]

It is estimated that 'about 30% (of masochists) participate in sadistic behaviour as well.'[42] There are different theories as to the cause of sexual masochism, among them childhood trauma (including sexual abuse – though there is no evidence of this in Hitler's case).

Langer ended his report to the OSS by postulating a number of different ways in which Hitler might meet his end: he might die of natural causes, seek refuge in a neutral country, be killed in battle, be assassinated, go insane, be seized by the German military in a revolt, or be captured by the Allies. *In Langer's opinion, the most plausible outcome was suicide, Hitler having threatened this on a number of occasions.*

In all probability however, it would not be a simple suicide. He has much too much of the dramatic for that, and since immortality is one of his dominant motives, we can imagine that he would stage the most dramatic and effective death scene he could possibly think of.[43]

This illuminating report by Langer was then locked away and forgotten for more than twenty-five years!

***

In 1944 after an acquaintance of fifteen years, Eva Braun was still Hitler's mistress. Even as late as June 1944 when Eva's sister Gretl married SS General Otto Hermann Fegelein, Hitler still declined to marry her.

On 7 March 1945 Eva, intensely frustrated at her long separations from Hitler, went to Berlin to be with him, even though this was against his wishes. It was here, on 28 April in the 'Führer bunker' of the Reich Chancellery, that they finally married. Two days later, they would take their own lives.

Homosexuality

Lothar Machtan has written extensively on the question of whether or not Hitler was homosexual, pointing to a number of homosexual and homosexually inclined men amongst Hitler's acquaintances including Kubizek, Hanisch, Röhm, Eckart and Hess. Machtan concludes however that, 'It is doubtful that Hitler was sexually active in any way (gay or straight) after 1933 ....' Hitler's homosexual past, nevertheless, was his Achilles heel which 'threatened him politically and left him open to blackmail by his most intimate associates'.[44]

Drugs

Between 1936 and 1944 Hitler's personal physician, Theodor Morell, was believed to have been prescribing psychotropic drugs, including opiates and amphetamines. Could these have affected Hitler's personality? The answer is probably not, since his mindset appears to have been well established many years prior to this.

Syphilis

The fact that Hitler devoted several pages of *Mein Kampf* to the subject of syphilis has led to speculation that he himself suffered from this disease.

A person who contracts syphilis develops an ulcer within ten days to three months (chancre); this is known as the primary phase. Three to six weeks later, the patient develops a skin rash with generalised symptoms of fever, fatigue, headache, sore throat and swollen lymph nodes. These symptoms may persist for up to one to two years. This is known as the secondary phase.

Approximately one third of those who develop secondary syphilis will go on to experience the complications of the tertiary phase, where the bacterium which causes the disease may affect any organ of the body, in particular the heart, eyes, brain, nervous system and bones. This phase can last for many years.

The final phase can result in mental illness, blindness, heart disease and stroke. A small percentage of sufferers develop neuro-syphilis (the symptoms of which may present up to twenty years after the initial infection), with sensory loss, ataxia (lack of coordination), bladder dysfunction and finally, dementia, general paralysis and death.

There was no cure for this disease, because although penicillin was discovered in 1928 (by Alexander Fleming) it was not until 1939 that Howard Florey and Ernst Chain perfected a method of producing the drug, which was not generally available until after World War II.

Although it cannot be said for certain that the Führer was NOT suffering from syphilis, taking the clinical picture as a whole, the diagnosis of Parkinson's Disease is far more likely.

Body Language

Many hours of cinematographic footage exist of Hitler showing him either on public view, or relaxing at his retreat at the Berghof. Is it possible therefore, from his body language, to make any deductions about the man himself, bearing in mind that most of the footage was taken on occasions when Hitler was on public view, and therefore not relaxed?

In his speeches, the pattern is usually fairly predictable. He begins in a reasonably controlled manner, allowing himself a flicker of a smile as his adulatory audience yells out the familiar, 'Sieg heil!' greeting. He then becomes more and more animated and agitated; the tone of his voice grows louder, sometimes menacing and sometimes hysterical. He clenches his hand or hands, the fist signalling conviction and determination (but this gesture can also, 'be deliberately exploited by public speakers and politicians who might, in reality, have neither').[45]

He uses chopping, or slicing movements with his arm or arms as if to (metaphorically) cut through obstacles, and makes jabbing movements with his forefinger as if to stab the person whom he is verbally attacking.[46] At the end of the sentence there is often an involuntary tilt of the head to one side.

When he travels in his motorcade he is to be seen standing up in his car with his arm outstretched in the classic Nazi salute. At other times he uses the right hand to make the palm up salute, a gesture so repetitive in his case as to look almost comical. As the arm is returned to his side, the palm once again faces downwards, a gesture intended to calm, quieten or even control.

More information can be deduced about the Führer's body language from his quieter moments at say, the Berghof mountain retreat. Here it is clear that he likes formality, both in his own dress and that required of his staff and visitors, and also at the tea table. It is true that he is sometimes to be seen smiling, or even laughing, but in the main, even when surrounded by a host of close associates, he gives the appearance of being somehow detached, both physically and mentally, from the events going on around him. Apart from a handshake, he studiously avoids any physical contact, except with his Alsatian 'Blondi', whom he loves to stroke. His face is often morose and his piercing blue eyes linger on their subject, as if to see right through them, as it were. He does, however, become more animated when studying maps, presumably in anticipation of executing his warlike intentions; or architectural plans for the proposed buildings of his new Reich.

***

The overriding impression is that Hitler is a person who is unable to engage with others on a personal, social or emotional level, but only in the capacity of master and servant; he of course, invariably being the master. The fact that in today's parlance, Hitler was and always had been 'a loner' is borne out by the statements of fellow soldiers who had fought alongside him in World War I.

Aside from describing the way in which Hitler thought and acted, and attempting to attach a psychological or psychiatric label to him, is it possible to probe more deeply and establish WHY he behaved as he did?

Notes

1. Rauschning, Hermann, *Hitler Speaks*, p. 250.
2, 3.*The Diagnostic and Statistical Manual of Mental Disorders*, 4th edn. 1994. Washington DC: American Psychiatric Association Press Inc. pp. 657–8.
4. WHO. 1992. *The ICD-10 Classification of Mental and Behavioural Disorders*, Geneva.
5. *General Criteria for Personality Disorders*, www.geocities.com./morisson9x/personality. htm.
6. Wagener, Otto, *Hitler–Memoirs of a Confidant*, p. xix.
7. Ibid, p. x.
8. Ibid, p. ix.
9. Ibid, p. xiii.
10. Ibid, p. xiv.
11. Ibid, p. 150.
12. Ibid, p. 151.
13. Ibid.
14. Ibid, p. 325.
15. Rauschning, op. cit., p. 181.
16. Ibid, p. 220.
17. Ibid, p. 253.
18. Ibid.
19. Ibid, p. 255.
20. Wagener, op. cit., p. xv.
21. Ibid, p. xvi.
22. Ibid.
23. Ibid, pp. xvi, xvii.
24. Ibid, p. xvii.
25. Hitler, Adolf, *Mein Kampf*, p. 22.
26. Bloch, Dr Eduard, *My Patient Hitler*, p. 36.
27. *History of Childhood Quarterly* 1, 1973, p. 201: *Hitler's concept of Lebensraum*.
28. Bloch, op. cit., p.36.
29. Toland, John, *Adolf Hitler*, p. 28.
30. Hitler, op. cit., p. 118.
31. Ibid, p. 120.
32. Ibid, p. 118.
33. Ibid, p. 119.
34. Toland, op. cit., p. 925 (from Dr Karl Kronor, 1943. *A Psychiatric Study of Hitler*, in OSS files at National Archives, Washington DC, USA).
35. Joy, R J T, 1997, *Historical Aspects of Medical Defense Against Chemical Warfare*, Washington DC: Office of the Surgeon General.

36. Smith, William J, 2002, (in *Chemical Warfare and Chemical Terrorism: Psychological and Performance Outcomes of 'Military Psychology'*. 40(2), p. 83, 2177.

37. Perrotta, Dennis M, 18 July 1996. *Long Term Health Effects Associated with Sub-clinical Exposures to GB and Mustard*. A Review conducted by the Environmental Committee, Armed Forces Epidemiological Board.

38. *The Oxford Companion to The Mind*, p. 333.

39. Speer, Albert, *Inside the Third Reich*, p. 182.

40. Rauschning, op. cit., p. 257.

41. *The Merck Manual of Diagnoses and Therapy*, Section 15, *Psychiatric Disorders*, Chapter 192, *Psycho-sexual Disorders*.

42. Morrison, J, 1995, *The Clinician's Guide to Diagnosis*. New York: The Guilford Press.

43. Langer, Walter, *The Mind of Adolf Hitler*, p. 212.

44. Machtan, Lothar, *The Hidden Hitler*.

45. Lambert, David, *Body Language*, p. 35.

46. Ibid, p. 38.

CHAPTER XXXIII

Hitler's Genetic Make Up

Herbert Richter (German soldier of World War I) made the following observations about Hitler.

> He began to speak, and I immediately disliked him. I didn't know then what he would later become. I found him rather comical with his funny little moustache. He had a scratchy voice and a strange appearance; and he shouted so much. He was shouting in this small room and what he was saying was really quite simplistic. I thought he wasn't quite normal. I found him spooky.[1]

Richter's simple and straightforward observation about the Führer may give a clue to the answer to the perennial unanswered question: why did Hitler behave as he did? Could it be that there was a *genetic basis* to the extraordinary convolutions of the Führer's mind?

***

No records exist of Hitler's family tree in the Oberösterreichisches Landesarchiv of the Austrian town of Linz. However, as August Kubizek, a friend of Hitler's from his youthful Vienna period points out, it was because of the closeness of the family relationship between Hitler's father Alois and his mother Klara, that the couple were required to obtain a special Ecclesiastical Dispensation from the Pope, before the marriage could take place. An attachment that accompanied the couple's application (dated 27 October 1884), indicates exactly what this relationship was.

The Hitler Family Tree.[2]

Johann Georg Hiedler	-----	Johann von Nepomuk Hiedler
Alois Hitler		Johanna Hiedler
(Adolf's Father)		(married Pölzl)
		Klara Pölzl
		(Adolf's Mother)

From this it can be seen that *Hitler's paternal grandfather, Johann Georg Hiedler, and Hitler's maternal grandfather, Johann von Nepomuk Hiedler, were brothers.*

***

August Kubizek described the young Hitler as someone who

> wallowed deeper and deeper in self-criticism. Yet it needed only the slightest touch ... for his self-accusation to become an accusation against the times, against the whole world; choking with a catalogue of hates, he would pour his fury over everything, against mankind in general who did not understand him, who did not appreciate him, and by whom he was persecuted.[3] Quite trivial things, such as a few thoughtless words [presumably on Kubizek's part], could produce in him [Hitler] outbursts of temper which I thought were quite out of proportion to the significance of the matter [in hand].[4]

Kubizek described the

> outstanding trait in my friend's [i.e. Hitler's] character [as], the unparalleled consistency in everything that he said and did. There was in his nature something firm, inflexible, immovable, obstinately rigid, which manifested itself in his profound seriousness and was at the bottom of all his other characteristics. Adolf simply could not change his mind or his nature. Everything that lay in these rigid precincts of his being remained unaltered forever.[5]

The explanation for this, according to Kubizek, was *'that the biological effect of the intermarriage [i.e. inbreeding] in the family was to fix certain spheres, and that those "arrested complexes" have produced that particular type of character'.*[6]

***

Now (presumably because of this inbreeding), Hitler's family was to be struck by a series of catastrophes. Of the five children born to his parents Alois and

Klara, four died prematurely: Gustav (1885–7), Ida (1886–8), Otto (born 1887, but lived for only three days)[7] and Edmund (1894–1900).[8] As for Hitler's younger sister Paula (1896–1960), family physician Dr Bloch testified to members of the American OSS that she was considered to be 'a little on the stupid side, perhaps a high-grade moron'.[9] Bloch also stated that, 'there was a daughter, slightly older than Adolf, who was always kept hidden when he [Bloch] came to visit, and who was 'an imbecile'. (He was probably referring to Ida, who lived for only two years.)[10]

By contrast, Hitler's half-siblings (the offspring of his father Alois and Franziska Matzelbergher), *who were apparently not inbred*, fared somewhat better. Angela, for example, married a Professor Hammitsche at Dresden, and Alois junior became a waiter in London and later opened his own restaurant in Berlin.[11]

The Genetic Effects of Inbreeding

English scientist and mathematician Sir Isaac Newton (1642–1727) once modestly compared himself to 'a boy playing on the sea-shore, and … now and then, finding a smoother pebble or a prettier shell than ordinary, whilst the great ocean of truth lay all undiscovered before me'.[12] As far as the subject of Hitler and Genetics is concerned however, the 'ocean' is slowly but surely yielding up its secrets.

'Inbreeding' is defined as 'the mating of individuals related by common ancestry', and it has 'its most conspicuous effect on the frequency of appearance of rare recessive characteristics, which most often are of an undesirable nature'.[13]

> Inbreeding has its most conspicuous consequences in increasing the relative frequency of appearance of physical and mental defects due to rare recessive genes, an effect that is extremely accentuated in consanguineous [of the same family], and especially in incestuous [father-daughter and brother-sister] matings'.[14]

In the nucleus of each human cell are normally to be found 46 chromosomes (23 pairs), half of which are inherited from each parent. Each chromosome is composed of a length of DNA, in which the genes are arranged in a linear fashion – like beads in a necklace – the gene being instrumental in directing the synthesis of the specific proteins that play a structural or functional role in the cell. The position of a gene on the chromosome is called the 'gene locus' (each chromosome having between approximately 400 and 4,000 gene loci).

Adolf Hitler, therefore, like the vast majority of other human beings, would have had a total of 46 chromosomes, each with an average of say 2,000 gene loci, making approximately 100,000 gene loci in all.

Genes (like chromosomes) occur in pairs, each member of the pair being called an 'allele'. If the two alleles are identical, then the gene pair is described as 'homozygous' for that particular gene; if they are different, then the gene pair is described as 'heterozygous'.

Inbreeding may be deleterious to the offspring because,

> it greatly increases the probability of producing homozygous recessives [genes which are usually suppressed], and since *most deleterious characteristics are recessive*, inbreeding increases the risk of defects in the progeny …. [This phenomenon is known as 'inbreeding depression' and] is manifested in many quantitative human characteristics: birth weight, height, head circumference, chest girth, muscular strength, foetal and infant viability and so forth. Mental ability is similarly subject to inbreeding depression to as great, or even greater degree than most of the physical features mentioned above.[15]

The *coefficient of inbreeding* is defined as the probability that for any given gene locus, the inbred individual resulting from inbreeding will receive the same allele (form of gene) on both homologous chromosomes (i.e. of the same essential nature) from the common ancestor.

Given that Hitler's coefficient of inbreeding (calculated from his family tree) was 1/32, then the possibility would exist that *in excess of 3,000 of his 100,000 gene loci would be occupied by recessive genes*.[16]

Inbreeding may have positive as well as negative effects on the offspring. For example, although it tends to depress the mean IQ of the inbred individual ('inbreeding depression'), it also has the effect of increasing the variance (deviation) of that mean with the effect that the inbred progeny may have an IQ higher than normal. (This might explain why in some aspects of his make up, e.g. his prodigious memory for detail – viz. in relation to the weaponry used by his armed forces, Hitler was superior to his colleagues.)

Hitler's Eye Colour

The colour of a person's eyes depends on the amount of a pigment called melanin that is present in the iris of the eye. Eye colour varies according to the genetic make-up of the individual, and at present three genes are known to control human eye colour. (There may be more, that are as yet undiscovered.) These are: 'Bey 1' (located on chromosome 15), 'Bey 2' (also located on chromosome 15), and 'Gey' (which is located on chromosome 19). The genes direct the production of enzymes, which in turn direct how much of the brown pigment melanin is produced in the iris; hence they determine the colour of the eyes.

If the melanin-producing allele is present and strongly dominant, then the only pigment present in the iris will be brown – hence brown eyes. If however, the melanin-producing pigment is present but less strongly dominant, then the amount of brown pigment in the iris will be less, and (unlike with brown eyes) some light will penetrate and be reflected off the rear of the eye (retina); this will result in hazel, green, grey or blue eyes.

'A great deal is written about his [Hitler's] eyes,' said psychologist Walter Langer of the American OSS, 'which have been described in terms of almost every colour of the rainbow. As a matter of fact, they seem to be rather a bright blue – bordering on the violet.'[17]

The fact that a person (such as Hitler) has blue eyes indicates that the two alleles present at the relevant gene loci are identical and of the recessive (non melanin-producing) type. This should not be taken to mean that everyone who has blue eyes is inbred. It is simply that inbreeding greatly increases the probability of the offspring acquiring homozygous, recessive genes. Also, not all recessive traits are disadvantageous, and a person with blue eyes is no more advantaged or disadvantaged than a person with eyes of another colour.

***

Was Hitler aware that his family was inbred? The answer is 'yes'. In the words of the author Benjamin B Wolman, Hitler himself,

> seems to have suspected that 'incestuous poisoning of the blood' – to use one of his favourite expressions in condemning the Jews – was responsible for certain striking peculiarities about his own family, and in 1937 during a speech to his propaganda leaders, Hitler's topics, according to author Max Domarus, included the following: 'He, Hitler, would not live much longer, at least as far as this was accessible to the human mind. In his family, men did not grow old. Also, both his parents had died young.'[18]

Hitler, referring to Wagner's opera *Parsival*, also said:

> It is not the Christian-Schopenhauerist religion of compassion that is acclaimed, but pure, noble blood in the protection and glorification of whose purity the brotherhood of the initiated has come together. The king [Amfortas] is suffering from the incurable ailment of corrupted blood. [and he went on to say] *All of us are suffering from the ailment of mixed, corrupted blood.*[19]

***

How ironic therefore, that Hitler, one whose primary aim was to eliminate anyone with the slightest physical or mental defect, may himself have been the recipient of defective genes! Furthermore, under the rules which he and his Party laid down, *he himself ought by rights to have been eliminated as a 'defective'*.

(There has been speculation that Hitler had a condition called monorchism – i.e the possession only one testicle. This is discounted by his physician Dr Theodor Morell, who made a full medical examination of the Führer and recorded that in fact Hitler possessed the normal number of testicles – i.e. two.)

***

Just as in the 19th and 20th centuries the principal challenge to mankind was how to overcome diseases caused by bacteria, viruses and malnutrition, so in the 21st century the spotlight has shifted to a large extent to genetics.

With the completion of the 'Human Genome Project' in 2003, all the genes in human DNA – approximately 30,000 have been identified, and the sequence of the three billion chemical base pairs that make up this DNA have been determined. This now offers a unique tool in the diagnosis of disease, and with the advance of techniques of genetic engineering it may be possible one day to offer treatment for diseases caused by genetic defects present in an individual's make up.

David Woodrow sums up the current situation thus:

> Scientists currently believe that single gene mutations [alterations] cause approximately 6,000 inherited diseases. These diseases are called single gene or 'monogenic' diseases, because a change in only one gene causes the disease. [Examples cited are: cystic fibrosis, sickle cell anaemia and haemophilia.][20]

However, the rules that underlie the inheritance of most major common diseases such as heart disease, diabetes, Alzheimer's, osteoarthritis and psychiatric disorders are not as straightforward.

> These common diseases result not just from a change [mutation] in one, or a few genes, but from a combination of the effects of the environment and a number of 'susceptibility genes' [defined as genes which contribute to an individual's risk of developing a specific disease, but which usually are not enough to cause the disease].

Woodrow cites the 'APOE gene on chromosome 19' as,

> one example of a disease susceptibility gene. An individual who has two copies of one variant [mutant] allele of APOE is more likely to develop Alzheimer's Disease at an earlier age than an individual with a different APOE genotype.[21]

***

In the latter stages of the war, Hitler began to show some of the classic signs of Parkinson's Disease, a rhythmically shaking left arm and hand, together with staring eyes, a shuffling gait and an increasing absence of facial expression.

Parkinson's Disease appears to be caused by an accumulation of proteins in the brain which would normally be disposed of (i.e. there is a defect in the brain's method of disposing of these proteins), and there are now strong indications that this may have a genetic basis.

For example, in 1996 scientists at the National Human Genome Research Institute (NHGRI), located a gene that causes some rare forms of familial Parkinson's Disease [and the following year they], identified the alteration [mutation] which was in the gene that produces the protein alpha synuclein. The alteration may cause the protein to fold abnormally, thus forming a misshapen protein that is difficult to break down and dispose [of].[22]

In 1998 researchers at The National Institute of Health (NIH) discovered in two German siblings (brother and sister) with Parkinson's Disease, an alteration in the gene that produces ubiquitin carboxyl-terminal hydrolase (UCH-L1), 'a protein that is involved in the tagging of other proteins for routine disposal in the brain'.[23]

It is therefore possible that Hitler inherited (perhaps through inbreeding) two recessive (and therefore disadvantageous) alleles on one or more of the gene loci mentioned above, and that this is what caused him to develop Parkinson's Disease in later life.

***

But what of mental disease? Research into the genetic basis of mental disorders is at an early stage. For example, in *Bipolar Disorder* (where the mood swings between mania and depression),

more than two-thirds of people … have at least one close relative with the disorder or with unipolar major depression [i.e. depression without mania], indicating that the disease has a heritable component. Studies seeking to identify the genetic basis of bipolar disorder indicate that susceptibility stems from multiple genes. Scientists are continuing their search for these genes, using advanced genetic analytic methods and large samples of families affected by the illness.[24]

Schizophrenia

Morrison describes the symptoms of *Schizotypal Personality Disorder* as follows:

Beginning by early life, these patients experience isolation and discomfort with social relationships …. Behaviour is influenced by odd beliefs …. [There is] odd speech [which may be] impoverished. [There are] paranoid or suspicious ideas, [and] 'affect' [i.e. mood] [that is] constricted in range, or inappropriate to the topic [with], odd behaviour or appearance. Other than close relatives [the patient has], no close friends or confidants. In social situations [there is], marked anxiety that is not reduced by familiarity. This is associated with paranoid fears rather than negative self-judgements.[25]

These symptoms may herald the onset of schizophrenia, the diagnosis of which is reached by observing a pattern of signs and symptoms which may include:

> hearing internal voices or experiencing other sensations not connected to an obvious source [hallucinations], and assigning unusual significance or meaning to normal events, or holding fixed, false, personal beliefs [delusions].[26]

These symptoms would appear to fit Hitler *like the proverbial glove.*

Bearing these criteria in mind, there is a prima facie case for believing that Adolf Hitler did indeed suffer from schizophrenia. This is a disease which generally presents in young adulthood – the mid-twenties for men. As Hitler was born in 1889, the onset of the disease in his case (had it occurred at the typical age) would have coincided with his joining the German army to fight in the First World War. *Crucially, it would explain how the seemingly innocuous, even charming youth described by family physician Eduard Bloch became transformed into a totally different character – i.e. that of the Führer.*

However, it has to be said that even prior to 1914 (after which date the florid symptoms of overt schizophrenia were becoming increasingly apparent in Hitler), there were signs that all was not well, as evidenced by August Kubizek's description of Hitler's uncontrolled outbursts of temper and vituperation, and Dr Bloch's description of him as 'this strange boy'.

***

Researchers at the USA's National Institute of Mental Health (NIMH) have recently identified a 'GRM 3 gene', which is responsible for regulating a substance found in between brain cells, known as glutamate, which is in turn responsible for the transfer of information from cell to cell.[27] It is known that patients with schizophrenia are more likely to inherit a variant of this gene, which may therefore be responsible for the disease.[28] This again fits in with the theory of Hitler having inherited recessive genes.

Notes

1. *The Nazis: A Warning from History, Part 1.
2. Linz. 1884. *Archives of the Episcopate*: No. 6.911/II/2, in Kubizek. p. 29.
3. Kubizek, August, *Young Hitler*, p. 111.
4. Ibid, p. 10.
5. Ibid, pp. 29–30.
6. Ibid, p. 30.
7. Ibid, p. 29.

8. Heiden, Konrad, *Hitler: a Biography*, p. 41.
9. Langer, Walter, *The Mind of Adolf Hitler*, p. 96.
10. Ibid, p. 106.
11. Bloch, Dr Eduard, 'My Patient Hitler' in *Colliers*. p. 35.
12. Brewster, D, 1855, *Memoirs of the Life, Writings and Discoveries of Sir Isaac Newton*. Thomas Constable & Co./Hamilton Adams & Co. Vol.II, ch.27.
13–16. Osborne, R Travis, Clyde E Noble and Nathaniel Weyl (eds), 1978, *Human Variation: The Biopsychology of Age, Race, and Sex*, New York: Academic Press. pp. 95, 85, 95, 85, 59.
17. Langer, op. cit., p. 44.
18. Domarus, Max, Hitler, *Speeches and Proclamations 1932–1945*, Vol.2. p. 959.
19. Rauschning, Hermann, *Hitler Speaks*, p. 227.
20. Article for GlaxoSmithKline entitled *Genes and Diseases*, 2004, www.msu.co.uk.
21. Ibid.
22–23. National Human Genome Research Institute, September 1998, Release: *Parkinson's Disease Gene and The Brain*, in www.genome.gov/pagecfm?pageIG=10000577.
24. National Institute of Mental Health. www.nimh.nih.gov.publicat/manic.cfm, 08.07.03.
25. www.geocities.com/morrison94/personality.html1, 18.7.2003.
26. *Schizophrenia Overview*, www.surgeongeneral.gov/library/mentalhealth/chapterfour/sec4.html, 9.7.2003.
27. National Institute of Mental Health Press Release: *Schizophrenia Gene Variant Linked to Risk Trait*. www.nimh.nih.gov/press/prschizgene.cfm).
28. Egan, Michael, Daniel Weinberger, and colleagues in Proceedings of the National Academy of Sciences. 24 August 2004.

CHAPTER XXXIV

Finale

Bernd Fryetag von Loringhoven (of Hitler's General Staff) described Hitler's appearance in July 1944:

> I saw a wreck standing in front of me … a stooped man, already dragging one leg, who could only offer his shaky left hand because his right hand was more or less unusable owing to a contusion from the attempt on his life [in the July plot of 1944]. I saw no shining eyes able to hold one spellbound. His eyes were dull. And a worn out figure stood in front of me.[1]

(In fact, Hitler at this time was suffering from Parkinson's Disease, and this is why his left arm and hand were shaking.)

In early December 1944 Hitler (against the advice of his generals) made Himmler Commander-in-Chief of the Army Group Upper Rhine. When Himmler duly failed to stem the tide of Germany's collapse, he was reassigned (in January 1945) to command Army Group Vistula, which by mid-January 1945 was also overrun by the Red Army. Himmler now retired to the SS military hospital at Hohenlychen, from where he claimed to be suffering from influenza.

As the final months of World War II played themselves out, Hitler, from 16 January 1945, took up permanent residence in Berlin at the so-called 'Führer bunker', situated some 15 metres beneath the gardens of Berlin's Reich chancellery building. 'I expect every German to do his duty to the utmost,' said the Führer, and, 'to take upon himself every sacrifice which must be required of him.'[2]

On 30 January 1945 Hitler made his last broadcast to the German people:

> However grave the crisis may be at the moment, through our unalterable will, our readiness for sacrifice and our own abilities, we will overcome the crisis. We will endure. It is not Central Asia that will win, but Europe, led by this nation, which for 1,500 years has defended and will continue to defend Europe against the East – our greater German Reich – the German nation.[3]

Hitler's words applied not only to adults, for he was anxious that those members of the Hitler Youth 'who can fight, do fight, and that we sacrifice ourselves together'.[4] Referring to the fact that the defence of Berlin was being carried out mainly by children, Baldur von Schirach, who had been instrumental in their military training, declared: 'I didn't know ... that young people were deployed there. I had no influence any more. But on looking back, I can't understand how people could send children into battle. I feel you can't justify it, not biologically.'[5]

These sentiments were echoed by Walter Goergen (formerly of the Hitler Youth). Referring to boys of just 16 or 17 who had fought for Germany at the end of the war against hopeless odds, he said: 'They didn't realise that the war had been lost long before. Those lads sacrificed themselves for Germany for nothing.' Hans Jurgen Habenicht (formerly of the Hitler Youth) said: 'I am furious that we were used in a hopeless situation, just to prolong Hitler's life by a couple of days.'[6] Said Ingeborg Seldte: 'That's what I reproach Hitler for most. He led the youth astray. He betrayed them and he took their lives'.[7]

However, because Hitler was both Chancellor of Germany and Supreme Commander of her armed forces, there was no one who felt able to intervene, to take his place and sue for peace, even at this late stage.

**

With the advance of the Soviets, Hitler issued on 19 March 1945 the so-called 'Nero Decree': the implementation of a 'scorched earth' policy, designed to deprive the Allies of any facilities which might be useful to them. At the same time, all traces of the concentration camps were to be removed. The following day, Himmler was dismissed by his disillusioned Führer.

On 20 April 1945 Hitler, who had been joined by Bormann and Goebbels for the final few days of the battle, celebrated (if that is the correct word) his 56th birthday. Camera footage shows him shaking hands with his soldiers with his right hand, while the left hand is held behind his back, shaking rhythmically and uncontrollably from the elbow down at the rate of about five times per second.

Himmler would now play his last card, for on that very day, he crept away from the Führer bunker, to a prearranged meeting in a mansion north of Berlin with Norbert Masur, a Jew, who was spokesman for the Jewish World Congress. To save Germany from total defeat, Himmler proposed a new alliance between Nazi Germany and the western Allies against the Soviet Union. Part of the bargain would be the release by the Nazis of some 15,000 women prisoners (including some 2,000 Jews) from Ravensbrück concentration camp. Himmler also used Hungarian Jews as bargaining counters, and as a result of this meeting, the lives of approximately 350,000 inmates of the camps were saved. Others were not so fortunate, and as the camps were evacuated by the SS, many Jews died as a result of forced marches.

When Himmler began making peace overtures in the direction of Winston Churchill, they were rejected out of hand. As for Hitler, when he learned that Himmler had offered Great Britain and the United States (but not the Soviet Union) unconditional capitulation, he stripped the latter of all his offices of state.

On 23 April 1945 Albert Speer, having said his goodbyes to Hitler, unexpect-edly flew back to the besieged city of Berlin's Reich Chancellery. It has been sug-gested that Speer was anxious NOT to be named by the Führer as his successor, as he felt that this might adversely prejudice the part that he hoped to play in the new, post-Hitler Germany.

On the night of 28 April 1945 Hitler married Eva Braun in the Führer bunker. Only two days previously, his wartime ally Mussolini, along with his mistress Clara Petacci, had been executed by Italian partisans. After the executions, the angry mob in Milan had hanged both bodies up by their feet.

Lieutenant General Hans Baur, Hitler's personal pilot (who was interrogated by the Soviets), said that on the morning of his death, Hitler sent for him. The Führer,

> ... talked about being betrayed by his generals [and said] that his soldiers refused to fight for him. ... 'You must see to it that my body is burned so that it cannot be carried to Moscow and displayed like Mussolini's' [said the Führer].[8]

Hitler's valet, Heinz Linge (who was also interrogated), stated that there were no eyewitnesses to what happened after Hitler and his wife Eva entered their sitting room, at about 3.30p.m. on the afternoon of 30 April 1945. However, Hitler had in his possession two pistols; Eva had one, and each had a small box of cyanide cap-sules. When they were discovered moments later, it appeared that Eva had bitten on a cyanide capsule and died swiftly; whereas Hitler had put a cyanide capsule between his teeth, and shot himself at the precise moment when he bit into it.

Linge described how Hitler had ordered that after he had shot himself, his body was to be burned. Linge was also to burn Eva's body. (Hitler had previously ordered that Blondi, his Alsatian, be used as a guinea pig for testing the cyanide capsules which he and Eva intended to used on themselves.)

Rochus Misch, the Führer bunker's switchboard operator, is adamant that the bodies were buried in a bomb crater near the exit to the bunker. 'The bodies of Hitler and Eva Braun were placed here. They were wrapped in blankets and petrol was poured over them ... that's how Hitler was burned.'[9]

German radio announced, 'Soldiers of the German army. Our Führer Adolf Hitler is dead. The German people bow in grief and reverence.' According to Ulrich de Maizière (General Staff Officer, Hitler's headquarters 1945) however, Hitler had said shortly before his death that, '... after the end of him [i.e. Hitler] and of National Socialism, the German people could not survive. It would be destined to collapse.'[10]

On 1 May 1945 Admiral Karl Dönitz, having learned of Hitler's death, made a radio broadcast to the German people, telling them that the Führer had perished, and that he [Dönitz] had been appointed his successor.[11] Dönitz had joined the submarine service of the Imperial German Navy in World War I. In 1943 he had been appointed Commander-in-Chief of the German navy.

From the Naval Academy at Mervik-Flensburg (where Field Marshal Wilhelm Keitel, Chief of the High Command of the Armed Forces (OKW), and Colonel General Alfred Jodl, Chief of OKW's Operations Office, were also in attendance), Dönitz made the decision to surrender in the West, but to carry on fighting in the East in order to save as many Germans as possible from capture by the Russians.

Himmler, now dressed as a soldier and disguised with an eye patch, intermingled with retreating troops. It was to no avail. He was captured by the Allies and confessed to his identity, but before he could be tried he took poison. Himmler was buried by the British in an unmarked grave near Lüneburg.

On 2 May 1945 Soviet troops reached the Reich Chancellery and entered the Führer bunker, where only twenty or so personnel remained alive. Here they found the charred bodies of Josef Goebbels and his wife Magda; he had shot himself and his wife, and their bodies had been burned by his adjutant. As for their six children, they were all found dead, having been poisoned by their mother. The charred corpses of Hitler and Eva were found buried about three metres from the bunker doorway.[12]

On 4 May 1945 Field Marshal Bernard Law Montgomery of Alamein, Deputy Commander of Ground Forces (under General Dwight D Eisenhower), accepted the partial surrender of the Wehrmacht (Armed Forces) at Lüneburg Heath in northern Germany. On 7 May Jodl agreed to unconditional surrender on all fronts.

***

When on 8 May 1945 an autopsy was carried out by five forensic scientists of the Red Army, the bodies of Hitler and his wife were found to be so badly damaged, that they could only be identified with certainty from dental records. It was reported that part of Hitler's skull was missing, and that only one testicle was present. The Soviets also discovered a sketchbook of Hitler's, containing drawings which he had made between 1910 and 1921.

The two bodies finally arrived at Magdeburg, the East German headquarters of 'Smersh' ('Smert Shpiovam' – 'Death to Spies' – the Soviet Assassination Department of the KGB), where they were buried. In 1970 the Soviets affirmed that the remains had now (finally) been completely destroyed by incineration.[13]

In the subsequent examination of the cause of Hitler's death, German prisoners of war, who had been present in the Reich Chancellery bunker at the time, were taken back in 1946 by the 79th Smersh Counter Intelligence Unit, to the place where they alleged Hitler's body had been buried. Here, four fragments of a man's skull were exhumed, one of which clearly had a hole in it made by a bullet. Even the marks of the flames from the fire which had burnt the body were visible.

Notes

1. *Hitler: a Profile: The Commander*.
2. Ibid.
3. *The Nazis: A Warning from History, Part 5*.
4. *Hitler's Henchmen: Schirach, the Corrupter of Youth*.
5. Ibid.
6. Ibid.
7. *Hitler: a Profile: The Commander*.
8. *Hitler's Death: The Final Report*.
9. Ibid.
10. *The Nazis: A Warning from History, Part 5*.
11. *Hitler's Henchmen: Karl Dönitz*.
12. *Hitler's Death: The Final Report*.
13. Ibid.

CHAPTER XXXV

Aftermath

Twenty-two major defendants stood trial before the International Military Tribunal (convened at the Palace of Justice in the German town of Nürnberg, from November 1945 to October 1946 – where the Nazis had previously promulgated their racial laws), having been indicted for crimes against peace, war crimes, and crimes against humanity.

Hermann Göring

At Nürnberg, Göring told his doctor:

I'm determined to go down in German history as a great man. If I can't convince the court, I shall at least convince the German people that everything I did was done for the greater German Reich. In fifty or sixty years there will be statues of Hermann Göring all over Germany.

Unlike his fellow accused who admitted their guilt, or blamed Hitler for their crimes, having been confronted with cinematographic evidence, Göring told the Tribunal that he would accept guilt neither for himself, nor for his country.[1] Göring was due to be executed on 15 October 1946 but hours before his execution he committed suicide by taking cyanide.

Rudolf Hess

In his address to the court Hess said:

It was my privilege to spend many years of my life working for the greatest son whom my people have produced in their thousand year history. Even if I could …, I would not want to erase that time from my life. I am happy in the knowledge that I did my duty towards my people, my duty as a German as a National Socialist and as a loyal follower of the Führer. I regret nothing.[2]

Hess was found guilty at Nürnberg and sentenced to life imprisonment.

By 1966 Hess was the only prisoner remaining in Berlin's Spandau Prison. He remained unrepentant: 'If I had my time again I would act as I have acted, I regret nothing,' he said.[3] Only in 1969 did he permit himself to receive visits from his family, including his son Wolf. On 17 August 1987, while still a prisoner in Spandau, Hess committed suicide by hanging. He was aged 93.

Heinrich Himmler

Himmler, despite having disguised himself as an ordinary German soldier, was arrested by British forces. On 23 May 1945 however, before he could be brought to trial, he committed suicide by taking a cyanide capsule.

Albert Speer

At Nürnberg, Speer was the only defendant to accept collective responsibility for Hitler's deeds. However, to the end of his life, he claimed to have had no knowledge of the crimes of the Nazi regime (though this was demonstrably untrue, viz. his visits in the capacity of Armaments Minister to the slave labour camp of Dora-Nordhausen). He was sentenced to twenty years imprisonment, and was released in 1966. He died in 1981.

Martin Bormann

Bormann, who in the final phase of hostilities had managed to escape from the Reich Chancellery, was sentenced in his absence to death by hanging. In 1972 construction workers in Berlin unearthed two bodies. By comparison of teeth and dental records, and by DNA testing (although there was no corroborative confirmation, because no samples were sent to an independent laboratory), one of these bodies was positively identified as being that of Bormann (who is believed to have committed suicide).

Alfred Rosenburg

Rosenburg was found guilty of crimes against humanity and hanged in October 1946.

Joachim von Ribbentrop

In a statement made to the Nürnberg Tribunal, Joachim von Ribbentrop said:

> For years Hitler tried to counteract the danger from the East by concluding an alliance with Britain. The Naval Agreement of 1935 and the waiving of German claims to Alsace-Lorraine were, among other things, an earnest [indication] of the intentions of German foreign policy; they showed that Germany was ready to make sacrifices. But Britain could not be won over. She regarded Germany's growing strength not as a reasonable correction [of the Treaty of Versailles] and as a safeguard against the East, but only as a threat to the 'balance of power'. I worked for an understanding between Germany, France and Britain for twenty years of my life, and later wrestled with Britain to achieve an alliance. Up to the last hour I made efforts to avoid the war. Britain, fully resolved to prevent the further growth of Germany's strength, concluded her alliance with Poland. This made a peaceful German–Polish settlement impossible.[4] [As for the current charges] I declare myself not guilty as charged.[5]

Ribbentrop, however, had intervened with Mussolini to deport Italian Jews to concentration camps, and on this count alone he was found guilty of crimes against humanity and sentenced to death by hanging.

Baldur von Shirach

With the Red Army on the outskirts of Vienna (where he was 'Gauleiter'), Schirach left his command post and fled into the mountains of the Austrian Tyrol, but was captured nevertheless. At Nürnberg, he said, 'I declare myself not guilty as charged.' When confronted with graphic pictures of the concentration camps however, he put the blame on Hitler. 'I'm guilty of having trained young people for a man who was a murderer a million times over. I believed in this man. That's all that can be said in my defence.'[6] Schirach was found guilty and would serve a term of twenty years imprisonment in Spandau Prison.

Karl Dönitz

Grand Admiral Dönitz was captured by the British when the German fleet surrendered. In his trial at Nürnberg, Dönitz said, 'I think the conduct of this war was justified – and I acted according to my conscience. I would do exactly the same again.' He served a ten-year sentence in Spandau Prison, and was released in October 1956.

Josef Mengele

On 18 January 1945, with the approach of the Russian Army, Dr Mengele disappeared from Auschwitz, exchanged his SS uniform for that of an ordinary German soldier, and joined a retreating German army unit as a doctor. Despite being captured by the Allies, his true identity remained a secret, because for some reason his blood group had not been tattooed on to his skin, as was normal procedure for the SS.

Mengele made his way to his home town of Gunzburg in southern Germany, where he worked on a farm. He then fled to Italy and from there to Buenos Aries, choosing Argentina because of a secret organisation called 'Odessa', which helped former SS members to evade capture. Here he set up in medical practice. In the early 1950s he found employment in the Argentine branch of his family's farm implement retailing business. When the German government tried to extradite former Nazis from Argentina, Mengele fled to Paraguay; a 3.4 million dollar reward was offered for his capture.

When in June 1985 in Brazil, a body (said to have been buried in 1979) was exhumed from a cemetery, subsequent DNA analysis revealed that this was the remains of Mengele.[7] Eye witnesses at the time stated that he had drowned, having suffered a stroke while swimming in the sea.

Hjalmar Schacht

Schacht was one of only three to be acquitted at Nürnberg (the other two being former Chancellor Franz von Papen and Hans Fritzsche – an official in the Propaganda Ministry). However, with the coming of the new Federal Republic of Germany in 1949, Schacht was arrested once more, and it was not until 13 September 1950 that he was finally cleared on the charge of being a Nazi.

Subsequently, the energetic Schacht not only went on to found two banks of his own, but he became financial consultant adviser to various governments, including those of Egypt, Syria and Indonesia. A resident of München, he died on 4 June 1970 at the age of 93.

The Windsors

When his brother King George VI died on 6 February 1952, Edward attended the funeral, but without Wallis, his wife. When Queen Mary died on 24 March 1953, once again the Duke attended the funeral, but again without Wallis.

The new Queen, Elizabeth II, was crowned on 2 June 1953. On this occasion, Edward watched the ceremony on television at the home of some American friends in Paris. In June 1967 the Queen invited the Windsors to accompany herself and her husband, the Duke of Edinburgh, to the dedication of a plaque outside Marlborough House in memory of Queen Mary; which they did. However, when the Queen invited Edward to the investiture of Charles, Prince of Wales, held on 1 July 1969 Edward declined, presumably on the grounds that Wallis had not been invited.

In May 1972 the Queen visited Edward in Paris; her uncle was now terminally ill with cancer of the throat. He died in Paris in the early hours of the morning of 28 May, aged 77. His body was flown back to Britain for the funeral at Windsor in the presence of the Queen, his widow the Duchess of Windsor, the Archbishops of Canterbury and York, and Prime Minister Sir Edward Heath. Edward was buried at Frogmore, the royal mausoleum in the grounds of the castle. When Wallis died on 24 April 1986 she too was buried at Frogmore, beside her husband.

The Mosleys

Despite all his setbacks as a would be political leader, Sir Oswald Mosley's spirit was undimmed. In 1947 he published *The Alternative* in which he portrayed himself as a European, with a vision of a new Europe, 'beyond both fascism and democracy'.

In February 1948 he founded yet another political party, the 'Union Movement', which campaigned for a unified Europe, trading exclusively with the continent of Africa, which would provide her with basic raw materials. Now he appeared to reject anti-Semitism by, 'refusing to recognise a Jewish question'.[8]

The Mosleys were in the habit of spending the winters in Ireland, from March to July in France, and August in Venice. However, they would return to Paris for Christmas, where they would be invited to parties, including those given by the Duke and Duchess of Windsor (who were also living in exile at nearby Gif-sur-Yvette). Mosley also found time to maintain links with his fascist friends in Spain, South Africa, Argentina, Italy and Germany.

From 1951 the couple chose to reside permanently in France and to this end they purchased a house in the Chevreuse Valley some fifteen miles from Paris, there to live out the remainder of their lives in luxury. This was much to the chagrin of their former followers back in Britain, many of whom had sacrificed everything, and had even gone to prison for the cause.

In 1952 Mosley's Union Movement was producing two periodicals, *Comrade* and *Action*. This was now followed by *The European* of which Diana became the editor, with Mosley writing the editorial column.

In 1959 Mosley stood as parliamentary candidate for Notting Hill, campaigning strongly for the end of non-white immigration. His efforts were in vain and in the election, held in the aftermath of the Notting Hill race riots, he not only failed, but lost his deposit. Diana went on to publish several books, including her memoirs and a biography of the Duchess of Windsor.

In 1962 the indefatigable Mosley represented Britain in Venice at a congress of extreme right wing groups. (By now he was resigned to the fact that his vision of Europe as a one-nation state was a non-starter.) In 1966 Mosley attempted to re-enter Parliament, this time as Member for Shoreditch, but again without success.

In 1980 Mosley, now suffering from Parkinson's Disease, died in France at the age of 84. So ended the life of a man who, had Germany been successful in her attempted invasion, might have had a major role to play in the new 'Nazi Britain'. In 1994 Mosley's wife Lady Diana, who even now could not bring herself to make a full and unreserved apology (for supporting Hitler and the Nazis) told writer Brian Masters:

> They will go on persecuting me until I say Hitler was ghastly. Well, what's the point in saying that? We all know that he was a monster, that he was very cruel and did terrible things, but that doesn't alter the fact that he was obviously an interesting figure. It was fascinating for me at 24, to sit and talk to him, to ask him questions, and get answers, even if they weren't true ones. No torture on Earth would get me to say anything different.[9]

William Joyce

Joyce was captured in Denmark by an observant British officer, and was tried at the Old Bailey in September 1945. At the trial, the prosecution claimed, that having acquired a British passport in 1933 (albeit fraudulently), he therefore owed his allegiance to the Crown.

In his diary, Joyce wrote, 'I yield nothing of my political opinions, nor do I believe I have acted wrongly, but I hate dying as England's enemy.' On 3 January 1946 Joyce was hanged at Wandsworth Prison. In 1976 his body was reburied at Galway in the Irish Republic, where he was regarded as something of a local hero.

Arnold Leese

As a writer, and publisher of a monthly newsletter *Gothic Ripples*, Leese continued his attacks upon the Jews. In 1947 he was convicted of being involved in a conspiracy to assist escaping Nazis (who were on the wanted list for war criminals) to evade capture and escape to South America.[10] He died in 1956.

Archibald Ramsay

Ramsay was defeated in the General Election of 1945. He died on 11 March 1955.

The British Free Corps

At the end of the war, most returning members of the British Free Corps were rounded up by MI5 and prosecuted. Thomas Cooper, who had boasted to his comrades that he had killed eighty Jewish women and children in a single day, was given the death sentence; this was later commuted to life imprisonment.

Frank Wood was also sentenced to life, and John Wilson to ten years. Robert Chipchase, who emigrated to Australia, was never charged.

As for John Amery (whose brainchild the BFC had been), he laughed as he was found guilty of high treason. He was executed on 19 December 1945 at Wandsworth Prison.[11]

Josef Stalin

Russian historian Dmitri Volkogonov, head of a special Russian parliamentary commission (and Stalin's official biographer), has concluded from newly available Soviet KGB documents, that under Stalin's twenty-nine year leadership, '21.5 million (Soviet) people were repressed. Of these, ⅓ were shot, and the rest sentenced to imprisonment, where many also died.'[12] In fact, it was only by his death from a stroke on 5 March 1953 that another purge of the Jews was avoided. He was buried in the same tomb as Lenin, in Moscow's Red Square.

Following Stalin's death, Marshal Lavrenti Beria attempted to seize power in a failed coup. Nikita Khruschev now became First Secretary of the Soviet All Union Party. At the 20th Party Congress in 1956 Khruschev astonished the world by his frankness in condemning much of what Stalin had done. Soon he would introduce greater freedoms, relax press censorship, and free the prisoners from the gulags.

Shortly after the 22nd Party Congress of October 1961, Stalin's body was removed and reburied near the Kremlin wall (close to those of the former leaders of the Bolshevik Revolution).

Czechoslovakia

Following Germany's defeat in May 1945 Eduard Beneš and his government returned from exile to the Czech capital Prague. Now, in excess of two million Sudeten Germans were expelled from Czechoslovakia, thereby increasing the population of Germany (and thus achieving the opposite of what Hitler had intended by his policy of 'Lebensraum'). Against this however, must be offset the total German dead of World War II – estimated to be in the region of 4 million.

Communism Worldwide

Communism was finally dismantled in Eastern Europe in 1989 and in the USSR at the end of 1991. Elsewhere, it had failed to take root in more than a handful of countries, such as North Korea and Cuba. As for China, 'which was never slavishly soviet in its ideology and practices', that country has, 'quietly abandoned its beliefs in everything except the dictatorship of the Party, particularly after the death of Deng Xiao Ping in 1997. The same is broadly true of the communist regime in (North) Vietnam.'[13]

Simon Wiesenthal

Simon Wiesenthal was born in Galicia, Poland in 1908. When the Nazis overran that country in September/October 1939 they sent his family to the ghetto. He himself would spend a period of four years being moved from one concentration camp to another, finishing up in Mathausen in Austria (where over 100,000 prisoners would be murdered).

Wiesenthal, however, was among the 18,000 Mathausen prisoners who survived, the camp having been liberated in May 1945 by the American army. Amazingly, Wiesenthal's wife Cyla (a Jew, a former schoolfriend, and like him, a concentration camp internee), also survived the war. However, from their combined families, a total of eighty-nine people had perished at the hands of the Nazis.

Wiesenthal, whose gift of memory was legendary, compiled and sent hundreds of dossiers on Nazi war criminals to Yad Vashem, the Holocaust Centre in Jerusalem. He then concentrated his energies on tracking down Adolf Eichman, whom he regarded as the architect of 'The Final Solution'. On 11 May 1960 the Israeli Intelligence Service, Mossad, captured Eichman in Argentina (Wiesenthal having alerted them to the fact that he had become a citizen of that country and was living there), and brought him back to Israel. There he was tried, convicted and executed.

Another prominent Nazi was Franz Stangl, who as commandant of the Treblinka concentration camp, had ordered the deaths of 40,000 Jews. Wiesenthal located him in Brazil, from where he was extradited to Germany, tried and sentenced to life imprisonment.

Wiesenthal was quick to acknowledge that it was not only Jews who died in the holocaust, but also 'gypsies, homosexuals, and Jehova's Witnesses [who], when they were murdered, all ended up in the same mass grave. My aim was to work for everybody in that mass grave, not just those buried in the Jewish corner,' he said.[14]

In June 2004, at a private ceremony at his home in Vienna, the 95-year-old Simon Wiesenthal was awarded an honorary knighthood by the British Government. He died on 20 September 2005, aged 96.

The Holocaust in Perspective

'The Holocaust', as it came to be known, resulted in the murder of an estimated 16 million people by Hitler and his regime between 1933 and 1945. They included around 6 million Jews (of whom 3 million were from Poland), and 10 million Ukranians, Russians, Romanies, socialists, homosexuals, and those labelled mental or physical 'defectives'.

With regard to the Jews, not only working people, shopkeepers and businessmen, but also doctors, chemists, musicians, composers, teachers, artists, philosophers and so forth were eliminated; i.e. those who had most to contribute when it came to enriching the culture and civilisation of the society in which they lived, and of course, children.

The loss to the world was incalculable and the degree of human suffering unquantifiable. As for mankind in general, the holocaust produced not one single benefit, but instead would taint those who planned and perpetrated it for all time.

To the credit of the majority of the German people, they have not tried to hide the fact that the holocaust actually took place. In fact since the war, numerous Germans have come forward to describe exactly what they saw, both inside and outside the labour camps and the extermination camps (in the proximity of which, the stench of death was all pervading). Also, German school children are deliberately taken to see the camps as part of their educational curriculum.

Hitler's Legacy

In his will, Hitler left everything he owned to the Nazi Party or, 'If that does not exist any more, then to the State ....'[15]

For him, as for his henchmen, there would be no monument or memorial. His beloved Berghof was bombed to destruction by the Allies; his Reich Chancellery bunker is now the site of a children's playground.

The Hitler Family

Hitler's sister Paula remained unmarried and bore no children during her lifetime. She died in 1960.

His half-sister, Angela, married Leo Raubal, an assistant tax collector, and bore him three children: Leo Rudolf Raubal, born 1906; Angela (Geli) Raubal, born 1908, died 1931 (suicide); Elfriede, born 1910. Leo Rudolf went on to have a son of his own, Peter.

Hitler's half-brother Alois visited Ireland in 1909 where he married an Irish girl Brigid Dowling, by whom she had a son William Patrick Hitler. Heinz Hitler was Alois' son by his second marriage to Maimee. Heinz became an army officer and died in captivity, having been captured by the Russians on the Eastern front.

William Patrick, having lived for a time in England and also in Germany, moved with his mother to the USA, and between 1944 and 1946 served in the US Navy. He then decided to shun public life and live under an assumed name. He married and had four sons, of whom Howard (the only one to marry) was killed in a car accident.

The three remaining sons made a positive decision never to have children of their own. They also steadfastly refused to contest Hitler's will, describing any royalties to which they might have been entitled from the sale of Hitler's book *Mein Kampf* as 'blood money'.

***

Notes

1. *Hermann Göring: Ambition without Conscience.*
2. *Hitler's Henchmen: Hess, The Deputy.*
3. Ibid.
4. *Joachim von Ribbentrop.* www.spartacus.schoolnet.co.uk/GERribbentrop.htm.
5. *Hitler's Henchmen: Ribbentrop, the Puppet.*
6. *Hitler's Henchmen: Schirach, the Corrupter of Youth.*
7. *Josef Mengele: Medical Madman of Auschwitz.*
8. Dalley, Jan, *Diana Mosley: A Life*, p.275.
9. Woods, Audrey, *British World War II Fascist Dies*,
   www.news.com.au/common/story_page/0,4057,6941452%5E13780,00.html.
10. Royal Archives, KV (King George V) 2/1365–7 and KV2/60–3.
11. *The Brits who fought for Hitler*
12. 'The Jewish Role in the Bolshevik Revolution and Russia's Early Soviet Regime'. [This essay appeared in the Jan.-Feb. 1994 issue of the *Journal of Historical Review*, published by the Institute for Historical Review].
   www.ihr.org/jhr/v14/v14n1p-4Weber.html.
13. *Chambers Dictionary of World History.*
14. *Simon Wiesenthal.*
15. *Hitler's Henchmen: Bormann – the Shadow Man.*

CHAPTER XXXVI

Epilogue

The Germany of the 1920s was a country damaged by war, and wounded even more by the iniquitous Treaty of Versailles, the harsh terms of which she was completely incapable of fulfilling. When the 'messiah', Hitler, came along with the promise of salvation, the German people embraced him with open arms, seduced as they were by Hitler's oratory, Goebbels' propaganda, Himmler's mythology, Wagnerian music and Nazi pageantry.

Meanwhile, guided by their misguided masters, his legions of jack-booted, goose-stepping, robotic minions struggled frantically to obey the Führer's every whim, while at the same time unleashing a reign of unmitigated terror on a world which had done precious little to deserve it.

***

Four facts about Adolf Hitler have been established beyond reasonable doubt.

Firstly, that he possessed copies of the journal *Ostara* and was familiar with this and other teachings of Lanz von Liebenfels. Also, that a substantial number of Liebenfels' core sentiments (articulated by him in *Ostara*) were adopted by Hitler and his Nazi regime and put into practice with catastrophic results.

Secondly, many who were acquainted with Hitler, even if only slightly, attest to the fact that he was not 'normal', either in appearance or in manner.

Thirdly, that because of the close inbreeding of his recent forebears, Hitler had inherited a large percentage of recessive (and therefore deleterious) genes.

Fourthly, Hitler suffered from a severe personality disorder, the evidence pointing to schizoid tendencies, and probably to frank schizophrenia. Certainly Hitler's body language as displayed during his speeches – the agonised contortions of face and limbs, often with hands cradling head – suggest strongly that here was a man *possessed by some irresistible force*. Were these four facts connected in any way? The answer is 'yes'.

***

Thousands, if not millions, of Germans, must have realised that what Hitler was preaching was unscientific, historically inaccurate and cruel beyond belief. Yet very few spoke out against him. Why? Because his was a 'terror state', where the slightest deviation was punishable by incarceration, enslavement and probably death.

On the other hand, bearing in mind that the whole philosophy and ethos of Nazism was built on a number of palpably demonstrable myths, it is astonishing how many people did actually believe it! The question is, did Hitler himself believe what he preached?

Certainly the Führer was cunning enough to convince the Germans, in the early days at least, that he had their interests at heart. What they did not realise was that he was driven by irrational forces beyond his control – those of paranoia and hatred – made real to him by the voices which he (and only he) heard in his head.

Hermann Rauschning's statement (as previously mentioned) referring to Hitler, that 'He hears voices. I have met him when in this mood', together with the Führer's own admission (as reported by Wagener) that 'something speaks through me', and his reference to an 'inner voice' makes the diagnosis of schizophrenia virtually certain.

These were the voices therefore, which, in all probability, were responsible not only for Hitler's pathological hatreds, particularly of Slavs and Jews, but also of his (previously unexplained) fatal hesitancy at Dunkerque, or for the mishmash of contradictory orders which he issued during the disastrous 'Operation Barbarossa'. In other words, evil and irrational notions such as those instilled into him by Lanz von Liebenfels and the like were impinging, in Hitler's case, *not on a normal mind, but on one which would hungrily assimilate their poison, before translating them into a ghastly reality.*

The corollary to this is that from the time of Hitler's seizing of power on 30 January 1933 until the day of his death on 30 April 1945, the entire German nation, both in peace and war, was being orchestrated by a man whose actions were determined by the voices which he heard in his head, rather than by his own intelligence, experience and emotions, and the wise council of experts in the field.

***

Hitler, by his own admission, was aware that his family, and himself in particular, were the victims of the effects of inbreeding or 'incestuous poisoning of the blood'. However, he would have had neither knowledge nor understanding of those recessive genes which he had inherited as a result, and which were wreaking such havoc with his personality: being instrumental, in all probability, in causing his self-loathing, disgust of anyone with a physical or mental defect, and irrational and exaggerated fear and hatred (paranoia) in respect of Bolsheviks, Slavs, Jews and others.

It is also unlikely that he had any realisation of the fact that he was mentally deranged, one of the features of schizophrenia being a lack of insight on the part of the subject.

***

By a strange coincidence, it appears that Hitler was not alone amongst the 'dramatis personae' of World War II in possessing recessive genes.

The great-grandmother of Edward VIII (King of the United Kingdom from January to December 1936) was Queen Victoria, who in 1840 married Albert of Saxe-Coburg. Victoria and Albert were very closely related – first cousins in fact, Victoria's mother (Victoria of Saxe Coburg Saalfeld) and Albert's father (Ernst I of Saxe Coburg Saalfeld) being sister and brother.

Edward's coefficient of inbreeding was 1/156. Therefore, approximately 650 (i.e. 0.65%) of his 100,000 or so gene loci would be occupied by recessive genes (compared to Hitler's 3,000, or 3%) including of course the one for blue eyes, which he had! At first glance, this figure seems small; however, if those particular recessive genes were concerned with such functions as choice of wife and political inclination, then their effect on the outcome of world, and in particular British, history may have been considerable.

**

A Jew who was forced to flee the Nazi persecution was Austrian neurologist and founder of psychoanalysis Sigmund Freud (1856–1939). In 1938 after the Anschluss (annexation of Austria) and prior to the Nazi persecution of Austria's Jews, Freud and his family escaped to London. He died the following year.

Under the Nazi regime, psychoanalysis was banned; had he been given the opportunity to psychoanalyse the Führer, what a field day Freud would have had!

**

An irony is that had Hitler himself been held up to the same type of scrutiny as those whom his Nazis selected for elimination in the death camps, then by rights *he himself ought to have been eliminated under the very criteria which he had laid down for others.* (Perhaps it is not too fanciful to imagine that one day genetic loci will be discovered, the genes of which bestow on their owner the capacity for humanity, compassion and most importantly of all, love?)

Another irony is that had World War II not occurred, then it is unlikely, as has been shown, that communism would have spread much beyond the Soviet Union. However, by invading the Soviet Union, Hitler provoked a huge backlash, which ended up with the Soviets overrunning much of Eastern Europe. An 'Iron Curtain' came down (this term was first coined by Nazi Propaganda Minister Joseph Goebbels in 1943: and subsequently in a speech by Winston Churchill in 1946), which was only lifted in the year 1990 with the ending of the so-called 'Cold War'. Therefore, for a period of almost half a century, the countries of Eastern Europe laboured unnecessarily under the yoke of the communist invader.

**

Even now the Führer continues to fascinate, but often for the wrong reasons. The question is, could the 'Hitler phenomenon' happen again? The answer is regrettably, yes it most certainly could. To consider the phenomenon of Nazism alone (and to ignore, for the time being, the host of tyrants, fundamentalists, and fanatics who have held sway – and continue to do so – repeatedly throughout the history of mankind on this Earth), then the forces which swept Hitler to power have by no means been extinguished. Far from it: they lurk, like pre-cancerous cells, occasionally coming to the surface like sulphurous bubbles from a smouldering volcano.

For example, in France today, the land of 'Liberté, Egalité and Fraternité' (which has, at 600,000, the world's largest population of Jews outside Israel and the USA) there is a growing problem of anti-Semitism, many Jews feeling, 'under siege both from the country's 6 million-strong Muslim population and from far-right political movements like the National Front'.[1]

**

Humanity's hold on Democracy and Freedom (so taken for granted by those who enjoy its privileges, and yet so yearned after by those to whom they are denied) is always under threat, and has to be continually defended. In the words of John Philpot Curran (1750–1817), 'The condition upon which God hath given liberty to man is eternal vigilance ....'[2] However, vigilance alone is not enough. Other factors are involved; not least courage, such as that shown by Pastor Martin Niemoller, Archbishop Jan de Jöng of Utrecht, and 'July plotter' Klaus von Stauffenberg. Only a recipe containing the appropriate 'ingredients' will produce, as it were, a satisfactory 'cake'.

Notes

1. Graff, James, *Time*, London and Paris, 6 September 2004.
2. Speech to the Right of Election of Lord Mayor of Dublin, 10 July 1790.

Bibliography

Books, Papers, Articles

Aarons, Mark and John Loftus. 1994. *The Secret War Against the Jews*. New York: St Martin's Press.

Allen, Gary. 1976. *The Rockefeller File*. CA, USA. Seal Beach: '76 Press.

Barker, Alan. 2000. *Invisible Eagle: The History of Nazi Occultism*. London: Virgin Books.

Barnett, Correlli. 1989. *Hitler's Generals*. London: Weidenfeld & Nicolson.

Binion, Dr Rudolph. 1973. *Hitler's Concept of Lebensraum, in History of Childhood Quarterly*, 1, p. 251.

Bloch, Dr Eduard. 1941. *My Patient Hitler, in Colliers Magazine*, Vol. 1, March 15, pp. 11, 35–9; and March 22, pp. 69–73.

Bloch, Michael. 1997. *The Duchess of Windsor*. London: Phoenix Illustrated.

Bloch, Michael. 1988. *The Secret File of the Duke of Windsor*. London: Bantam Press.

Bryan III, J and Charles J B Murphy. 1979. *The Windsor Story*. New York: William Morrow and Company Inc.

Bullock, Alan. 1973. *Hitler: A Study in Tyranny*. London Book Club Associates (by arrangement with the Hamlyn Publishing Group.)

Bullock, Alan. 1991. *Hitler and Stalin: Parallel Lives*. London: Book Club Associates (by arrangement with HarperCollins Publishers.)

Campbell, Christy. 1985. *The World War II Fact Book*. London: Macdonald (Publishers).

Chambers Biographical Dictionary. 2002. Una McGovern (ed.). Edinburgh: Chambers Harrap.

Chambers Dictionary of World History. 2000. Bruce P Lenman (ed.). Edinburgh: Chambers Harrap.

Colliers Magazine. 1905–1957. New York: P F Collier & Sons.

Daim, Dr Wilfried. 1985. *Der Mann, der Hitler die Ideen gab*. 2nd edn. Vienna/Cologne/Graz,

Dalley, Jan. 1999. *Diana Mosley: A Life*. London: Faber & Faber.

Degrelle, Leon. May/June 1994. *The Enigma of Hitler, The Journal For Historical Review*.

Devrient, Paul. 2003. *Mein Schuler Adolf Hitler*. München: Universitas.

Domarus, Max. 1992. *Hitler, Speeches and Proclamations 1932–1945*. 4 vols. London: I.B. Tauris.

Douglas-Hamilton, James. 1993. *The Truth about Rudolf Hess*. Edinburgh and London: Mainstream Publishing.

Encyclopaedia of World War II. 1977. John Keegan (ed.) CT, USA: Bison Books Corp.

Flood, Charles Bracelen. 1989. *Hitler: The Path to Power.* Ma. Boston, Houghton Mifflin Company.

Fest, Joachim. *Hitler.* 1974. Middlesex, UK: Penguin.

Gilbert, Martin. 1981. *Winston Churchill – The Wilderness Years.* London: Macmillan.

Goodenough, Judith, Robert A Wallis, and Betty McGuire. 1998. *Human Biology.* New York and London: Saunders College Publishing, Harcourt Brace College Publishers.

Goodrick-Clarke, Nicholas. 1992. *The Occult Roots of Nazism.* New York University Press.

Göring, Emmy. 1967. *An der Seite meines Manne: und Begebenheiten und Bekenntuisse.* Gottingen: Schutz.

Gregory, Richard L 1987. *The Oxford Companion to The Mind.* Oxford University Press.

Greiner, J. 1949. *Das Ende des Hitler-Mythos.* Zurich/Leipzig/Vienna.

Griffiths, Richard. 1998. *Patriotism Perverted: Captain Ramsay, the Right Club and British Anti-Semitism 1939–40.* London: Constable.

Hamann, Brigitte. 1999. *Hitler's Vienna: a Dictator's Apprenticeship.* Oxford University Press.

Hamilton, General Sir Ian. *The Hamilton Papers.* London. King's College: Liddell Hart Centre for Military Archives.

Hanisch, Reinhold. 1939. *I was Hitler's Buddy.* New York. The New Republic. April 5, 1939, pp. 239–42 (I); April 12, pp. 270–2 (II); April 19, 1939, pp. 297–300 (III).

Heer, Friedrich. 1968. *Der Glaube des Adolf Hitler.* München/Esslingen.

Heiden, Konrad. 1936. *Hitler: a Biography.* London: Constable.

Higham, Charles. 1984. *Trading With The Enemy.* New York: Dell Publishing.

Higham, Charles. 1988. *Wallis: Secret Lives of the Duchess of Windsor.* London: Sidgwick & Jackson.

History of the Communist Party of the Soviet Union: Bolsheviks. 1943. Edited by a Commission of the CC of the CPSU (B). Moscow: Foreign Languages Publishing House.

Hitler, Adolf. 1942. *Mein Kampf* (Unexpurgated Edition). London: Hurst & Blackett.

Hougan, Jim. 1978. *Spooks.* New York: Bantam Books.

Jenkins, Roy. 2001. *Churchill: A Biography.* London: Macmillan.

Jenks, William A 1960. *Vienna and the Young Hitler.* New York: Columbia University Press.

Kershaw, Ian. 1998. *Hitler 1889–1936: Hubris.* London: Alan Lane, The Penguin Press.

King, Greg. 1999. *The Duchess of Windsor.* London: Aurum Press.

Kogon, Eugen. 1980. *The Theory and Practice of Hell.* New York: Berkeley Books.

Krause, Karl. *Die Fackel* (satirical journal, 922 issues of which were published between 1899 and 1912).

Kubizek, August. 1973. *Young Hitler.* Maidstone, Kent, UK: George Mann Books.

Lambert, David (and the Diagram Group). 1996. *Body Language.* Glasgow: HarperCollins Publishers.

Langer, Walter. 1973. *The Mind of Adolf Hitler.* Great Britain: Book Club Associates.

Liebenfels, Dr Jorg Lanz von. 2003. *Theozoology.* Sandusky, Ohio, USA: Europa Germanic Traditions.

Liebenfels, Lanz von. 1931. *Bibliomystikon oder Die Geheimbibel der Eingweihten.* 10 vols. 1930–38. Pforzheim.

List, Guido von. 1988. *The Secret of The Runes.* (Edited, introduced and translated by Stephen E Flowers,) Vermont, USA: Destiny Books.

Lloyd George, David. 1938. *War Memoirs of David Lloyd George,* vols. I,II. London: Odhams Press.

Lovell, Mary S. 2001. *The Mitford Girls.* New York: Little, Brown.

Lumsden, Robin. 1995. *SS Regalia: A Collector's Guide to Third Reich Militaria*. London: Ian Allan.

Machtan, Lothar. 2001. *The Hidden Hitler*. Oxford: The Perseus Press.

Matthews, John. 1981. *The Grail*. London: Thames & Hudson.

McLeod, Kirsty. 1999. *Battle Royal*. London: Constable.

Mintz, Morton and Jerry S Cohen. 1977. *Power, Inc.* New York: Bantam Books.

Morrison, James M 1995. *DSM-IV Made Easy: The Clinician's Guide to Diagnosis*. New York: Guilford Press.

Mosley, Sir Oswald. 1968. *My Life*. London: Thomas

Muhlen, Norbert. 1939. *Schacht: Hitler's Magician*. New York: Alliance Book Corp.

National Archives: *Release of Security Service (MI5) Material*. (File refs. KV)

Nedava, Joseph. 1972. *Trotsky and the Jews*. The Jewish Publication Society of America [with the permission of the publisher, The Jewish Publication Society].

Osborne, R Travis, Clyde Noble and Nathaniel Weyl, (eds). 1978. *Human Variation: the Biopsychology of Age, Race, and Sex*. New York: Academic Press.

Overy, Richard. 1989. *The Road to War*. London: Macmillan.

Pia, Jack. 1974. *SS Regalia*. New York: Ballantine Books.

Pick, Heller. 1997. *Simon Wiesenthal: a Life in Search of Justice*. London: Phoenix.

Prange, Gordon W (ed.). 1944. *Hitler's Words*. American Council on Public Affairs.

Ramsay, Archibald M. 1955. *The Nameless War*. London: Britons Publishing Co.

Rauschning, Hermann. 1939. *Hitler Speaks*. London: Thornton Butterworth.

Schacht, Hjalmar. 1955. *76 Jahre meines Lebens*. London.

Schwarz, Dr Paul. 1943. *This Man Ribbentrop*. New York: Julian Messmer.

Seldes, George. 1943. *Facts and Fascism*. New York: In Fact Inc.

Service, Robert. 2000. *Lenin: a Biography*. London: Macmillan.

Shirer, William L. 1972. *The Rise and Fall of the Third Reich*. London: Book Club Associates (by arrangement with Secker & Warburg).

Speer, Albert. 1971. *Inside the Third Reich*. London: Sphere.

Sutton, Antony C 1974. *Wall Street and the Bolshevik Revolution*. N.Y. New Rochelle, Arlington House.

Toland, John. 1977. *Adolf Hitler*. London: Book Club Associates.

Trevor-Roper, H R (ed.) 1953. *Hitler's Secret Conversations, 1941–1944*. London: Weidenfeld & Nicolson.

Vorres, Ian. 1964. *The Last Grand-Duchess*. London: Hutchinson.

Wagener, Otto. [Ed. Henry Ashby Turner, Jr.] 1985. *Hitler – Memoirs of a Confidant*. New Haven and London: Yale University Press.

Walther, Herbert (ed.). 1978. *Der Führer*. London: Bison Books.

Weitz, John. 1977. *Hitler's Banker*. New York: Little, Brown.

Weitz, John. 1992. *Joachim von Ribbentrop: Hitler's Diplomat*. London: Weidenfeld & Nicolson.

Wheen, Francis. 1999. *Karl Marx*. London: HarperCollins.

Wiedemann, Fritz. 1964. *Der Mann, der Feldherr werden wollte*. Velbert/Kettwig.

Williams, Susan. 2003. *The People's King*. London: Allen Lane.

Windsor, the Duke of. 1947. *A King's Story*. New York: G P Putnam's Sons.

Wolman, Benjamin (ed.). 1971. *The Psychoanalytic Interpretation of History*. New York: Harper Torchbooks.

Ziegler, Philip. 1990. *King Edward VIII, the Official Biography*. London: Collins.

Film Documentaries

Betrayal: Oswald Mosley, the English Führer. © 2003. AP Traitor Productions Limited.
    History Channel.
Churchill, Pt.1. Renegade and Turncoat. © BBC 1992. UK History.
Eva Braun. © ZDF 2001. History Channel.
Hermann Göring: Ambition without Conscience. © 2002. A&E Television Networks.
Hitler: a Profile: The Betrayer. © 1995. ZDF.
Hitler: a Profile: The Blackmailer. C.2001. Channel Five Broadcasting Limited,
Hitler: a Profile: The Commander. © 1995. ZDF.
Hitler: a Profile: The Criminal. © 1995. ZDF.
Hitler: a Profile: The Dictator. © 1995. ZDF, DiscoveryChannel.
Hitler: a Profile: The Seducer. © 1995. ZDF.
Hitler's Britain. © 2002, Lion Television
Limited, Sea Lion Productions, Inc. History Channel.
Hitler's Death: The Final Report. © 1995. BBC.
Hitler's Henchmen: Hess, The Deputy. © 1996. ZDF Enterprises. Discovery Channel.
Hitler's Henchmen: Karl Dönitz. © 1984. Granada UK,
Hitler's Henchmen: Freisler: the Executioner. © 1998. Discovery Communications, Inc.
Hitler's Henchmen: Schirach, the Corrupter of Youth. © 1998. Discovery Communications Inc.
Hitler's Henchmen: Speer, the Architect. © 2001 Atlantic Alliance Inc. The History Channel.
Hitler's Henchmen: Ribbentrop, the Puppet. C.1998. Discovery Communications Inc.
    Discovery Channel.
Hitler's War: Air War over Germany. © 2002. ZDF. History Channel.
Hitler's Women. © 2001. Spiegel TV. History Channel.
Josef Mengele: Medical Madman of Auschwitz. © 1996. A&E Television Networks.
Kristallnacht: November 9, 1938. © 2003. BBC.
Nazis: The Occult Conspiracy. © 1998. Discovery Communications Inc. Discovery Channel.
Pius XII: the Pope, the Jews, and the Nazis. © 1994. BBC. Reputations.
Russia: Land of the Tsars. © 2003. A and E Television Networks. History Channel.
Secret History: The Nazi Expedition. © 2004. MMIV Ifage Productions.
Sex and the Swastika: The Making of Adolf Hitler. © 2002. BBC. Timewatch.
Simon Wiesenthal. © 1997. A BBC/A&E Network co-production.
History Channel.
Stalin. © 1990. Thames Television plc. History Channel.
The Brits who fought for Hitler. © Channel Five Broadcasting Limited, 2002. History
    Channel.
The Last Nazi Secret. © 2002. Channel Four Television Corporation.
The Nazis: A Warning from History –
    Pt.1 'Helped into Power.
    Pt.2 'The Wrong War.
    Pt.3 'The Wild East.
    Pt.4 'The Road to Treblinka.
    Pt.5 'Fighting to the End.
© 1997. BBC.
The SS: Himmler's Madness. © 2002. ZDF. History Channel.
The Third Reich in Colour. © 1999. Spiegel TV. History Channel.
World at War: Hitler's Germany: the Only Hope, 1933–1936. © 1975. Thames Television Limited.

Appendix

Ostara Index

The Author (if other than Liebenfels) is indicated in brackets.

First Series (1905–16)

Titles:

1. The German / Austrians and Election Reform. 1905.
2. Economic Trade and Law Reform. March 1906.
3. Revolution or Evolution: A Free Conservative Easter Prayer: The Supremacy of the European Race. April 1906.
4. Hungary's Economic Bankruptcy and how to bring it under control. May 1906.
5. 'Be Hard, Lord' – An Old German story, retold in modern German (Hagen). June 1906.
6. The Empire's Treasure returns to the Empire! Guiding Humanitarian Principles for our Future. July 1906.
7. The Resurrection of Man (Harpf). August 1906.
8. The Austro–German regions of the Alps as Meat and Milk producers – A study of the Local Economy (Bernuth). August 1906.
9. The People's Thoughts – The Aristocratic Principle of our Time (Harpf). September 1906.
10/13. Anthropology – Primitive Peoples and Race in the Historical Literature. October 1906.
11/12. Women's Affairs – A Cultural Study (Harpf). January 1907.
14. Israel's Triumph (Freydank). March 1907.
15. Women's Earning Capacity and Prostitution. (Liszt). April 1907.
16. Judas' Monopoly of Money in the Ascendancy and Zenith (Wahrmund). June 1907.
17. The Technician's Headline. July 1907.
18. Race and Welfare Work – a call for a Boycott of Indiscriminate Charity. December 1907.
19/20. The Time of Eternal Peace: an Apology of War as a Cultural and Racial Purifier (Harpf). January 1908.
21. Race and Woman, and her Preference for an Inferior Breed of Man. March 1908.

22/23. The Statute of Emmanuel and Racial Cultivation. April 1908.
24. Patent Law and Unlawfulness of the Brain – Workers (i.e. white-collar workers). May 1908.
25. The Aryan and his Enemies (Jostenoode). July 1908.
26. Introduction to Ethnology.
27. An Account of Ethnology.
28. Countenance and Race: a summary of Ethnological Physiognomy.
29. Racial Theoretical Somatology.
30. Particular Ethnological Somatology I.
31. Particular Ethnological Somatology II.
32. From Tax Collection to the numerous State Dividends. 1909.
33. The Danger of Women's Suffrage and the Necessity of Master Ethics based on Men's Rights. 1909.
34. Racial Management as a solution to Sexual Problems. 1909.
35. New Physical and Mathematical Proofs for the Existence of the Soul. 1909.
36. The Purpose and Higher Living of the Blonds and the Darks. 1910.
37. Character Assessment, relative to the Shape of the Skull: An Elementary Racial Phrenology. 1910.
38. The Sex Life and Love Life of the Blonds and the Darks I. 1910.
39. The Sex Life and Love Life of the Blonds and the Darks II. 1910.
40. Racial Physiology in Industrial Life I. The Impoverishment of the Blonds, the Opulence of the Darks. 1910.
41. Racial Psychology in Industrial Life II. The Hidden Theft as an Industrial Principle of the Darks. 1910.
42. The Blonds and The Darks in Current Political Life. 1910.
43. Introduction to the Sexual Physiology or Love as Wasted Energy. 1911.
44. Comedy of Women's Rights – a Light Hearted Chronicle of a Woman's Life. 1911.
45. The Tragedy of Women's Rights – a Serious Chronicle of a Woman's Life. 1911.
46. Moses as a Darwinist: an Introduction to Anthropological Religion. 1911.
47. The Art of Good Living and in being Happily Married: a Racial Purity Breviary for People in Love. 1911.
48. Genesis or Moses as Anti-Semites – Fighters against the Ape People and Dark Races. 1911.
49. The Art of Happy Marriage: a Racially Pure Breviary for Newly Weds and Veterans of Marriage. 1911.
50. The Ancient Homeland and History of the Heroic Blond Race. 1911.
51. Callipaedics, or the Art of Deliberate Conception: a Racially Pure Breviary for Mother and Father. 1911.
52. The Blonds as Creators of Language – A Summary of the Creation of Ancient Languages. 1911.
53. The Rights of Men as a Saviour for the Sexual Needs of Women's Life. 1912.
54. Exodus or Moses as a Preacher of Racial Selection and Racial Morals. 1912.
55. The Social, Political and Sexual Life of Women in Our Time. 1912.
56. The Racial Upbringing and Liberation of the Blonds from the Reign of Terror of Dishonourable Education. 1912.
57. The Order of Races in the Economy and the Liberation of the Blonds from the Reign of Terror of Dishonourable Education as an Exploiter. 1912.
58. The Immoral and Criminal Woman's Lifestyle of Our Times. 1912.
59. The Aryan Christendom as a Racial Cult Religion of the Blonds – an Introduction to the Literature of the New Testament. 1912.

60. Racially Conscious and Unconscious Life and Lovemaking – a Breviary for the Ripe Blond Youth. 1912.
61. Racial Mixing and Racial De-mixing, 1912.
62. The Blonds and Darks as Commander-in-Chief and Commander. 1913.
63. The Blonds and Darks as Soldiers. 1913.
64. Many or Few Children. 1913.
65. Race and Illness: a Summary of General and Theoretical Racial Pathology. 1913.
66. Naked and Racial Culture in a Struggle against Hypocrisy and a Dishonourable Culture. 1913.
67. The Relationship of the Darks and Blonds to Illness: a Summary of Specialist and Practical Racial Pathology. 1913.
68. The Resurrection of the Blonds to Wealth and Power – an Introduction to Racial Sociology. 1913.
69. The Holy Grail as the Mystery of Aryan Christendom: a Racial Cult Religion.
70. The Blonds as Creators of Technical Culture. 1913.
71. Race and Nobility. 1913.
72. Race and External Politics. 1913.
73. The Blonds as Creators of Music. 1913.
74. Racial Metaphysics or the Immortality of Higher Peoples. 1914.
75. The Blonds as Bearer and Victim of Technical Culture. 1914.
76. Prostitution in Women, and Men's Rights – A Judgement. 1914.
77. Races and Architecture in Antiquity and the Middle Ages. 1914.
78. Racial Mystique – an Introduction to the Aryo–Christian Esoteric Doctrine, 1915.
79. Racial Physics of War. 1915.
80. An Introduction to Practical Racial Metaphysics. 1915.
81. Racial Metaphysics of War, 1914–15.
82. A Prayer Book for Enlightened and Spiritual Aryo–Christian I. 1915.
83. Race and Poetry. 1916.
84. Race and Philosophy. 1916.
85. Race and Architecture in the New Age. 1916.
86. Race and Painting. 1916.
87. Race and Internal Politics. 1916.
88. A Prayer Book for Enlightened and Spiritual Aryo-Christian II. 1916.
89. Racial Metaphysics of the Holy.
90. Abbot Bernhard of Clairvaux, praise prize of the new Knights Templar.
91. The Saint as Cultural and racially historical Hieroglyphs.
92. Race and Sculpture.
93. Racial metaphysics of the Saints.
94. The Language of the Aryo-heroic Flood.
95. Leviticus or Moses as a Racial Hygienist.
96. Information about the Names of Places
97. Numeri (Bible – Book of Numbers) or Moses as a Renewer of the Race.
98. Aryo-heroic Personal Names.
99. Deuteronomy or Moses as a Racial Law Giver.
100. Aryo-heroic Family Names.

Second Series. (1922)

1.Ostara and the Blond Empire.

Third Series. (1927–31)

1. Ostara and the Blond Empire. 1927.
2. World War as a Racial Struggle of the Darks against the Blond. 1927.
3. World Revolution as the Blonds' Grave. 1927.
4. World Peace as an Achievement and Victory for the Blonds. 1928.
5. Theozoology or Natural History of the Gods 1: the Old Testament and the Old God. 1928.
6/7. Theozoology or Natural History of the Gods 2: the Sodom Stone and Sodom Water. 1928.
8/9. Theozoology or Natural History of the Gods 3: Sodomfire and Sodomair. 1928.
10. Anthropology – Primitive Peoples and Race in the Historical Literature. 1931.
11. Economic Resurrection by the Blonds – an Introduction to Private Business in the Racial Economy. 1929.
12. The Dictator of the Blonds Patrician – an introduction to Political Economy of the Racial Economy. 1929.
13/14. The Zoological and Talmudish (i.e. Jewish traditional law) origin of Bolshevism. 1930.
15. Theozoology or Natural History of the Gods 4. The New Testament and New God. 1929.
16/17. Theozoology 5 – the Divine and Spiritual Father of Immortality in Substance and Spirit. 1929.
18. Theozoology or Natural History of the Gods 6: the Son of God and the Immortality of Origin and Race. 1930.
19. Theozoology 7: The Immortal Church of the Gods. 1930.
101. The work of J. Wolfl and L. Liebenfels – an Introduction to their Theories. 1927.

From Daim, pp. 311–14. (Kindly translated by Nicholas Dragffy and Martin Clay.)

Index

INDEX